Import Handbook

SUBSCRIPTION NOTICE

This Wiley product is updated on a periodic basis with supplements to reflect important changes in the subject matter. If you purchased this product directly from John Wiley & Sons, Inc., we have already recorded your subscription for this update service.

If, however, you purchased this product from a bookstore and wish to receive (1) the current update at no additional charge, and (2) future updates and revised or related volumes billed separately with a 30-day examination review, please send your name, company name (if applicable), address, and the title of the product to:

Supplement Department
John Wiley & Sons, Inc.
One Wiley Drive
Somerset, NJ 08875
1-800-225-5945

For customers outside the United States, please contact the Wiley office nearest you:

Professional & Reference Division
John Wiley & Sons Canada, Ltd.
22 Worcester Road
Rexdale, Ontario M9W 1L1
CANADA
(416) 675-3580
1-800-567-4797
FAX (416) 675-6599

John Wiley & Sons, Ltd.
Baffins Lane
Chichester
West Sussex, PO19 1UD
UNITED KINGDOM
(44) (243) 779777

Jacaranda Wiley Ltd.
PRT Division
P.O. Box 174
North Ryde, NSW 2113
AUSTRALIA
(02) 805-1100
FAX (02) 805-1597

John Wiley & Sons (SEA) Pte. Ltd.
37 Jalan Pemimpin
Block B # 05-04
Union Industrial Building
SINGAPORE 2057
(65) 258-1157

Import Handbook

A Compliance and Planning Guide

Edited by

Robert Feinschreiber and Charles L. Crowley

JOHN WILEY & SONS, INC.

New York • Chichester • Weinheim • Brisbane • Singapore • Toronto

This text is printed on acid-free paper.

This publication is designed to provide accurate and authoritative information in regard to the subject matter covered. It is sold with the understanding that the publisher is not engaged in rendering legal, accounting, or other professional services. If legal advice or other expert assistance is required, the services of a competent professional person should be sought.

Library of Congress Cataloging in Publication Data:

Import handbook: a compliance and planning guide / edited by Robert Feinschreiber and Charles L. Crowley.
p. cm.
Includes index.
ISBN 0-471-17742-3 (cloth : alk. paper)
1. Foreign trade regulation—United States—Handbooks, manuals, etc. 2. Tariff—United States—Handbooks, manuals, etc. 3. United States—Commerce—Handbooks, manuals, etc. I. Feinschreiber, Robert. II. Crowley, Charles L.
HF1455.I484 1997
658.7′2—dc21 97-12612

Printed in the United States of America

10 9 8 7 6 5 4 3 2 1

"You young gentlemen have entertained me royally, and in return I will give you a priceless secret. Tariffs! These are the politics of the future, and of the near future. Study them closely and make yourselves masters of them, and you will not regret your hospitality to me."

Winston S. Churchill—April 1902

About the Editors

Robert Feinschreiber is an attorney and practitioner in Miami. As a partner in the firm of Feinschreiber and Associates, his clients include foreign-owned U.S. businesses, U.S. exporters, and companies facing transfer pricing issues. He received a B.A. from Trinity College in Connecticut, an L.L.B. from Yale, an M.B.A. from Columbia Graduate School of Business, and an L.L.M. in Taxation from New York University. Mr. Feinschreiber was a CPA in Florida.

Mr. Feinschreiber is the editor of, and contributor to, *The Transfer Pricing Handbook* published by John Wiley & Sons. He has written and edited many books on taxation, including *Foreign Sales Corporations, Fundamentals of International Taxation, Domestic International Sales Corporations, Tax Incentives for U.S. Exports, Tax Depreciation Under the Class Life ADR System, International Tax Planning Today, Subpart F, Earnings & Profits, Allocation and Apportionment of Deductions,* and *International Reorganizations.* Mr. Feinschreiber is also the author of *Tax Reporting for Foreign-Owned U.S. Corporations,* published by John Wiley & Sons. Mr. Feinschreiber has written many articles on taxation and tax-related subjects, including international taxation. He has been quoted as an authority by *Tax Court, Business Week,* and *Forbes.* He has also been a consultant to several foreign governments and is the editor of *Special Economic Zones in Regional Development* published by the United Nations.

Mr. Feinschreiber is the editor of the *Interstate Tax Report.* He was the founding editor of the *International Tax Journal* and has been the editor of *Export Tax Report* and the United States editor of *Tax Haven* and *Shelter Report.* He was formerly the U.S. correspondent for *Tax News Service,* which is published by International Bureau of Fiscal Documentation.

He has taught accounting at Yale and law at Wayne State University Law School. He was director of the International Tax Institute. Mr. Feinschreiber has lectured at various tax conferences on such topics as Foreign Sales Corporations, DISC, intercompany pricing, Subpart F, the foreign tax credit, research credit, and depreciation. He has lectured for the American Management Association, International Business Seminars, the International Tax Institute, the World Trade Institute, where he was the Senior International Tax Advisor, and other organizations. He is the editor of the *Export Handbook* and co-editor of the *Import Handbook,* both published by John Wiley & Sons.

Charles L. Crowley is the leader of the largest Customs and International Trade Consulting practice among the major accounting and consultation firms at Ernst & Young LLP. He was formerly an attorney with the U.S. Customs Service, Office of Regulations and Rulings, in Washington, D.C., and practiced law in the areas of customs and international trade for several years in Washington, D.C., and New York.

Mr. Crowley advises numerous multinational corporations concerning global customs and international trade activities. He focuses primarily on the areas of customs audits, foreign trade zone reviews, duty refunds, duty reductions, regulatory compliance, and penalty-related matters. He advises companies involved in the importation and exportation of such products as pharmaceuticals, chemicals, electronics, textiles and apparel, steel, machinery, footwear, computers, and eyewear. He also has extensive experience as a technical consultant for major corporations in antidumping and other unfair trade law and foreign labor proceedings.

Mr. Crowley is an author on the subject of export issues in the *Export Handbook,* published by John Wiley & Sons. A former president of the Customs Lawyers Association, Mr. Crowley is coauthor of "The Impact on Canada-United States Free Trade Agreement on the Accounting Profession" in *The Journal of Corporate Accounting and Finance,* Autumn 1989, published by John Wiley & Sons, and "Retail Tax Developments" in *Retail Control* magazine, May 1992. He is admitted to the bars of New York, Washington, D.C., and Massachusetts, as well as the U.S. Court of International Trade, U.S. Tax Court, and the U.S. Court of Appeals for the Federal Circuit. He is a member of the board of directors for the Association of American Exporters and Importers, technical advisor to the National Transportation Organization, an active member of the Customs and International Trade Bar Association, and a regular lecturer for various international trade associations.

About the Contributors

Frank Chioccola, a licensed customs broker, is a consultant with Ernst & Young LLP Customs and International Trade Practice. He advises multinational companies on various customs and international trade matters, including regulatory compliance, customs valuation, tariff classification, country of origin marking, and eligibility for tariff preference programs, such as NAFTA and the Generalized System of Preferences. Mr. Chioccola has coordinated and conducted internal audits for several Fortune 500 companies to reclaim value-added tax.

Joseph F. Donohue Jr. is a partner in the New York office of Donohue & Donohue, a law firm specializing in customs and international trade law. He advises U.S. and foreign corporations on customs and trade matters and represents such clients in administrative and judicial proceedings. He is a former president of the Customs and International Trade Bar Association and is a member of the Advisory Committee of the United States Court of International Trade.

Edward L. Farrell, Jr., CPA, is an international tax consultant to global business organizations. He is an author and lecturer on international taxation.

James A. Geraghty, JD, LLM, is a director of the Customs and International Trade Practice at Deloitte & Touche LLP. Previously, he was a partner in a New York City law firm specializing in customs law. He is a past member of the Board of Directors of the Customs and International Trade Bar Association, a former adjunct professor at Hofstra University School of Law, and a lecturer on customs audits for the MIS Training Institute. Mr. Geraghty is also a licensed Custom House Broker.

Patrick D. Gill is a partner in the customs and international trade law firm of Rode & Qualey. He is the immediate past president of the Customs and International Trade Bar Association.

Ronald C. Glowzinski, MBA, a licensed customs broker, is a Customs Administrator with General Motors Corporation in Detroit, Michigan, where he is responsible for coordination of all U.S. customs audits and the development of customs compliance review programs. He is the chairman of the Drawback Revitalization

Committee for Customs Modernization Act and NCITD Drawback Committee. Mr. Glowzinski was also a participant in the negotiations to establish NAFTA rules of origin and drawback provisions. For his contributions to drawback regulations, he was a recipient of the Hammer Award.

Harry L. Isacoff, JD, is a senior manager at Ernst & Young LLP. He also served as a vice president of a national freight forwarding and customs brokerage company. He advises multinational corporations in the areas of international trade matters, including NAFTA and GATT, marking, quota, first sale rule, export compliance programs, and customs brokerage reviews. Mr. Isacoff is a contributing author to the export guide *Expanding Your Business Globally* and has published several articles on customs issues. He is a member of the Association of Exporters and Importers, the New York County Lawyers Association, and has lectured at customs and international trade conferences.

Joseph S. Kaplan, LLB, is a partner at Ross & Hardies in New York. He also serves as a member of the Advisory Committee to the United States Court of International Trade and as director of the American Association of Exporters & Importers. Mr. Kaplan is former Director of the USCIT Bar Association.

Seth T. Kaplan, Ph.D., is Director of Economic Research at Trade Resources Company, Professorial Lecturer in Economics at The George Washington University, and a former International Economist at the U.S. International Trade Commission.

Peter W. Klestadt, JD, a licensed customs broker, is a partner with the law firm of Grunfeld, Desiderio, Lebowitz & Silverman, where he counsels importers, foreign manufacturers, trading companies, trade associations, and foreign governments regarding the customs and related laws governing the importation of merchandise into the United States. Mr. Klestadt is a member of the New York County Lawyers Association, the Customs and International Trade Association, and Consulegis, an international network of law firms. He is an adjunct professor at New York University and the World Trade Institute.

Beril J. Lapson, Ph.M., MBA, CMC, is cofounder of Trade Resources Company, providing economic, cost accounting, valuation, and data analysis services to attorneys in antidumping and transfer pricing procedures.

M. Barry Levy is the senior partner at the firm of Sharretts, Paley, Carter & Blauvelt, P.C. He is a past president of the Customs and International Trade Bar Association and currently serves as chairman of the Committee on Customs and International Trade Law of the New York County Lawyer's Association. He is the coeditor of the *Handbook on Customs and International Trade Law,* 1996 edition, prepared by the New York County Lawyers' Association. For the past 20 years, Mr. Levy has served as Industry Advisor to the U.S. Trade Negotiators. His firm practices exclusively in the area of customs and international trade law.

Michael P. Maxwell, JD, LLM, is a partner in the Los Angeles firm of Grunfeld, Desiderio, Lebowitz & Silverman LLP. He was formerly a law clerk and trial attorney in the International Trade Field Office of the U.S. Department of Justice, where he tried cases concerning Customs and International Trade before the Court of International Trade.

David M. Murphy is a senior associate with Grunfeld, Desiderio, Lebowitz & Silverman LLP, one of the nation's largest firms dedicated solely to the practice of customs and trade law issues. Mr. Murphy is a member of the New York, Connecticut and Washington, D.C., bars. He is a licensed customs broker and leads a customs broker license examination preparation course in New York.

Jill D. Murray is the Customs Director at J. Crew Corporation, is a licensed customs house broker, and has worked with importers, brokers, and freight forwarders in excess of ten years. She is a member of Women in International Trade and the International Trade Council. She has promoted awareness in the trading community by developing automated testing for customs house broker examination and a placement program for international business majors. She has studied abroad at the University of Salamanca, Spain, and participated in the Fulbright program in German studies.

Susan Kohn Ross has been practicing law in the areas of Customs, International Trade, and Transportation for almost 20 years. She is a former member of the NAFTA Advisory Committee on Private Commercial Disputes, as well as the U.S. Customs NAFTA Advisory Committee. Ms. Ross assists clients through the management and legislative consulting services her firm provides. She is a prolific author and frequent speaker on trade issues and is a member of the American Association of Exporters and Importers, Women in International Trade of Los Angeles, and the Border Trade Alliance.

Matthew G. Shaw is a senior manager at Ernst & Young LLP. Mr. Shaw has assisted overseas and domestic companies involved in the importation and sale of wearing apparel, consumer electronics, chemicals, machinery, and footwear. He advises multinational corporations on various aspects of customs and trade law, with a concentration on duty savings and reductions, tariff classification, merchandise valuation, country of origin determinations, and regulatory requirements and compliance. Mr. Shaw is a member of the International Law and Practice Section of the New York State Bar Association, the Customs and International Trade Bar Association, and the American Association of Exporters and Importers. He is coauthor of *Latin American Development Strategies: Opportunities for U.S. Exports.*

Andrew L. Siciliano, CPA, is a licensed customs broker and a consultant with Ernst & Young LLP Customs and International Trade Practice. He conducts on-site customs audits of multinational companies and has an extensive understanding of transaction flows. In addition, Mr. Siciliano advises multinational companies on all customs and international trade matters, including product valuation, tariff classification, duty drawback, country of origin marking, and recordkeeping compliance requirements.

Kenneth C. Stanhagen, MBA, is a senior consultant at Trade Resources Company, providing economic, cost accounting, valuation and data analysis services to attorneys in antidumping and transfer pricing proceedings. He was formerly an international trade analyst at the U.S. Department of Commerce.

Sidney N. Weiss is an international trade, commercial, and customs lawyer in New York. A member of the California and New York bars, he has been practicing in the customs area for over 20 years. He served as a trial attorney with the United States Department of Justice, specializing in customs classification, valuation, and antidumping cases. He is a member of the Customs and International Trade Bar Association, Director and Chair of the nationwide Association of Customs and International Trade Lawyers' Trial and Appellate Practice Committee. He has also been named by the Chief Judge of the United States Court of International Trade as a member of its advisory committee.

Steven C. Wrappe, JD, CPA, LLM, is an international tax partner in the National Tax Office of Deloitte & Touche LLP in Washington, D.C. He is a former senior attorney with the IRS Advance Pricing Agreement Program and an adjunct professor at George Mason University School of Law.

Richard P. Wulwick is a senior consultant with KPMG Peat Marwick LLP. He assists multinational companies on a variety of customs and international trade issues, including structuring international transactions, valuation, duty drawback, export restrictions, duty preference programs, quota and unfair trade law restrictions, and tariff classification. Mr. Wulwick is a member of the Customs and International Trade Bar Association, American Association of Exporters and Importers, New York State Bar, and the Court of International Trade.

Douglas P. Zuvich is a manager in the KPMG Trade and Customs Practice. Mr. Zuvich was vice president of a customs brokerage firm that specialized in duty drawback. He was an auditor with the U.S. Customs Service, Regulatory Audit Division and coordinated and conducted import and export audits. Mr. Zuvich is a Certified Public Accountant in the State of Maryland and is a licensed customs broker.

Preface

The authors and editors have produced a volume we hope you will find to be useful, practical, and entertaining. We are confident that we perhaps succeeded in all three of our goals! Nothing like *The Import Handbook* has ever been written for the import community. The book is divided into 17 chapters, as discussed below.

Both newcomers to U.S. importing and old-hands in the field should benefit from Chapter 1, entitled "Overview of Customs Procedures and Considerations." Customs consultant Matthew G. Shaw, assisted by Richard P. Wulwick, explain the general procedures all importers must follow to enter products into the United States. These include invoicing and entry documentation, customs bonds, special product requirements (FDA, USDA, CITA, DOC, EPA and myriad other federal government agencies), clearance of cargo, payment of duties and taxes, and other import considerations.

How do you fix a value on products for customs and tax purposes? What is the proper value for barter/trade, consignments, leases, and other ways parties may import goods? The steps required to answer these questions are addressed in Chapter 2, "Customs Appraisement," by James A. Geraghty. This subject is one of the most important and complex areas of importing. Businesses constantly find new and creative ways to engage in trade. The government tries to find equally creative ways to obtain additional tax and duty based on the "proper" value of merchandise.

Chapter 3 addresses the tactics used by government to encourage importers to obey import rules. The discussion focuses on the traditionally punitive measures at U.S. Customs' disposal, and on some of the newer ways fines are assessed against importers. Susan Kohn Ross mentions in "Fines, Penalties, and Forfeitures" the ways to defend your company against this exposure.

Many recent international trade seminars and articles have dealt with the dramatic rise and significance of customs audits. In practical business language, Chapter 4, "U.S. Customs Audits," by Andrew L. Siciliano and Douglas P. Zuvich, lists the criteria for audit targets, ways to prepare for and possibly avoid such audits, and techniques to survive these experiences. In their capacity as customs auditors, they explain the purpose and objective of the U.S. customs auditor. This analysis is invaluable to any company involved in importing.

"The First Sale Rule" (also known as the *Nissho Iwai* or "Chain of Sale") valuation technique is discussed in Chapter 5. This technique presents an opportunity to save duties by valuing goods based on the sale from an overseas manufacturer to an overseas middleman, rather than the higher price paid when the importer pays the middleman. Of course, many recordkeeping, legal, accounting, and procedural conditions must be met to qualify for this benefit, as discussed by customs lawyer M. Barry Levy.

A significant concern of an importer is whether its products are subject to taxes, duty, quotas, or special requirements. These concerns are discussed by Sidney N. Weiss in Chapter 6, "Tariff Classification of Goods and Services."

NAFTA, the North American Free Trade Agreement, is the focus of Chapter 7. Customs lawyer Michael P. Maxwell explains that for many companies NAFTA is more a highly regulated trade agreement than an easy to apply free trade panacea.

Chapter 8 addresses the growing importance of foreign trade zones in the United States. Foreign trade zones and subzones are essentially geographic and legal fictions that allow importers to lawfully reduce taxes and duties without having to enter their goods into the stream of commerce, while also encouraging the flow of products in and out of the United States. Many of the recordkeeping, accounting, and legal demands are explained by customs lawyer Joseph F. Donahue Jr.

Chapter 9 explains how to obtain duty refunds for goods exported from the United States with duty paid imported components, or for duty paid products previously imported and then exported. "Duty Drawback and Exportation of Imported Goods" is written by Ronald C. Glowzinski, a leader in this field and a well-regarded professional in the customs department of one of the world's largest automotive companies. Mr. Glowzinski shares his wealth of knowledge of duty drawback, especially in complex cases involving manufacturing, to explain a potentially lucrative source of untapped revenue.

Jill D. Murray explains the practical and legal side to importing with the benefit of "U.S. Customs Bonded Warehouses and Temporary Import Bonds." As a customs leader for a well-known U.S. apparel importer, catalog company, and retailer, Ms. Murray outlines in Chapter 10 ways to save duties and hassles by using these privileges.

Customs lawyers Peter W. Klestadt and David M. Murphy discuss the often complex and occasionally incomprehensible U.S. system of import quotas. Chapter 11, entitled "Import Quotas," is mandatory reading for textile and apparel importers.

U.S. Customs is increasingly focusing its attention on import and export documentation and recordkeeping compliance. In Chapter 12, authors Frank Chioccola, Harry Isacoff, and Richard P. Wulwick explain pragmatic ways for importers to comply with these demands. As customs and international trade consultants for one of the Big Six consulting firms, the authors reflect on the need for companies to understand and master this requirement if they intend to import successfully.

"Unfair Trade Remedies," the title of Chapter 13, is written by international trade lawyer Joseph S. Kaplan. "Dumping and Transfer Pricing," the title of Chapter 14, is written by lawyers Edward L. Farrell, Seth T. Kaplan, Beril J. Lapson, and Kenneth C. Stanhagen. Both chapters are must-reads for those defending against unfair actions or for those planning an offensive against allegedly unfair foreign business competition.

"Country of Origin Making Requirements" is the title of Chapter 15 written by customs lawyers Peter W. Klestadt and David M. Murphy. This chapter discusses the especially onerous demand placed on importers. "U.S. Customs Rulings, Litigation, and Appeals," written by customs lawyer and litigator Patrick D. Gill, is the title and subject of Chapter 16.

Lastly, Chapter 17 is the icing on the import cake. Entitled "Importing Merchandise—The Tax Issue," highly regarded authors Robert Feinschreiber and Steven C. Wrappe speak on the interrelationship between U.S. Customs valuation and U.S. Internal Revenue Service transfer pricing in related party transactions. The future points to a coordination of IRS and Customs activities. This chapter helps define and clarify the complex rules of this subject.

Import rules are changing rapidly. Readers are encouraged to contact the Editors as these changes evolve. Contact Robert Feinschreiber at Suite F-301, 1121 Crandon Boulevard, Key Biscayne, Florida 33149, telephone 305-361-5800, fax 305-361-7722. Contact Charles L. Crowley at Ernst & Young, LLP, 787 Seventh Avenue, New York, N.Y. 10019, telephone 212-773-1270, fax 212-773-5583. A supplement to the *Import Handbook* is planned. Readers are welcome to provide suggestions. We also recommend you read *The Export Handbook,* and *The Transfer Pricing Handbook,* published in 1996 by John Wiley & Sons, to discover new ways to save money and insure regulatory compliance.

Edward Nash said it well when he penned these words: "If you are not competing globally, you are not competing at all." We hope this book leads to professional success by helping you adapt to the global marketplace.

Robert Feinschreiber
Charles L. Crowley

Acknowledgments

A book is a collaboration of efforts. While many fine individuals have contributed to the process of making the *Import Handbook* a valued resource for importers and others, three individuals stand out: Charles L. Crowley, my co-editor, provided continuing insight into the import process and to the creation of the book itself; my wife, Margaret Kent, a best-selling author and attorney, provided her input into this editorial process; finally, Sheck Cho at John Wiley & Sons, encouraged the process from initiation to rendition.

Robert Feinschreiber

Faith and inspiration for this endeavor came from a variety of treasured sources, including my lovely wife, Diane Ferrara; our children, Alyssa Nicole and Drew Elizabeth; our friends and clients (usually one and the same); my parents, Norma and Charles L. Crowley Sr.; and my mother-in-law, Lucille Ferrara. A special thanks to my co-editor Robert Feinschreiber and his wonderful wife, Margaret, for their support and consideration. Finally, thanks to the entire Ernst & Young International Tax and Customs team, our fellow authors, and Sheck Cho and Anne Brunell for their inspired editing and patience.

Charles L. Crowley

Contents

1 Overview of Customs Procedures and Considerations 1
Matthew G. Shaw
Richard P. Wulwick

2 Customs Appraisement 19
James A. Geraghty

3 Fines, Penalties, and Forfeitures 31
Susan Kohn Ross

4 U.S. Customs Audits 51
Andrew L. Siciliano
Douglas P. Zuvich

5 The First Sale Rule 71
M. Barry Levy

6 Tariff Classification of Goods and Services 87
Sidney N. Weiss

7 NAFTA 105
Michael P. Maxwell

8 Foreign Trade Zones in the United States 127
Joseph F. Donohue Jr.

9 Duty Drawback and Exportation of Imported Goods 151
Ronald C. Glowzinski

10 U.S. Customs Bonded Warehouses
and Temporary Importation Bonds 179
Jill D. Murray

11 Import Quotas **205**
Peter W. Klestadt
David M. Murphy

12 Import and Export Documentation and Recordkeeping Compliance **221**
Frank Chioccola
Harry L. Isacoff
Richard P. Wulwick

13 Unfair Trade Remedies **241**
Joseph S. Kaplan

14 Dumping and Transfer Pricing **273**
Edward L. Farrell, Jr.
Seth T. Kaplan
Beril J. Lapson
Kenneth C. Stanhagen

15 Country of Origin Marking Requirements **301**
Peter W. Klestadt
David M. Murphy

16 U.S. Customs Rulings, Litigation, and Appeals **317**
Patrick D. Gill

17 Importing Merchandise—The Tax Issues **343**
Robert Feinschreiber
Steven C. Wrappe

Index **365**

CHAPTER 1

Overview of Customs Procedures and Considerations

Matthew G. Shaw
Richard P. Wulwick

1.1 Introduction
1.2 Import Transactions: What to Import and From Where
1.3 Consideration of Overseas Laws
1.4 Choosing a Port of Entry
1.5 Choosing a Customs Broker and Freight Forwarder
1.6 Posting a Bond
1.7 Obtaining an Importer Number
1.8 Special Concerns—Quotas and Special Duties
(a) Import Quotas
(b) Special Duties
1.9 Calculating Customs Duties
(a) Tariff Classification
(b) Product Valuation
(c) Modification
(d) Binding Rulings
1.10 Special Tariff Preference Programs and Duty Deferral Mechanisms
(a) Special Tariff Preference Programs
(b) The Generalized System of Preferences
(c) The Caribbean Basin Initiative
(d) The North American Free Trade Agreement
(e) Duty Deferral and Duty Avoidance Mechanisms
(f) Foreign Trade Zones and Customs Bonded Warehouses
(g) Temporary Importation Under Bond
(h) Duty Drawback
1.11 Country of Origin Marking
1.12 Other United States Government Requirements

1.13 Merchandise Entry
1.14 Liquidation
(a) Challenging Liquidation
1.15 Inquiries from Customs
1.16 Recordkeeping

1.1 Introduction

Significant opportunities and vast rewards await those willing to participate in today's global economy and the international trade arena. Success, however, hinges on thorough homework and consideration of many issues before imports commence. This chapter provides an overview of many of these considerations in the United States.

1.2 Import Transactions: What to Import and From Where

Import transactions can take various forms and can include differing terms, but the primary and most obvious consideration is the product to be imported. Added to this are potential markets and consumer preferences. The importer should consider whether it is more prudent to source domestically or overseas, the availability of the article, and the reliability and consistency of this supply. Without this reliability, the importer may be unable to meet obligations, such as a holiday deadline, and incur significant liabilities.

The importer must also consider the merchandise itself, since certain products are subject to United States import restrictions, licensing requirements, high duty rates, or other special regulations. Examples include textiles and apparel, foodstuffs, drugs and cosmetics, alcoholic beverages, wildlife, pets, watches and watch movements, medical devices, radioactive materials, arms, ammunition and explosives, and others. Importation of certain other items are prohibited, including cultural property, switchblades, products made by slave labor, and obscene material.

Once the product is selected, the importer must decide on the country or countries from which to export. Choices are limited if the article is a raw material or is a natural resource grown or extracted in a finite number of countries. The importer should search for sources where labor costs are low if the article is produced from raw materials and this production is labor intensive. In any case, the importer must also consider the infrastructures of the exporting countries and their proximity to the United States. These factors are critical because the time and cost of international and overseas inland freight can be substantial factors in any import transaction.

Importers will also need to consider U.S. costs, such as customs duties, antidumping duties, countervailing duties, and quota expenses. As discussed later in greater detail, these factors may significantly increase the cost of an import transaction.

1.3 Consideration of Overseas Laws

The United States importer must determine whether any laws in the country of exportation affect the transaction. Export licenses and controls, quotas, or other requirements may delay, prevent, or add dramatically to a product's cost.

Information about overseas laws can be obtained from the party supplying the merchandise, or from government officials in the relevant country. The United States can be of help as well, through the Country Desk Program of the United States Department of Commerce. This program supplies specific commercial, industry, and country information on many of the world's trading nations to the country's embassy or consulate in the United States. The Department of Commerce's main telephone number is (202) 482-2000. The telephone number for a specific country desk can be obtained from a locator at this number.

1.4 Choosing a Port of Entry

The United States port of entry may seem to be an elementary choice, but importers should fully consider each port's facilities and any special needs for their merchandise. The location of unlading from an ocean vessel or aircraft may not necessarily be the same as where the customs entry will be made and release from Customs' custody will occur. Merchandise can be unloaded at a particular place and transported in bond to the chosen place of entry.

Factors for consideration in choosing a port of entry include its proximity to the importer's United States warehouse or other storage facility, congestion and traffic at the port where the merchandise lands, and the customs broker's ability to efficiently operate at the location. With the advent of remote entry filing, a new program that allows customs brokers to clear merchandise electronically with Customs at a location different from where it entered the country, the latter concern is less important.

1.5 Choosing a Customs Broker and Freight Forwarder

Once the importer has selected the location of merchandise entry, the importer must determine whether to employ a customs broker and/or freight forwarder. A customs broker is the importer's agent responsible for filing any necessary import-related documents, paying duties and fees, and clearing the merchandise. A freight forwarder is typically responsible for moving merchandise from the port of exportation to the importer's facilities. Both may play crucial roles in the import transaction and can help ensure compliance and minimize expenses relating to the import.

A customs broker may not be necessary if the importer is entering small quantities on a limited basis or possesses the requisite import expertise. The importer may enter merchandise on its own, but most importers use brokers because of their expertise and familiarity with complicated laws and procedures. Because Customs has moved toward electronic transmission of entry information, importers may have little choice but to use brokers because of their ability to electronically interface with Customs.

When choosing a broker, importers should consider the broker's expertise with the merchandise, financial stability, and referrals from other importers. The broker is the importer's agent, so that the importer remains fully responsible for duties, fees, and the broker's actions. For example, the importer is liable to Customs should the broker fail to pay the required duties, even though the importer may have advanced the duties to the broker.

For the broker to act on the importer's behalf, the importer must sign a power of attorney, typically granted through a Customs Form 5291. Importers should be aware of power of attorney forms prepared by the customs broker, because these may contain provisions protecting the broker at the importer's expense. Importers should carefully review powers of attorney to ensure that their interests are adequately protected.

A freight forwarder should be considered if the importer will be moving significant quantities of merchandise or using several locations. A forwarder is responsible for addressing freight concerns, such as packing containers, and for hiring carriers. Using a freight forwarder can, in certain cases, drastically reduce freight costs. As with customs brokers, a variety of freight forwarders exist in the marketplace, so that the importer should carefully choose one that can meet its particular needs. This choice should be made after interviewing candidates, reviewing the forwarder's rates, and consulting other parties who have used the forwarder.

1.6 Posting a Bond

Importers must pay the United States Customs Service to import merchandise, which will typically include duties, merchandise processing fees, and harbor maintenance fees. Before an import occurs, the importer must obtain a bond to ensure that Customs will receive all lawfully owed duties and other fees. The cost of a bond, which can cover a single transaction or a continuing series of transactions, varies depending on the kind of bond. Customs brokers possess their own bonds, and importers may, with the broker's permission, import merchandise under this authority.

Bonds must be filed with the District Director of Customs at the location of merchandise entry in the United States. Evidence of the bond's existence must be filed with the entry documents, as demonstrated by a Customs Form 301.

1.7 Obtaining an Importer Number

U.S. Customs uses the importer number to track import transactions and importer compliance. Such numbers must appear on all import documents presented to Customs when merchandise enters the United States.

New importers must obtain an importer number from Customs before the first import and must include this number on all subsequent importations. Often an importer number is its company Federal Employer Identification Number. For an individual, the number is typically the importer's Social Security Number.

1.8 Special Concerns—Quotas and Special Duties

In addition to taking necessary steps relating to logistics, the importer must consider whether the merchandise is subject in the United States to any quotas, or to countervailing duties, antidumping duties, or other special duties. Quotas and special duties can be significant and, if applicable, can substantially increase the cost of a transaction.

(a) Import Quotas

The United States government imposes quotas, or quantity limitations, on certain merchandise imported to the United States. Two types of quota exist, (1) absolute quantitative[1] and (2) tariff-rate.[2] Importers are required to submit to Customs, with the other required entry documents, a Quota Charge Statement attesting to the merchandise's quota treatment.

Absolute quantitative quotas limit the number of units that can be entered or withdrawn for consumption during a specified period. Once an absolute quota is filled for a certain period, no further imports of that merchandise are permitted in that calendar period. Merchandise arriving after a quota is filled will be denied entry (embargoed) to the United States and must be exported, destroyed, or, if possible, placed in a bonded warehouse or foreign trade zone until the quota opens. Certain absolute quotas apply only to merchandise from specific geographic areas, while others apply to a total number of items of imported merchandise, irrespective of origin. Merchandise subject to absolute quotas include textiles and apparel, raw cotton, meat, sugar, syrups, certain wheat products, and peanuts.

Tariff rate quotas, unlike absolute quotas, do not limit the amount of product that can be imported to the United States but, rather, affect the duty rate for the product. Tariff-rate quotas permit a specified amount of product to be entered or withdrawn for consumption at a reduced duty rate. Once the quota is filled, the merchandise can be imported, but at a significantly higher rate of duty. Examples of merchandise subject to U.S. tariff rate quotas include tuna fish, olives, and wool apparel.

(b) Special Duties

Like quotas, special duties can significantly impact an import transaction. Special duties are usually in the form of antidumping or countervailing duties imposed under special orders by the United States Department of Commerce and administered by

---

[1]19 C.F.R. § 132.1(a).

[2]19 C.F.R. § 132.1(b).

the Customs Service, or sanctions imposed under a United States law, such as Section 301 of the Trade Act of 1974.

Antidumping duties are imposed in situations where an exporter is selling merchandise in the United States at a price below that in the home market, and this trade has caused injury or poses a threat of injury to a domestic industry. Countervailing duties exist to protect the American market from overseas governments that bestow bounties, grants, or subsidies to facilitate the exportation of goods. Countervailing duties are imposed, "to offset the unfair comparative advantage that overseas producers would otherwise enjoy from export subsidies paid by their governments." Actionable export subsidies can take the form of cash rebates, credits, preferential financing, remission of customs duties, and other benefits under governmental programs.

Special duties can exceed 150% of the imported merchandise's appraised value and must be paid in addition to any regular customs duties. Importers of merchandise subject to these special orders must pay these duties themselves and cannot seek compensation from overseas suppliers. Any reimbursement is a violation of the Customs regulations and may result in penalties.

In some cases, special duties are not imposed when an importer initially imports merchandise, but may apply at some future date. To protect against this risk, importers should consult with qualified professionals to evaluate potential risks.

1.9 Calculating Customs Duties

Once the importer has determined whether the merchandise is subject to any special conditions or treatment, the importer should calculate the amount of customs duties that can be assessed. All merchandise imported to the United States is subject to duty. Duty rates vary from duty free to over 100% ad valorem, that is, as a percentage of the merchandise's appraised value. The two critical factors in determining duties owed are the merchandise's tariff classification and value of the merchandise.

There are four types of duty:

1. Free
2. Specific (the amount of duty is charged on a per unit basis—for example, $1.407/kg)
3. Ad valorem (for example, 6.9%)
4. Compound (based on a specific/ad valorem combination—for example, $.0807/kg + 9.8%)

(a) Tariff Classification

All merchandise imported to the United States must be properly classified under the Harmonized Tariff Schedule of the United States, or HTS. The HTS is a common commodity identification system that has been adopted by most of the world's major trading nations. The text consists of 99 chapters in 22 sections. For specificity purposes, each chapter is further divided into headings and subheadings.

There is a provision for every product in the tariff schedule. When merchandise is not specifically described by use or name, it is classified under a basket, catch-all provision. Besides determining the duty rate, classification also determines the availability of preferential tariff treatment and the applicability of quotas, antidumping and countervailing duties.

The HTS is comprehensive and requires significant technical expertise to master. Accordingly, importers often require assistance from qualified professionals, such as customs consultants, counsel, or brokers. It is also advisable for importers to confirm their merchandise's classification through a written binding ruling request properly submitted to the Customs Service. Only written opinions from the Customs Service are binding on the importer and the government as to that importer and its merchandise.

While importers are legally obligated to properly classify their merchandise, the classification system provides opportunities for importers to lawfully reduce duty liability. This reduction can be accomplished by:

1. Seeking alternative classifications with more favorable tariff treatment
2. Modifying merchandise at the design or production level to change the classification to a more favorable designation, or
3. Proactively structuring the transaction; for example, to take advantage of the rules for sets or composite goods.

(b) Product Valuation

The value of imported merchandise is equally as important as tariff classification in determining the duties owed, because most duties are assessed on an ad valorem basis; that is, as a percentage of the imported product's value. Importers are required by law to properly value their merchandise even when no duty is owed.

Valuation methodologies include the transaction value of identical or similar goods sold at or about the same time as the goods being appraised: deductive value, which is the imported merchandise's United States sale price less certain clearly defined deductions; and computed value, which is a value determined from manufacturing costs, such as materials, fabrication, general expenses, and profit. These alternative methodologies are applied hierarchically when transaction value cannot be used.

In the vast majority of importations the dutiable value is the transaction value, which is the total payment, whether direct or indirect, made or to be made for the imported merchandise by the buyer to the seller. Added to this must be sums covering the following:

1. Packing costs incurred by the buyer for the imported merchandise
2. Selling, but not buying, commissions incurred by the buyer for the imported merchandise

3. The value, properly apportioned, of any assists
4. Any royalty or license fee related to the imported merchandise that the buyer is required to pay, directly or indirectly, as condition of the imported merchandise's sale for exportation to the United States
5. The proceeds of any subsequent resale, disposal, or use of the imported merchandise that accrues, directly or indirectly, to the seller

An assist is any of the following, if supplied by the buyer to the seller, free of charge or at a reduced cost:

1. Materials, components, parts, and similar items
2. Tools, dies, molds, and similar items used in production
3. Merchandise consumed in production
4. Overseas engineering, development, artwork, design work, and plans and sketches

A royalty or license fee is a payment made for the right to use, produce, or sell a given item. Additions to transaction value for royalties or license fees are limited to those that the buyer is required to pay, directly or indirectly, as a condition of the sale of imported merchandise for exportation to the United States. Royalties or license fee payments may not be dutiable if the importer can demonstrate that the fee paid (1) was separate and distinct from the price actually paid or payable and (2) was not a condition of the sale of the imported goods for export to the United States.

(c) Modification

The price paid or payable excludes any charges or expenses incurred for transportation, insurance, and services incident to the international shipment of the merchandise. In addition, when separately identifiable and properly supported, the following charges are not necessarily a part of the merchandise's dutiable value:

1. Bona fide buying agency commissions
2. Certain royalties
3. Interest charges
4. Overseas inland freight costs
5. Quota charges
6. A middleman's markup

Duty exclusions may provide excellent opportunities for importers to lessen duty liability by lawfully reducing dutiable value. Caution is required, though, since customs valuation is quite complex and may also have tax ramifications. As a result, unsuspecting importers that adjust value may be found to be in violation of the valuation or tax laws or may experience unintended negative consequences. Accordingly, importers would be wise to seek guidance before recharacterizing cost components and to confirm any planning ideas with a written binding ruling request to Customs.

Transaction value is not an acceptable basis for valuation in some circumstances. Transactions between related parties will be questioned if the relationship influences the price. Related parties include those who are members of the same family, partners, employer and employee, and any person who, directly or indirectly, owns, controls, or holds with power to vote, 5% or more of the outstanding voting stock or share of the other organization. Customs expects the parties to be able to substantiate the pricing methodologies and elements when the transaction involves related parties.

(d) Binding Rulings

Importers should seek written resolution and confirmation of value, classification, or origin from the United States Customs Service through a formal binding ruling request if uncertainty exists. Only in this way can an importer be assured of conformity with Customs regulations and the exercise of reasonable care.

A binding ruling must be prepared and submitted in accordance with the Customs regulations[3] and must sufficiently describe an issue to permit Customs to issue a decision. For example, when tariff classification advice is sought, the ruling request must sufficiently describe the merchandise's composition and fabrication to permit Customs to analyze and rule on the item. Moreover, a binding ruling does not offer protection if the importer deviates from the scenario(s) presented in the ruling request and decision. For example, a classification ruling is valid only for merchandise identical to that described in the ruling. If changes are made to the merchandise's composition, design, or manufacture, the ruling is no longer effective and the importer should obtain a new ruling under the altered facts.

Importers can obtain binding rulings under the requirements stated in the Customs regulations by submitting a completed request to the District Director at the port where the merchandise will be imported. Alternatively, the importer can seek informal assistance from his customs broker, outside consultant, or qualified legal counsel.

1.10 Special Tariff Preference Programs and Duty Deferral Mechanisms

Once the importer has determined the tariff classification and value of the merchandise, the importer should determine whether the merchandise is eligible for special treatment under a tariff preference program, such as the North American Free Trade Agreement (NAFTA), the Generalized System of Preferences (GSP), or the Caribbean Basin Initiative (CBI). Qualifying for one of these programs can allow the importer to enter the merchandise duty-free or at a reduced rate.

---

[3]19 C.F.R. Pt. 177.

Even if merchandise does not qualify for preferential tariff treatment, an importer may minimize duty liability through a lawful duty deferral or avoidance mechanism, such as customs bonded warehouses, foreign trade zones, temporary importations under bond, or duty drawback. Successful use of customs bonded warehouses and foreign trade zones permits importers to defer duty payments, while use of a temporary importation under bond and duty drawback permits importers to avoid or recover duty.

(a) Special Tariff Preference Programs

Determining whether a product is eligible for a special tariff program often depends on its country of origin. An importer must ensure that its merchandise is validly considered a product of an eligible country prior to claiming preferential treatment. In addition, origin in an eligible country does not guarantee preferential treatment. Specific products may be denied preferential treatment because of their tariff classification. Information regarding eligibility under particular tariff subheadings is contained in the tariff code.

Merchandise may be required to meet certain other requirements for duty preferences, such as "value content," direct transit, and documentary requirements. See Chapter 15, "Country of Origin Marking Requirements," for specific requirements.

(b) The Generalized System of Preferences

GSP is a worldwide tariff preference program enacted to promote economic revitalization in, and develop trade from, lesser developed nations. Under the United States program, over 100 nations are considered "beneficiary developing countries" for GSP purposes, and many articles from these countries are afforded duty-free treatment upon their United States importation.

(c) The Caribbean Basin Initiative

CBI is a United States government program under which qualifying merchandise from most Caribbean nations is afforded preferential tariff treatment upon United States import. Although similar to the GSP program, its requirements are generally less stringent.

(d) The North American Free Trade Agreement

Under the NAFTA, merchandise originating in Mexico or Canada may be entitled to preferential tariff treatment upon importation to the United States. Many articles are entitled to duty-free treatment, and the duty rates for most other products are being reduced over either a five, ten or fifteen year phase-out period.

(e) Duty Deferral and Duty Avoidance Mechanisms

Importers may be able to defer or avoid virtually all duty payments on imported merchandise if they can use foreign trade zones, customs bonded warehouses, or temporary importations under bond or duty drawback. Each of these mechanisms provide differing benefits and costs. Therefore, before choosing one importers should consult with a qualified professional.

(f) Foreign Trade Zones and Customs Bonded Warehouses

A foreign trade zone (FTZ) or subzone is a secured area that is geographically within the United States, but considered outside it for customs purposes. Importers may enter merchandise into an FTZ for storage or processing without being subject to the usual customs entry procedures or duties, fees, and tax payments. Duties are owed only when merchandise leaves the zone and enters the United States customs territory. No duty is due when the goods are exported instead of entered into the United States.

Merchandise entered to a foreign trade zone may be manufactured, exhibited, repackaged or unpacked, manipulated or assembled, sorted or cleaned. Merchandise may not, however, be put up for retail sale. Imported merchandise may remain in an FTZ indefinitely. Merchandise may remain in a bonded warehouse for up to five years. Manufacturing is permitted in certain types of bonded warehouses where the merchandise is destined for exportation.

Depending on how the merchandise is designated when entering a zone, importers may elect the merchandise's duty treatment. For example, duties can be assessed on the merchandise on the date and in the condition when it either enters or leaves the zone. Proper utilization of this designation system can result in significant duty savings.

Customs bonded warehouses are similar in several respects to foreign trade zones, since importers can store, manipulate, or, in some cases, manufacture imported merchandise in a customs bonded warehouse without incurring duty liability. Duties are owed only when merchandise is withdrawn for entry to the United States. Unlike FTZs, though, with a customs bonded warehouse entry duties are based on the duty rate in effect when the merchandise is withdrawn from the warehouse. In addition, entry to a customs bonded warehouse requires filing certain entry documents, including a warehouse entry. Importers can apply to bond their own storage facilities, or they can rent space in an existing customs bonded warehouse.

Customs bonded warehouses may be used to store merchandise whose duty rate is expected to be reduced, or become duty free, until the rate becomes effective. The warehouse is also useful to enter articles subject to quota or other import restrictions until the quota reopens or restrictions lift, and for merchandise that will not be used in the United States until a significant period after importation.

FTZs and customs bonded warehouses are similar in several respects, but the following significant differences exist:

1. *Storage.* Merchandise can be stored in a bonded warehouse for up to five years. There is no time limitation for FTZs.
2. *Manufacturing.* Manufacturing is permitted in customs bonded warehouses only for merchandise to be exported from the United States. Manufacturing is permitted in an FTZ without restriction.

3. *Administration.* The application process for customs bonded warehouse status generally takes several months and is relatively inexpensive, as compared with FTZ designation, which can require at least a year for approval by the foreign trade zones board and is fairly political and costly.
4. *Duty Rate.* Merchandise in a customs bonded warehouse is dutiable at the rate in effect at the time of withdrawal from the warehouse into the United States. The duty rates for FTZ merchandise may be chosen to be either the rate when entered or the rate when withdrawn from the zone.
5. *Cost.* Space in a customs bonded warehouse is considerably less expensive than in an FTZ.

(g) Temporary Importation Under Bond

Products to be imported for a short duration may be entered without duty liability into the United States using a temporary importation under bond, or TIB. Situations when TIBs are permitted include articles being entered to be repaired, altered, processed, as samples for taking orders, and articles to be tested.

Importers using a TIB must post a bond with United States Customs to ensure the payment of duties should the importer breach the bond's terms. The amount of this bond is generally twice the estimated duties payable in a typical importation. In certain circumstances, the amount of the bond may be 110% of the estimated duties or any amount the District Director of Customs deems necessary to protect Customs' interests. Merchandise entered under a TIB must be exported from (or properly destroyed in) the United States within one year of entering the country. To be properly exported for TIB purposes, merchandise must be physically exported "with the intention of uniting it to the commerce of some other country." Shipping merchandise abroad, intending to return the goods and simply circumvent a limitation or restriction in the tariff laws, or to secure a benefit, is not a valid exportation. This time limit may, with permission from Customs, be extended for up to two additional one-year periods. If the merchandise remains in the United States for more than one year without authorization, or past any extended deadline, Customs will consider the TIB breached. This will result in importer liability for liquidated damages (forfeiture of the bond), along with payment of all duties and fees owed and possible penalties.

(h) Duty Drawback

Duty drawback is unlike the aforementioned mechanisms that lawfully defer or avoid customs duties in that parties claiming duty drawback obtain a refund of 99% of duties already paid on materials and products imported and subsequently exported. To use duty drawback, it is critical for Customs to be able to match imported to exported merchandise to ensure that proper refunds are given.

The four most common types of drawback are as follows:

1. *Manufacturing—Direct Identification Drawback* applies to articles manufactured in the United States from imported components. A claimant may re-

cover 99% of the duties paid on the imported components that are subsequently exported as part of a finished product.

2. *Manufacturing—Substitution Drawback* applies to articles manufactured in the United States from domestic and imported materials that are of the "same kind and quality." A claimant may recover 99% of the duties paid on the imported materials, even if they have not specifically been exported. The claimant may substitute domestic materials for imported materials up to the total amount imported.
3. *Unused Merchandise—Direct Identification Drawback* applies to merchandise exported or destroyed within three years of its importation to the United States. In such case, a claimant may recover 99% of the duties paid on the imported merchandise. Although the merchandise must be unused for this type of drawback, incidental operations, such as inspecting, cleaning, testing, repackaging, and replacing components, may be performed.
4. *Unused Merchandise—Substitution Drawback* applies to domestic merchandise that is "commercially interchangeable" with imported merchandise exported within three years of importation. If, at the time of exportation, the domestic merchandise is in the same condition as the imported merchandise, then the claimant may recover 99% of the duties paid on the imported merchandise.

Duty drawback is a privilege, not a right, so persons utilizing it must adhere to strict recordkeeping requirements in support of a drawback claim. These records include:

1. Documents verifying the importation and receipt of imported merchandise
2. Records confirming any manufacturing
3. Documents verifying that substituted merchandise was commercially interchangeable with imported merchandise
4. Documents verifying exportation from the United States (air waybills or ocean bills of lading)

In sum, customs bonded warehouses, foreign trade zones, temporary importations under bond, and duty drawback provide tangible, duty-saving benefits. Importers considering any of these mechanisms should do their homework and consult with a qualified professional before implementation to determine which best and properly meets their needs.

1.11 Country of Origin Marking

In most cases, articles made abroad—or their containers—imported to the United States must be conspicuously marked with name of the item's country of origin. This marking must be legible, indelible, and permanent and must indicate to the ultimate purchaser in the United States the article's country of origin in

English.[4] The term "ultimate purchaser" is generally the last person in the United States who will receive the article in its imported form.[5]

There are several exemptions to the country of origin marking requirements, including those on the "J-List."[6] Examples of J-List articles include works of art, screws, and barbed wire. Other exempt articles include those incapable of being marked without economic hardship and articles whose containers, when the product reaches the ultimate consumer in its container, are reasonably marked to indicate the article's origin. Some articles are exempt from marking, but in those rare cases their outermost containers must indicate country of origin. These regulations exist to permit the ultimate purchaser to easily determine the article's origin and buy or refuse to buy based on this knowledge.

Customs is empowered to seize improperly marked merchandise. Seized merchandise can either be exported or destroyed, or released to the importer for proper marking after the payment of additional marking duties (10%). If the improper marking is not discovered until after the merchandise's release, Customs can order the articles redelivered to Customs for proper marking, exportation, or destruction. An importer who fails to redeliver improperly marked merchandise can be assessed liquidated damages amounting to the merchandise's entered value, plus estimated duties. Substantial penalties will be levied for the intentional removal or defacement of a country of origin marking.

The marking regulations require all importers to verify that their merchandise is sufficiently marked, and that the marking accurately indicates the merchandise's country of origin. This information can be verified through a binding ruling request to Customs, often preceded by consultations with experienced professionals.

1.12 Other United States Government Requirements

In addition to its own regulations, Customs enforces other governmental requirements with regard to imported merchandise. For example, the Food and Drug Administration has regulations involving the safety and purity of foodstuffs, health care products, and sunglasses, and the Federal Trade Commission regulates wearing apparel and textiles. Importers should determine whether any of these requirements apply to their merchandise and ensure compliance.

1.13 Merchandise Entry

Imports can begin once the importer has:

1. Chosen a product and a source
2. Selected a country of origin and considered that country's laws

---

[4] 19 C.F.R. § 134.11.

[5] 19 C.F.R. § 134.1(d).

[6] 19 C.F.R. § 134.33.

3. Determined whether quotas or special duties exist
4. Calculated duties
5. Evaluated tariff preference programs
6. Analyzed duty deferral or avoidance mechanism

The importer must generally arrange to transport the merchandise from the country of exportation to the United States. Depending on the terms of sale, the importer's responsibilities and risk of loss may commence at the time the merchandise leaves the exporter's facility (ex-factory), at the port of exportation, or upon leaving the transporting vessel at the port of importation.

Commercial shipments are typically made through a common carrier, such as an airline or ocean vessel line. When a common carrier is used, prior to entry the importer will receive a bill of lading from the carrier indicating that it has received the merchandise for transportation to the United States. A properly completed bill of lading must be submitted to Customs as part of the merchandise's entry documents, evidencing that the person making entry has the right to do so. The bill of lading is used to obtain the merchandise's release from the carrier in ocean shipments.

In addition to the bill of lading, the importer will also receive a commercial invoice itemizing the merchandise and its cost, and often a packing list detailing the merchandise contained in the shipment. Both must be filed with U.S. Customs as part of the entry documents.

Once the merchandise arrives at the U.S. port of entry, the carrier will send notice to the importer or its agent (usually a customs broker) informing it of the merchandise's arrival. That party must typically present the required entry information, along with estimated duties, to Customs within five days to make a formal import entry and obtain the release of merchandise.

Under the proper circumstances, the importer may obtain the immediate release of its merchandise by filing an Entry/Immediate Delivery Form (Customs Form 3461). When immediate release is granted, the importer must file the other required documents within ten working days of filing the Customs Form 3461. Failure to do so can result in penalties.

The imported merchandise is released for delivery to the importer's facilities, bonded warehouse, or foreign trade zone, whether immediate release is requested or a regular entry is filed, assuming no problems exist, such as improper markings. Customs involvement has not ended yet, though, because the merchandise must still be liquidated.

1.14 Liquidation

Generally within one year of importation Customs will liquidate the entry. *Liquidation* is the process by which the importer's final liability (for example, adjusted duties) on a specific entry is determined. All entries, except those for a temporary importation under bond, transportation in bond, or immediate exportation, must be liquidated. Unless properly challenged, liquidations are final, conclusive, and binding on all persons.

(a) Challenging Liquidation

The primary way to challenge a decision on liquidation is by timely filing with Customs an administrative protest. Depending on the facts involved, protests must be filed within 90 days of the date of liquidation, the date of notice of liquidation, or the date of the decision about which the protest is made. Untimely protests will be summarily denied, regardless of their validity or merits.

Alternatively, other mechanisms exist to challenge liquidation. For example, reliquidation may occur when the Customs Service voluntarily, or at the request of an interested party, reexamines the liquidation. Voluntary reliquidation must occur within 90 days of the initial liquidation.

Importers may obtain reliquidation through use of a 520(c) claim to correct a clerical error, mistake of fact, or other inadvertence not amounting to an error in the construction of a law.

A clerical error occurs when a person intends to do one thing but does something else. For example, clerical errors include arithmetic mistakes or mistakes made in copying or typing figures. The exercise of poor judgment is not considered a 520(c) clerical error.

A mistake of fact occurs when a person believes the facts to be other than they really are and takes some action based on that erroneous belief. The basis for the belief may be that a fact exists, but is unknown to the person, or the person may be convinced that something is a fact when in reality it is not.

"Other inadvertences" is a broad term that connotes inattention, oversight, or carelessness. For example, an article might be classified properly under a tariff code subheading providing for it by name, but thorough *oversight* is given a duty rate different from any rate provided under that subheading.

An "error in the construction of a law" occurs when a person knows the true facts but has a mistaken belief of the legal consequences and acts on that mistaken belief. Errors in the construction of a law cannot be corrected by a 520(c) claim.

A 520(c) claim must be made within one year after the date of liquidation or extraction. Ultimately, an aggrieved importer may seek satisfaction in the United States Court of International Trade, although judicial review is limited in many cases.

1.15 Inquiries from Customs

At any time after entry, an importer may receive a Customs Form 28—Request for Information from Customs. A CF-28 is the primary device by which Customs learns more about an importation, and it may involve detailed questions about the transaction. Unless an extension is granted, importers must respond to a CF-28 within 30 days. Failure to timely or accurately respond can result in merchandise seizure, liquidation at nonpreferential tariff rates, or other significant problems.

Importers should be aware that any information released on a CF-28 can be used against them to reclassify or revalue imported merchandise or to commence an audit. Accordingly, importers must carefully and accurately complete CF-28 documents and understand the consequences of the information contained in their responses.

1.16 Recordkeeping

The Customs Modernization and Informed Compliance Act, enacted as part of the NAFTA implementation legislation, has established comprehensive recordkeeping regulations. These require all persons involved in import transactions to maintain, store, and produce when lawfully requested virtually all import related records they generate. The *Mod Act* permits Customs to examine these records to ascertain entry correctness, determine fine and penalty liability, and ensure general compliance. Failure to follow the recordkeeping requirements can result in recordkeeping penalties plus general customs penalties. As a result, importers should develop a recordkeeping program and internal controls to ensure that all required documents are saved and retrievable.

CHAPTER 2

Customs Appraisement

James A. Geraghty

2.1 Introduction
2.2 Appraisement Bases
2.3 Transaction Value
- (a) General Considerations
- (b) Invoice Prices
- (c) Related Parties
- (d) Remedies

2.4 Exclusions from Transaction Value
- (a) Inland Freight
- (b) Post-importation Costs
- (c) Limits on Exclusions
- (d) Interest
- (e) Buying Agents' Commissions

2.5 Additions to Transaction Value
- (a) Selling Agents' Commissions
- (b) Assists
- (c) Royalties

2.6 Determining the Price
- (a) Quota Costs
- (b) Formula Pricing
- (c) Currency Issues
- (d) First Sale
- (e) Unrelated Credits

2.7 Deductive Value
2.8 Computed Value
2.9 Derivative Value
2.10 Conclusion

2.1 Introduction

Duty assessment is a function of the value or the quantity of imported merchandise and the applicable duty rate. Duty rates are determined under the Harmonized Tariff Schedule of the United States (HTSUS) nomenclature. A relatively small percentage of merchandise is subject to duty based on quantity (e.g., per pound, barrel, or square yard). However, the vast majority of imports are dutiable on a percentage of their appraised value. Customs appraisement is an objective exercise, prescribed by stature, rather than an evaluation of what the goods would be worth in some market or in the opinion of an expert. Instead, imported merchandise is appraised under hierarchically arranged bases, each of which has criteria or elements of value.[1]

The primary basis of appraisement seeks an actual arm's length price, with adjustments depending on the price terms. Alternative appraisement bases tend to approach what such a price would have been had it existed. In the past, Customs appraised at a price at which imported merchandise was freely sold or offered for sale for exportation to the United States. This standard was often difficult to establish and has been eliminated. Moreover, Customs is proscribed from appraising at the price at which the merchandise was sold in the home market or to third countries, the price at which comparable domestically produced merchandise was sold in the United States, or under the higher of alternative bases of appraisement. Appraisement parameters have narrowed since Congress adopted the international value agreement or code in 1980. Nevertheless, Customs appraisement can be complex, and undervaluation may subject an importer to draconian penalties.

This chapter presents an overview of Customs appraisement principles as well as a discussion of problems that arise frequently. Importers must be sensitive to the nuances of Customs appraisement to fulfill their obligation to use reasonable care in the entry of imported merchandise. Of the various Customs compliance issues, appraisement has become more significant inasmuch as Customs audits, by their nature, focus on value and price issues. Yet a good working knowledge of appraisement will mitigate an importer's anxieties about interacting with Customs officials and allow the importer to take advantage of all legitimate means to minimize duty assessment.

2.2 Appraisement Bases

The primary basis of appraisement is transaction value, which is the price actually paid or payable for the merchandise when sold for exportation to the United States. The price is the total payment, whether direct or indirect, made by the buyer to the seller. If, for whatever reason, the transaction value of the merchandise undergoing appraisement does not exist, or is not determinable, the secondary and tertiary bases are the transaction values of "*identical merchandise*" and "*similar*

---

[1] § 402 of the Tariff Act of 1930, as amended, 19 U.S.C. § 1401a.

merchandise," respectively. Identical merchandise is produced in the same country by the "same person" as the merchandise undergoing appraisement. Similar merchandise is produced in the same country by the same person, is similar to the imported merchandise in characteristics and component material, and is commercially interchangeable with the merchandise undergoing appraisement. Merchandise meeting the definitions of identical or similar, but made by another producer in the country of manufacture, may still meet the criteria.

If there is no transaction value for the imported merchandise, the next alternative in sequence is "*deductive value,*" which is a post-importation price in the United States, with deductions to yield what theoretically would have been a FOB-level transaction value if it had existed. If deductive value cannot be determined, or if the importer affirmatively chooses to avoid deductive value, the next basis is "*computed value,*" which is not a price, but rather the sum of the costs of production in the country of manufacture. Finally, the residual basis is "*derivative value,*" which is a value derived from one of the preceding bases but for which an element of value is not determinable.

2.3 Transaction Value

The sine qua non of transaction value is a "*price for exportation,*" which presumes that the goods were shipped subject to a sale. Goods shipped on consignment and inventory transfers to a branch do not constitute sales. In-transit sales are not sales for exportation since the goods already have been exported at the time of sale. Goods imported under lease likewise cannot be appraised under transaction value.

(a) General Considerations

The locations of the buyer and the seller are not determinative of transaction value. An owner in a third country can sell goods from the country of exportation to the United States. Likewise, a buyer may be located outside the United States and have such goods "drop shipped" to a resale customer or to an agent within the United States.

Transaction value applies as a general matter provided that there are no restrictions on the disposition or use of the imported merchandise, except those required by law, or the restriction does not affect the value of the goods. Territorial restrictions on distribution likewise would not obviate transaction value. For example, a proscription on resale before the commencement of a model year would not be considered to affect the value.

(b) Invoice Prices

Transaction value is often thought to be equivalent to invoice price. However, the invoice price is actually a representation by the seller of the price at which the goods were sold. Depending on its terms, that price might be subject to adjustment, and there may be dutiable elements of value not included in the price.

The invoice price might not be the full price. The transaction value price reflects what is known in contract law as consideration, that is, that which is given or promised in a bargain. Consideration need not include money and might not even be calculable. However, the transaction value price must be determinable in terms of money. For this reason, tie-in arrangements under which the importer agrees to buy goods different from those undergoing appraisement, or to remit something to the seller that cannot be valued, vitiate transaction value.

(c) Related Parties

If the parties are unrelated, transaction value applies assuming that the other criteria are present. Related party transfer prices may constitute transaction value if the prices meet certain test values or if there is evidence that the relationship did not affect the price. The test values include the transaction value of identical or similar merchandise in sales to unrelated buyers, or the deductive value or computed value of identical or similar merchandise. The test values must reflect actual transactions that have been accepted by Customs under the indicated bases, and must have been contemporaneous with the related party sales. If related party transactions are acceptable under a test value, the test value is not substituted in the appraisement, but rather stands as a benchmark concerning the propriety of the related party transaction price.

In the absence of a test value, Customs will accept information showing that the related parties did business as if they were at arm's length. The importer has the burden of proof on this issue. Unlike transfer pricing for income tax purposes, there are no agency guidelines or other published criteria for customs purposes. Moreover, there is no judicial precedent, although the current value law is over 15 years old.

The Customs regulations state simply that a related party transaction would be acceptable if the parties settle the prices in a manner consistent with industry practice or in sales, if any, to unrelated parties. A related party price would be acceptable if it includes all costs plus a profit equivalent to the seller's overall profit realized over a representative period of time. Customs has taken the position that, in certain circumstances, a price that does not include a profit may be satisfactory as transaction value.

The dearth of precedent in this highly significant area can be attributed to the fact that Customs had routinely accepted conclusory representations concerning price negotiations, the propriety of relative markups in the country of export and in the United States, as well as the lack of a motive to suppress export prices because of a relatively lower income tax rate in the country of exportation. Also, for many years Customs had been predisposed to accept related party transfer prices unless there was an affirmative reason to suspect price suppression. However, that practice is changing and Customs now performs transfer price audits with greater frequency.

(d) Remedies

If Customs concludes that the relationship affected the price, and that transaction value does not apply, the imported merchandise would be appraised under another, presumably higher, basis. It is an open issue whether Customs could assess penalties for purported undervaluation. Customs might take the position that an importer whose transfer price was found to have been influenced by the relationship failed to use due care in selecting an appraisement basis and thereby committed what might be characterized as a false practice by making entry accordingly. The alternative, and probably better, view is that importers do not actually choose an appraisement basis, but rather submit value information required by regulation. Under this approach, it is Customs that has the responsibility to conclude whether a relationship affected the price and, therefore, whether transaction value applies. Nevertheless, to avoid this predicament, and in view of the fact that importers have the burden of establishing the propriety of the related party transfer price, prudence dictates that transfer prices be established based on sound appraisement and income tax planning in accordance with Customs standards, however imprecise.

2.4 Exclusions from Transaction Value

International freight and insurance premiums are excluded from transaction value if otherwise included in, but identified separately from, the price paid or payable. Therefore, an appreciation of Incoterms, the internationally recognized standard price terms, is essential.[2] For Customs purposes, international freight includes all incidental charges such as freight forwarder and/or Customs brokers' fees.

(a) Inland Freight

The duty status of foreign inland freight has been controversial. Customs considers foreign inland freight to be incidental to the international freight and, therefore, nondutiable if the cost of the inland freight occurred after the sale for exportation, and the goods were shipped on a through bill of lading that included the foreign inland leg of the shipment. So, for example, the total freight on a through bill of lading from the foreign point of shipment in a CIF sale is nondutiable. In contrast, if goods are purchased at an ex-factory price, and the buyer pays the foreign inland freight directly to the carrier, there is no adjustment since the price does not include the freight.

The freight on sales for export to the United States from inland points in contiguous countries is all international freight. Thus, the entire freight from Montreal on a through bill to Dallas is nondutiable. However, presale foreign inland freight from the factory to a stocking point is not deducted from the export price since it is not incidental to an international shipment.

---

[2]Incoterms are published by the International Chamber of Commerce.

(b) Post-importation Costs

Post-importation costs included in an export price are not dutiable. Equipment may be imported under a "turnkey" contract at a price that includes the cost of assembly and technical assistance in the United States. The post-importation costs may be deducted from the transaction value if they can be separately identified in the contract or invoice, as the case may be.

United States inland freight, as well as Customs duties and other federal taxes, if applicable, are not dutiable. Therefore, a duty-paid delivered price (DDP) term would indicate that the price includes all costs to the point of delivery in the United States. To determine dutiable value, the United States inland freight plus any other nondutiable charges are deducted from the price. The resultant figure includes duty. If that figure is divided by one plus the duty rate, the quotient is the appraised value.

(c) Limits on Exclusions

Customs' position, which has been endorsed by the courts, is that the total amount remitted directly or indirectly to the seller is the transaction value price, and that only nondutiable elements specified in the statute may be excluded. It is irrelevant how the parties derived the price or allocated cost elements for purposes of negotiation or, for that matter, how these elements are enumerated on an invoice. This principle has given rise to two pitfalls in structuring import transactions that involve buying agents' commissions and finance charges.

(d) Interest

Interest is a payment for the use of money, not for the purchase of goods per se. Therefore, import financing done through financial institutions or any party unrelated to the seller is not dutiable. However, any finance charges included in the price, or paid to the seller of the goods in addition to the price, are not deducted from transaction value unless the buyer can establish that:

1. The finance charges are separable from the price,
2. The financial arrangement was reduced to writing, and
3. If required by Customs, that the goods have actually been sold at the net price and/or the interest rate does not exceed the prevailing rate in the country where the financing was arranged.

This scenario must be distinguished from delayed payment terms which, theoretically, reduce the price by the time value of money. In the latter case, there is no adjustment.

(e) Buying Agents' Commissions

A buying agent's commission is compensation for services, not for goods. It has become a rule of thumb that selling agents' commissions are dutiable, while buying agents' commissions are not. Also, it is sometimes difficult to so distinguish an agent from a principal buying and selling on its own behalf. As a principal, the would-be commission is considered nothing more than the principal/seller's markup and, therefore, dutiable. Generally, the primary feature of the principal/agent relationship is control. Therefore, if the buyer controls the actions of the buying agent, and remits the commission directly to the agent, Customs probably would recognize its status, and the commission would not be dutiable. However, if the agent submits an invoice to the buyer enumerating the cost of the goods and all other charges including the commission, Customs requires a copy of the factory invoice to verify the price from the seller.

This practice is salutary in that it keeps an agent honest, as it were. On the other hand, if the seller controls the agent who, in effect, solicits sales on the seller's behalf, the agent's commission is dutiable. Even a bona fide buying agent's commission is dutiable if the commission is remitted to the seller of the merchandise who disburses the commission to the agent. This last circumstance does no more than underscore the basic principle that the transaction value is the total payment to the seller of the merchandise, as well as the fact that there is no specific statutory exclusion for buying agents' commissions.

2.5 Additions to Transaction Value

If not already included in the price, the transaction value price is increased by selling commissions, packing costs, "assists," certain royalties, and resale proceeds that inure to the benefit of the seller of the imported merchandise. Packing includes the cost of labor and materials used in placing the merchandise ready for shipment to the United States. However, packing does not include international containers, such as those used in consolidation.

(a) Selling Agents' Commissions

Selling agents' commissions are dutiable, whether included in the price, paid separately to the seller of the merchandise, or paid directly to the selling agent. An importer's buying agent who is related to the seller of the merchandise by family or by corporate affiliation might be deemed to be a selling agent. However, such a relationship is not conclusive, and there have been rulings in which Customs has held that an agent was a bona fide buying agent despite the relationship with the seller. Nevertheless, these relationships are scrutinized and should be avoided in the absence of a contract requiring full disclosure to, and approval by, the importer/principal.

(b) Assists

Probably the most fruitful area for the assessment of Customs penalties is the failure to declare assists. An assist is a production factor furnished free of charge or at reduced cost by the buyer to the manufacturer for use in the production of the imported merchandise. By the nature of things, the price of the goods would not embrace the assist. Therefore, importers are obliged to declare assists to Customs at the time of entry of the imported merchandise. There are four exclusive assist categories:

1. Materials, components, and like items,
2. Tools, dies, molds, and similar items,
3. Merchandise consumed in production, and
4. Engineering, design, and R and D undertaken outside the United States.

Category 2 could include capital equipment such as machine tools. Category 4 does not include such work undertaken within the United States or done abroad by United States domiciliaries incidental to work done in the United States. Costs that might be categorized as general and administrative expenses are not in nature of assists. For example, management consultants' fees and computer equipment furnished free of charge need not be declared to Customs.

Assists are valued at their purchase price or cost of production, and include freight and other related expenses to the place of manufacture of the imported merchandise. Customs' current position is that materials assists should be valued based on the quantity used in production, not the quantity appearing in the manufactured product. In short, there is no deduction for waste, except to the extent that the value of recovered scrap may be factored out of the material cost.

The value of assists may be allocated

1. Over the number of units included in the first entry of the affected merchandise,
2. Over the total number of units produced at the time of entry of the first shipment, or
3. Over the total number of units anticipated to be produced.

Customs may accept an alternative method proposed by the importer. If the goods to be produced are for sale in markets other than the United States, Customs may accept a per unit allocation over the entire amount to be produced, thus reducing the amount to be allocated to the goods exported to the United States.

(c) Royalties

The dutiable royalty issue has been controversial, complex, and intertwined with the question as to whether a certain payment may be considered to be a separately dutiable resale proceed benefiting the seller. Royalties that pertain to the manufacturing process or that are required as a condition of sale for exportation to the United States are dutiable whether they are paid directly to the foreign producer or to a third party on behalf of the producer. On the other hand, a royalty paid to an unrelated third party for trademark rights to resell in the United States would not be dutiable.

If any resale proceeds are payable to a party related to the seller, Customs would consider them to be dutiable as resale proceeds regardless of whether they would be considered royalties in the technical sense. Subtle differences between transactions can change the dutiable status of a particular payment. Therefore, it is difficult to generalize in this area, except that if the importer could buy the product without paying a royalty fee at that time or subsequently as a condition of importation, any later payment predicated upon a separate liability probably would not be dutiable.

2.6 Determining the Price

Before price adjustments may be considered, the initial task is to identify and calculate the transaction value price paid or payable. A price list price or invoice price would not be the transaction value if the buyer remitted to or credited the seller with a different amount. Customs recognizes discounts if the buyer actually paid the net amount and as long as the discount was available at the time of exportation. The reason for the discount is immaterial. Quantity discounts and those that are sometimes characterized as loyalty discounts are not uncommon. However, deferred discounts whereby a buyer qualifies for the discount only after purchasing a minimum value or quantity are not allowed by Customs if the buyer has not yet qualified at the time of exportation.

As indicated in Section 2.4 of this chapter, it has been Customs' consistent position that the transaction value price is the total amount paid or payable to the seller of the merchandise in the absence of a specific statutory exclusion. Although Customs has recognized exceptions in limited cases for finance charges and foreign inland freight, Customs makes no exception for quota payments or warranty charges that are deemed to be bound up in the price of the goods. The former have been controversial.

(a) Quota Costs

Generally, the price for quota merchandise includes the value of a visa or export license. A seller who has utilized its quota allotment, purchases additional quota on the market, and charges the buyer an amount therefor, has, in effect, raised the price of the goods. The transaction value includes the total payment since the buyer has remitted the additional charge to the seller of the imported merchandise. However, if a buyer purchases quota rights from a third party directly or through its buying agent, there is no addition to the transaction value since the payment did not benefit the seller. Importers must be cautious when using a buying agent to purchase quota, because if the buying agent furnishes the funds to the seller of the imported merchandise to purchase the quota rights, that payment, albeit indirect, is part of the transaction value price.

(b) Formula Pricing

Transaction value may exist even if the price is not calculable at the time of entry. This situation entails what is often referred to as formula pricing. The formula must be in place at the time of exportation and must include variables over which the parties have no control. So, for example, a price pegged to the unit value of an item on a recognized commodity exchange at a particular time subsequent to importation would be a classic example of a formula price. Price escalation clauses in contracts based on, for example, changes in a labor cost index, would be another type of formula pricing.

The statute proscribes adjustments based on price decreases effected after importation regardless of the reason. However, a true formula price does not entail a proscribed post-importation price decrease as such, although the price is not calculable until after importation. Post-importation price increases are part of the transaction value price and must be declared to Customs. Price changes in either direction prior to export constitute the transaction value price for exportation.

(c) Currency Issues

Appraised value always is expressed in United States dollars. Merchandise sold in a foreign currency is appraised at the published exchange rate in effect at the date of exportation. Currency conversion rates fixed by the parties that yield an amount payable in dollars are recognized by Customs and viewed as a type of formula pricing. Currency hedging itself is immaterial. If the payment is made in a foreign currency, it does not matter what it cost the buyer in dollars to obtain the currency at any particular time, but rather what the exchange rate was at the date of exportation.

(d) First Sale

Occasionally, more than one price could constitute the transaction value, especially in what are sometimes known as back-to-back sales, both occurring prior to exportation. In a series of judicial decisions, the courts have held that it is the first or earliest sale that constitutes the transaction value, provided that the goods had been earmarked for exportation to the United States in some demonstrable way. There are practical difficulties with what has become the first sale rule because of the understandable reluctance of an unrelated middleman to disclose to his customer, the importer, the price at which the merchandise was purchased from the manufacturer.

(e) Unrelated Credits

Transaction value is the total payment for the imported merchandise regardless of how the payment was effected. If a seller credits a buyer for defects relating to previous shipments, and reverses the credits by lowering the invoice price for subsequent shipments, the transaction value for a subsequent shipment is the invoice price plus the credit, regardless of whether the only funds remitted reflected the net invoice price. A failure to declare the credit at entry is viewed by Customs as a variation on the double invoicing theme, that is, a classic fraudulent undervaluation.

2.7 Deductive Value

The next appraisement basis in sequence is the price at which the merchandise being appraised, or identical or similar merchandise, is sold in the United States in the greatest aggregate quantity at the time of the importation of the merchandise undergoing appraisement or within 90 days. If the merchandise being appraised is further processed in the United States before sale, the deductive value is the post-processing price within 180 days of importation. The sale in the United States must be to unrelated parties.

The deductive value price is adjusted by subtracting the cost of the post-importation processing, if applicable, as well as the non-dutiable charges that would apply in the case of transaction value, that is, international freight and insurance, United States inland freight, and duties and federal taxes. The price also is reduced by either selling commissions or the profit and general expenses incurred in connection with sales of imported merchandise of the same class or kind as the merchandise undergoing appraisement. State and local taxes are deductible as a part of general expenses. A sale to a party who supplies an assist is disregarded in determining deductive value.

Unlike transaction value, selling agents' commissions are not an addition, but rather a deduction from the deductive value price. However, in this context, the commissions cannot be deducted twice—once as such, and again as a component of the general expense and profit factor. As in the case of adjusting a duty-paid delivered transaction value price to yield the appraised value, all nondutiable charges are subtracted from the deductive value price before applying the arithmetic formula for excluding the duty. These deductions include the cost or value of American origin fabricated components eligible for exclusion from appraised value under subheading 9802.00.80 HTSUS. Thus, the duty is calculated on a lower base if the imported products include such components.

2.8 Computed Value

Computed value is not a price, but rather the sum of the costs of production. It includes the costs of materials and fabrication plus an amount for profit and general expenses equal to that usually reflected in sales of merchandise of the same class or kind in the country of production. The value of assists and packing costs are included, but foreign internal taxes remitted or forgiven by virtue of exportation are excluded. Customs will accept the foreign producer's actual general expenses and profit unless inconsistent with those incurred and realized by other producers of the same class or kind of merchandise. There are no minimum additions for general expense and/or profit as had been the case under previous statutory appraisement regimes.

2.9 Derivative Value

The residual basis of appraisement is derived from a previous basis in the hierarchy. The standards of derivative value are not precise, and this basis is not open-ended, but Customs is required to use reasonable ways and means in deriving a value. In some cases, Customs has applied what is essentially a deductive value method without the 90-day time period constraint.

In one ruling, Customs approved appraising components imported from a related party for repair at a percentage of the standard cost for new components. Here there was no sale after repair in the United States and there was insufficient information for appraisement under computed value. Merchandise imported under a lease/purchase agreement has been appraised under derivative value by applying what would be a transaction value method, despite the absence of a sale for exportation. In rulings involving used goods, Customs has appraised at a depreciated value under the residual basis.

2.10 Conclusion

Under the Customs Modernization Act, as passed by Congress as part of the legislation implementing NAFTA, importers are required to use reasonable care in entering merchandise with Customs. The Act also requires importers to maintain pertinent documents and records or be subject to a new penalty scheme. Therefore, it is essential for importers to plan import transactions with a sense of the appropriate appraisement basis and a declared value that includes all applicable adjustments. Moreover, importers should establish a compliance program and document the steps taken to properly reckon dutiable value.

The legislative history of the Act indicates that Congress expects importers to seek guidance from knowledgeable professionals and to create a document trail that will facilitate verification by Customs auditors and other agency officials. This approach is termed *shared responsibility.* To implement the "shared responsibility" and "informed compliance" themes of the Act, Congress has established a recordkeeping compliance certification program to limit the liability of importers who are making a good faith effort to comply, but who have inadvertent recordkeeping discrepancies. Importers will need the protection offered by certification as a component of an overall proactive compliance program to avoid penalties and to ensure that no more than the required duty has been paid.

CHAPTER 3

Fines, Penalties, and Forfeitures

Susan Kohn Ross

3.1 Introduction
- (a) Scope
- (b) Impact

3.2 Penalties
- (a) Computer Chip Example
- (b) Opportunities

3.3 Prior Disclosures
- (a) Procedure
- (b) Timing Issues
- (c) Consequences
- (d) Negligence, Gross Negligence, and Fraud

3.4 Petitions
- (a) Timing
- (b) Settlement
- (c) Other Issues

3.5 Liquidated Damages
- (a) Disputes
- (b) Consequences

3.6 Seizures

3.7 Copyrights

3.8 Trademarks

3.9 Patents

3.10 Customs' Detention Policy

3.11 Marking Violations
- (a) Initial Remedies
- (b) Second-Stage Remedies
- (c) Repeated Marking Violations
- (d) Multiple Suppliers
- (e) Shipments

3.12 Textiles
- (a) Quotas
- (b) Origin
- (c) Questionnaire
- (d) Recommendations and Consequences

3.13 Exports

3.14 Customs Modernization Act
- (a) Reasonable Care
- (b) Use of Experts

3.15 Recordkeeping
- (a) List of Records
- (b) Records Defined
- (c) Violations
- (d) Summons
- (e) Drawback

3.16 NAFTA
- (a) Exports
- (b) Eligibility
- (c) Records and Penalties

3.17 Conclusion

3.1 Introduction

Fines, penalties, and forfeitures are important civil enforcement tools used by Customs to enhance compliance with the law regarding imports and exports. The following example illustrates the impact of this process: When a company's import manager opened the day's mail, it included a certified letter from U.S. Customs demanding payment of $10,000,000 as satisfaction for a penalty case proposed against the company!

The stated scenario actually happened. This case was settled several years after a voluntary payment by the importer of $400,000 in underpaid duties. The importer was ultimately forced out of business. What seems a simple unintentional error, when viewed from the importer's perspective, often turns out to be a major violation to Customs. The aim of this chapter is to describe mistakes that can happen and their consequences with Customs.

(a) Scope

Fines, Penalties & Forfeitures (FP&F) is the section within the agency that oversees Customs' civil enforcement activities. This section has exclusive jurisdiction regarding Customs' civil enforcement actions. It works with appropriate authorities in the event of a criminal case.

The focus of this chapter is on Customs' civil enforcement tools; however, it is worth mentioning some of the circumstances in which a criminal prosecution may arise. Most often, criminal cases arise because of smuggling; a failure to declare imported items; or when a traveler fails to accurately declare the amount of money and/or other monetary instruments on his or her person, whether inbound or outbound. This transaction applies to travelers' checks, securities, checks, or other negotiable instruments being transported when the amount involved is $10,000 or more. Criminal prosecution could also arise in the context of commercial fraud, such as in the classification or valuation of goods, and with textile importations.

(b) Impact

In the civil context, importers usually deal with Customs enforcement either because goods have been seized or because Customs has initiated a penalty action. Customs enforces the law on behalf of over 60 other federal agencies. Therefore, any shipment could become the subject of enforcement activity by Customs.

3.2 Penalties

(a) Computer Chip Example

Fraud penalties occur when Customs contends that there has been a material misstatement or a material omission in conjunction with an importation.[1] For example, an importer gets into trouble by failing to declare the full value of a shipment at time of importation. In the situation mentioned at the start of this chapter, the importer was importing motherboards. The importer obtained computer chips on a consignment basis in the United States. Those chips were then shipped to an Asian factory, where they were mounted on locally made motherboards. Foreign-made chips were mounted, too. Before undertaking this computer chip import project, the importer called a professional and asked whether goods exported from the United States could be returned to the United States on a duty-free basis. Without asking any more questions, the adviser stated that it was possible—a correct statement, as far as it went—and the conversation ended.

The importer was exporting foreign origin computer chips from the U.S. The full value of those exported chips had to be declared to Customs at the time of entry of the finished motherboards, even if brought in on a duty-free basis. The importer was not aware of this requirement. The importer provided Customs with an invoice from the Asian factory which stated only the value added. As a result, the value of the shipments was severely understated. This situation occurred because of a misunderstanding about the requirements. In the end, the importer was required to pay duty on the foreign chips when they were returned, mounted on the finished motherboards, because he failed to meet the recordkeeping requirements for duty free entry.

The situation came to light when Customs inspected some of the motherboard shipments. Upon inspection, it became clear to Customs that the full value was not

[1] 19 U.S.C. §1592.

being declared. To confirm its suspicions, Customs insisted that the importer's manager meet with an inspector to discuss the particulars of one shipment. Customs spent just a few minutes with the manager. The only direct question asked was whether or not the invoice submitted to Customs, which stated only the Asian value added, included the full value of what the importer paid for the finished motherboards. The importer's representative answered in the affirmative because the importer was not paying for the consigned chips.

Customs would not release the shipment until the details were provided. Once having gotten the desired details, Customs ended the meeting and promptly released the shipment. This question and answer process was repeated a total of three times with the ultimate result being an additional duty bill of $400,000. The importer thought this would end the matter, but a sizable penalty case came much later. The duty problem put the importer out of business. Cessation of business, however, did not stop Customs.

(b) Opportunities

The importer could have avoided these problems by learning the requirements and by fully advising his customs professional about all the terms of the deal. The adviser should also have asked more questions. Had the adviser been told that the exported product was foreign-made computer chips, duty on those chips might have been avoided through special recordkeeping. Further, the adviser should have cautioned the importer about the need to state the value of the consigned chips shipped from the United States on the commercial invoices declaring the value of the returned finished motherboards.

3.3 Prior Disclosures

An importer may need to obtain advice before making entry or, at least, before any meeting with Customs. This importer's entire problem, however, could have been avoided if the importer had fully understood the legal requirements. Even if the importer was unfamiliar with the requirements at time of entry, had it learned of its error before Customs opened an investigation, the two filings of a Prior Disclosure could have prevented Customs from imposing a penalty.

(a) Procedure

Prior Disclosures are provided for by statute and regulations.[2] The purpose of the law is to encourage compliance. If an importer finds it has not properly declared its transactions and does not otherwise have reason to know that a Customs' investigation has begun, it may file a Prior Disclosure.

In a Prior Disclosure, the importer identifies a number of details, including the nature of the violation and the specific entries involved. The importer recalculates

---

[2] 19 C.F.R. §162.74.

the duties and taxes due and eventually tenders those sums. Some Customs officials try to disqualify submissions as Prior Disclosures because these officials feel that granting Prior Disclosures allows violators to get away with breaking the law. Nonetheless, the procedure is provided by law and should be used by importers when applicable. Prior Disclosures are limited to cases involving §592 violations.[3] After disclosure, the importer should wait for Customs to demand payment of the amount involved so that if later there is a dispute over the correct amount, the importer retains its right to court review of the matter.

(b) Timing Issues

A submission can qualify as a Prior Disclosure if the importer is not aware that Customs has opened an investigation. Investigations are handled by Customs agents and are opened on the date when the agent records initial information about the violation as having been received. If the importer acts after that date, it may still be able to file a successful Prior Disclosure if he or she meets the second requirement—that the importer did not have knowledge of the investigation.

If the agent speaks directly to the importer, that importer has knowledge of an investigation. It is unclear whether the importer is deemed to have knowledge of an investigation if the agent simply states the importer is under investigation for misclassifying or under valuing goods. It is unclear whether it is required that the agent specify the precise nature of the claimed misclassification, including the goods and tariff numbers involved, or the specifics of the claimed under declaration of value, such as that an assist is in issue. One of the unanswered questions is how precise the agent must be in advising the importer about the nature of the investigation.

Suppose the agent subpoenas records from the importer's bank. Does that act alone convey knowledge of an investigation to the importer? Probably it does not, because issuing a subpoena does not involve immediately providing a copy of it to the importer. However, if the importer instructs its broker to file corrected papers with Customs and the broker speaks with the agent, then the right to a Prior Disclosure is probably precluded.

(c) Consequences

A Prior Disclosure limits Customs' recovery to collecting the underpaid duties and taxes plus interest if the Prior Disclosure is successful. The underpaid duty and taxes plus one time the loss of revenue can be collected by Customs if fraud is present. This measure of importer liability should be weighed against what can happen if a fraud penalty case is initiated.

(d) Negligence, Gross Negligence, and Fraud

Customs has the power to refuse to mitigate a case. However, cases are generally mitigated in the absence of repeated violations. There are three possible levels

[3] 19 U.S.C. §1592.

of fault: negligence, gross negligence, and fraud. Typically, each has the same definition as provided through general state and federal legal interpretations.

In the case of negligence, Customs' mitigation guidelines call for an ultimate fine in the range of one-half to two times the otherwise underpaid duties and taxes, or 5 to 20% of the Customs' value of the goods, where there is no revenue loss. In the case of gross negligence, the ranges are two and one-half to four times the underpaid duties and taxes, or 25 to 40% of the value. Finally, where there is fraud, the ranges are five to eight times the underpaid duties and taxes, or 50 to 80% of the value. These fines are in addition to paying all underpaid duties and taxes plus interest.

Customs considers the importer's overall record and experience in importing, as well as any prior occurrences of the same type of violation, in making its final decision. Prior identical violations are considered to be aggravating factors, resulting in larger fines. On the other hand, mitigating factors, such as inexperience in importing and remedial activities, may reduce the fine.

3.4 Petitions

The importer is given written notice of the allegations and its right to file a petition, which is a written explanation of the facts and circumstances that led to the violation.

(a) Timing

The importer is limited in the amount of time within which a petition must be filed, generally 30 or 60 days, depending on the nature of the case. There is no time limit for Customs' decision, which is conveyed to the importer in writing.

If the importer is dissatisfied with that decision, a Supplemental Petition may be filed. However, the Supplemental Petition cannot rehash arguments already made. A Supplemental Petition must be filed within 30 days of the decision letter, and the Supplemental Petition is allowed only when there are new issues of fact or law, or both, to address. Again, Customs has unlimited time in which to make its decision.

If the importer is still dissatisfied, it must first pay the amount demanded in order to be able to file a Second Supplemental Petition, the last administrative remedy.

(b) Settlement

The importer is free to propose a settlement to Customs at any time during the petitioning process. Called an offer in compromise, in order to do so, the importer is required to submit a check in payment of the proposed settlement amount, accompanied by whatever written materials the importer believes are helpful to persuade Customs to accept the offer. If the argument being made is inability to pay, the importer will also be required to provide copies of at least three years of tax returns to support his or her claim.

(c) Other Issues

Disputes with Customs over how to properly classify goods can lead to penalty action. For example, goods misdescribed and misclassified over a number of entries might lead to the conclusion that the error was made with intent to evade the lawful payment of duties. Such conduct could be viewed as a falsification giving rise to a fraud penalty.[4]

3.5 Liquidated Damages

Customs also seeks liquidated damages as an enforcement tool. A liquidated damage case arises when an importer breaches the terms of its Customs bond.

(a) Disputes

A quota is a quantitative limitation set by category of goods on a bilateral basis, authorizing specific goods to be exported to the United States. An importer must have a valid visa, that is, the document from the exporting country that validates the transaction as legitimate. The visa must state that there is sufficient quota. Quotas and visas generally apply to imported textiles and wearing apparel.

A dispute may arise between Customs and the importer over the validity of a particular visa submitted at time of entry. If the problem is repetitive, a seizure results prior to release of the goods. Unfortunately for importers, such a dispute may also arise after goods have been released for distribution. If such a circumstance occurs, under the terms of its bond, the importer is obligated to redeliver the shipment to Customs' custody until the matter is resolved. Customs is required to issue the Notice of Redelivery within a limited time period. If the importer fails to redeliver the goods and the matter is not otherwise resolved, Customs may proceed to levy a fine against the importer's bond. A liquidated damage claim is usually accomplished by first issuing notification of the proposed fine to the importer and giving the importer an opportunity to mitigate the claim through the petition process.

Liquidated damages may occur for goods subject to regulation by the Food and Drug Administration (FDA). Such a shipment is required to be held intact until the FDA gives its written approval that the shipment meets the applicable sanitary or other health standards. If the goods fail to meet those necessary standards, the importer is required to either re-export the goods or destroy them under Customs' supervision, both within a set time frame. If the importer fails to do so, Customs may proceed with a liquidated damage claim for breach of the bond, that is failure to comply with the applicable FDA and Customs requirements in a timely fashion.

An importer who fails to pay timely duties due has also breached the bond. A liquidated damage case will follow.

---

[4] 19 U.S.C. §1592.

(b) Consequences

If the importer pays the finalized liquidated damage claim, that ends the matter. If not, court action follows.

The petition and supplemental petition process is the same in the context of liquidated damage cases as it is with penalty cases. The ultimate outcome, however, is potentially quite different. In a penalty situation, the resulting court action is against the importer. In the liquidated damage context, the claim is against the surety, which has a claim for reimbursement from the importer after satisfying customs.

3.6 Seizures

Seizures are another enforcement tool for Customs but a potentially large problem for importers. Seizures occur in a variety of contexts, all of which involve an allegation that the goods being offered for entry are in violation of the law. A typical seizure might involve allegations of intellectual property rights violations. For example, a shipment of bottled wines bears the name or logo of a company that is protected by a properly recorded copyright. The wine is, however, imported by an unrelated entity. As a result, the wine is seized.

Industry may record both copyrights and trademarks with Customs. Customs makes its database of information available to all Customs personnel. A seizure can occur simply because a mark has been recorded with Customs, whether or not the holder of the mark is aware that infringing goods are actually being imported. Customs will also enforce marks that are not recorded with it so long as those marks are recorded with the U.S. Patent and Trademark Office. A fine is assessed by Customs against the importer for the underlying violation, if the importer is eventually able to arrange the release of goods.

3.7 Copyrights

Copyright protection is available for a specified period of time when original works of authorship are fixed in a tangible medium of expression. A bottled wine may have a protected brand name, including possibly its script design. Customs seizes the shipment and gives written notification of the seizure to the importer. If the importer claims the copyright is not infringed, Customs must give notice to the copyright holder. The holder then has a limited period of time in which to object, stating that the copyright is indeed infringed. The copyright holder must also post a bond to make the importer whole if the shipment is found to be noninfringing. As a bond needs to be posted, the question of infringement occurs after the goods are released to the importer. There is no basis upon which to mitigate Customs' actions if it is clear that the goods involved are counterfeit. Counterfeit goods are subject to forfeiture and are ultimately destroyed by the government.

3.8 Trademarks

A trademark is a word, name, symbol or device, or combination thereof, adopted by a manufacturer to identify its goods. In the trademark context, the issue of infringement is tested by determining the "likelihood of confusion," that is, whether the typical consumer is likely to confuse the two products. This test is subject to interpretation. What might seem confusingly similar to one person may be clearly distinguishable to another.

What makes things even more confusing is that trademarks are also subject to analysis as "strong" versus "weak" marks. For example, courts have held that the use of the word *xerox* is allowed when referring to the process of reproducing copies on a photocopier because the process of photocopying has come to be widely referred to as *xeroxing*. However, use of the name Xerox© in relation to copiers themselves is not allowed because the name is considered a strong mark. The name Xerox is not widely used except by the Xerox company.

Goods bearing counterfeit trademarks will not be returned to the importer if seized by Customs. Intellectual property rights cases routinely are referred to the Intellectual Property Rights Branch at Customs Headquarters in Washington, D.C. for determination. Customs handles the processing of trademark and copyright cases similarly.

3.9 Patents

Machines, processes, and devices are examples of tangible items that are protected by patents. Unlike copyrights and trademarks, Customs protects a patent only after being directed to do so by an independent agency of the U.S. government, the International Trade Commission (ITC). Once the ITC makes a finding of patent infringement, Customs enforces that finding by excluding imported goods so identified, that is, barring them from entry into the United States.

3.10 Customs' Detention Policy

In some instances, Customs inspects a particular shipment, suspects a violation of law, and needs more time and information to make a final decision. For those circumstances, Customs has developed a national detention policy. While Customs remains committed to making its decisions as quickly as possible, there are circumstances where information from the importer is helpful in making the final determination.

For example, an inspector suspects a shipment violates a copyright. If the importer can show that its goods are sufficiently different from the copyrighted goods, both parties benefit. Customs has the opportunity to consider the matter, while, at the same time, the importer gains the release of its goods without having to bear the time and cost associated with a formal seizure. However, if the importer is unsuccessful, its goods are seized.

Under the terms of Customs Directive 3550-43, Customs is obligated to give the importer written notice within five days that its shipment is being detained. Customs is to provide the reason for the detention, its anticipated length of the detention, and the nature of the information that would be helpful to Customs in reaching its final decision. The Directive states that a final decision should be made wherever possible within 30 days from the date of detention.

3.11 Marking Violations

A contentious area between Customs and the trade has been marking. Each imported item must be marked with its country of origin as indelibly, conspicuously, and permanently as the article will allow,[5] a standard that is subject to interpretation.

By way of example, a dispute arose as to whether frozen foods were properly marked if the country of origin designation was on the back of the outer package, where the bar coding is located. Customs found it to be inadequate marking. It was "permanent" in that it was printed with other information on the outer packaging. It was "indelible" for the same reason, it was part of the printed information. However, it was not conspicuous. It was not something the consumer would easily find unless the package was turned backwards. If the product itself mentions or the brand name implies an American locality or address, the country of origin marking then has to be stated in close proximity to and in similar type size as the American name and/or address.

(a) Initial Remedies

Customs is changing the procedures by which it enforces country of origin marking. Customs has the power to refer for criminal prosecution any person who defaces, destroys, removes, alters, covers, obscures, or obliterates any country of origin mark with the intent to conceal that information.[6] However, criminal prosecution is rare for this offense because the consequences are relatively modest.[7]

Customs has a number of strong civil options available to it to enforce the marking requirement. If an importer brings in a shipment that is not properly marked, typically for a first offense Customs will allow the importer to take the goods into its facility and properly mark them. However, before the importer may remove those goods, they must be made available so Customs can confirm that proper re-marking has occurred. Customs typically approves this method on a Notice to Mark as Redeliver.[8]

---

[5] 19 U.S.C. §1304.

[6] 19 U.S.C. §1304(i).

[7] 19 U.S.C. §1304(f).

[8] C.F. 4647.

The Notice to Remark requires the importer to certify that the remarked sample being submitted for review is identical to the relabeled goods in the shipment. There have been instances in which an importer failed to fully comply. For example, the importer remarks a sample and submits it to Customs with the certified Notice to Remark, thinking Customs will approve the sample before the entire shipment has to be relabeled. Instead, Customs visits the importer's premises, only to find the shipment has not been remarked. Fraud cases[9] have resulted because the importer signed the Notice[10] stating the entire shipment had been remarked when, in fact, it was not.

(b) Second-Stage Remedies

As a second-stage remedy to ensure proper marking, Customs will again issue a Notice to Mark a Redeliver but will now require the importer to remark the goods at the site where they are located, usually a commercial warehouse specially designated for inspection purposes by Customs, called a Centralized Examination Station. These warehouses assess a fee for their services. The additional cost and delay is itself usually a deterrent against future inadequate marking of goods.

(c) Repeated Marking Violations

If an importer has a history of importing goods that are not properly marked, Customs may seize the importers' shipments and force the importer to remark the goods under Customs' supervision as a condition of mitigation and in addition to a penalty. The most extreme remedy available to Customs is the issuance of a fraud penalty.[11] A number of marking cases have relied on this fraud penalty.

Improper marking as to origin is a material misstatement, such as when a product is labeled "Hong Kong" but is actually made in China. Therefore, a fraud penalty lies. However, the basis on which Customs may assert that a material misstatement or omission has been made is not clear if the product fails to indicate any origin at time of entry. It will be up to the courts to settle the question of whether or not Customs is correct in relying on the fraud statute, where there is no marking at all on a product at time of importation.

(d) Multiple Suppliers

Adequate marking is contentious because of the manner in which seizures arise and mitigation is granted. Customs directs further its personnel to consider an importer's history in deciding which remedy to use to enforce proper marking. Customs also directs that if an importer has had previous problems with one supplier and now has problems with a different supplier, the problems with the second supplier are treated as a first offense. Nonetheless, there have been numerous cases in

[9] 19 U.S.C. §1592.

[10] C.F. 4647.

[11] 19 U.S.C. §1592.

which previous problems with unrelated suppliers are treated as grounds for seizure of subsequent shipments.

(e) Shipments

In-transit shipments can be problematic, too. If a marking problem is discovered on shipment A but shipments B and C are already en route, together the three shipments are to be treated as one violation. The remedy that applies to one shipment should apply to all three. Here a problem arises in establishing what is "en route." Goods that are already in the air or on the water are clearly en route. However, it is uncertain at what stage in the transportation stream, from the manufacturer's facility to delivery to the importer, the goods have to be in order to be considered en route. It may be sufficient that the goods have been manufactured and have left the manufacturer's premises. It is uncertain whether the goods must actually be in a shipping container to be considered en route. These unanswered questions leave much to the discretion of the individual Customs inspector handling the transaction.

3.12 Textiles

(a) Quotas

There is friction between Customs and the trade concerning quota authorization through the issuance of visas by the exporting country. Recent trade disagreements with China, for example, have involved claims by the United States that large quantities of Chinese-made textile products are being shipped to third countries. The garments are then relabeled, stating their origin to be the third country. The mislabeled garments are then shipped to the United States. According to U.S. government sources, the reason for this scheme is that China does not have enough quota available. China is apparently producing and shipping more textile products than are authorized under its bilateral agreement with the United States.

As a result of quota authorization issues, many American importers find themselves buying garments or fabric in good faith but unable to obtain the release of their shipments in the U.S. because of documentation problems. At time of publication, the United States is in the midst of a series of facility visits in Hong Kong. The purpose of these visits is to allow U.S. Customs personnel to determine whether these Hong Kong factories actually have the ability to produce the numbers of garments they claim to export. If the factories do not and the goods are already released, the importer's goods must be returned to Customs' custody for seizure action due to the lack of a valid visa.

(b) Origin

If Customs finds the origin of fabric or garments to be suspect, it has the power to seize shipments prior to their release. Importers can run into trouble, however, because such a situation may also arise after goods have been delivered to customers. In an effort to aid American companies, part of the Uruguay Round enabling legislation included the requirement that twice a year Customs publish a list of foreign companies accused of transhipping their goods, that is, improperly shipping and relabeling their goods as previously described.[12] In addition to publishing the list, Customs also made specific recommendations about how importers can protect themselves from transhipped goods. Importers are advised by Customs to address each question separately but consecutively.

(c) Questionnaire

Customs and textile importers use the following recommended questions:

1. Does the importer have a prior relationship with the supplier?
2. Has the importer had prior seizures or detentions of goods that were produced, supplied, or transported, directly or indirectly, by any of the suppliers identified on Customs' published list?
3. Has the importer visited the supplier's premises and ascertained the capability of the factory to produce its merchandise?
4. If the factory claims it uses fabric from third countries, has the importer ascertained that the factory actually manufactures the merchandise in question?
5. Is the seller operating from the same country as the goods originate?
6. Has the quota closed from the shipping country or is it near closing from the major producing countries for the category of goods involved?
7. What is the history of the producing country regarding this category of quota?
8. Has the importer asked questions of his supplier regarding origin?
9. Has the importer verified the validity and accuracy of the visa, license, or permit documents provided by the supplier/seller?

(d) Recommendations and Consequences

The biggest problems with the list of recommendations are the inability of most importers to determine the accuracy of a given visa, license, or permit, plus the sheer cost of compliance. For large companies, it is feasible to perform on-site visits and to have technical personnel on staff who can monitor quota activity. These steps are impossible for smaller companies due to associated costs.

Many of the questions posed by Customs do not stand up to closer scrutiny. For example, having an existing relationship with a supplier does not guarantee there will not be future problems. Having a vendor located in one country but sourcing in another is also common, as for example, in the case of Hong Kong and China. In short, none of these factors guarantees results.

[12]Uruguay Round Agreement Act §333 (P. Law 103–465, Dec. 8, 1994).

3.13 Exports

Customs routinely enforces the law concerning exports on behalf of other agencies. Export licenses are issued by a variety of agencies, notably the Departments of Commerce and State. The State Department licenses munitions, while the Commerce Department licenses high-technology goods. If an export requires a license, but it has not been issued, Customs will seize the shipment. With a first violation, Customs usually allows the exporter the opportunity to obtain the missing export license, assesses a fine, and then releases the goods. However, if multiple violations occur, not only may Customs withhold release of the goods, but the Commerce or State Department may take action as well. In the case of both of these agencies, their first recourse is criminal prosecution.

Customs also enforces the requirements of the Bureau of Census regarding export declarations. Export declarations state shipment details including value, product description, and method of conveyance. Government sources estimate that approximately half of all export declarations currently being filed are erroneous. In an effort to stem these problems, Customs is developing the Automated Export System. While not currently in operation, it is expected that regulations will be enacted that will extend the existing penalty statutes to exporters and their agents if they fail to make proper declarations on export paperwork.

Another area that is receiving a high degree of interest is harbor maintenance fees (HMF). Every importer and exporter is required to pay the HMF on each international shipment by sea. The current rate is 0.125% of the value of the goods. In early 1996, the HMF was found to be an unconstitutional tax on exports. The case is on appeal. The lower court found that if refunds are due to exporters, interest must also be paid. A similar case has been filed challenging the application of the HMF on imports. However, it is new and different principles are involved.

3.14 Customs Modernization Act

The ground rules for dealing with Customs changed dramatically at the end of 1993. The Customs Modernization Act (Mod Act)[13] passed Congress and was signed into law as part of the NAFTA legislation. Prior to its enactment, the law required Customs to determine the proper classification and fix the value. Customs also determined admissibility; that is, Customs had to figure out the special rules with which an importer had to comply to import a particular category of goods and make sure there was compliance with those product-specific rules.[14] The Mod Act requires the importer to make these initial determinations.

[13] P. Law 103–182, Dec. 8, 1993.

[14] 19 U.S.C. §1484.

(a) Reasonable Care

An importer is now also required to use "reasonable care," which remains to be statutorily defined. An importer is expected to act prudently in the preparation and filing of entries so that Customs may:

1. Determine whether goods should be released;
2. Assess whether the proper classification and value have been stated; and
3. Determine if any product special requirements exist and have been met.

Customs is mandated to inform the trade community about what is expected of it. Customs has begun its "informed compliance" efforts by establishing its own Internet web site, obtaining input from the trade community regarding regulatory changes prior to their implementation, publicizing regulatory interpretations through the issuance of timely rulings, and attending trade functions in order to inform the trade community about the status of various regulatory efforts and other substantive issues.

(b) Use of Experts

The Mod Act intends that an importer may discharge its obligation to exercise reasonable care if it consults with an expert, makes full disclosure about the transactions under discussion, and then follows that expert's advice. An importer may obtain direction from Customs through the use of preimportation or formal rulings or can exercise reasonable care by consulting with its customs broker or consultant, certified public accountant, or attorney, or using in-house personnel with similar knowledge and experience. Reasonable care can be exercised by obtaining laboratory analyses or reports from other scientific experts regarding the technical qualities of the product at issue, if appropriate. If threatened with a penalty, the importer must be able to prove to Customs that reasonable care was exercised, including that an expert had been consulted. Prudent importers ensure that they state all the pertinent facts in writing to their expert and insist upon receiving a written opinion in response.

An importer can benefit by consulting with an expert, but it is unclear how Customs handles experts with whom it regularly disagrees. Experts must be expert in trade issues. For example, an experienced trade lawyer or CPA may have opinions that disagree sharply with those of Customs. Customs does not currently intend to take any adverse action against an expert, but its position could change. For importers, the question could turn out to be whether reasonable care has been exercised if there are repeated substantive differences between the importer's chosen expert and customs.

While reliance on expert advice is an exercise of reasonable care, it is not enough. Importers are also expected to be familiar with their imported product(s), with the Customs regulations, rulings, and statutes, and with the tariff and applicable judicial decisions. Familiarity with merchandise includes knowing the terms of the transaction, the description, use, and composition of the goods, their origin, and sometimes even the production process.

3.15 Recordkeeping

Under the Mod Act, one of the ways in which an importer may take steps to minimize liability is to become a certified recordkeeper. No regulations are yet in place. However, Customs has released a number of proposals that make its intentions clear. While some of the specifics remain to be decided, it appears Customs will require an importer to make its processes and procedures available in advance for review and approval. These processes and procedures must be maintained in a written manual and be followed by the appropriate personnel.

If the processes and procedures are acceptable, that is, are such that Customs is sure transactions are being properly reported, then an importer becomes certified as a recordkeeper. Once certified, if there is a failure, Customs is expected to issue a warning letter rather than initiating a penalty case. However, a penalty will result if the error was fraudulent. Importers may also turn to third parties, such as customs brokers, to maintain some or all of the required records.

(a) List of Records

The records to be maintained are referred to as the "(a)(1)(A)" list, from their section number in the Mod Act. The obligation to retain records pertains to importations, drawback claims, and the transportation or storage of merchandise held under bond, all of which are required by regulations. However, an importer is not required to create documents simply to respond to a subpoena. For example, if Customs requests a cash disbursal journal, or the (a)(1)(A) list, and the importer does not ordinarily maintain one, it is not necessary to create one to satisfy the subpoena. However, if the record is subpoenaed and it exists, it must be produced.

(b) Records Defined

"Records" are defined by Customs to include statements, declarations, books, papers, correspondence, accounts, technical data, automated storage devices, computer programs necessary to retrieve information in a usable form, and other information that pertains to an importation or is otherwise required under law or regulation. If an importer makes special claims, such as drawback or NAFTA, whatever records are needed to support those claims are to be maintained, in addition to those previously mentioned. The minimum amount of time records must be maintained is five years from date of entry. However, a longer period may apply, depending on the nature of the transaction and the type of entry filed.

In the past, to view the records maintained by an importer, Customs would first make a request that the importer voluntarily provide access to those records. If that effort failed, Customs was forced to issue a summons to obtain the records. If the importer still refused to comply, Customs' only recourse was to enforce the summons through the courts. Under the Mod Act, if Customs requests a record required by the (a)(1)(A) list and the importer is unable to produce it, Customs may now impose a recordkeeping penalty.

(c) Violations

Customs will issue a formal notice of violation to a certified record keeper that is unable to produce the requested records at the first such occurrence. Additional remedies are possible if violations recur:

1. Suspension from the program,
2. Records subject to a summons,
3. Contempt of court, and
4. Imposition of sanctions as to the goods involved.

The penalty for each release of goods (i.e., each entry) is the lesser of $10,000 or 40% of the value of the goods involved if a company is not a certified record keeper or its certified status has been revoked and the failure to produce the documents is the result of negligence. In the case of willful violations, the penalty per entry is the lesser of $100,000 or 75% of the value of the goods. In addition, if the goods are the subject of a duty reduction or elimination program (e.g., NAFTA or GSP), Customs may liquidate or reliquidate the entry at the regular rate of duty. However, no penalty is to be issued if the information is unavailable due to an act of God, or other natural cause or disaster, or there was substantial compliance through other evidence, or the requested information was previously filed with and retained by Customs.

(d) Summons

Customs may proceed against those who imported or caused the goods to be imported in issuing a summons for records, including:

1. Importers,
2. Officers, employees, or agents of those persons or entities,
3. Persons having possession, custody, or care of import-related records, or
4. Anyone else deemed proper to produce records or give testimony or both.

An importer's broker, CPA, or attorney could also be required to produce the importer's records in its possession.

(e) Drawback

A special certified record keeper program can apply if a company claims drawback. The drawback recordkeeping program is similar to the recordkeeping program that applies to all U.S. importers, and is expanded to include drawback related documents. However, the penalty consequences are considerably higher. The ultimate penalty may be up to 20% of the refunds received if a claim is negligently filed. The fine may go as high as 50% of the refunds received if there are repeated violations. The penalty may be up to 300% of the refunds paid, if fraud is involved.

3.16 NAFTA

NAFTA provides Customs with its own set of enforcement tools. NAFTA applies to both U.S. importers and exporters of raw materials, parts, components, goods, and anything else that is shipped claiming NAFTA benefits. It also applies to anyone who prepares and signs a NAFTA Certificate of Origin, Customs Form 214.

Anyone who makes a NAFTA claim or provides documents that support a NAFTA claim must provide corrected details if that party becomes aware that an error was made with the original claim. Amending an existing claim must be done within 30 days of when the party becomes aware or should have become aware that an error was made. No penalty applies if corrected information is provided in a timely fashion and no investigation has been commenced. As in the Prior Disclosure Context, penalties apply if an investigation has been commenced and the importer has knowledge of it.

(a) Exports

The exporter is required to provide a copy of the Certificate of Origin and all related documents to its own Customs service on request. The exporter must correct an erroneous Certificate within the appropriate time frame. Finally, the exporter must maintain NAFTA supporting paperwork for five years after the date the Certificate of Origin was signed. Under certain circumstances an even longer record retention period may apply. These same time frames apply to importers.

NAFTA claims may be denied if the exporter fails to comply. In addition, penalty action may follow. If the required records are not retained, what is presently unclear is whether any enforcement action will involve only the recordkeeping penalties or whether it will be applied in concert with other possible violations, for example, seizure of the goods in question. Recordkeeping penalties will not apply in concert with fraud or broker discipline penalties.

NAFTA allows records to be maintained in hard copy, microfilm, microfiche, or automated record storage devices, for example, magnetic discs or tapes. However, these records are permitted only if the associated computer programs are available to allow retrieval of the data.

(b) Eligibility

Eligibility for NAFTA benefits is determined through a verification audit undertaken in the exporter's home country. Failure or refusal of the importer to provide information is not considered a failure by the exporter to comply, nor is it grounds for denial of NAFTA benefits. However, NAFTA benefits may be denied if local

Customs has contacted the exporter and it fails to respond. In addition, if a U.S. company certifies NAFTA eligibility but fails to use generally accepted accounting principles, NAFTA may again be denied. However, before denial may take place, the local Customs service must give the company 60 days to bring its records into conformity. U.S. Customs has already indicated that such failures by U.S. companies will lead to recordkeeping penalties.

(c) Records and Penalties

If U.S. Customs demands records from a company to support its NAFTA claims and the company cannot comply, the only legitimate excuses are bankruptcy, other financial distress resulting in the loss of records, or natural disasters, such as flooding or fire. Inability to produce the demanded records may be excused if:

1. The company can establish there is an advance ruling in place,
2. An outside authority has confirmed the accuracy of its value statements,
3. There has been a prior verification audit of identical or similar materials that resulted in a favorable determination,
4. Due diligence was exercised,
5. Partial records are sufficient, or
6. There are other sources for the relevant information and the company will bear the cost to assist Customs to obtain the needed information from those sources.

All existing civil, criminal, and administrative penalties under NAFTA apply to U.S. exporters and producers. Under the Prior Disclosure regulations, even fraudulent claims may be corrected. However, NAFTA fraudulent claims cannot be voluntarily corrected without the imposition of a penalty. Further, penalty action may be taken if an advance ruling is sought and there is, in the application, a misrepresentation or a material fact is omitted.

3.17 Conclusion

Violations can lead to criminal referrals by Customs if the circumstances are sufficiently egregious. The ultimate decision as to whether or not to prosecute is made by the local U.S. Attorney's office. Defending even the threat of a criminal prosecution can be costly and worrisome.

There is nothing more frustrating for an importer than to receive a duty increase bill from Customs long after a transaction has been concluded. It completely alters the profit margin. What makes matters even worse is that the importer may also become the subject of a fines, penalties, and forfeiture action by Customs. In the new regulatory environment, it has become even more important for international traders to carefully select competent advisers, make full disclosure regarding the facts involved, and then follow that adviser's counsel, action which was prudent even before the Mod Act.

CHAPTER 4

U.S. Customs Audits

Andrew L. Siciliano
Douglas P. Zuvich

4.1 Introduction
- (a) Regulatory Audit Division, U.S. Customs Service
- (b) The Auditors—Their Scope, Objectives, Power, and Authority
- (c) Audit Selection Process

4.2 The Audit
- (a) Becoming Audit-Ready
- (b) Recordkeeping

4.3 Periodic Reviews

4.4 Controls and Procedures
- (a) Periodic Internal/Independent Customs Reviews
- (b) Electronic Data
- (c) Post-Entry Document Reviews
- (d) Contract and Agreement Logs
- (e) Customs Compliance and Import Procedures Manual
- (f) Product Classification
- (g) Consultation with Outside Consultants
- (h) In-House Training
- (i) Coordination Within Departments
- (j) Customs Liaison
- (k) Marking
- (l) Transshipment
- (m) Preference Duty Programs and Special Tariff Provisions

4.5 Continuing the Audit
- (a) CAT Reviews
- (b) Opening Conference
- (c) Audit Procedures
- (d) Assessment of the Importer's System of Internal Controls

4.6 General Ledger Review

4.7 General Journal Review
(a) Purchase Journal Review
(b) Cash Disbursements Journal Review
(c) Entry Analysis
4.8 Exit Conference
(a) The Audit Report
(b) Audit Issue Resolution

4.1 Introduction

Customs relies on post-entry audits to ensure the accuracy and completeness of the information provided to Customs by the trade community. This shift toward audit dramatically changes the importers' responsibilities. In understanding the shift to Post-entry audits, we examine the role of Customs auditors—who they are, their power, and their goals. We also explain the audit process from both Customs' perspective—the steps it will follow to gather information and reach conclusions, and an importer's perspective—what an importer should expect and how it should respond to Customs audits.

(a) Regulatory Audit Division, U.S. Customs Service

The Regulatory Audit Division was established in the Customs Service on July 15, 1973. Prior to that time, many of the audit functions were undertaken by the Office of Security and Audit (now called the Office of Internal Affairs and Treasury Inspector General) and by the Office of Investigations (now called the Office of Enforcement). The change in audit function was designed to provide a clear distinction of external audit from internal audit. This change provides Regional Commissioners with direct control over an audit function. The Commissioners can review commercial activities under their geographical control. The 1995 reorganization of the Customs Service shifted the direct control of the audit function from the former Regional Commissioners to Customs Headquarters in Washington, D.C., providing the Commissioner of Customs with direct control over the audit function.

The Regulatory Audit Division of the United States Customs Service provides Customs with the capability to verify transactions and related claims of importers, carriers, and their agents. Verification comes through on-site audits of the records, accounts, and operating facilities of persons and companies. Third-party customs audits secure "compliance by selectivity." In the past, Customs operated on the assumption that to secure compliance, it was necessary to physically examine and individually process each importation. Under the third-party audit approach, Customs is able to establish credibility and veracity of accounts and records of firms doing business with Customs on an operation entity basis, as opposed to an examination of specific transactions. This new methodology permits Customs to concentrate its limited resources on the high-pay-off and high-risk transactions. Customs is also relying on the threat of audits and severe penalties to persuade parties with whom they do business to voluntarily comply with Customs laws and regulations.

(b) The Auditors—Their Scope, Objectives, Power, and Authority

The staff of the Regulatory Audit Division consists of approximately 350 auditors, located in over 20 major cities. These auditors possess varied backgrounds of education, accounting expertise, and knowledge of Customs laws. Customs auditors are required to have, at a minimum, a bachelor's degree—not necessarily in accounting. Some auditors have master's degrees or hold professional certification, such as Certified Public Accountant (CPA), Certified Internal Auditor (CIA), and Certified Fraud Examiner (CFE).

The scope of Regulatory Audit's authority has been consistently expanding to where their responsibilities now include:

- Importers
- Customs Brokers
- North American Free Trade Agreement Reviews
- Bonded Warehouses
- Express Courier Reviews
- User Fee Payers
- Foreign Trade Zones
- Automotive Product Trade Act Reviews
- Drawback Claims
- Generalized System of Preferences Reviews
- Caribbean Basin Initiative Special Access Program Reviews
- Importations from Insular Possessions
- Temporary Importation Bonds
- Importations Under the Special Trade Programs
- Duty-Free Shop Reviews
- Vessel Repair Entry Reviews
- Assists to Other Customs Offices and/or Other Government Agencies

The primary objectives of customs audits are fourfold:

1. To ensure protection of government revenues,
2. To ensure compliance with customs laws and regulations,
3. To establish the credibility and accuracy of company records, and
4. To protect the rights of the public transacting business through customs brokers.

In securing these customs objectives, audits provide a means of identifying opportunities to improve existing regulations and their administration by Customs.

Customs encourages the improvement of recordkeeping and necessary documentation on the part of firms and individuals.

As Customs moves toward increased automation, Customs relies more on post-entry audits to ensure the accuracy and confidence of the information provided to Customs upon entry. Customs audits are directed exclusively toward the activities of third parties and complement the work of Customs personnel in all areas of operations, providing supportive services in areas where examination of third-party activities by professional auditors is essential.

Customs auditors have only an advisory function; they are merely fact finders. Customs auditors work closely with customs import specialists, who are the decision makers responsible for appraisement and classification issues. At the conclusion of an audit, the auditors forward a report detailing their findings and recommendations to various customs officials. The customs officials to whom audit reports are forwarded (Office of Enforcement, Customs Broker Licensing, Trade Enforcement, Port Directors, etc.) have the option to act or not on the recommendations made by the auditors. However, these reviewers are required to review the reports carefully, to take action promptly where it is needed, and to advise the auditors in writing of corrective action taken or indicate why action has not been taken.

(c) Audit Selection Process

U.S. Customs utilizes a formal selection process to identify audit candidates for inclusion in its annual audit plan. This process, which occurs each fiscal year, is dependent on referrals, suggestions, and other information obtained from a variety of sources. The audit plan ensure, that importers selected for audit are appropriate, based on Customs' overall priorities and the availability of audit resources. Some sources of information and the rationale for selection include:

- Top 1,000 importers, based on import values
- Strategic industries; textiles and apparel items; advanced displays; autos, trucks, and parts; chemicals and pharmaceuticals; critical components; manufacturing equipment; steel products; and telecommunication
- Referrals from other disciplines within Customs: local import specialists, special agents
- Customs audit history
- Importer with no Customs audit history
- Informant tips: disgruntled company employees and others
- Data developed internally within Regulatory Audit: source countries, duty rates, broker errors, classification and valuation discrepancies
- Prior disclosures

With an ever-increasing number of importers and Customs' increasing workload, coupled with new audit priorities generated by new or revised programs and commercial systems, U.S. Customs is relying more on selectivity and automation to facilitate and improve the audit selection process. The audit division has the capability to research and analyze vast amounts of information from Customs' commercial databases with the assistance of its computer audit specialists. This helps to ensure that the selection process is accomplished in the most effective and efficient manner possible.

A company's conduct frequently triggers a customs audit. Commonly, an audit is commenced based on an audit referral by a local import specialist requesting Regulatory Audit to assist in obtaining information needed in an appraisement issue. All too often, import specialists submit requests for information (Customs Form 28) to importers, which are unanswered, incomplete, and/or inconsistent. The import specialist then turns to Regulatory Audit for help. Upon examining an importer's books for one reason, Regulatory Audit may decide that a broader examination of the records is in order. This decision may be based on issues spotted during a visit or on the location—if within the vicinity of the auditor's home.

Prompt, consistent, and complete responses to Custom's requests for information will minimize the risk that a company will be selected for a U.S. Customs audit.

4.2 The Audit

Prior to notifying a company that it has been targeted for a customs audit, the customs audit team gathers information about the company and its operations from a variety of sources, including:

- The local import specialist team who handles the company's importations on a daily basis—the auditors and import specialists review prior correspondence and entry files to identify potential areas of concern.
- The Office of Enforcement through its national data base ensures that the audit will not interfere with an ongoing criminal investigation.
- Searching Customs databases to gather data on importing activities. Customs auditors usually attend the opening conference equipped with an understanding of the merchandise imported, the countries of origin and export, the vendors used, the total entered value, and the annual duties paid.
- On-line information services such as Dun and Bradstreet to obtain financial information.
- The Internal Revenue Service's files to obtain financial, transfer pricing, and other tax information.

The first contact a company will have with the customs auditor is by telephone. A company official, usually the Chief Financial Officer or Corporate Controller, is notified of the audit, its purpose, preliminary audit requirements, and records required. This discussion will be followed by an engagement letter providing detailed information regarding the types of records and documentation required during the audit.

These records and documents may include the following:

1. The chart of accounts,
2. Purchase journals,
3. Contracts,
4. Royalties,
5. Marketing agreements,
6. Price lists,
7. Product descriptions,
8. Company organizational structure,
9. Cost of manufacturing, and
10. Allocation of general and administrative expenses.

In addition, the engagement letter will state the proposed start date of the audit and provide the name of the customs auditor to whom inquiries should be addressed.

Customs encloses a "General Questionnaire for Importer Audits" with the engagement letter. The general questionnaire inquires about information on the company's structure, related party transactions, methods of payment, valuation, and many other items concerned with customs transactions. This questionnaire also identifies the general areas of interest to auditors at the start of the audit. Companies should exercise extreme care in preparing the questionnaire responses; well-prepared responses will facilitate the audit. Inaccurate responses will assist customs auditors to argue negligence, or even fraud, if the audit discloses compliance issues.

Unless the company has been informed of an investigation, the period between the initial contact and the entrance conference is the last chance the company has to ensure it becomes audit ready and to reduce its penalty liability. This time period is usually 3-6 weeks, but can be extended if necessary.

(a) Becoming Audit-Ready

Many corporations are unaware of the costs involved in facilitating a customs audit, especially when the company is not customs audit-ready. These costs can be overwhelming and detrimental to a company's bottom line. They may consist of potential (sometimes significant) penalties, additional duty payments, costs of responding to Customs' inquiries and requests (such as salaries of company personnel, legal counsel, outside consultants, or temporary help), as well as the opportunity costs of the company's personnel.

Being audit-ready prior to audit notification, provides numerous benefits that far outweigh the costs.

1. Being audit-ready demonstrates "reasonable care" and encourages maximum trade compliance with customs laws and regulations.
2. Being audit-ready provides a means to detect and correct issues before they are discovered by Customs while reducing potential penalty liability.

3. The process of becoming audit-ready provides information to company management about the company's internal controls and procedures as they relate to international operations, which may lead to suggestions for improved efficiency.
4. The process of becoming audit-ready will expedite Customs' verification efforts in the event of an actual audit by Customs.

(b) Recordkeeping

An important part of being audit-ready is ensuring compliance with U.S. Customs recordkeeping requirements. Customs has identified and published a list of records and information that is required to be maintained and produced by importers that import merchandise into the United States. This list is commonly referred to as the "(a)(1)(A) list." This list is Customs' attempt to identify all the documents and information required to substantiate claims made by importers upon entry.

In addition to the (a)(1)(A) list of entry information, the importer is required to maintain and produce documents and information that support, reflect, or relate to importation, exportation, or other activities or transactions requiring compliance with customs regulations. These records and supporting documents, kept in the normal course of business, should substantiate information provided to Customs upon entry of imported merchandise. Such records include, but are not limited to, accounting documents, books, financial statements, and similar records. Although these records are not listed in the (a)(1)(A) list, importers must be aware of, and understand, the requirements for the maintenance and production of these records.

An importer can consider itself "audit recordkeeping-ready" if its recordkeeping system is able to provide, in a timely manner, all information required to make entry of merchandise into the customs territory of the United States. Such systems can be maintained either manually or electronically and must retain original documents or electronic information in the form received from the originating source. In addition, each of the required records must be complete with all required information. The general list of records required for most entries include, but are not limited to, the following:

- Evidence of right to make entry (airway bill/bill of lading)
- Declaration of entry (usually contained on entry summary or warehouse entry)
- Power of attorney (if applicable)
- Packing list (where appropriate)
- Bond information

Customs auditors commonly use a checklist to ensure that a company is in compliance with the (a)(1)(A) list requirements. This checklist is appropriately named "Verification of the (a)(1)(A) List." This list is composed of two columns, one column for compliance and the other for remarks of noncompliance.

Customs requires that each document requested be provided by the company in a timely manner. Customs regulations also require that records be maintained for a minimum of five years. These records are required to be readily accessible and stored in a safe area. The following are practices and procedures that will demonstrate to Customs that records are safe and readily accessible for a Customs review.

1. Maintain written recordkeeping procedures and ensure that they are current.
2. Conduct periodic and recurring reviews of employee knowledge of written recordkeeping procedures during internal and external reviews.
3. Make available periodic and recurring training programs that explain the proper recordkeeping procedures for employees who prepare, maintain, and produce entry documents and information.
4. Designate at least one dependable individual to be a recordkeeping compliance officer. This officer must remain current on customs recordkeeping requirements and act as a liaison for managing all customs requests for records and documents.
5. Establish procedures and controls to ensure the integrity of the information.
6. Consult with customs consultants for assistance with recordkeeping matters.
7. Ensure that all parties involved with the handling of company documents—namely, brokers, freight forwarders, vendors, and agents—understand the company's recordkeeping procedures.

4.3 Periodic Reviews

An importer can gauge its level of audit-readiness by undertaking a customs compliance review to measure compliance and to detect errors and violations. By undergoing an internal or external compliance review, the company will have an opportunity to detect and examine issues prior to Customs' scrutiny. If deemed appropriate, the company can submit a prior disclosure to Customs detailing any compliance issues. A valid prior disclosure will significantly limit the company's potential penalty liability. In addition, a customs review may disclose duty saving opportunities that may result in significant savings and duty refunds.

A comprehensive customs review should determine whether information the company has submitted to U.S. Customs complies with applicable laws and is properly supported. A customs review determines the efficiency of operating procedures, recordkeeping, and internal controls as they relate to the company's import program and determines whether a company is taking fullest advantage of customs provisions to lawfully minimize the amount of duties the company pays.

When a company hires an outside firm to perform a customs review or to assist the company in performing the review, the importer should engage a firm that is proficient in customs auditing. To properly detect customs compliance issues, similar to the issues Customs would detect, customs consultants and company employees should use procedures that mirror those used by U.S. Customs auditors.

Customs compliance reviews are most proficiently performed by qualified CPA firms who specialize in customs auditing. Many of these firms are staffed with former U.S. Customs auditors and attorneys who are experts in customs and international trade.

A customs compliance review should include a review of the general ledger, purchase journal, cash disbursements journal, randomly selected customs entries, and an analysis of the company's recordkeeping procedures. It should also include interviews with selected company personnel responsible for logistics, finance, accounting, tax, legal, customs, marketing, and related departments concerning customs matters.

A customs review should seek to determine if the importer has maximized its duty saving opportunities, minimized its penalty liability, and followed U.S. government regulations. In addition, procedures for tariff classification and product valuation, among other matters, should be analyzed.

The importer should analyze books, records, and documentation during the course of customs compliance reviews:

- *Chart of Accounts and General Ledger*—The chart of accounts and general ledger should be analyzed to determine whether any accounts reflect additional funds of payments transferred overseas. Overseas payments are important because these payments may be part of the dutiable value of the company's imported merchandise. Accounts reviewed include material purchases, research and development, discounts, commissions, variances, foreign exchange currency adjustments, intercompany transfers, equipment depreciation overseas, freight to suppliers, molds, and samples.
- *Cash Disbursements Journal*—The cash disbursements journal or accounts payable distribution should be analyzed to identify any miscellaneous or additional payments pertaining to imported items over and above amounts listed on the vendor's invoices.
- *General Journal*—The general journal should be analyzed to determine if journal entries affect the cost of goods sold accounts or any other journal entries that may affect import transactions. For example, a company may adjust its costs of goods sold at year end to account for a retroactive price adjustment.
- *Monthly Statements* (such as statements from overseas offices or buying agents)—Monthly statements from various parties should be reviewed to determine if any expenses incurred affect the value of imported merchandise.
- *Agreements Affecting Importations* (such as buying agency, royalty, or licensing agreements)—Agreements and contracts should be examined to determine the effect of any payments on the dutiable value of imported items.
- *Letters of Credit Schedule*—Letter of credit schedules should be analyzed to determine the nature, frequency, and volume of funds flowing overseas.
- *Debit and Credit Notes*—Debit and credit notes should be analyzed for any price adjustments or other changes made.

- *Supplemental Logs and Schedules* (if any)—Logs and schedules pertaining to such areas as costs for assists, tooling, samples, and the like should be reviewed to verify that entries are proper and complete.

A customs compliance review should be performed using the same or similar sampling techniques used by Customs during its audits. Historically, Customs chose a sample based on dollar amounts, vendors, country of exportation, or imported merchandise. However, with the recent enactment of Compliance Assessment Team (CAT) audits, Customs now uses a statistical sample of transactions from certain accounts.

Once the transaction sample is chosen and the audit trail for the shipments selected is established, the following supporting documents should be reviewed:

- Purchase Orders
- Sales Confirmations/Amendments
- Price Lists
- Invoices
- Bills of Lading (review of actual freight charges and terms)
- Receiving Reports (verification of quantities received versus quantities declared)
- Inventory Reports
- Customs Entry Declarations [Customs Forms 7501 and 3461]
- Correspondence, telexes, and facsimile transmissions
- Proofs of payment (bank advices, checks, accounts payable documents)
- Liquidation Notices

The review of compliance documents should determine compliance in the following five core areas:

1. Classification
2. Valuation
3. Quantities (overages and shortages)
4. Recordkeeping
5. Duties and Fees

A customs compliance review should also determine compliance with any special trade programs utilized by the company, such as the North American Free Trade Agreement (NAFTA), Caribbean Basin Initiative (CBI), General System of Preferences (GSP), Harmonized Tariff Schedule (HTS), and other special programs. A customs compliance review should also determine whether country of origin declarations and information are complete and accurate, and whether they comply with the U.S. country of origin laws. Customs compliance reviews should demonstrate that the company is using "reasonable care" in efforts to comply with customs laws and regulations, as required by the new Customs Modernization Act.

4.4 Controls and Procedures

The company's internal controls play a significant role in determining the extent of scrutiny undertaken by customs auditors during a customs audit. The auditor's first step during an audit is to evaluate the company's internal controls as they relate to customs-related activities. If Customs determines that sufficient internal controls exist to ensure that accurate information is provided to Customs, the auditors will be more likely to accept the validity of the company's information. Strong internal controls are a positive factor in future penalty mitigation with Customs. Customs will increase the audit's scope due to lack of confidence in the importers data where company controls are lacking.

All importers and exporters are required to have adequate controls and safeguards which help ensure complete customs compliance. International traders should consider implementing various controls to help promote full customs compliance.

(a) Periodic Internal/Independent Customs Reviews

Companies should conduct periodic (annual or semiannual) customs reviews of their international operations. These periodic reviews should be conducted by personnel or consultants proficient in customs auditing.

(b) Electronic Data

Companies with international operations should have electronic systems and procedures that enable the company to link records and certain financial information to customs entry submissions and declarations. The company's computer systems should have the capability to track import shipments and provide various information about each shipment. A proficient computer system, coupled with proper recordkeeping, will ensure that future customs audits are less costly and time-consuming.

(c) Post-Entry Document Reviews

Each set of documents should be reviewed by company personnel upon receipt of the various import documents from the customs broker and other sources prior to the filing of the documents. These reviews should ensure that the correct value of the merchandise has been declared, the merchandise has been classified correctly, all duties and fees have been paid, and all other information submitted to Customs is accurate. During the same review, company personnel can also conduct freight reviews to verify that the charges for freight are accurate. The post-entry review function should identify discrepancies in a timely manner. This will provide the company with an adequate time period, upon discovery of a discrepancy, to file for a duty refund by protest or submit a voluntary tender, if necessary.

(d) Contract and Agreement Logs

Many companies use logs to detail various contracts and agreements with overseas vendors and agents. These logs should be maintained and kept current. In addition, all licensure and royalty agreements should be kept in an orderly manner. Customs consultants should review the actual agreements and the circumstances surrounding related transactions. The agreement can be added to the log prior to the initiation of such contracts or agreements once a customs professional acknowledges that an agreement has no customs implications. This procedure should clarify any ambiguity concerning these relationships and their customs implications.

(e) Customs Compliance and Import Procedures Manual

More companies are putting their controls and procedures explicitly in customs compliance manuals as they are becoming aware of Customs' standards for reasonable care and the potential penalties for noncompliance. A customs compliance and import manual should demonstrate a good faith attempt to comply with the recently enacted Customs Modernization and Informed Compliance Act. This manual should explicitly detail the company's controls, systems, and procedures for international operations. A Customs compliance manual helps to ensure effective communication between often diverse and geographically dispersed corporate divisions and informs all company employees about the customs implications of their actions.

(f) Product Classification

Product classification is of utmost importance. Failure to properly classify merchandise may result in civil and criminal penalties. Moreover, improper classifications may result in duty overpayments and/or underpayments. Product classification is very subjective—two or three knowledgeable people could conceivably classify one item three different ways. However, Customs requires that importers correctly (according to Customs) classify their imported merchandise.

Classification responsibilities fall on various departments depending on a company's structure. For example, many importers rely on the buyers to classify items they order, while some rely on the import department and others rely exclusively on the customs broker. The most important thing is that the individual classifying the item is familiar with the item and the Harmonized Tariff Schedule. Companies should submit binding ruling requests for questionable classifications to Customs to confirm the company's position. Ruling requests can be informally submitted to the customs broker where the classification question involves basic issues. However, when classification issues are complex, binding ruling requests should be formally submitted to Customs by either the company, a customs broker, or a customs consultant.

(g) Consultation with Outside Consultants

International traders should continually communicate with outside experts, such as customs consultants, to keep up to date on trade issues, to perform operational reviews, and to suggest lawful duty savings strategies. Customs considers the consultation with outside experts as evidence that a company is using reasonable care in its customs-related operations.

(h) In-House Training

Seminars and training courses should be conducted on a periodic basis for company personnel because of the continuing changes in Customs rules and regulations. These courses should educate new employees about various customs issues, as well as assist in keeping all cognizant employees up to date with current trade issues. Attendance at these seminars should be mandatory for relevant personnel.

(i) Coordination Within Departments

It is essential for company personnel in different departments to coordinate and communicate with each other concerning customs issues. For example, personnel involved with the sourcing of merchandise must continuously communicate with personnel in the import department to ensure their actions do not jeopardize the company's relationship with U.S. Customs. Enhanced interdepartmental communication will help to ensure that the people responsible for customs issues and other government regulations are aware of the action of other company individuals.

(j) Customs Liaison

Company personnel responsible for interacting with Customs should ensure that their relationships with the various customs officials are courteous, friendly, and professional. The company should assign particular (internal or external) individuals to communicate and coordinate with customs officials regarding customs matters. Customs contacts can prove to be valuable resources of information and insight.

(k) Marking

Improper country of origin marking of imported merchandise may result in customs penalties and/or the seizure or forfeiture of merchandise. Knowledgeable company officials or representatives should periodically instruct manufacturers on how to mark imported merchandise.

During periodic reviews by outside consultants, as well as during internal reviews, the country of origin information contained within the merchandise's entry documents should be reviewed for consistency and accuracy. In addition, company personnel or outside consultants should routinely examine imported merchandise to ensure proper marking.

(l) Transshipment

Transshipment is the undisclosed transporting of an article through another location after exportation from its country of origin. Transshipping, coupled with incorrect labeling, is a serious violation of United States law.

To protect against the unauthorized transshipment of merchandise, companies should employ some or all the following procedures:

1. Periodically distribute information to company personnel and buying agents containing the names of companies that U.S. Customs has identified as "being guilty of transshipping merchandise" to ensure that the company does not transact with such companies.
2. Include a clause in all buying agency agreements, if applicable, requiring the buying agent to warrant that "the genuine and true origin of all merchandise" is stated on any country of origin declaration, invoice, visa, or other document made in conjunction with the merchandise's importation to the United States, and that no shipment has been illegally transshipped from any other country. In conjunction with this responsibility, buying agents should be required to verify, through personal visits memorialized by pictures, that manufacturers and subcontractors have the production capacity, machinery, and labor force necessary to produce the merchandise, and further verify that such entity produced the merchandise by completing inspection of production forms.
3. Execute purchase agreements and purchase orders with sellers that place the burden of proving country of origin on the seller and make the seller ultimately responsible for any customs penalty on transshipped merchandise.
4. When ordering from a new vendor, company personnel or the company's agent should inspect production facilities to verify production capabilities. After such inspection, the inspectors should be required to keep and file an inspection certificate that provides specific details on the number of employees, number of knitting and/or sewing machines, and the factory's production capacity.
5. Require all purchases to include a written certification from the vendor or manufacturer attesting that the subject merchandise was actually produced within the designated country of origin.
6. Maintain an internal program aimed at ensuring that all employees involved in merchandise purchase and importation, and all buying agents, are aware of the company's customs compliance procedures and transshipment prevention measures.

(m) Preference Duty Programs and Special Tariff Provisions

Companies should employ procedures that ensure compliance with the various rules and regulations of duty preference and special tariff provision programs to continue obtaining benefits under such programs. Control procedures assist the company in avoiding improper participation, which could result in denial of reduced duty treatment, access to quota, and significant penalties. Controls vary for each special tariff provision.

4.5 Continuing the Audit

When an importer is notified of a customs audit, the company should initiate a team to manage the audit. If the company has undergone a recent customs compliance review, the customs consultants who performed the review are most likely to be most familiar with the company's import operations and accounting techniques. Therefore, the customs consultants may be best fit to act as a liaison between the company and Customs. The company's audit team must be familiar with the company's accounting records and systems. This knowledge of the company's accounting systems is of extreme importance, considering that Customs will focus approximately 75% of its resources on analyzing accounting-related transactions.

(a) CAT Reviews

The compliance assessment team (CAT) is a unified Customs team led by the Regulatory Audit Division. The CAT team will visit larger importers by appointment. The CAT team has preselected issues to review and requests documentation from the importer's books and records, perhaps in an automated format, for testing. The tests are performed in accordance with professional statistical sampling techniques and encompasses areas of the importer's internal controls over such customs transactions as trade priorities, value, quantities, classification, antidumping and countervailing duty, quota, transshipment, and special trade agreements.

(b) Opening Conference

The opening conference is usually attended by a company senior executive (to demonstrate company dedication to customs compliance), the controller (to answer accounting-related inquiries), import-related personnel (who know the day-to-day import operations), and customs consultants (who liaison with the auditors), the auditors, import specialists, and other customs officials assigned to the audit or compliance assessment team. The audit team should use the entrance conference to obtain key information. The audit team should attempt to obtain the audit's scope, objectives, time frame, and any special/covert issues the auditors want to address. Most consumption entry and CAT audits continue for at least eight months after the entrance conference and even longer if the auditor lives nearby. In preparation for this conference, company officials should have ready the completed questionnaire and any other responses to expedite the audit.

(c) Audit Procedures

Audit procedures employed by customs auditors during CAT and consumption audits are similar. The main difference between CAT and consumption audits is the size of the transaction sampling, which is influenced by the importer's industry, internal controls, volume of transactions, and the auditor's desired confidence level. Most CAT reviews require a 95% confidence level of compliance.

The primary audit steps conducted in CAT and consumption entry reviews are similar to those suggested in the compliance review section of this chapter (see Section 4.3). We now discuss these audit steps from the perspective of customs auditors.

(d) Assessment of the Importer's System of Internal Controls

One of the more important audit reporting standards to be addressed during an audit or CAT review is the assessment of the company's internal control structure as it relates to customs transactions. The assessment begins at the commencement of the audit, because of its importance in establishing the sample size of importer transactions to be examined during the audit, and is required to be commented on in the audit report.

The auditors must report on the assessment of policies, procedures, practices, and controls that have specific bearing on the company's international business practices as they relate to the audit objectives of determining compliance with customs laws, regulations, and rulings. At a minimum, their report includes the scope of the auditor's work in obtaining an understanding of the internal control structure as that structure relates to the audit objectives. The report indicates how the controls provide a reasonable assurance that the audited entity is able to properly support its business transactions with Customs. The report should indicate any material weakness and its impact on the conduct of the audit toward the achievement of the audit objectives.

There are instances in which the auditor may choose to limit the review of the internal control structure for a variety of reasons. Some are:

1. Adequate internal control structure does not exist because of the company's small size. However, the auditor can still assess the adequacy of the company's recordkeeping.
2. The auditor may conclude that it would be inefficient to evaluate the effectiveness of the controls and that the audit can be conducted more efficiently by expanding the substantive testing.
3. There may be an existing audit report (by an internal or independent auditor) that attests to the company's internal control structure, strengths, or weaknesses. Such reports can be evaluated for the purpose of the customs auditor's statement on the control system as it relates to the audit objectives.
4. The internal control structure may contain so many weaknesses that the auditor has no choice but to rely on expanded substantive testing, thus ignoring the control structure.

In any event, if assessment of internal controls is not conducted, the audit report must still comment on the reasons for not conducting such a review and further comment on the degree of expanded substantive testing as a result.

Based on studying and analyzing the company's operations and internal controls, the auditor should have a solid understanding of the company's importing operations and potential risk and problem areas. The auditor will know:

1. How the company orders, receives, stores, accounts for, and pays for imports
2. Who the foreign suppliers are and their relationship to the auditee
3. What the company imports and the volumes, values, and duties from each country

With a good perspective of the company in mind, the auditor will next move to analyzing and testing the company's transactions.

4.6 General Ledger Review

The general ledger review is viewed as a quick way for the customs auditors to overview the company and its accounting systems. This review will allow the auditors to analyze the summary information of all subsidiary accounts and help the auditors understand which records feed the general ledger. The analysis of the general ledger may disclose accounts that reflect activities that have potential customs implications.

The transactions in selected accounts will then be analyzed and tested further to determine if the transactions were correctly handled for customs purposes. Examples of the types of accounts reviewed are material purchases, research and development, discounts, commissions, variances, foreign exchange (currency adjustments), intercompany transfers, equipment depreciation (overseas), freight (to suppliers), molds, and samples.

4.7 General Journal Review

Customs' primary purpose of reviewing the general journal is to analyze intercompany transactions that may not be disclosed during the purchase journal review. Their reasoning is that in related party transactions purchases or purchase price adjustments will not flow through the purchase journal. Such transactions will frequently be recorded in the general journal. For example, a related party purchase or purchase adjustment may be recorded as follows:

Purchases	\$100.00
Intercompany	\$100.00
Retroactive Price Adjustment from Parent Co.	

In addition, the auditors will be looking for any debt to an expense account that may affect the customs dutiable value of imported merchandise.

(a) Purchase Journal Review

Customs auditors view the purchase journal review as an opportunity to select transactions. Depending on the size of the importer, the samples may be composed of over 200 transactions. They can be compared to the applicable purchase orders, commercial invoices, entry summaries, and payment advices. The primary purpose of the purchase journal review is to compile a list of purchase transactions that can be compared to customs entries during the entry analysis. Auditors compile the purchase journal selections both statistically and/or manually. Customs auditors are trained to select transactions based on the following criteria: mode of transportation (ocean or air), quantity imported, value of merchandise, date of importation, country of origin, and vendor. They also focus their selection efforts on transactions with revised invoices, debit notes, and odd invoice amounts and numbers.

(b) Cash Disbursements Journal Review

During the cash disbursements journal review, the auditors will select various disbursement transactions to scrutinize. The primary purpose of the cash disbursements journal review is to analyze payments that are not reflected during the purchase journal review. This review is meant to focus on payments by checks and wire transfers for accessories and the like. The selected transactions are scheduled and either traced to customs entries, if applicable, or to supporting documents, which should provide the auditor with enough information to determine if the payment has been correctly declared to Customs.

(c) Entry Analysis

Customs requests the importer to provide all import, accounting and payment documentation relating to the samples selected during general ledger, general journal, purchase and cash disbursement journal reviews. Each documentation is analyzed and tested for the accuracy of the information provided to Customs upon entry of the company's imported merchandise. Their audit steps will analyze:

- *Valuation of Imported Merchandise*—The auditors compare the purchase order unit price to the commercial invoice price, to the value declared to Customs, to the price paid to the overseas vendors.
- *Accuracy of Declared Quantities*—The auditors, on a sample basis, trace and reconcile imported merchandise quantities on consumption entries and accompanying commercial invoices to the respective receiving reports and inventory records.
- *Classification and Admissibility*—The auditors determine whether the imported merchandise is accurately classified and in conformity with all admissibility requirements (trademarks and trade names, copyrights, marking, import quotas, currency conversions).
- *User Fees*—The auditors verify the payment and accuracy of the merchandise processing fee and the harbor maintenance fee as they pertain to imports and exports.

- *Recordkeeping*—The auditors review the company's records supporting the selected transactions to determine whether the company is in compliance with the (a)(1)(A) list and other customs recordkeeping requirements.

In the event that any of the aforementioned tests indicate a compliance level below the required level (usually 95%—statistically about 5 errors in 220 transactions), a decision will be made to expand the compliance assessment into a wider audit of the importer's transactions. At that time, the CAT leader or auditor should communicate these issues to the importer (unless there is evidence of fraud). In addition, if any problems resulted in an underpayment of duty, Customs will require the importer to calculate such underpayments for the past five years and tender the duties due.

Any problems discovered may result in Customs requiring the importer to provide a written plan of action to improve the customs processes, and the plan is subsequently reviewed by Customs for compliance. If future reviews disclose continued noncompliance, Customs may attempt to prove gross negligence or even fraud and assess penalties up to eight times the duties due.

4.8 Exit Conference

At the conclusion of the audit fieldwork, the CAT team holds an exit conference with the importer, providing a full explanation of the procedures employed, tests taken, and results of the audit. There should be no surprises at the exit conference. If handled correctly by Customs, the company should be informed of any and all findings during the course of the review.

If the auditors take a position on an issue that the company does not agree with, it is unlikely that this conference will influence the auditors' or import specialist's position. By this time, the customs audit team has dedicated a vast amount of time and resources to supporting their position. Furthermore, customs auditors traditionally have difficulty seeing beyond their initial opinions, especially in front of their peers and company officials—their pride clouds their objectivity.

(a) The Audit Report

The audit report is required to be completed 90 days following the exit conference unless Customs notifies the importer of the reason for the delay. A copy of the report is also required to be issued to the company within 30 days following a completion of the report. However, if a formal investigation is initiated, the report may not be released to the company immediately.

Customs audit reports are available to the public via the Freedom of Information Act. Audit reports frequently contain information that is sensitive to a company's operations. Therefore, an importer has the right to request that certain information be deemed "business confidential" and blacked out of all reports issued via the Freedom of Information Act. The company has the burden to prove to Customs that the information requested to be kept business confidential is sensitive to its operations.

The audit report contains descriptions of the company's audit history, accounting systems, international activities, and corporate structure. The audit report also describes the audit's scope, objectives, and findings. However, audit recommendations concerning further action, such as penalty action, are not released outside the Customs Service.

(b) Audit Issue Resolution

If, at the conclusion of an audit, the company does not agree with the position(s) taken by the customs audit team, Customs or the company may request advice from Customs' Office of Regulations and Rulings in Washington, D.C.

If the company is not satisfied with the internal advice received from the Office of Regulations and Rulings, the company may lodge a timely protest with Customs. Finally, if the protest is not successful, the company may attempt to litigate the issue before the Court of International Trade.

CHAPTER 5

The First Sale Rule

M. Barry Levy

5.1 Introduction
- (a) Appraisement
- (b) Basic Exceptions
- (c) First Sale Rule

5.2 Historical Background
- (a) Early Litigation
- (b) 1956 Amendments
- (c) 1979 Amendments
- (d) 1983 Reversal by Customs
- (e) Hong Kong Tailors' Litigation
- (f) Customs' Non-Acquiescence
- (g) *Nissho Iwai*
- (h) Customs' Acquiescence

5.3 Bona Fide Sale
- (a) Transfer of Title and Risk of Loss
- (b) No Single Factor
- (c) Sale Established
- (d) Failure of Proof
- (e) Assists
- (f) Manufacturer Involvement in Resale
- (g) Relevant Factors

5.4 Sale for Exportation to the United States
- (a) Identification
- (b) Admission
- (c) Customer
- (d) Physical Characteristics
- (e) Made to Order
- (f) Notification
- (g) Letter of Credit

(h) Shipment In-Bond
(i) Failure of Proof
(j) Summary
5.5 Transaction at Arm's Length
(a) Related Parties
(b) No Relationship
(c) Reviewing Related Party Transactions
(d) Consequences of Related Party Characterization
5.6 Conclusion

5.1 Introduction

When importing goods into the United States, U.S. companies often rely on middlemen to facilitate their commercial transactions rather than dealing directly with manufacturers located overseas. Middlemen are especially useful in international business dealings because of the physical distance and the differences in language, culture, and currency separating a foreign manufacturer and a United States importer.

(a) Appraisement

As a general rule, the United States Customs Service will appraise imported merchandise (that is, determine the price on which ad valorem duties are calculated). Appraisement is determined pursuant to Section 402(b), Tariff Act of 1930, as amended by the Trade Agreements Act of 1979 (Tariff Act amended by TAA); and is based on transaction value, represented by the price paid for the goods to a foreign seller by the American importer, adjusted in accordance with law.[1]

Alternative bases of appraisement (for example, transaction value of identical or similar merchandise, deductive value, computed value) are utilized whenever the Customs Service determines, for any number of reasons specified in the Tariff Act, that merchandise cannot be appraised on the basis of transaction value; that is, the price paid or payable by the buyer (whether the importer, middleman, or ultimate purchaser) to the seller for exportation to the United States. A discussion of these alternatives is beyond the scope of this chapter.

(b) Basic Exceptions

Three basic exceptions to the general method of determining statutory transaction value could apply.

[1] Adjustments to transaction value are specified in §402(b)(1) of the Tariff Act.

First, if Customs concludes that the United States importer is not a buyer for its own account, but instead is merely a selling agent for a purchaser at the next level of distribution in the United States, appraisement may be based on the middleman's sales price to the ultimate purchaser, thereby *including* both the middleman's and the importer's markup in appraised value.

Second, if the middleman is acting as the importer's buying agent, and the importer provides the Customs Service with sufficient documentation to support this relationship, appraisement will be based on the price paid by the importer to the manufacturer, thereby *excluding* the middleman's commission.

Third, even if Customs concludes that the middleman is acting as a buyer and reseller for its own account, appraisement can be based on the price paid by the middleman to the manufacturer, thereby excluding the middleman's markup, provided that the Customs Service is satisfied that the manufacturer's transaction with the middleman is a bona fide sale, at an arm's-length price, for exportation to the United States.

(c) First Sale Rule

The final option of the three mentioned previously, which is the subject of this chapter, has been the source of considerable controversy for many years. However, as a result of a December 28, 1992, decision by the Court of Appeals for the Federal Circuit in *Nissho Iwai American Corp. v. United States,*[2] which reaffirmed the Federal Circuit's March 1, 1983, decision in *E.C. McAfee Company v. United States,*[3] the Customs Service has belatedly and reluctantly accepted the premise that:

> [I]f the transaction between the manufacturer and the middleman falls within the statutory provision for valuation, the manufacturer's price, rather than the price from the middleman to his customer, is used for appraisal.[4]

After a brief review of the history of this so-called first sale or middleman pricing rule, this chapter examines the criteria utilized by the Customs Service in determining whether appraised value should be based on the manufacturer's sales price to a middleman.

5.2 Historical Background

The issue as to whether imported merchandise could be appraised on the basis of a foreign manufacturer's sales price to a middleman was first subjected to judicial scrutiny nearly 60 years and two value laws ago.

---

[2] 982 F.2d 505 (Fed. Cir. 1992).

[3] 842 F.2d 314 (Fed. Cir. 1988).

[4] 842 F.2d at 318.

(a) Early Litigation

In *United States v. S.S. Kresge Co., Inc.*,[5] the Court of Customs and Patent Appeals reasoned that sales by manufacturers to commissionaires and dealers could be utilized as statutory export value,[6] as the price at which such or similar merchandise is freely offered for sale for exportation to the United States. Ten years later, in *Melba B. Rodriguez v. United States,*[7] the Court reaffirmed the principle that a manufacturer's price to a reseller, rather than the reseller's price, could be utilized for appraisement purposes. The Court reasoned that "when it has been found that the manufacturer's prices . . . meet the requirements of the statute . . . there is no need to consider the dealer's resale prices."[8]

(b) 1956 Amendments

In 1956, Congress amended the appraisement provisions of the Tariff Act of 1930 by substituting the term "freely sold or, in the absence of sales, offered for sale" for the term "freely offered for sale." As had been the case prior to this amendment, the relevant offers and sales were required to be "for exportation to the United States." In *United States v. Getz Bros.*,[9] the Court of Customs and Patent Appeals applied the *S.S. Kresge, Melba B. Rodriguez,* and *R.J. Saunders* rationale to the "new value law," holding that:[10]

> [If] a manufacturer, or original seller, i.e., a mill, and a dealer, i.e., a "trading house," both sold plywood at a price which met the statutory standards for "export value," the manufacturer's price is the basis of reappraisement.

Getz and *Mitsui* were accepted by the Customs Service as controlling precedent in decisions rendered pursuant to Section 402 of the Tariff Act. For example, Customs Service Headquarters cited these judicial decisions for the proposition that not only *could* a sale to a buyer located in a foreign country be a sale for exportation within the meaning of the value law, but also that this initial sale represented statutory appraised value.[11]

(c) 1979 Amendments

In 1979, Customs appraisement law was amended by the Trade Agreements Act, or TAA value law, which remains in effect today. Pursuant to the TAA, "transaction value" replaced "export value" as the primary basis of appraisement. While

---

[5]26 C.C.P.A. 349, C.A.D. (1939).

[6]Defined in §402(d), Tariff Act of 1930.

[7]23 Cust. Ct. 296, Reap. Dec. 7752 (1949).

[8]*Id.* at 300. *See also* R. J. Saunders & Co. v. United States, 42 C.C.P.A. 55, 59, C.A.D. 570 (1954).

[9]55 C.C.P.A. 11, 18, C.A.D. 927 (1967).

[10]*See also* Mitsui & Co. v. United States, 68 Cust. Ct. 266, Reap. Dec. 11767 (1972), *rev'd on other grounds,* 70 Cust. Ct. 301, A.R.D. 315 (1973).

[11]Internal Advice 55/77 (541495 TLL), HQ 541033, May 19, 1977, and HQ 541591 (date unknown).

the new law based appraisement on "the price paid or payable," rather than on a "freely sold" sales price, the critical requirement that the sale be "for exportation to the United States" remained unchanged.

There was absolutely no indication anywhere in the legislative history of the Trade Agreements Act of 1979 that Congress intended to overrule the basic principles established in *Kresge, Rodriguez, Sanders, Getz,* and *Mitsui.* For these reasons, immediately upon enactment of the TAA, the Customs Service accepted prior judicial decisions as controlling precedent. Customs held that a manufacturer's sale to a foreign reseller could be used as statutory transaction value provided that the merchandise was being sold for exportation; that is, that the merchandise was irrevocably and undeniably destined for export.[12]

(d) 1983 Reversal by Customs

Shortly thereafter, however, the Customs Service reversed its position on middleman pricing.[13] Headquarters reasoned that the TAA value law differed "conceptually and in . . . operation" from its predecessors. Customs held that the term "when sold for exportation to the United States," as it appeared in the new law, refers to "the transaction which most directly causes the merchandise to be exported to the United States."[14] In practice, this most-direct-exportation test resulted in the Customs Service's appraising imported merchandise on the price paid by the importer to a foreign-based middleman, rather than on the price paid by the middleman to the manufacturer.

(e) Hong Kong Tailors' Litigation

Customs' test was first challenged in the Court of International Trade (CIT) by importers of custom-made men's suits from Hong Kong, who argued that appraised value should be based on the Hong Kong tailors' sales prices to distributors in Hong Kong, rather than on the distributors' prices to the importers. By decision dated March 20, 1987, the CIT, in *America Air Parcel Forwarding Company Ltd. v. United States,*[15] rejected the importers' position without reaching the legal issue as to whether a manufacturer's price, in appropriate circumstances, *could* represent statutory appraised value. Thus, the Court held that the sales by the tailors were not "for exportation to the United States" since the tailors "may or may not know the identity or address of the customer."[16]

The Federal Circuit reversed its position. In *E.C. McAfee Company v. United States,*[17] the appellate court held that *Saunders, Kresge, Rodriguez,* and *Getz Bros., supra,* compelled a conclusion that, as a matter of law, if:

---

[12]*See, e.g.,* HQ 542416, July 31, 1981; HQ 542406, July 23, 1981.

[13]HQ 542928 BLS, January 21, 1983, *published as* C.S.D. 83-46.

[14]17 Cust. Bull. at 813.

[15]664 F. Supp. 1434 (Ct. Int'l Trade 1987).

[16]864 F. Supp. at 1437.

[17]842 F.2d 314, 318 (Fed. Cir. 1988).

the transaction between the manufacturer and the middleman falls within the statutory provision for valuation, the manufacturer's price, rather than the price from the middleman to his customer, is used for appraisal.

The Court then reasoned that the lower court erred when it held that the sales in issue were not for exportation. The Appellate Court reasoned that the "tailors' actual knowledge that the particular suits were destined for the United States was irrelevant," and that

> where clothing is made-to-measure for individual United States customers and ultimately sent to those customers, the reality of the transaction between the distributors and the tailors is that the goods, at the time of the transaction between the distributor and tailors, are "for exportation to the United States."[18]

(f) Customs' Non-Acquiescence

The Customs Service, as it does periodically when it disagrees with a decision of the Court, refused to follow this decision.[19] Customs Service Headquarters notified the public that the "principles set forth within [*McAfee*] should only be applied with regard to the importation of made-to-measure clothing when the distributor and tailor are located in the same country."

As a result, in its published decisions, the Customs Service continued to apply the "sale which most directly caused the exportation" test and continued to uniformly hold that this sale was between the middleman and the United States importer.

The Customs Service's position was implicitly accepted by the CIT in *Brosterhous Coleman & Co. v. United States,*[20] wherein the Court noted that:

> when there is more than one sale for exportation, Customs policy is that transaction value should be calculated according to the sale which most directly caused the merchandise to be exported to the United States.[21]

(g) *Nissho Iwai*

Two years later, in *Nissho Iwai American Corp. v. United States,*[22] the CIT expressly accepted Customs' policy. The Court held that the appraised value of certain imported subway cars was based on the price from the middleman, Nissho Iwai Corporation ("NIC") to the United States purchaser, the Metropolitan Transportation Authority ("MTA"), rather than on the price paid by NIC to the manu-

---

[18](*Id.* at 319).

[19]General Notice dated April 1, 1988, and published in the Cust. Bull., Vol. 22, No. 18, at 7–8 (May 4, 1988).

[20]737 F. Supp. 1197 (Ct. Int'l Trade 1990).

[21]737 F. Supp. at 1199.

[22]786 F. Supp. 1002 (Ct. Int'l Trade 1992)

facturer, Kawasaki Heavy Industries Inc. ("KHI"). The Court reasoned that it was this second sale "which most directly caused the goods to be exported to the United States."[23]

Although the Court acknowledged that "a more doctrinaire reading of [the MTA-NIC] contract in the context of the *McAfee* case might [lead] to a different conclusion," it distinguished *McAfee* based on its belief that "the Master Contract" between the MTA and NIC "controlled the export transaction," and "was the transaction which most directly caused the export to the United States."[24]

The appellate court reversed. First, the court held that, as a matter of law, the *McAfee* "first sale" rule controlled, that is:

> Once it is determined that both the manufacturer's price and the middleman's price are statutorily viable transaction values, the rule is straightforward: the manufacturer's price, rather than the price from the middleman to the purchaser, is used as the basis for determining transaction value.[25]

In reaching this conclusion, the court expressly and unequivocally overruled *Brosterhous* insofar as, in that decision, the CIT had based appraised value on the transaction which "most directly caused the exportation."

The *Nissho Iwai* court held that the transaction between KHI and NIC constituted the basis of appraisement, since it was a sale for exportation between unrelated parties. In reaching this conclusion, the court emphasized the following factors: (1) the transaction unquestionably was for exportation to the United States, since the subway cars in issue "were manufactured for a specific United States purchaser" and "had no possible alternative destination,"[26] and (2) KHI and NIC were not related parties under 19 United States Code, Section 1401a(g), and the KHI-NIC sales price accurately reflected the price that would exist in a true arm's-length transaction.[27] The Court then dismissed the government's contention that its decision would "open the floodgates":

> Conceivably, mechanical application of the rule whenever there is a three-tiered distribution system could lead to inequitable results where the manufacturer's price is set artificially low. However, the rule only applies where there is a legitimate choice between two statutorily viable transaction values. The manufacturer's price constitutes a viable transaction value when the goods are clearly destined for export to the United States and when the manufacturer and the middleman deal with each other at arm's length, in the absence of any non-market influences that affect the legitimacy of the sales price. As the government itself recognizes, that determination can only be made on a case-by-case basis.[28]

---

[23] *Id.* at 1006.

[24] *Id.* at 1007.

[25] (982 F.2d at 509.)

[26] 982 F.2d at 509.

[27] *Id.* at 510.

[28] *Id.* at 509.

(h) Customs' Acquiescence

Unlike its reaction to *McAfee,* the Customs Service has accepted and followed the *Nissho Iwai* decision. In precedential ruling letters issued from 1993 through the present, Customs held that, in appropriate circumstances, transaction value can be based on a sale between a foreign manufacturer and a foreign middleman. This transaction value applies provided that the importer can establish to Customs' satisfaction that:

1. The transaction between the manufacturer and middleman, in fact, is a sale;
2. The sale, in fact, is for exportation to the United States; and
3. The manufacturer and middleman, in fact, deal with each other at arm's-length.

An examination of this three-prong test, as discussed in Customs Service Headquarters rulings, follows.

5.3 Bona Fide Sale

(a) Transfer of Title and Risk of Loss

The Customs Service has held that, for customs purposes, a sale is a transfer of ownership in property from one party to another for a consideration.[29] Customs reasoned that a sale had not taken place, and that the price paid by the middleman to the manufacturer could not be used as the basis of appraisement, when "title and risk of loss passed from the seller to the supplier, then immediately thereafter from the supplier to the ultimate purchaser."[30] The terms of sale between the seller and supplier were "ex works," while those between the supplier and ultimate purchaser were "FOB ex-cellars," which, according to Customs was synonymous with "ex works." Thus, Customs held that the supplier merely acted as a selling agent, resulting in the supplier's commission being subject to duty.

While this decision has not been expressly overruled, in subsequent ruling letters the Customs Service has not applied a per se rule that a sale can never take place where there is an instantaneous transfer of title and risk of loss. This issue was not raised in *Nissho Iwai* since the transfer between KHI and NIC was FOB Kobe, Japan, with risk of loss and title being assumed by NIC until the subsequent delivery of the subway cars to the MTA in the United States.

---

[29]HQ 546091, January 3, 1996, citing with approval J.L. Wood v. United States, 62 C.C.P.A. 25, 33, C.A.D. 1139 (1974).

[30]HQ 545105, November 9, 1993.

(b) No Single Factor

Headquarters reasoned that "no single factor is determinative" as to whether a bona fide sale has taken place. Customs concluded that "the relationship is to be ascertained by an overall view of the entire situation."[31]

Customs noted that the immediate transfer of title and risk of loss from the manufacturer to the middleman and the shipment of the goods directly from the manufacturer to the ultimate purchaser constituted "indications that there may not be a valid sale." However, Customs also stated that the importer had presented evidence—for example, documents such as purchase orders, invoices, payments, and so forth—which "otherwise indicate that the parties transact business as buyer/seller." After discussing these factors, Customs refused to issue a binding ruling, holding that "there is insufficient information to determine . . . the roles of the parties and the circumstances of the transaction."

(c) Sale Established

Headquarters held that a bona fide sale had taken place, notwithstanding the fact that the "shipping terms . . . are inconclusive" on the transfer of title and risk of loss issue.[32] In reaching this conclusion, Customs examined the roles of the parties and the circumstances of the transactions as evidenced by purchase orders, invoices, and an affidavit submitted for review. Customs reasoned that the middleman was acting for its own account and was not subject to the control of the manufacturer or ultimate purchaser, based on its understanding that the middleman:

1. Gave instructions to the manufacturer;
2. Was free to resell the merchandise at any price it desired;
3. Was able to select its own customers and to negotiate with them without consulting the manufacturer; and
4. Was able, if it so desired, to have the merchandise delivered from its own inventory.[33]

(d) Failure of Proof

Customs reasoned that an importer had failed to present sufficient evidence to establish that a bona fide sale had taken place because "no purchase orders or contracts relating to any of these alleged sales were provided."[34] Similarly, Headquarters rejected an importer's claim that appraisement should be based on the manufacturer's sales price, since the manufacturer's visaed invoice did not indicate the

---

[31]HQ 545967, July 7, 1995.

[32]HQ 545709, May 12, 1995.

[33]*See also* HQ 545474, August 25, 1995.

[34]HQ 545648 of August 31, 1994.

name of the buyer and the letter of credit failed to state who actually received payment for the merchandise.[35]

(e) Assists

An issue relating to the "sale" requirement is whether a sale for customs purposes can take place where the middleman supplies the manufacturer with component parts. This situation arises when the manufacturer's sole role in the transaction is as an assembler of imported goods, or where the manufacturer merely processes materials supplied free of charge. Customs has answered this question in the affirmative.[36] Appraised value will be based on the price paid by the middleman to the manufacturer plus the value of any materials, component parts, or other assists supplied free of charge or at a reduced cost, directly or indirectly, by the middleman to the manufacturer.[37] Materials supplied free of charge by the importer to the manufacturer will be categorized as assists, as they are being supplied indirectly by the buyer (the middleman).

In fact, both *McAfee* and *Nissho Iwai* involved situations in which the manufacturer was provided with component parts ("assists") free of charge. In *McAfee,* the Hong Kong tailors performed cut, make, and trim ("CMT") operations on fabric provided to them by the distributors, and in *Nissho Iwai,* the middleman (NIC) provided the manufacturer (KHI) with a significant number of component parts while KHI manufactured other components itself. In both instances, the appellate court expressly held that these facts did not preclude basing appraised value on the sales price from the manufacturer to the middleman.

The *Nissho Iwai* court noted that Section 152.103(a)(3) of the Customs Regulations expressly mandated that a sale could be found where "the price actually paid or payable . . . represent[s] an amount for the assembly of imported merchandise in which the seller has no interest other than as assembler." The Court reasoned that the fact that the manufacturer (KHI) was more than a "mere assembler" did not "mandate a different result."[38]

(f) Manufacturer Involvement in Resale

In *Nissho Iwai,* the government argued that a bona fide sale and resale had not taken place because the manufacturer was extensively involved in negotiations between the middleman and ultimate purchaser and, therefore, "possessed a significant stake in the ensuing contract."[39] The court summarily rejected this argument, reasoning that this fact did not "take this case out from the rule in *McAfee*" and that "in fact, it emphasizes KHI's role in the export of the merchandise to the United

[35] HQ 545499, October 13, 1994.

[36] *See* HQ 545368, July 6, 1995.

[37] §§ 402(b)(1) and 402(h)(1), Tariff Act of 1930, as amended. *See, e.g.,* HQ 545368, July 6, 1995; HQ 545979, August 24, 1995.

[38] 982 F.2d at 510.

[39] 982 F.2d at 505.

States, supporting the conclusion that its sale to NIC is the legally controlling transaction."[40]

(g) Relevant Factors

In sum, Customs will base its decision as to whether a sale has occurred on a case-by-case evaluation of "all relevant factors," and will not reject the manufacturer-to-middleman price simply because the manufacturer was merely an assembler or processor of materials owned by another party to the transaction or because the manufacturer was involved in the negotiations leading to the resale contract. While the middleman's assumption of title and risk of loss will constitute significant factors in the determination as to whether a sale and resale have taken place, instantaneous transfer of title and risk of loss will not, by themselves, prevent an importer from establishing to Customs' satisfaction that the merchandise, in fact, has been sold by the manufacturer to the middleman.

5.4 Sale for Exportation to the United States

Once the Customs Service has determined that the manufacturer and middleman have acted as a buyer and seller, Customs will evaluate whether the sale, in fact, is for exportation to the United States.

(a) Identification

In *McAfee,* the lower court had reasoned that an "export sale" had not taken place because the manufacturers (the tailors) "may or may not know the identity or address of the customer."[41] The Federal Circuit held that this particular knowledge was irrelevant, and that an export sale had taken place because the goods in question (men's suits) "were being made [to order] for a specific United States consumer."[42]

(b) Admission

In *Nissho Iwai,* the "for exportation" requirement was not difficult to satisfy, since the Government had admitted, in its Answer to plaintiff's Complaint, that the subject subway cars were made to order and dedicated for use in the New York City subway system. Thus, the Federal Circuit found that the imported merchandise was "unquestionably intended for exportation to the United States and had no possible alternative destination."[43] The court noted that this requirement would be

---

[40] *Id.*

[41] 664 F. Supp. at 1437.

[42] 842 F.2d at 319.

[43] 982 F.2d at 509.

satisfied "when the goods were clearly destined for exportation to the United States."[44]

(c) Customer

In *Synergy Sport International, Ltd. v. United States,*[45] the Court of International Trade held that the "for exportation to the United States" criteria had been satisfied where the goods were shipped directly by the manufacturer to the United States and that labels placed on the garments by the manufacturers "reflect[ed] the fact the goods are destined for the United States and always for a particular customer."[46]

In its precedential decisions, the Customs Service has followed the "clearly destined" test articulated by the *Nissho Iwai* and *Synergy* courts and has concluded that goods have been sold "for exportation to the United States" where sufficient evidence has been provided.

(d) Physical Characteristics

The exportation criterion is most easily established when the imported products are, by nature of their peculiar physical characteristics, manufactured for the U.S. market. For example, Headquarters reasoned that the "for exportation" test had been satisfied because:[47]

1. The packaging was exclusively in English;
2. The products bore the Underwriters' Laboratories (UL) trademark;
3. The products were made to operate on 110-volt electrical current, which is not used outside North America;
4. The products had a circuit control device required in the United States, but not in other countries;
5. The products bore a U.S. trademark; and
6. The products were to be shipped from the manufacturer directly to the United States.

Similarly, Headquarters held that this criterion was satisfied where the merchandise:[48]

1. Was manufactured as a result of an order from the U.S. importer;
2. Was made specifically for the U.S. market using U.S. shoe sizes;

---

[44] *Id.*

[45] 17 CIT 18 (Ct. Int'l Trade 1993).

[46] *Id.* at 20.

[47] HQ 545368, July 6, 1995.

[48] HQ 545967, July 7, 1995.

3. Was accompanied by a form prepared by the manufacturer used to assist in U.S. tariff classification; and
4. Was shipped directly from a foreign consolidator to the importer.[49]

(e) Made to Order

The "for exportation" test is satisfied when the goods were produced to order for a particular U.S. importer. Headquarters relied on the following factors:[50]

1. The goods were designed and manufactured according to the importer's specifications;
2. The goods had the importer's stock number and bar-coded string tag when shipped from the factory;
3. The goods and their containers contained all the requisite marking for importation into the United States; and
4. The goods were shipped directly from the manufacturers to the importer.

Evidence included fact that warranty applied solely to merchandise sold in the United States.[51]

(f) Notification

An identical conclusion was reached wherein Headquarters held that the importer had presented sufficient evidence to satisfy this test, notwithstanding that there did not appear to be any evidence that the merchandise itself (Waterford lead crystal glassware) could not be used in other markets.[52] Specifically, Customs reasoned that the submitted affidavits established that both the manufacturers and middleman knew, prior to production, that the product was being produced for exportation to the United States. Similarly, Customs held that a sale for exportation had taken place where the middleman notified the manufacturers that the merchandise was destined for the United States and the manufacturers prepared visaed invoices.[53]

(g) Letter of Credit

Headquarters found a "sale for exportation" where all submitted documents indicated that the goods were to be shipped to the United States and the letter of credit from the middleman to the manufacturer specified that the goods were to be

---

[49] *See also* HQ 545262, March 11, 1994. (Evidence included statement on purchase order that goods must conform to standards set by the American Iron and Steel Institute or American Society for Mechanical Engineers.)

[50] HQ 545612, May 25, 1995.

[51] HQ 545474, August 25, 1995; HQ 545508, January 20, 1995; HQ 545420, May 31, 1995. *See also* HQ 545979, August 24, 1995.

[52] HQ 545709, May 12, 1995.

[53] HQ 545360, May 31, 1994.

transported to New York.[54] Customs reasoned that the letter of credit restriction was especially significant "because unless the conditions in the letter of credit are met, [the manufacturer] would not be paid."

(h) Shipment In-Bond

Customs held that the "clearly destined" requirement had been satisfied when the imported goods were shipped through a third country prior to importation into the United States. Customs reasoned that goods specially ordered by one U.S. customer remained destined for the United States notwithstanding the fact that they were initially shipped to Canada, since "the evidence indicates that they were shipped in-bond and there is no indication there was any planned or actual use of the bags in Canada."[55]

(i) Failure of Proof

In contrast, the opposite result was reached, as the middleman sold its products to many countries, had the capability of diverting the shipments to other markets after the transactions occurred, and was under no contractual obligation to deliver specific merchandise to the U.S. importer at a certain time.[56] Similarly, Customs reasoned that the presence of an export visa, issued on the date of exportation, did not satisfy the "clearly destined" requirement since there was no evidence that the goods were destined for the United States at time of the alleged sale between the manufacturer and middleman.[57]

(j) Summary

The "sale for exportation to the United States" criterion can be satisfied by providing the Customs Service with credible evidence that the physical characteristics of the goods render them clearly destined for the U.S. market or that the goods are being manufactured to order for a particular U.S. importer. In contrast, off-the-shelf articles, which a middleman could sell worldwide, would not satisfy this test since they are not clearly destined for exportation to the United States when sold by the manufacturer to the middleman.

5.5 Transaction at Arm's Length

The final requirement for appraising merchandise on the basis of the manufacturer's sales price to the middleman is to determine whether the "manufacturer and middleman deal with each other at arm's length, in the absence of any non-market influences that affect the legitimacy of the sale price."[58]

---

[54]HQ 545898, June 12, 1995.

[55]HQ 545254, November 22, 1994.

[56]HQ 546091, January 3, 1996.

[57]HQ 545648, August 31, 1994.

[58]982 F.2d at 509.

(a) Related Parties

In *Nissho Iwai,* the government had argued that KHI and the middleman, NIC, were related parties, as that term is defined in Section 402(g) of the Tariff Act, and that a sale between a related manufacturer and middleman could not support statutory transaction value. The CIT rejected the government's position on this issue, reasoning that the interaction between these companies in negotiating the Master Contract with the ultimate purchaser (the MTA) "did not constitute a partnership or joint venture to produce" within the meaning of Section 402(g).[59] The Court further noted that the manufacturer and seller did not share overall profits and losses, or pool their resources or expertise, and that since each did not own more than 1% of the other, they were not "related parties within the meaning of the cross ownership provisions" of Section 402(g)(1)(F).[60]

On appeal, the Federal Circuit held that the arm's-length criterion had been satisfied because the trial court had rejected the government's claim that the manufacturer and middleman were related parties, as defined in the value law. No additional evidence substantiating the arm's-length nature of the relationship was required.

(b) No Relationship

In its precedential decisions on this issue, the Customs Service has consistently held that the arm's-length test will be satisfied when the manufacturer and middleman are not related parties, as that term is defined in Section 402(g). For example, Customs held that the sales were at arms-length prices because the parties were not related and there was no evidence presented to show that the transaction was not at arms length.[61] Customs accepted the manufacturer-middleman price based on the manufacturer's certified statement that it was not related to the middleman and the middleman's statement that it had no financial interest in the manufacturer.[62] ("The information submitted reveals that the middleman and the foreign manufacturer are not related; accordingly, we will assume that the sales between the manufacturers and [the middleman] are independent, arm's-length transactions.").[63,64]

(c) Reviewing Related Party Transactions

In those instances in which the manufacturer and middleman are related, Customs has examined the bona fides of the sale price in the same manner as it examines all related party transactions.[65]

---

[59]786 F.Supp. at 1009.

[60]*Id.*

[61]HQ 545368, July 6, 1995.

[62]HQ 545898, June 12, 1995.

[63]HQ 545474, August 2, 1994.

[64]HQ 545709, May 12, 1995; HQ 545967, July 7, 1995.

[65]*See generally* "Transfer Pricing; Related Party Transactions," Cust. Bull. & Dec., vol. 27, no. 4, at 4 (January 27, 1993).

For example, Customs held that, in order for a sale between related companies to be acceptable as an arm's-length sale under *Nissho Iwai,* the sale must satisfy the statutory requirements in Section 402(b)(2)(B).[66] An examination of the circumstances of sale between the manufacturer and middleman must indicate that the relationship did not influence the price actually paid or payable, *or* the sales price must closely approximate one of the test values (transaction value of identical or similar merchandise, computed value, deductive value).

Customs held that the sale between the manufacturer and middleman could not be utilized as the basis of appraisement since the parties were related and they had not submitted sufficient information to establish that the relationship did not influence the price or that the price closely approximated a test value.[67] Customs rejected the importer's argument that a 4% margin, which the manufacturer realized on its sales, was sufficient to establish the bona fides of the sales price. Customs was unable "to verify that the price inclusive of this profit margin is consistent with the normal pricing practice of the industry in question." Customs then noted that the importer had *not* established that the related party sales price (1) was negotiated at arm's length, (2) was consistent with the industry in question, (3) contained all costs plus a profit equivalent to the firm's overall profit on sales of the same class or kind of merchandise, or (4) closely approximated a test value.[68]

(d) Consequences of Related Party Characterization

In sum, as a general rule, and in the absence of any evidence to the contrary, the final criterion, the arm's-length test, will be satisfied whenever the manufacturer and middleman are not related parties, as that term is defined in Section 402(g) of the Tariff Act. In contrast, if the manufacturer and middleman are related, the importer must satisfy the Customs Service as to the bona fides of the sales price based on traditional criteria utilized in all related party sales transactions.

5.6 Conclusion

After more than a decade of uncertainty, including two appellate court decisions, appraisement based on middleman pricing has become the law of the land. The Customs Service has followed the principles set forth in *Nissho Iwai* and, through its precedential decisions, has established guidelines that importers can follow to prove that a sales price from a manufacturer to a middleman represents the proper basis for appraising imported goods.[69]

---

[66]HQ 546091, January 3, 1996.

[67]HQ 544579 of September 30, 1993.

[68]*See also* HQ 545272, August 17, 1995.

[69]In November 1996, Customs Service Headquarters published an advanced level informed compliance booklet, "What Every Member of the Trade Community Should Know About: Bona Fide Sales and Sales for Exportation," summarizing Customs' current position on this issue.

CHAPTER 6

Tariff Classification of Goods and Services

Sidney N. Weiss

6.1 Introduction
- (a) Basic Aspects
- (b) Classification
- (c) Subclassification

6.2 Harmonized Tariff System
- (a) Tariff Schedule
- (b) Types of Duty Rates
- (c) Specific Rules
- (d) Most Favored Nation
- (e) General System of Preference

6.3 General Rules of Interpretation
- (a) General Rules of Interpretation–1
- (b) General Rules of Interpretation–2
- (c) General Rules of Interpretation–3
- (d) General Rules of Interpretation–4
- (e) General Rules of Interpretation–5
- (f) General Rules of Interpretation–6

6.4 Additional U.S. Rules of Interpretation
- (a) Classifications Controlled by Use
- (b) Classifications Controlled by Actual Use
- (c) Tariff Provisions for "Parts" and "Accessories" of Other Articles
- (d) Classification of Articles Consisting of a Mixture of Textile Articles

6.5 Pre-Importation Determination
- (a) Two Programs
- (b) Pre-Entry Classification
- (c) Binding Classification

6.6 Administrative Protests
- (a) Timing

(b) Further Review
(c) Justification
(d) Headquarters
(e) Correcting Clerical Errors
(f) Remedies for Domestic Manufacturers

6.7 Judicial Review
(a) Powers
(b) Judiciary
(c) Procedure
(d) Test Procedure
(e) Appeals

6.8 Conclusion

6.1 Introduction

Customs must know both the value of the merchandise and the category, or classification, of the merchandise to properly assess duty on merchandise. Classification is the process by which the United States Customs Service determines the category and duty rate of the merchandise being imported. Customs must also determine the origin of the goods because of the myriad of duty-reduction and forgiveness programs, duty-free programs, quota programs, free trade area programs, and the like. All of these programs are controlled by the country of origin of the imported merchandise. Origin almost always turns on the classification of the merchandise for almost all manufactured goods.

(a) Basic Aspects

The proper duty depends upon origin, classification, rate of duty, and appraisal. Under the Customs Modernization Act, it is now the importer's legal obligation to enter the merchandise at the proper duty rate or classification and value. Customs may assess severe penalties amounting to as much as many times the value of the merchandise and the duty rate for failure to comply with the Mod Act. Customs may review classification of merchandise up to five years after the merchandise has been entered and liquidated. To this end, Customs may demand to see documents relating to the merchandise being imported for up to five years after entry and liquidation. Failure to keep and produce such records constitutes a separate offense, punishable by penalties of as much as $100,000 per violation.

(b) Classification

Classification of the merchandise is determined by the Harmonized Tariff Schedule of the United States (HTSUS). This law[1] categorizes and classifies every

[1] 19 U.S.C. 1202.

article of commerce entering into the United States. The HTSUS is divided into chapters, beginning with live animals, Chapter 1, and meat, Chapter 2, and advancing with the degree of sophistication, processing, and manufacturing to edible products, Chapter 4; prepared foods, Chapters 16 to 24; mineral products, Chapters 25 to 27; chemicals, plastics, textile products, steel products, and so on, through optical equipment and armaments in Chapters 90 through 93. The balance of the chapters, through Chapter 99, concern miscellaneous articles and special tariff provisions.

The HTSUS classification is given as a ten-digit number. The first two numbers indicate the chapter of the HTSUS in which the article is classified. Thus, an import whose classification begins with "01" would be in Chapter 1; that is, the merchandise would be a live animal of some sort.

The HTSUS is identical to the Harmonized Tariff Code, adopted by more than 130 countries around the world in 1988 to govern Customs classification. The Harmonized Tariff Code (also known more simply as the Harmonized Code) ensures uniformity and predictability in international trade transactions. Merchandise exported from one country under a particular Harmonized Code classification should enter another country under the same Harmonized Code classification.

(c) Subclassification

Like the HTSUS, the Harmonized Code is divided into identical chapters, but its classifications are given in six-digit categories. For example, the Harmonized Code classifies

> Instruments and appliances used in medical, surgical, dental or veterinary sciences. . . : electro-diagnostic apparatus . . . other than EKGs.

under item 9018.19. This provision, consisting of six digits in the Harmonized Code, should be the identical provision, in the identical language and nomenclature, by which the merchandise is classified in each of the countries that use Harmonized Code systems. Moreover, each country's Harmonized Code Tariff classifying such merchandise must begin with the first six numbers of the Harmonized Code classification, in this case 901819.

The Harmonized Code itself provides only nomenclature and the first six digits of the classification. All countries are free to impose whatever tariff rate they wish for each tariff classification. Each country is also permitted to further classify its products.

The United States has chosen in the HTSUS to subclassify products into ten digits, and to assess duties at the eight-digit level. To take the example we have been discussing, HTSUS item 90.18.19.40 provides for:

> Instruments and appliances used in medical, surgical, dental or veterinary sciences. . . : electro-diagnostic apparatus . . . other than EKGs. . . :
>
> Apparatus for functional exploratory examination, and parts and accessories thereof

and the duty rate is set at this eight-digit level. The duty rate in the HTSUS is unique to U.S. law, and so is the suffix ".40," but the language and the first six numbers are common to all tariffs around the world using the Harmonized Code.

The United States sets the tariff at the eight-digit level and uses a ten-digit system in the HTSUS. The additional two digits are used for statistical purposes. The last two digits are used for some import-sensitive products such as textiles and apparel for quota purposes.

Thus, to return to our example, under the HTSUS all electro-diagnostic medical and surgical instruments and appliances other than EKGs, and other than apparatus for functional exploratory examinations (item 90.18.19.40), would be classified in the HTSUS under the eight-digit item 90.18.19.80, with further subdivisions to the ten-digit level for blood pressure apparatus (item 90.18.19.80.30), EEGs (item 90.18.90.80.35), ultrasonic scanning equipment (90.18.19.80.45), and so on. In this example, all the items carrying the same first eight digits pay exactly the same rate of duty, the last two digits being used for statistical purposes only.

6.2 Harmonized Tariff System

The desirability of having a uniform, internationally accepted classification system brought about the Harmonized Commodity Description and Coding System. This system went into effect in the United States on January 1, 1989. The Harmonized Tariff Schedule is codified at Title 19 of the U.S. Code at Section 1202.

The implementing legislation authorizes the president, upon the recommendation of the U.S. International Trade Commission, to proclaim modifications to the U.S. tariff schedule to reflect changes in the harmonized system. Modifications become necessary as a result of classification opinions issued by the Harmonized System Committee of the Customs Cooperation Council (CCC).

(a) Tariff Schedule

The tariff schedule contains 22 major subdivisions or sections, numbered from I to XXII. The sections consist of general product groupings based on a branch of a particular industry. These sections each contain one or more subsections, which are called chapters, and they comprise narrower groupings of related product categories. Altogether, there are 99 chapters in the schedule. Generally, the headings and subheadings in each chapter are arranged sequentially according to the degree of processing performed on the basic raw material. A heading refers to a four-digit number, and a subheading refers to a six- or eight-digit number.

In the HTSUS, the first eight digits are the subheading numbers that represent the item. There is also a two-digit statistical suffix after the eight-digit numbers. Every eight-digit rate level has its own particular general rate of duty. The entire schedule has about 8,500 tariff descriptions and tariff numbers at the eight-digit rate level.

In addition to the product categories in the sections, the HTSUS also consists of

General Notes;
Section Notes;
Chapter Notes;
General Statistical Notes;
General Rules of Interpretation;
Additional U.S. Rules of Interpretation;
Chemical Appendix;
Statistical Annexes; and the
Alphabetical Index.

These provisions will be discussed in more detail later.

(b) Types of Duty Rates

Three different types of duty rates are found in the HTSUS. The most common type of duty is known as an ad valorem rate and is expressed as a percentage of the value of the merchandise. Thus, duties that are calculated as a percentage of value of the merchandise being imported are ad valorem duties. When an item's duty rate is 5% of its value (ad valorem), in order to assess duty properly, it is essential to determine the item's value.

(c) Specific Rules

The next most common type of duty rate is the specific rate of duty. Examples of specific rates of duty are duties denominated as 2.5 cents per kilogram, 15 cents per gross, or $1.67 per cubic meter, for example. As may be expected, specific rates of duties tend to be charged on commodity items, but there are some items, such as textiles and clothing, for which specific rates of duties are also charged, either alone or in combination with other types of duties.

When both an ad valorem rate and a specific rate of duty are levied on merchandise, the rate is known as a compound rate of duty. For example, imports of certain textiles may be dutiable at 3.5 cents per square meter (or per kilogram) *plus* 10% ad valorem. All measurements in the HTSUS are given in metric terms to keep the HTSUS uniform with the tariff systems of the other countries in the world.

(d) Most Favored Nation

Under the General Agreement on Tariffs and Trade (GATT), all member countries of GATT are entitled to receive the rate of duty no less favorable than the most favorable rate of duty afforded to the imports of any other country. This is known as the "Most Favored Nation" rate, or MFN rate. By way of explanation, if Japan, a GATT member, exports widgets to the United States (another GATT member) and pays duty at the rate of 5%, all other GATT members who export widgets to the United States must pay duty at a rate no greater than 5%. Conversely, the rate that Japan pays must be no greater than the rate any other GATT member state pays for its exports of a particular product to the United States. This rate, or the MFN rate, is listed in Column 1 of the HTSUS. Therefore, it is also known as the "Column 1 rate."

The MFN rate was quite meaningful especially after the Second World War. The communist world was precluded from receiving MFN benefits, and many non-communist countries were not signatories of GATT. The distinction between the MFN rate and the non-MFN rate (or as it became known, the "Column 2 rate") was significant. With the passage of time, various multilateral trade agreements reduced the Column 1, MFN, rates, while leaving the Column 2 rates at extremely high protectionist levels. MFN treatment became increasingly desirable, and the United States used this as leverage to obtain political concessions from its cold war adversaries. With the end of the cold war, only a handful of countries were not entitled to Column 1, MFN, rates. Almost all countries are now entitled to MFN, the main exceptions being Cuba and North Korea, with whom the United States has trade embargoes of another sort.

The Column 1 rate, or the MFN rate, is subdivided into two categories. Contrary to the plain meaning of MFN, GATT does permit rates more favorable than MFN rates. Exceptions are permitted for free trade areas and special programs to assist the development of less developed countries. Exports from our major GATT trading partners enter the United States paying the MFN rate. Exports from Canada, Mexico, and Israel—with all of whom we have free trade area agreements—enter the United States free of duty.

(e) General System of Preference

The United States has two major trade programs to assist developing countries. Under the Generalized System of Preferences (GSP), most products (except import-sensitive products like steel and textiles, apparel and shoes) entering the United States pay no duty at all. The coverage of GSP has been somewhat broadened and extended to the countries of the Caribbean in a program called the Caribbean Basin Initiative (CBI), so that most of their exports enter the United States duty free.

As a result of these special programs, Column 1 is divided into two categories. The first, called "General," contains the regular MFN rate. The second, called "Special," contains the special GSP, MFN, and free trade area rates.

6.3 General Rules of Interpretation

Since there are a great number of product categories and descriptions in the HTSUS, a product often falls under more than one product description in the tariff schedule. In determining the applicable duty rate, a single product category needs to be selected. Accordingly, the HTSUS contains rules of interpretation to guide classification.

The General Rules of Interpretation (GRI) consist of six rules found in the international system. In addition to these rules, the U.S. tariff schedule contains additional U.S. rules of interpretation consisting of one rule subdivided into four parts. Of the six rules of the GRI, Rules 1 through 4 must be applied sequentially, while Rules 5 and 6 may be used when applicable.

(a) General Rules of Interpretation–1

GRI 1 provides that the table of contents, alphabetical index, and the titles of sections, chapters, and subchapters of the tariff schedules do not have any legal significance in determining the proper classification of merchandise. GRI 1 also provides that the tariff headings and any relevant section or chapter notes are the primary materials used in classifying goods. If these headings and legal notes do not assist in classifying the specific item, the remaining rules, GRI 2 to 6, must be used. GRI 1 provides that the tariff schedule must be interpreted according to the common meaning of the terms used in the tariff schedules. The common meaning is presumed to be the same as the commercial meaning. In ascertaining the common meaning of a tariff term, dictionaries, scientific authorities, and other reliable sources may be consulted.

Another guide of interpretation, the *Explanatory Notes,* is issued by the Customs Cooperation Council in Brussels. The Explanatory Notes provide further guidance as to how goods are classified under the HTSUS. These notes contain extensive explanations for each heading, subheading, and the General Rules of Interpretation. The Explanatory Notes are not legally binding in the United States, but both Customs and the courts consult them for guidance in interpreting the HTSUS provisions.

(b) General Rules of Interpretation–2

GRI 2 guides classification of merchandise when the merchandise consists of unfinished and incomplete articles, mixtures, and combinations of articles. Rule GRI 2 is divided into two subsections: GRI 2 (a) applies to incomplete or unfinished articles, while GRI 2 (b) applies to mixtures and combinations of articles.

GRI 2 (a), which controls the classification of unfinished or incomplete articles, provides that a heading or a subheading applies to the article described, whether or not the article is complete or incomplete, or finished or unfinished. Thus, when a tariff item refers to "furniture," by force of GRI 2 (a) it refers as well to unfinished and incomplete furniture. Furthermore, the rule also applies to incomplete or unfinished articles having the essential character of the finished version. GRI 2 (a) provides that if an article is unassembled or disassembled, it is classified as the completed article.

GRI 2(b) controls the classification of mixtures and combinations of materials or substances. Any tariff heading that provides for classification of a substance under that heading is read to include classification of all articles that may consist of mixtures containing that substance. However, the classification of goods containing more than one material or substance is governed by GRI 3.

(c) General Rules of Interpretation–3

GRI 3 governs the classification of goods that may be classifiable under two or more headings of the tariff. As a practical matter, GRI 3 is used in most classifications under the HTSUS. GRI 3 is the rule that will be referred to and examined more than any other in questionable areas. The rule provides three ordering rules to determine the proper classification. These rules are listed in descending order of priority and provide that an article may be classifiable under two or more headings:

1. The heading that provides the "most specific description" is preferred over other headings. The basis of comparison is made at the level of headings, not at the subheading, chapter, or item level. Therefore, a comparison is not made between eight- or ten-digit classifications, but at the heading level.
2. In the case of mixtures, sets composed of different components or articles, and the like, if classification cannot be made by resort to GRI 3 (a), then the component that gives the mixture or sets its "essential character," governs classification.
3. Finally, and arbitrarily, if no prior GRI results in the proper classification of the merchandise, then the tariff *heading* "which appears last in numerical order" in the HTSUS, governs classification.

Example

We may see use of GRI 3(a) in U.S. Customs Ruling HQ 958995 of May 6, 1996. This ruling involved the correct classification of six-wheeled vehicles capable of traversing rough terrain and inland water. These vehicles were fully amphibious and used as armored supply vehicles in the British army. The competing headings at issue were 8704: Motor Vehicles for the transport of goods, and 8710: Tanks and other armored fighting vehicles.

Customs reasoned that "for purposes of GRI 3(a), a Heading which more clearly identifies goods shall be preferred to one where identification is less complete." Since Heading 8710 encompassed fighting vehicles that are armored and capable of transporting people and goods, this heading more clearly identified the goods than did Heading 8704.

The "determination of essential character," referred to in GRI 3 (b) varies among different kinds of goods. According to the *Explanatory Notes,* essential character may, for example, be determined by the nature of the material or component, its bulk, quantity, weight or value, or by the role of a constituent material in relation to the use of the goods. Customs has ruled that under HQ 958955, in general, essential character has been construed to mean the attribute that strongly marks or serves to distinguish what an article is; that which is indispensable to the structure, core, or condition of the article.

(d) General Rules of Interpretation–4

GRI 4 provides that goods that cannot be classified in accordance with the foregoing rules are classified under the heading appropriate to the goods to which they are most akin. According to the Explanatory Note for this rule, kinship can depend on factors like description, character, and purpose. This rule is intended to serve as a last resort and is utilized only on rare occasions. This is the last rule that must be applied in sequential order. The two remaining rules are not applied in sequential order.

(e) General Rules of Interpretation–5

GRI 5 is divided into two parts. GRI 5 (a) pertains to the classification of specially shaped or fitted cases. GRI 5(a) states that:

> Camera cases, instrument cases, gun cases, drawing instrument cases, necklace cases, and similar containers, specially shaped or fitted to contain a specific article or set of articles, suitable for long-term use and entered with the articles for which they are intended, are classified with such articles when of a kind normally sold therewith. This rule does not, however, apply to containers that give the whole its essential character.

According to the Explanatory Note for this rule, this rule requires that:

1. Containers that are shaped or fitted to contain a specific article or set of articles must be designed to accommodate the articles for which they are intended.
2. Containers suitable for long-term use and having a durability analogous to that of the articles they are designed to hold.
3. The containers are imported together with the articles for which they are intended, whether or not they are packed separately from the articles for which they are contemplated.
4. The containers are normally sold with such materials.
5. The articles do not bestow to the whole its essential character.

GRI 5(b) governs the classification of packing materials and containers imported together with the goods. The rule provides that such packing materials are to be classified under the same heading as the goods with which they are imported. This rule does not apply to containers that are clearly suited for repetitive use.

Example

An example of the application of rule 5(b) can be found in Customs Ruling NY 813637 of September 1, 1995. This ruling involved the classification of plastic hangers imported with garments by having the hanger inserted into the garment. The hangers in question were to be reused if they were removed from the garments upon their sale. The issue in this case was whether the hangers are separately classified as hangers or whether they are subject to the duty of the garments with which they are imported.

The ruling applied GRI 5(b) and is quoted in the course of the analysis. The use of the hangers at issue was found to be "incidental and fugitive relative to the . . . scale of operations." Accordingly, the reuse of hangers here was not viewed as a repetitive use in the commercial sense since the function of the hangers was for shipment and the presentation of garments to the consumer. Therefore, the hangers were classified with the garments with which they were imported, and assessed a duty at the same rate as the garments.

(f) General Rules of Interpretation–6

GRI 6 governs the classification of goods in the six-digit and eight-digit subheadings. The rule states that "the classification of goods in the subheadings of a heading shall be determined according to the terms of those subheadings and any related subheading notes." This Rule is consulted only when it is agreed that the correct classification is between two subheadings under the same heading.

6.4 Additional U.S. Rules of Interpretation

In addition to the GRIs which apply to the HTSUS as well as to all tariff codes that are identical to the Harmonized Code, the United States has promulgated special rules of interpretation that apply to classification of goods only pursuant to the HTSUS.

(a) Classifications Controlled by Use

Additional U.S. Rule of Interpretation 1 (a) provides that in cases of a tariff classification "controlled by use, other than actual use," the "the applicable use" is that use in the United States at the date of importation, or immediately prior thereto, of goods of the same class or kind as the imported goods. The rule defines the "controlling use" as the principal use. Therefore, the principal use of the imported article will be the use of the merchandise of the same class or kind of the imported merchandise that supersedes every other use, not all other uses combined. Consequently, the principal use might be less than 50% of the total possible uses. In cases of classifications governed by use, it is the obligation of the importer to show the principal use of the product. This U.S. Rule of Interpretation continues the practice of prior United States tariffs going back at least a century and codifies U.S. case law relative to classification controlled by use.

(b) Classifications Controlled by Actual Use

Additional U.S. Rule of Interpretation 1 (b) provides that a classification governed by *actual* use requires that:

1. The actual use is intended at the time of importation,
2. The goods are actually so used after importation, and

3. Documentation of the actual use of the goods is presented to Customs within three years after the date of entry of the goods.

(c) Tariff Provisions for "Parts" and "Accessories" of Other Articles

Additional U.S. Rule of Interpretation 1 (c) provides that when a tariff provision refers to "parts of an article," that provision "covers products solely or principally used as a part of such articles." Nevertheless, provisions for "parts" or "parts and accessories" are not to control classification when a more specific tariff provision applies to such part or accessory. A part is merchandise that cannot be utilized by itself, but must be used together with other merchandise to form an article permitting the achievement of its intended function.

However, "accessories" are not necessary for the article they accompany to achieve their intended purpose. Yet accessories must be identified as being intended for use with a specific article. Therefore, if a heading specifically covers the article in question by name, then that heading supersedes a provision for "parts" or "parts and accessories."

(d) Classification of Articles Consisting of a Mixture of Textile Articles

Additional U.S. Rule of Interpretation 1 (d) governs the classification of items composed of a mixture of textile materials. The rule states that the principles of Section XI regarding mixtures of two or more textile materials apply to the classification of goods in any provision in which a textile material is named.

The rule also provides that articles of specified textile materials which are classified as "of textile materials" will be classified in accordance with the provision of Note 2 to Section XI. This note states that articles composed of a mixture of two or more textile materials are to be classified as if consisting wholly of the textile material which predominates by weight over each other single textile material. For example, a textile jacket with an outer surface made up of a textile material which is—by weight—75% man-made fiber and 25% cotton fiber would be considered a jacket of man-made fiber. Therefore, the value of the respective component materials is not taken into account.

This analysis is precisely the opposite of the practice which controlled in the United States prior to the enactment of the HTSUS.

This rule applies to articles that are partially composed of textiles.

6.5 Pre-Importation Determination

The import process is completed within two months by a process known as liquidation, including presentation of entry papers to Customs, payment of estimated duties, and Customs' review of the entry. At that time, the classification, rate of duty, and appraisement become fixed and final for all parties. At liquidation, excess monies paid at entry are refunded to the importer, and any underpayments are collected by Customs. The importer is unaware of Customs' final decisions as to the importations until months after shipment. In addition, under the Customs Modernization Act, Customs may review entries for up to five years after entry to determine whether fraud or misstatements have been committed as to the entry of merchandise.

(a) Two Programs

Customs has set up two programs, the pre-entry classification program and the binding ruling program, to avoid problems that may occur after importation and to encourage importers to tell Customs what is being imported prior to importation. Under these programs, importers and other interested parties can receive written binding tariff classifications on their merchandise.

The pre-entry classification program within Customs is administered by National Import Specialists (NIS) in New York City or by Deputy National Import Specialists (DNIS) located at several ports of entry throughout the United States. The NIS or the DNIS reviews and examines the importer's merchandise and issues written tariff classifications. By participating in this program, Customs is bound by its tariff classifications at all ports of entry.

(b) Pre-Entry Classification

Pre-entry classifications are binding on Customs unless they are examined and nullified by the Office of Regulations and Rulings at Customs Headquarters in Washington, D.C. Such a reversal of a binding ruling can occur only after Customs publishes its intent to revoke or change the ruling in the *Customs Bulletin* and gives the affected importer 60 days' advance notice of the revocation. The importer is protected for its already-purchased imports for a period of at least 60 days after publication of the ruling. A change in classification cannot be enforced by Customs to the extent that an importer can prove reliance on the ruling when placing orders.

Importers have a right to protest classification decisions even if they participate in the pre-entry classification program. However, until the protest is reviewed, importers must enter their merchandise at the higher rate of duty.

Under the tariff classification ruling program, the Customs Service furnishes written binding rulings to the importer relating to the imported merchandise's classification. These rulings are issued by the NIS in New York City or by the Office of Regulations and Rulings in Customs Headquarters. This program is confined to transactions that are not already pending before a Customs Service office by reason of arrival, entry, or otherwise.

(c) Binding Classification

A binding tariff classification ruling can be obtained from Customs by an importer with a written application at any district where the importer has reason to do business. Customs requires a full description of the merchandise and a sample if possible. Then Customs will promulgate its ruling, which takes 30 days, or 120 days if Headquarters is involved.

The ruling requests are limited to five items of the same class or type of merchandise. These rulings are binding on Customs officials unless overturned by Headquarters in Washington, D.C. As in the pre-entry classification program, an importer does not waive his right to file a protest by participating in the binding tariff classification ruling program.

6.6 Administrative Protests

After liquidation—that is, after the merchandise has entered the United States and duty has been paid—administrative review may be obtained by the filing of a protest. A protest may be filed against a decision of the Customs Service as to "the classification and rate and amount of duties chargeable." The protest may be filed by an importer, consignee, agent, surety, or any person paying any charge or exaction, or anyone seeking entry, delivery, or drawback. The protest may be filed in writing or electronically under an electronic data interchange system. The protest must set forth the specific decisions being contested, each category of merchandise affected, and the reasons why Customs was wrong in its classification determination.

(a) Timing

The protest must be filed within 90 days after the date of liquidation. The 90-day period begins on the date of the liquidation in the *Customs Bulletin.* Any bill for additional duties does not have any effect on the commencement of the 90-day period. The protest must be filed with the district director whose decision is being contested and also may be filed with the port director of the port where the entry was filed. The date of filing is deemed to be the date on which Customs received the protest. If a protest is filed before liquidation, it will be deemed premature and will be dismissed.

The protest may be amended only before the expiration of the 90-day period during which the protest can be filed. After the 90-day period, Customs can consider alternative claims and arguments presented in writing before the disposition of the protest.

Only one protest may generally filed per entry. An exception is made for entries covering different categories of merchandise. One protest may be filed for more than one entry if there is a same protestant, the same category of merchandise, and a common decision to the entries that are subject to the protest.

Customs has up to two years to review the protest unless the importer requests accelerated disposition or the protest relates to the exclusion of merchandise. An accelerated disposition of a protest can be obtained at any time after the 90-day period for the filing of the protest. If a request for accelerated disposition is filed, and the protest is not acted upon within 30 days, it is deemed denied.

(b) Further Review

The protest may be further reviewed by another Customs officer upon the request of the protesting party. This officer is usually at a higher administrative level than the officer who made the original determination. This further review is also subject to the two-year limitation on the review of protests. This protest undergoes a preliminary examination by the district director to determine if the protest will be denied in whole or in part. If the district director determines that the protest will probably be denied, it is forwarded to the Commissioner of Customs.

Further review is granted if certain requirements are met by the protesting party. To obtain such review, the protesting party must state whether:

1. The importer currently has a request pending for an administrative ruling concerning the same claim and merchandise;
2. An adverse administrative decision was issued by Customs involving the same claim and merchandise;
3. A legal action is pending in one of the Customs courts involving the same claim and merchandise;
4. An adverse decision was issued by a court involving the same claim and merchandise;
5. A prior request for further review was made involving the same claim and merchandise.

If item 1, 3, or 5 in the preceding list applies, further review may not be granted. If either 2 or 4 applies, further review will be denied unless the requesting party can show certain facts or legal arguments exist that were not considered at the time of the adverse decision.

(c) Justification

The party requesting further review must show that further review is justified. This may be shown by demonstrating that the adverse decision is incompatible with a previous decision by the Commissioner of Customs, or by a District Director concerning the same or substantially the same merchandise, or it involves questions of fact or law that have not been ruled upon by Customs or the courts. If further review is not granted at this point, the request for further review is forwarded to either a regional office of Customs or to the Commissioner of Customs.

(d) Headquarters

The documents will be sent to Headquarters if the protest raises any of the following issues: inconsistent Customs decision, an unannounced change of a prior practice by Customs over a long period of time, and questions of law and fact that have not yet been ruled upon by the courts or Headquarters.

After the further review, the protest is either granted in whole or in part, or denied. If it is granted, the documents are sent back to the district director for reliquidation of the entry. If denied, the only available remedy is judicial review by the Court of International Trade.

(e) Correcting Clerical Errors

An entry may be reliquidated more than 90 days after liquidation (but not more than one year after liquidation) to correct a clerical error, mistake of fact, or inadvertence. Inadvertence does not include an error in the construction of law, in an entry, liquidation, or customs transaction. Clerical error includes errors in arithmetic or transcription. A mistake of fact refers to a situation in which a person believes that something is a fact when in reality it is not. Inadvertence happens when one intends to do one thing, but does something else. If Customs denies the request for reliquidation, a formal protest may be filed within 90 days of the date of the official denial. Furthermore, the Customs Service may reliquidate an entry for fraud within two years after the date of liquidation.

(f) Remedies for Domestic Manufacturers

A "domestic interested" party may petition Customs, arguing that the classification of competitive imports is erroneous. A "domestic interested" party refers to a manufacturer, producer, or wholesaler in the United States of a product like the imported product. If the petition is approved, the Commissioner of Customs determines the proper classification or the rate of duty. If the petition is denied, the petitioner has 30 days to contest the classification. Then the Customs Service will provide the petitioner with information relating to the entries and consignees of the merchandise.

6.7 Judicial Review

A person whose protest has been denied, in whole or in part, may contest the denial by bringing a civil action in the Court of International Trade within 180 days after (1) the date of mailing of a notice of denial of a protest, in whole or in part, or (2) the date a protest for which accelerated disposition was requested is deemed to have been denied. The court also has jurisdiction in cases in which a petition filed by a domestic interested party is denied. In such a case, the petitioner has 30 days from the date of the mailing of the notice of denial to file a summons in the Court of International Trade. Here, review is by trial de novo.

(a) Powers

The Court of International Trade has been designated by Congress to have exclusive subject matter jurisdiction over all civil actions arising from import transactions or out of federal laws that affect international trade. The Court of International Trade consists of nine judges appointed by the president with the advice and consent of the Senate. Each judge holds office for life and good behavior. A chief judge is designated by the president, who then serves in that office until he reaches the age of 70; then another judge is appointed as chief judge. The former chief judge is allowed to continue serving as a judge. The chief judge supervises the clerical force of the Court.

All filings of legal papers or other documents are received by the office of the clerk. All actions filed are given a docket number. The clerk keeps a docket of all civil actions filed with the Court of International Trade. Accordingly, all papers filed in an action must include this docket number and conform to Court rules relating to means of production, duplication, form, and number of copies. To actually commence a civil action, a summons and a complaint together must be filed with the clerk, except for certain actions that may be commenced only with a summons, which involves court challenges to the denial of a protest, such as an action under 28 U.S.C. 1581(a).

(b) Judiciary

The chief judge then assigns actions to a single judge for decision. An action may be assigned to a panel of three judges if the chief judge finds that a constitutional issue is raised by a statute or has significant implications in the administration or interpretation of law. The Court of International Trade has power to afford appropriate relief including a money judgment and equitable relief. Except for cases in which the government sues an importer—relatively rare in the Court of International Trade—trials are bench trials, not jury trials.

The Court of International Trade has jurisdiction over a variety of matters. In addition to administrative decisions involving classification, the Court's jurisdiction includes review of decisions involving valuation, assessment of duties, the refusal to grant drawback or reliquidate for clerical error, and the exclusion of merchandise from entry. The Court has jurisdiction over countervailing and antidumping duty actions, and country of origin determinations. Further jurisdiction includes review of administrative decisions concerning suspension or revocation of custom brokers' licenses, rulings issued prior to importation, and actions brought against the United States concerning issues relating to revenue from imports, tariffs, duties, fees, or taxes on merchandise, embargoes, and other quantitative restrictions.

The Court of International Trade has exclusive jurisdiction over civil actions commenced by the United States to recover civil penalties for fraud and negligence relating to the importation of merchandise. The Court has exclusive jurisdiction to recover customs duties, to recover bonds relating to importation, and for violations of agreements relating to subsidies and dumping. The Court also has residual jurisdiction, which means that if a cause of action arises out of any law dealing with imports, it may be heard in the Court of International Trade, rather than in a federal district court.

(c) Procedure

All liquidated duties and charges must be paid before an action is commenced in the Court of International Trade. The standard of review for classification cases is by trial de novo, which is defined as trying a matter anew; the same as if it had not been heard before and as if no decision had been previously rendered. Either party may introduce new evidence to support its position and defeat the opponent's assertions. The plaintiff is allowed to introduce a claim differing from the one in the protest as long as the claim is related to the administrative decision being challenged.

It is presumed that the decision of the Customs Service is correct, and the plaintiff importer has the burden of proof in proceedings before the Court of International Trade. In classification cases the plaintiff must prove that the original decision was incorrect, and prove the correctness of the claimed classification.

Actions commenced under the Customs Courts Act are initiated by filing a summons, which is served by the Court's clerk upon the Secretary of the Treasury and the Department of Justice. Consequently, it is not necessary for the plaintiff to serve those governmental parties. In addition, a complaint does not have to be filed with the summons. This summons is placed on the reserve calendar of the Court for one year.

This procedure enables the Court to act upon subsequent actions brought by plaintiff on the same type of merchandise at the same time. This operation enables the importer to preserve a claim for a year without actual litigation. During this time, the plaintiff can examine the merits of the case and save the expense of going through a trial before committing to active litigation.

(d) Test Procedure

The Court tries to avoid repetitious litigation arising out of protests relating to importations of the same type of merchandise or raising the same issues of classification and affecting more than one importer. The method used by the Court is called the test case method of adjudication. Under this procedure, the plaintiff selects a summons covering a representative entry or entries, files a complaint, and after the government files an answer within 60 days, moves to designate the civil action as a test case.

A plaintiff that filed a summons involving the same legal issue may move to have that case suspended pending the outcome of the test case. In the latter scenario, it does not matter whether a complaint has been filed or not. Now only the test case needs to be tried.

After the Court's decision on the test case is final, all suspended cases are acted upon. If the test case is won by the importer, the suspended cases are stipulated for judgment by the parties on the basis of that decision. If the test case is lost by the importer, the suspended cases are dismissed.

The Court has ruled that if the defendant files a counterclaim and argues that a higher rate of duty applies to the merchandise, the suspended cases will not be dismissed if the plaintiff loses the test case. The suspended cases will not always be dismissed when a test case is lost by the importer.

The Court of International Trade has remedial powers similar to any other federal district court. The Court may enter a money judgment for or against any party involved in the action. The Court may also order a retrial or remand the case for further administrative action if a decision cannot be made based on the available evidence.

Furthermore, the Court has equitable powers equal to other federal courts. This judicial power includes the power to grant declaratory judgments, orders of remand, injunctions, and writs of mandamus and prohibition. When injunctive relief is requested, the Court follows the tests developed in federal court. The Court weighs four critical factors: a threat of immediate irreparable injury, public interest considerations, the probability of success on the merits, and balancing the hardships on the parties.

(e) Appeals

A party may appeal an adverse decision by the Court of International Trade to the U.S. Court of Appeals for the Federal Circuit in Washington, D.C. The Court's jurisdiction is defined in terms of subject matter, rather than geography. An appeal may be commenced by filing a notice of appeal with the Court of International Trade within 60 days after entry of the judgment or order.

6.8 Conclusion

Classification of goods is an integral component of the importation process. Interpretive aids are necessary since the tariff schedules are extremely detailed and complex. Fortunately, the General Rules of Interpretation and the Explanatory Notes simplify the classification process. An importer must also follow precise procedural rules to contest Customs' decision. Administrative options less than a full blown lawsuit at the Court of International Trade are available to the importer.

CHAPTER 7

NAFTA

Michael P. Maxwell

7.1 Introduction
7.2 Tariff Elimination—Staged Rate Reductions
7.3 Basic Rules Governing NAFTA Eligibility
(a) Rule A—Wholly Produced Goods
(b) Rule B—Tariff Shift
(c) Regional Value Content
(d) Rule C—Goods Produced from Originating Materials
(e) Rule D—Parts and Components
(f) Rule E—Parts of Automatic Data Processing Equipment
(g) *De Minimis* Rule
7.4 Determining Regional Value Content
(a) Determination of RVC by Transaction Value Method
(b) Transaction Value
(c) Non-Originating Materials
(d) Applying the RVC Formula
(e) Net Cost Method
(f) *De Minimis* Rule
7.5 NAFTA Goods Directly Shipped
(a) Accumulation
(b) Determining Amount Accumulated
7.6 NAFTA Recordkeeping Requirements
(a) Exporters
(b) Importers
(c) Drawback
(d) Binding Rulings Procedure
7.7 Regulations Governing NAFTA Marking Rules
7.8 Marking Determinations—Special Rules
(a) Fungible Goods
(b) *De Minimis* Rule
(c) Disregarded Materials
(d) Parts

(e) Non-Qualifying Operations
(f) General Rules of Interpretation
7.9 Conclusion

7.1 Introduction

The North American Free Trade Agreement (NAFTA) is a multilateral agreement between the United States, Canada, and Mexico. NAFTA revolutionized the manner in which import and export transactions between these three countries are conducted. Most important, NAFTA provides that products that are produced in NAFTA member countries (Canada, Mexico, and the United States) and meet the NAFTA *eligibility* requirements are entitled to a duty preference. The preference is a reduced or a free rate of duty when products are imported into another NAFTA country and require that the goods must be imported directly from a NAFTA country. The principal rules governing the products that qualify for duty-free treatment are set forth in Annex 401 of NAFTA.[1]

NAFTA determines the manner in which an imported article is marked for country of origin. The United States customs law requires all articles to be individually marked to identify the country of origin. In the past, the country of origin of an article was determined by the country in which the article last underwent a substantial transformation. The "substantial transformation" test has now been replaced by rules based on "tariff shifts," which define the type of processing necessary to change an article's country of transformation.

In addition to NAFTA eligibility and country of origin marking requirements, NAFTA contains a large number of regulations regarding the documentation necessary to qualify for duty-free treatment and the "backup" necessary in the event that Customs seeks to verify the accuracy of country of origin certificates. The process of filling out the NAFTA certificate of origin requires substantial expertise and an understanding of the basic rules governing NAFTA eligibility. Both importers and exporters preparing certificates of origin should be aware of the documentation requirements and the backup that must be retained.

NAFTA contains important provisions governing drawback claims between the NAFTA member countries. In particular, substitution-same condition drawback has been eliminated. Drawback refunds are limited to articles exported from the United States to either Mexico or Canada over time. These matters are discussed further in this chapter.

7.2 Tariff Elimination—Staged Rate Reductions

Effective January 1, 1994, NAFTA eliminated tariffs on some articles originating in the United States, Canada, or Mexico, and reduced tariffs on other originat-

---

[1]HTS General Note 12.

ing goods imported into the United States from Canada or Mexico. Not all articles exported from a NAFTA country will qualify for these duty preferences. Articles must be eligible for these preferences—this requires that they have the status of "originating goods."

Not all duties were eliminated on January 1, 1994. In many cases, duty rates will be reduced in stages. These staged rate reductions will ultimately result in the elimination of tariffs. However, the staged reductions may require a 5, 10, or 15-year period to complete the tariff elimination. In addition, the duty rates and phases may differ, depending on whether the goods are imported into the United States from Canada or from Mexico.

In determining the applicable rate of duty under NAFTA preferences, an importer must refer to the Harmonized Tariff Schedule (HTS) and identify the tariff provision that describes the article being imported. Under the Column 1 "Special" rates, the rate of duty due on NAFTA eligible articles imported from Canada are designated by the letters CA, and the rate due for eligible products imported from Mexico are designated by the letters MX. For example, front panel assemblies of cathode ray tubes that are classified in 8540.91.15, HTS, are subject to a Most Favored Nation rate of duty of 6% (the MFN rate).

The "Special" rates in the duty column provide for duty-free treatment for originating goods in Mexico. The tariff rate "Free" is a parenthetical, indicating duty-free treatment is available for these articles under a number of different trade preferences, including products from Mexico. The duty rate has been reduced to 2.4%, assuming that the goods are eligible for the Canadian duty preference under NAFTA, if the same front panel assemblies are imported from Canada. Thus, the phase-out on tariff for panels imported from Canada will take place in staged reductions over a substantial period of time. Mexican originating panels are already eligible for duty-free treatment.

7.3 Basic Rules Governing NAFTA Eligibility

The most significant aspect of NAFTA is granting preferential duty treatment to merchandise imported into the United States from Mexico or Canada, if that merchandise is eligible as an "originating good" under the NAFTA rules for preferential treatment. The rules governing NAFTA eligibility are set forth in General Note 12 of the Harmonized Tariff Schedule (HTS) and Part II, Section 4 of the NAFTA regulations.[2]

Preferential treatment requires that a product satisfy the eligibility requirements, which are set forth in Annex 401 to NAFTA. There are four fundamental eligibility tests, and goods that meet any one of these four tests are deemed "originating in the territory of a NAFTA party" and are eligible for preferential duty treatment. These four rules cover:[3]

---

[2] 19 C.F.R. § 181 and Appendix.

[3] HTS General Note 12(b).

1. Goods that are wholly grown, produced, or manufactured in NAFTA territories;
2. Goods from which all nonoriginating materials incorporated in the imported articles have undergone the applicable tariff shift (formerly a substantial transformation). In addition, if applicable, the regional value content requirements must be satisfied. *Materials* means "a good that is used in the production of another good, and includes a part of ingredient."[4]
3. Goods that are produced from originating materials. "Originating materials" are articles composed of non-NAFTA materials that undergo the applicable tariff shift plus satisfying any applicable required regional value content (RVC in a NAFTA country) (formerly a *double substantial transformation* under other tariff preference programs).
4. Unassembled articles (classified pursuant to GRI 2(a)) or goods classified in the same heading as "parts" are assembled in NAFTA territory and have a regional value content of either (1) 60% by transaction value method or (2) 50% by net cost method.

In addition to these four rules, two special rules for originating goods govern parts of automatic data processing machines and agricultural products:

5. Special rule for electronic products (parts of automatic data processing equipment) in Annex 308.1.[5]
6. Certain agricultural goods, if originating, are exempted from quantitative quotas under Annex 703.2, NAFTA.

In addition to these eligibility requirements, articles eligible for NAFTA treatment must not be processed in third countries after production in a NAFTA country.

> *Transhipment.* A good shall *not* be considered to be an originating good by reason of having undergone production that satisfied the requirements of this note if, subsequent to that production, the good undergoes further production or any other operation outside the territories of the NAFTA parties, other than unloading, reloading, or any other operation necessary to preserve it in good condition or to transport the good to the territory if Canada, Mexico, and/or the United States.[6]

(a) Rule A—Wholly Produced Goods

These rules are comparatively simple in their application, except when regional value content (RVC) considerations are involved. Rule A, which covers goods that are "wholly obtained or produced" in a NAFTA country is both obvious and compelling in its simplicity.

---

[4] 19 C.F.R. p. 181, Appendix, p. 1, § 2.

[5] 58 Fed. Reg. 69,503.

[6] HTS General Note 12(l).

Wheat grown in Canada is obviously of Canadian origin—it could not possibly be a product of any other country. Wheat and similar fungible products need not be segregated to obtain NAFTA treatment. HTS General Note 12(g) provides that fungible articles such as wheat, plastic or metal parts, or chemicals may have their origin designated by inventory management methods such as LIFO and FIFO.

Similarly, a finished wooden panel produced in Canada that consists of Canadian lumber produced from Canadian logs is "wholly produced" in Canada. By definition, this is a product of Canada, and under Rule A, it is an originating good.

(b) Rule B—Tariff Shift

Rule B, in applying non-originating materials, is straightforward so long as it is unnecessary to determine regional value content. In most cases, RVC requirements are not imposed. Under Rule B, the article imported into the United States must have each of the non-originating materials used in its production undergo a tariff shift in one or more NAFTA countries. In addition to the tariff shift, the imported article may have to satisfy an RVC requirement to be eligible for duty preferential treatment as an originating good. In most cases, there is not an RVC requirement.

Example

A tariff shift determines an "originating good." The shift requires a comparison of the tariff description of the imported article with the tariff descriptions of the non-originating components of the article being imported. For example, if a computer is manufactured in Canada from stuffed printed circuit boards produced in Japan, a Canadian housing, and various U.S. components (a disk drive, etc.), the computer will be an originating good if the requisite tariff shift has occurred.

The tariff shift process occurs as follows in this example. First, the tariff classification of the computer must be determined, which is Heading 8741.2000, HTS. Second, the tariff shift rules found in General Note 12, HTS, for that provision must be located and analyzed. That tariff shift rule provides a change to subheadings 8471.20 through 8471.91 from any subheading outside that group.[7]

Rule A requires a tariff shift only for non-originating materials—in this case the Japanese printed circuit board subassemblies. Assuming the Japanese printed circuit board assemblies are classified in Heading 8473.30.10, HTS, and do not include a motherboard with microprocessor (which is considered an incomplete computer and classified in Heading 8471.9000, HTS), the requisite tariff shift has occurred. That is, Heading 8473.30 is outside subheadings 8471.20 through 8471.91. Accordingly, the Canadian computer is an originating article under Rule B.

(c) Regional Value Content

When there is a regional value content (RVC) requirement for originating goods, the process of determining eligibility requires two steps: (1) determining

[7]HTS General Note 12(t)(Chapter 84)(191).

whether the required tariff shift has taken place and (2) determining whether the imported article meets the RVC. RVC can be calculated under two alternative methods, the Transaction Value Method or the Net Cost Method. Both are complex determinations that involve determining the percentage of the imported article's value that is attributable to processing in NAFTA countries.

The purpose of regional value content (RVC) is to ensure that third-country producers cannot establish "pass-through" operations in NAFTA countries to obtain duty-free treatment without engaging in substantial manufacturing operations in a NAFTA country. In general, both transaction value and net cost calculations involve the determination of the percentage of the goods under Transaction Value or Net Cost (the total cost less marketing and after market service costs) that is attributable to processing in NAFTA countries and the costs of NAFTA materials.

Example

An example of the application of a tariff shift with regional value content illustrates the manner in which eligibility is determined for merchandise that is subject to both of these requirements. If the imported good is a calculator, classified in Heading 8470.10.00, HTS, manufactured in Canada from a Malaysian printed circuit board subassembly and from Canadian materials ("materials" includes components), it is necessary to refer to the eligibility rule.

1. A change to Heading 8470 from any other heading, except from Heading 8473; or
2. A change to Heading 8470 from Heading 8473, whether or not there is also a change from any other heading, provided there is a regional value content of not less than:
   a. 60% where Transaction Value is used; or
   b. 50% where the Net Cost Method is used.[8]

Here, the printed circuit board is classified in Heading 8473.21.00, HTS, as "parts of machines of Heading 8470." Accordingly, the change that takes place is from Heading 8473 to Heading 8471. The calculator must meet the regional value content requirement to be considered "originating" and thus eligible for duty-free treatment Column 1, Heading 8470.1000, HTS, determines the preference. If the transaction value of the calculator is \$10.00, and the transaction value of the non-originating material, the printed circuit board, is \$2.00, RVC is satisfied (i.e., 60% of \$10.00 is \$6.00). Here \$8.00 is the RVC (the transaction value of the calculator of \$10.00 less the value of the non-originating materials of \$2.00).

(d) Rule C—Goods Produced from Originating Materials

Rule C covers goods produced in NAFTA countries produced exclusively from originating materials. If the imported article is composed of both non-originating materials and originating materials, then eligibility must be determined according

[8]HTS General Note 12(t)(84)(189).

to Rule B. Under Rule C, the imported article must be manufactured from components that are wholly from growth or produce of NAFTA countries, or from components that were produced in NAFTA countries from non-originating materials. Non-originating (foreign) materials qualify if these materials underwent the necessary tariff shift (or tariff shift plus RVC) to transform the foreign materials into an originating good of a NAFTA country. Accessories, spare parts, and tools that are delivered with a good are considered originating if the good is originating, and disregarded in determining where the good originates.[9]

Under the originating materials rule, it is not necessary to examine the tariff shift of the components that are manufactured into the imported article. Rather, it is necessary to examine the tariff shift involved in manufacturing the NAFTA component that is incorporated in the imported article. For this reason, it is not necessary to determine the RVC of the imported good—it is each originating good's RVC that must be determined.

Example

Telephone sets are imported into the United States from Mexico under Heading 8517.10.00, HTS. These sets are manufactured from printed circuit board subassemblies that were stuffed in Mexico under Heading 8517.90.12, HTS. The printed circuit board subassemblies were manufactured from bare printed circuit boards under Heading 8534, HTS, and diodes and resistors under Heading 8541, HTS, which were manufactured in Taiwan. The telephones are classified in Heading 8517.10, and the tariff shift rule for articles classified in Heading 8517.10 provides that a telephone will be originating in NAFTA countries if there is:

> a change to subheading 8517.10 from any other subheading, except tariff items 8517.90.12, 8517.90.36, 8517.90.38, or 8517.90.44.

The change from the heading for printed circuit boards (Heading 8517.90.12) to telephones will therefore be sufficient if the printed circuit boards are originating articles. If they are not, there will not be the necessary shift. To make this determination, it is necessary to examine the tariff shift rules for printed circuit board subassemblies (Heading 8517.90.12, HTS). That rule provides:

> a change to subheading 8517.10 from any other subheading, except tariff items 8517.90.12, 8517.90.36, 8517.90.38, or 8517.90.44.

Here the tariff shift was from Heading 8534 to 8531, so the PCBAs were originating materials, and the telephones are eligible for NAFTA treatment.

(e) Rule D—Parts and Components

Rule D provides for special application when an article does not undergo a tariff shift because the components of the imported article are classified in a "parts" provision. Rule D applies in situations in which all the components of an article

---

[9]HTS General Note 12(h).

assembled in a NAFTA country are imported in a kit and classified as if assembled pursuant to General Rule of Interpretation 2(a), HTS. Rule D results in NAFTA eligibility if this situation arises, provided the regional value content of the imported article is not less than 60% under the transaction value method of determining RVC, or 50% under the net cost method of determining RVC.

For example, all the components necessary to manufacture a radio receiver are imported in a kit including bare circuit boards, resistors, and diodes to stuff the boards, speakers, batteries, and housing. These items are imported into Canada. These parts are classified as a radio receiver.[10] Accordingly, there will not be a tariff shift for any of the components when the radio receiver is assembled in Canada and then imported into the United States. Nevertheless, if the total cost of the radio receiver is such that the regional value content is greater than the required levels (60% by transaction value or 50% by net cost method), then the radio receiver will be eligible for duty-free treatment.

(f) Rule E—Parts of Automatic Data Processing Equipment

The special rule for parts of automatic data processing equipment is provided for under Annex 308.1 of NAFTA. This Annex provides that when all three NAFTA countries charge the same rate of duty for any of the specified tariff provisions, articles imported into one of the NAFTA countries that are classified in that provision will be deemed originating articles thereafter. The article that is imported into a NAFTA country is eligible for NAFTA tariff preferences if the article is exported to another NAFTA country. The value of the imported article is counted toward satisfaction of the RVC requirement if a component is incorporated in an article that is exported to a NAFTA country and that article has to satisfy an RVC requirement.

(g) *De Minimis* Rule

Several rules are intended to simplify NAFTA eligibility determinations. First, the NAFTA eligibility rules contain a *de minimis* exception, which permits an importer to disregard insubstantial non-originating materials (the definition of non-originating materials includes components) that do not undergo the applicable tariff shift.[11] This *de minimis* rule applies to non-originating materials that do not constitute more than 7% of the transaction value of the imported article (adjusted to an FOB basis). For textiles, the *de minimis* rule is applied to non-originating materials that constitute 7% *by weight* of the imported article.

7.4 Determining Regional Value Content

The regional value content (RVC) of an imported article is calculated by two different methods under NAFTA:

---

[10] HTS, GRI 2(a).

[11] HTS General Note 12(f); 58 Fed. Reg. 69,503.

1. By the Transaction Value Method, or
2. By the Net Cost Method.

Under the Transaction Value Method, the transaction value of the imported article (the producer's FOB price plus additions) is compared to the value of non-originating materials incorporated in the imported article to determine whether it meets the applicable RVC. Under the Net Cost Method, the total cost of the imported article, less excluded costs, equals net cost (the value of the article less the seller's profit). Net cost less the value of non-originating materials is divided by formula to derive the RVC.

As is the case under the Customs valuation statute, in certain circumstances the transaction value cannot be used, for example, there is no sale for export, or tied sales, and so on. Schedule III of the Appendix to the NAFTA regulations[12] sets forth the circumstances in which the Transaction Value Method of determining RVC cannot be used under NAFTA:[13]

1. There is no sale of the good;
2. There are substantial restrictions on the sale of the good other than geographic restrictions (including tied sales);
3. The sale is subject to a restriction for which a value cannot be determined (except marketing services);
4 Resale proceeds will accrue to the vendor and these amounts cannot be determined;
5. The parties are related and the relationship affects the price (must examine circumstances of sale and must accept test values).

(a) Determination of RVC by Transaction Value Method

The Transaction Value Method of determining RVC requires the exporter that executes the certificate of origin to determine the following three facts:

1. The transaction value of the imported article (the price paid to the producer);
2. The value of the non-originating materials incorporated in the imported article; and
3. The determination whether the article meets the stated RVC by applying a statutory formula.

Transaction value under the NAFTA rules is similar to transaction value under Customs valuation statute[14] and in most cases will be identical (it will generally

[12] 58 Fed. Reg. 69,539.

[13] HTS General Note 12(c)(iii).

[14] 19 U.S.C. §1401a.

equal the FOB price of the goods). The most significant difference is that the transaction value for purposes of calculating RVC is based on the producer's price—not the sale for export.

(b) Transaction Value

Transaction value of goods equals:

Price paid or payable to the producer, whether direct or indirect, plus specified additions (Schedule II, Section 4):

1. Commissions and brokerage fees, except buying commission;
2. Inland freight from sellers to point of direct shipment (if sale is not FOB);
3. Packing materials;
4. Assists furnished by buyer, which are defined as:
   a. Materials (other than indirect materials) used in production of the good;
   b. Tools, dies, and molds and similar indirect materials;
   c. Indirect materials (see General Note 12(i), HTS);
   d. Engineering, artwork, etc., regardless of where performed
5. Royalties (other than a right to reproduce goods in a NAFTA country);
6. Proceeds subsequently accruing to producer.

After calculating the transaction value of the imported article for NAFTA purposes (as distinct from Customs valuation purposes), it is necessary to determine the value of non-originating materials. The NAFTA regulations provide a specific method by which the value of non-originating materials is calculated.[15]

(c) Non-Originating Materials

The value of non-originating materials (VNM) may be determined in two ways:

1. If imported into a NAFTA country by the producer, the Customs value of the material from that importation; or,
2. If acquired in the NAFTA territory by the producer, the transaction value of the acquisition, or an alternative valuation method.

The non-originating material rules apply provided that the value of the non-originating materials includes:

1. International freight and insurance, and packing;
2. Duties and taxes and brokerage fees; and
3. Costs of waste and scrap, less value of reusable scrap.

[15] 19 C.F.R. pt. 181, Appendix IV.

The transaction value (TV) of non-originating materials is determined in similar fashion to the manner in which the transaction value of imported articles is determined.[16] The rule for determining RVC by the Transaction Value Method is set out in General Note 12, HTS, as:

$$RVC = \frac{TV - VNM}{TV}$$

(d) Applying the RVC Formula

This method is presented as a formula. It is easier to calculate the required RVC as a percentage of transaction value, and then determine whether the transaction value less the value of non-originating materials exceeds that amount. For example, if a product must have an RVC of 60% under transaction value, and the product costs $14.00, the RVC must be at least 60% of $14.00—that is, $8.40. If $8.40 is subtracted from $14.00, this leaves $5.60. Accordingly, if the value of the non-originating goods exceeds $5.60, the article will not meet the RVC requirements under transaction value.

The calculation example shows how RVC is determined. The transaction value of the calculator is $10.00, and the value of the printed circuit board from Malaysia is $2.00. Under the Customs method, the following calculation is used to derive RVC:

$$\frac{\$10.00 - \$2.00}{\$10.00} \text{ (8 divided by 10 = .8) = 80\%}$$

Sixty percent of $10.00 equals $6.00. The value of non-originating materials must be less than $10.00 minus $6.00, or $4.00. Here, since the value of the board is less than $4.00, the imported calculator meets the RVC.

(e) Net Cost Method

The second method of determining RVC is the Net Cost Method. This method is used if the importer chooses to use this method, or if transaction value is not applicable. To determine the RVC under the Net Cost Method, it is first necessary to determine the total cost of the imported good, and to subtract the excluded costs to arrive at net Cost.[17]

- Total cost is the total of all product costs (including costs of materials), period costs, and other costs incurred in one or more of the NAFTA territories, but does not include the producer's profit.[18]
- Excluded costs are sales promotion, marketing, and after-sale service costs, royalties, shipping and packing costs, and nonallowable interest costs.[19]

---

[16]The rules for determining the transaction value of materials is set forth at 19 C.F.R. pt. 181, Appendix, Schedule VIII (58 Fed. Reg. 69,547). The method to determine the transaction value of goods is found at 19 C.F.R. pt. 181, Appendix, Schedule V.

[17]HTS General Note 12((c)(vi)).

[18]58 Fed. Reg. 69,508.

[19]58 Fed. Reg. 69,497.

Net cost is derived by subtracting excluded costs from total costs. After calculating the net cost, the value of non-originating materials must be calculated, and the applicable formula applied to ascertain the RVC. The percentage of the cost of the imported article imported into the United States attributable to processing performed in NAFTA territories determines RVC.

Example

A Canadian producer of optical fibers, classified in Heading 9001.10.00, produces the optical fibers from glass rods, in subheading 7002.20.10, and sells the goods to a related U.S. buyer. The buyer must satisfy a regional value content to obtain duty-free treatment, and decides to calculate this value based on net cost, which requires a 50% regional value content. To calculate the regional value content of the imported optical fiber, the following steps are followed:

1. The total cost (product costs, period costs, and other costs) is determined on a per unit basis ($100.00).
2. The excluded costs (sales promotion, marketing, and after-sales service costs, royalties, shipping, packing, and non-allowed interest costs) are calculated on a per unit basis ($12.00).
3. The excluded costs are subtracted from the total costs to determine the net cost per unit ($ 88.00).
4. The value of the non-originating materials must then be calculated (their landed value—Customs value plus international freight, brokerage, and duties) on a per unit basis ($ 40.00). These costs made up part of the total costs of the article. In calculating the value of non-originating materials, goods produced by the Canadian producer that are produced in Canada from foreign materials are designated as intermediate materials. Intermediate materials are subject to accumulation requirements in designating their value toward the RVC, or the value of non-originating materials.
5. These figures are then plugged into the formula used to determine regional value content under the net cost method.

$$\text{TC} = \$100.00 - \$12.00 \text{ (excluded cost)} = \$88.00 \text{ (net cost)}$$

$$\text{RVC} = \frac{\text{NC} - \text{VNM}}{\text{NC}} = \text{RVC}$$

$$\text{NC-VNM} = \$88.00 - \$40.00 = \$48.00$$

$$\$48.00 \text{ divided by } \$88.00 = 0.54545$$

This amount could also be determined by dividing the $88.00 net cost by 50% to determine that the RVC had to equal $44.00, and the value of non-originating goods had to be less than $44.00. Here, since the value of the non-originating materials was $40.00, the RVC was satisfied. The principal distinction between transaction value and net costs is (1) their manner of derivation and (2) that the transaction value includes the producer's profit, and the net cost does not.

(f) *De Minimis* Rule[20]

An importer can avoid the need to calculate regional value content if the value of non-originating materials in the imported article is not more than 7% of the transaction value of the good, or of the total cost of the good, and the good satisfies all other applicable requirements.

This *de minimis* rule also applies to goods that are wholly the product of a beneficiary country, except for *de minimis* non-originating content.[21] For textiles, this rule applies by weight.

Example:

A producer of ceiling fans in Canada has all of the components in the fan undergo the applicable tariff shift, except for one component, which is classified in the same heading (8414.51) as ceiling fans as a part. If the value of this component does not exceed 7%, the rule of origin is satisfied. Note exceptions to the *de minimis* rule for certain designated tariff classifications and for printed circuit assemblies where the applicable tariff shift rule provides restriction, and for products in Chapters 1 through 27.[22]

7.5 NAFTA Goods Directly Shipped

Generally, to be eligible for NAFTA treatment, goods must be shipped directly from the NAFTA country in which they originate to the country in which the preference is claimed. It is permissible to transship merchandise if it merely undergoes loading, unloading, and operations to preserve the merchandise.[23] Duty-free treatment is disallowed if further production of other operations occur in third countries.

(a) Accumulation

The producer of an article produced in a NAFTA eligible country may add the costs of other NAFTA producers incurred in a NAFTA country and of NAFTA materials incorporated in the imported article.[24] The NAFTA costs of materials and production are aggregated so that the regional value content may be satisfied. However, non-originating materials and labor cannot be included in the aggregated amount.[25]

Producer A in Canada imports unfinished Japanese ball bearing rings that cost $0.75. Producer A manufactures them into finished ball bearing rings in Canada, and these rings are classified in the same subheading (8482.99) as the unfinished

---

[20]HTS General Note 12(f).

[21]19 C.F.R. pt. 181, Appendix pt. I, § 5.

[22]HTS General Note 12(r)(v).

[23]HTS General Note 12(1).

[24]HTS General Note 12(e).

[25]HTS General Note 12(c)(iii) and (viii).

rings. There is no tariff change, so the bearings are not originating materials. Their value cannot be counted toward satisfaction of the regional value content in articles in which they may be incorporated in Canada under Rule C for origin. The bearing rings are sold for $1.50 to a Canadian producer of ball bearings, Producer B. The value of Producer A's Canadian processing and the Canadian components in the bearing rings equals $0.55.

The ball bearing rings are used by Canadian Producer B to manufacture ball bearings in Canada, which are then imported into the United States. The non-originating bearing rings have undergone the requisite charge in tariff classification in Canada in the manufacture of the bearings, but the bearings do not satisfy the regional value content because of the $1.50 cost of the non-originating bearing rings.

Accumulation permits Producer B to allocate the Canadian costs of producing the bearing rings (the costs incurred by Producer A) as part of the value of originating materials. This permits the allocation of the cost of the unfinished Japanese ball bearing rings as non-originating materials.

(b) Determining Amount Accumulated

Several options are available to determine the amount of processing in a non-originating intermediate product that may be accumulated. This amount may be the net cost of the producer of the intermediate material (the bearing ring) plus freight, insurance packing, duties, brokerage (costs listed in Section 7 (c) through (e)). This amount may also be based on the transaction value of the materials (as determined in Section 7(1) less the value of non-originating materials.

7.6 NAFTA Recordkeeping Requirements

As to recordkeeping, Customs regulations govern the preparation of certificates of origin by both exporters and importers.

(a) Exporters

Exporters are required to prepare a certificate of origin for goods exported from the United States into Canada or Mexico.[26] The U.S. exporter must complete a certificate of origin[27] and furnish that certificate of origin to the Canadian or Mexican importer. If the U.S. exporter is not the producer of the good, the exporter can complete the certificate on the basis of knowledge that the good qualifies as an originating good, or on a reasonable reliance on the producer's written representation that the good is originating in NAFTA countries, or on a completed certificate provided by the producer. If there is a mistake in the certificate, the exporter is to notify all persons supplied with the certificate of the mistake.

---

[26]19 C.F.R. §181.11.

[27]Customs Form 434.

Exporters are required to maintain all records for five years relating to the origin of the good for which they executed certificates.[28] These records include records related to the purchase or cost or value of the good exported from the United States, the value of all materials, including indirect materials used in producing the good, and the production of the good in the form in which the good was exported. These records may be retained in hard copy, on microfilm or microfiche, or in automated record storage devices. The records must be made available to Customs upon a request by the district director. In addition, they may be subject to an origin verification visit by the Canadian or Mexican Customs administrations.

If an exporter fails to comply with these recordkeeping requirements, the exporter may be subject to penalties.[29] The regulations provide that a false certification by an exporter that a good qualifies as originating will have the same legal consequences that would apply to an importer for contravention of U.S. Customs laws. Exporters are presumably subject to civil penalties.[30]

(b) Importers

Importers are subject to specific recordkeeping requirements.[31] The U.S. importer must make a declaration claiming duty-free treatment by using the symbol CA or MX as a prefix to the HTS heading for which it is claiming a duty preference. This declaration must be based on a properly executed certificate of origin (CF 434) that is in the possession of the importer at the time of the importation.

Each importer is required to maintain all documentation relating to the importation, including a copy of the certificate of origin, for a period of five years after importation. The certificate of origin is to be signed by the exporter or producer or their agent and must be completed in English or in the language of the country from which the good is exported.

The certificate of origin may be applicable to a single importation of the good, or to multiple importations of identical goods in the United States within a period of 12 months. Thus, "blanket" certificates of origin may be used for one-year periods for importations of identical merchandise.

Customs regulations also provide for post-importation duty refund claims, authorizing an importer's right to amend an entry within one year after the date of the importation. The procedure for making such a claim is set forth in the Customs regulations.[32]

(c) Drawback

NAFTA affects the importer's rights to seek drawback. NAFTA eliminated substitution same condition drawback, and such claims can no longer be made. Moreover, drawback is limited on goods exported from the United States to Canada

---

[28] 19 C.F.R. §181.12.

[29] 19 C.F.R. §181.81.

[30] 19 U.S.C. §1592.

[31] 19 C.F.R. §181.21.

[32] 19 C.F.R. §181.32.

after January 1, 1996, and on goods exported to Mexico after January 1, 2001. Drawback is then limited to the refund of the lesser of the duties paid on the merchandise when imported into the United States, or the duties paid on goods exported to either Canada or Mexico incorporating the imported article for which drawback is sought.[33]

(d) Binding Rulings Procedure

NAFTA regulations provide that binding rulings can be obtained from U.S. Customs regarding NAFTA eligibility. The ruling requests may be addressed to the Office of Regulations and Rulings in Washington, D.C., or binding classification rulings can be sought from the Area Director of Customs at the New York Seaport. The specifics regarding the content of such rulings are set forth in the Customs regulations.[34]

7.7 Regulations Governing NAFTA Marking Rules

On January 3, 1994, Customs issued interim regulations governing the country of origin marking requirements under NAFTA and setting forth the required tariff shifts for determining origin for nonpreferential purposes (e.g., marking). Although these marking rules set forth the tariff shift required to have an article's country of origin transformed during manufacture, other rules govern country of origin determination in situations in which it is unnecessary to consider tariff shift rules, or when the tariff shift rules are not dispositive. For example, there is no need to consider tariff shift rules if an imported article is a product of a single country (e.g., Canadian wheat is a product of Canada and never undergoes a tariff shift).

The principal rules governing the determination of country of origin for marking purposes under NAFTA[35] provides six basic rules that govern the determination of an article's country of origin:

1. If an imported article is wholly the growth, product, or manufacture of a single country, that country is its country of origin (e.g., Canadian wheat).[36]
2. If an imported article is manufactured in a country exclusively from "domestic materials," then the country of origin is the place of manufacture.[37] A *domestic material* is defined as "a material whose country of origin as determined under these rules is the same as the country in which the good is produced."[38] This domestic materials rule applies when the *components* of the imported article are all produced in the country of manufacture, but the

[33] *See* 19 C.F.R. §§181.41–181.80.

[34] 19 C.F.R. §181.93.

[35] 19 C.F.R. §102.11.

[36] 19 C.F.R. §102.11(a)(1).

[37] 19 C.F.R. §102.11(a)(2).

[38] 19 C.F.R. §102.1(d).

components may be composed from materials that were produced in another country.

For example, Japanese steel sheet is imported into Canada and made into a Canadian tractor door panel. This is a sufficient tariff shift to change origin. This door panel is a Canadian domestic material when it is incorporated into a tractor that is manufactured in Canada.

3. Each of the "foreign materials" (the definition of foreign materials includes components)[39] incorporated in the article being imported into the United States has undergone the tariff shift required for the imported article.[40] A foreign material is defined as "a material whose country of origin as determined under these rules is not the same as the country in which the good is produced."[41]

   For example, a table lamp is produced in Brazil from a Brazilian light socket, Mexican steel tubing, and Bolivian insulated electrical wire. The lamp is imported into the United States and classified in Heading 9405.20.40, HTS. The Brazilian light socket is not a foreign material, so its classification need not be considered in determining country of origin. The rule governing the origin for articles classified as lamps in Heading 9405.20.40 provides: "9405.10–9405.60 . . . A change to subheading 9405.10 through 9405.60 from any subheading outside that group." Here, the Mexican tubing is classified in Heading 7304, HTS, and the Bolivian wire is classified in Heading 8311, HTS. Accordingly, there *is* a tariff shift of all foreign materials, and the country of origin for marking purposes is Brazil.

4. When origin cannot be determined under Rules 1 through 3, (e.g., there is not a tariff shift) and excluding merchandise classified as "sets" under GRI 3(b), the country of origin will be determined under two categories:[42]
   a. The country of origin of the material that imparts the essential character of the imported article For example, a Japanese motherboard imported to Canada is placed in a plastic housing. Then the complete computer is imported into the United States. For that reason, there is not a tariff shift of the motherboard. The essential character of the imported computer is imparted by the motherboard, and the country of origin is Japan[43]; or
   b. If the material that imparts the essential character of the article is fungible and commingled, the countries of origin may be determined by an inventory management method (For example, Hamburger Helper is produced in Italy by mixing Turkish and Canadian wheat with seasoning produced in India. There is not the requisite tariff shift, and the

[39] 19 C.F.R. §102.11(a)(3).

[40] 19 C.F.R. §102.20.

[41] 19 C.F.R. §102.1(e).

[42] 19 C.F.R. §102.11(b).

[43] 19 C.F.R. §102.18(b).

Canadian and Turkish wheat that provides the product's essential character is commingled and fungible.

5. If the article is a set, composite good, or mixture (as these terms are defined by the General Rules of Interpretation to the HTS), and origin cannot be determined by the rules set forth above (e.g., there is no component that imparts the essential character), the country of origin is the country or countries of origin of all the materials that merit equal consideration.[44] For example, a set consists of 12 French porcelain plates, 12 Italian cups and saucers, and 12 English knives, forks, and spoons. The goods are imported into the United States. The goods are prima facie classifiable in different tariff provisions, put up for retail sale, and designed for a specific purpose of activity, so they are a set under GRI 3, HTS. None of the materials imparts the essential character, and all the materials merit equal consideration, so the *set* is a product of France, Italy, and England.
6. If all the rules set forth above fail, then the following rules determine the country of origin:[45]
   a. The country of origin is the country where the imported article *last underwent production* that was more than simple assembly or processing;
   b. If the article is produced by simple assembly, the country of assembly *is* the country of origin if the materials that impart the essential character have different countries of origin; or
   c. If the country of the materials that impart essential character is the same country, their country of origin applies. For example, a crystal lamp is assembled in Canada from a lamp stem and fixture produced in Poland, an Irish crystal lamp body, and a French porcelain base. The assembly is simple (the joining of less than five parts), and none of the components imparts the essential character. The country of origin is Canada.

7.8 Marking Determinations—Special Rules

In addition to the regular NAFTA marking rules, additional rules may be applicable for certain products.[46]

(a) Fungible Goods[47]

Fungible goods are defined as goods or materials that are interchangeable for commercial purposes and whose properties are essentially identical.[48] Fungible articles include products such as wheat and crude petroleum, in which one batch of

---

[44] 19 C.F.R. §102.11(c).

[45] 19 C.F.R. §102.11(d).

[46] 19 C.F.R. § 102.11.

[47] 19 C.F.R. § 102.12.

[48] 19 C.F.R. § 102.1(f).

product cannot be distinguished from another when commingled. Fungible goods may also include indistinguishable manufactured products such as metal bolts, blue jeans, or plastic Lego blocks. When fungible goods are commingled, the country of origin of the commingled goods for marking purposes is all the countries of origin of the commingled product; or if the commingled product cannot be separated, the country of origin may be determined on an inventory management basis.[49]

(b) *De Minimis* Rule[50]

Foreign materials that do not undergo a change in tariff classification may be disregarded if the value of those materials is no more than 7% of the entered value of the imported article, or 10% of the value of a good in Chapter 22, HTS (beverages). The *de minimis* rule does not apply to live animals, vegetable products, sugar and confections, and preparations of fruits and nuts, which are goods of Chapters 1, 2, 3, 4, 7, 8, 11, 12, 15, 17, or 20, HTS. As to textiles in Chapters 50 through 63, the *de minimis* rule is not stated in terms of value, but in terms of weight. Under that rule, foreign materials may be disregarded if they do not exceed 7% of the total weight of the good.

(c) Disregarded Materials[51]

In determining whether there is the requisite tariff shift to change the country of origin, the following materials are disregarded:

1. Packaging of the imported article provided for its retail sale;
2. Accessories, spare parts, or tools delivered with the goods;
3. Packing materials for shipment; and
4. Indirect materials; these are goods used in production, testing, and inspection of a good, but are not incorporated in the good.[52] Indirect materials include fuel and energy; tools, dies, and molds; spare parts; lubricants; gloves, glasses, protective footwear, etc.; equipment to inspect merchandise; catalysts; and other products used in the production of a good.

(d) Parts[53]

In some instances a manufacturer may import a variety of parts that will be manufactured into a finished article, but the application of the tariff shift rules is frustrated because the importer's components are classified together as an "unassembled

---

[49] 19 C.F.R. § 181, Appendix (NAFTA eligibility rules).

[50] 19 C.F.R. § 102.13.

[51] 19 C.F.R. § 102.15.

[52] 19 C.F.R. § 102.1(k).

[53] 19 C.F.R. § 102.16.

article" pursuant to GRI 2(a), HTS, or else they are lumped together in a "parts" provision. The country of manufacture will be the country of origin, provided the parts undergo a substantial transformation.

(e) Non-Qualifying Operations[54]

Certain specified operations will not result in a foreign material being deemed to have undergone a tariff shift, although there is the requisite change in classification. These operations include:

1. A change in use
2. Disassembly
3. Packing or repacking
4. Mere dilution with water
5. Processes whose sole purpose is to circumvent these marking rules

(f) General Rules of Interpretation[55]

The Harmonized Tariff Schedule provides general rules of interpretation:

> Any reference in a heading to an article shall be taken to include a reference to that article incomplete or unfinished, provided that, as entered, the incomplete or unfinished article has the essential character of the complete or finished article. It shall also include a reference to that article complete or finished (or failing to be classified as complete or finished by virtue of this rule), entered unassembled or disassembled.

If this rule of interpretation is applied regarding the classification of unassembled articles, this may frustrate the use of a tariff shift to determine the origin of the imported article.[56] Similarly, if a component is classified as an "incomplete article" under the rules of interpretation, the tariff shift rules application may not work. The rules govern the determination of "essential character."[57] A multifactored weighing test is used to determine essential character, which includes consideration of:

1. The nature of the article
2. Its bulk
3. Its quantity
4. Its weight
5. Its value
6. Its role in relation to the use of the good
7. Any other relevant factors

---

[54] 19 C.F.R. § 102.17.

[55] 19 C.F.R. § 102.18.

[56] 19 C.F.R. § 102.18(a)(i) and (ii), § 102.18(b).

[57] 19 C.F.R. § 102.18(b).

If an imported article is eligible for duty-free treatment under NAFTA, but its origin is not a single NAFTA country, the country of origin for marking is the country in which the article last underwent production.

7.9 Conclusion

In sum, the application of the NAFTA marking rules contained in Part 102 of Customs Regulations is complex and requires a sophisticated application of the tariff classification rules in the HTS. Although these rules will often reach the same result as the "substantial transformation" test applied in the past, this is not always the case. Accordingly, importers should carefully review these rules and apply them to any products that they import.

CHAPTER 8

Foreign Trade Zones in the United States

Joseph F. Donohue Jr.

8.1 Introduction
- (a) Background
- (b) Zones and Subzones

8.2 Benefits from Using a Zone
- (a) Activities
- (b) Deferral of Customs Duties
- (c) State and Local Taxation
- (d) Option to Select Duty Rates
- (e) Summary of Benefits

8.3 Establishing a Foreign Trade Zone
- (a) Authority
- (b) Location
- (c) Subzones
- (d) Zone Grantees

8.4 The Application for a Zone Grant
- (a) Contents and Format
- (b) Executive Summary
- (c) Exhibits
- (d) Subzone Application
- (e) Review Process
- (f) Processing the Application

8.5 Conditions, Prohibitions, and Restrictions
- (a) Industry-Wide Restrictions
- (b) Denial of Grant
- (c) Statutory and Regulatory Restrictions
- (d) Revocation

8.6 Manufacturing and Processing Activities
- (a) Threshold Factors

(b) Economic Factors
8.7 Activation
8.8 Operations of the Zone
(a) Role of Customs
(b) Inventory Control and Recordkeeping System
(c) Admission of Merchandise into a Zone
(d) Status of Zone Merchandise
(e) Privileged Foreign Status
(f) Non-Privileged Foreign Status
(g) Domestic Status
(h) Zone Restricted Status
(i) Handling of Merchandise in a Zone
8.9 Transfer of Merchandise from a Zone
(a) Entry for Consumption
(b) Entry for Warehouse
(c) Classification—Privileged Foreign Merchandise
(d) Classification—Non-Privileged Foreign Merchandise
(e) Valuation
8.10 Transfer from a Zone for Exportation
8.11 Transfer of Zone Restricted Merchandise into Customs Territory
8.12 Equipment to be Used in a Zone
8.13 NAFTA Effect on Zones
8.14 Comparison of Zones with Other Duty-Deferral Programs
(a) Drawback
(b) Bonded Warehouses
(c) Temporary Importation Under Bond
8.15 Conclusion

8.1 Introduction

Businesses importing into the United States may find that foreign trade zones enable them to improve cash flow and to reduce or eliminate customs duties and certain local taxes. This chapter examines the benefits available through foreign trade zones, the procedure for obtaining foreign trade zone status, and operational procedures within a zone.

A foreign trade zone is a Customs-supervised enclosed area in or adjacent to a Customs port of entry that is treated as if it were outside the Customs territory of the United States.[1] Originally created as a means of expediting and facilitating for-

---

[1]The statute governing foreign trade zones is the Foreign-Trade Zones Act of 1934, as amended, codified at 19 U.S.C. § 81a-81u. Citations in this chapter to the law are to the U.S. Code unless otherwise noted. Implementing regulations appear in two titles of the Code of Federal Regulations (C.F.R.). 15 C.F.R. Pt. 400 contains the rules of practice and procedure of the Foreign-Trade Zones Board, including the substantive and procedural rules for authorizing zones and regulating zone activity. 19 C.F.R. Pt. 146 governs the admission of merchandise into a foreign trade zone, manipulation, manufacture, or exhibition in a zone; exportation of merchandise from a zone; and the transfer of merchandise from a zone into customs territory.

eign trade,[2] zones have as their policy objective today the creation and maintenance of employment through encouragement of operations in the United States which, for customs reasons, might otherwise have been carried on abroad.[3]

(a) Background

Zones have their earliest beginnings as far back as 1189, when Frederich I granted a charter to the City of Hamburg exempting it from the payment of customs duties.[4] Over the next several hundred years, the concept of duty-free port cities grew as a means of encouraging trade. In the last half of the nineteenth century, the Hanseatic cities of Hamburg, Bremen, and Lubeck formed a customs union, and the customs-free area of Hamburg was reduced but not eliminated. A portion of Hamburg was enclosed and made into a duty-free zone, thus leading to what are today known as "free zones."

Foreign trade zones are an outgrowth of the restricted duty-free zones. Most recently, the United Nations has expressed interest in zones.[5]

(b) Zones and Subzones

A zone must be located in or adjacent to a Customs port of entry[6] and is generally operated by a public utility or a quasi-public utility. If a company seeking to operate within a zone finds that it cannot accomplish its purpose at the zone located at the port of entry, it may seek permission to operate a subzone. A subzone is a special purpose zone established as part of a zone project for a limited purpose that cannot be accommodated within an existing zone.[7] A zone that is not a subzone is sometimes referred to as a general purpose zone. Unless otherwise indicated, references to "zones" or "foreign trade zones" in this chapter will include both general purpose zones and special purpose subzones.

Generally, subzones are manufacturing operations run by a single company.[8] At last report, there were 132 active zone projects and 156 active subzones operating in the United States.[9]

8.2 Benefits from Using a Zone

(a) Activities

Imported and domestic merchandise may be brought into a zone. Within the zone, the merchandise can be:

---

[2]*See* Fountain v. New Orleans Public Service, Inc., 387 F.2d 343 (1967).

[3]*See* 56 Fed. Reg. 50,790 (1991).

[4]Singer, *Foreign Trade Zones: A Means By Which the Businessman May Avoid Import Duties,* 29 Pitt. L. Rev. 89, 93 (1996).

[5]R. Feinschreiber, ed., *Special Economic Zones in Regional Development* (New York: United Nations, 1995).

[6]19 C.F.R. § 400.2(g).

[7]19 C.F.R. §§ 146.1(17), 400.2(p).

[8]15 C.F.R. § 400.28(a) (8).

[9]*56th Annual Report of the Foreign-Trade Zones Board to the Congress of the United States* (1994).

1. Stored
2. Sold
3. Exhibited
4. Broken up
5. Repacked
6. Assembled
7. Distributed
8. Sorted
9. Graded
10. Cleaned
11. Mixed with other foreign or domestic merchandise
12. Manipulated
13. Manufactured

These activities can take place without subjecting the merchandise to the Customs laws.[10]

(b) Deferral of Customs Duties

The merchandise may be removed from the zone for exportation or for entry into U.S. commerce. No customs duties or Internal Revenue taxes (where applicable) are assessed unless and until the merchandise is removed from the zone and entered into the commerce of the United States. The zone user thus is able to defer paying duties and Internal Revenue taxes (if applicable) while its goods are in inventory awaiting use in manufacture or sale. In contrast, an importer not operating a zone must pay duties and internal revenue taxes on importation.

(c) State and Local Taxation

State and local ad valorem taxes, such as inventory taxes, are precluded by federal law.[11] This provision applies to tangible personal property brought into a zone for one of the above-mentioned purposes, and to property produced in the United States and held in a zone for exportation. The property can be either in its original form or as altered by zone processing.

(d) Option to Select Duty Rates

When goods are manufactured in a zone with imported materials and then withdrawn for entry into U.S. commerce, the zone user has the option to pay duty based on either the condition of the material at the time it is entered into the zone, or the condition of the finished article.

[10] 19 U.S.C. § 81c(a).

[11] 19 U.S.C. § 81o(e).

Illustrative of a zone using this duty option was one granted in 1968 to the Equitable-Higgins Shipyard, Inc. (Equitable) of New Orleans, Louisiana. Equitable, a shipbuilder, had a contract to build over 200 barges for a U.S. company and planned to use Japanese steel. The duty on imported steel was 7.5% ad valorem. However, vessels were free of duty. Equitable produced the barges in its subzone with the imported steel and was able to withdraw the barges from the zone free of duty.

Armco Steel Corporation, a domestic steel producer, brought a court action to set aside the zone grant to Equitable on the grounds that it would be injured as a result of the grant. The court upheld the grant as within the discretion of the Foreign-Trade Zones Board.[12]

(e) Summary of Benefits

Zones thus offer the possibility of:

1. Avoiding duties and taxes on goods withdrawn from a zone for exportation
2. Deferring duties on imported merchandise placed in a zone until it is withdrawn for consumption in the United States
3. Selecting the lower of the two duty rates between the rate applicable to material used to produce an article in the zone and the rate applicable to the finished article

As will be discussed later in this chapter, the Foreign-Trade Zones Board can attach conditions or restrictions on a particular zone or an operation within a zone which may limit the realization of benefits otherwise potentially available.

8.3 Establishing a Foreign Trade Zone

(a) Authority

The authority to grant permission to operate as a foreign trade zone is vested with the Foreign-Trade Zones Board ("the FTZ Board" or "the Board"), which consists of the Secretary of Commerce (chairman), the Secretary of the Treasury, and the Secretary of the Army.[13]

(b) Location

Each port of entry is entitled to at least one zone project. The Board may authorize additional zones if it determines that existing projects will not adequately serve the public interest. The requirement that a zone must be in or adjacent to a port of entry is met if the general purpose zone is situated within 60 miles or 90 minutes' driving time from the outer limits of a port of entry.

---

[12]Armco Steel Corporation v. Stans, 303 F. Supp. 262 (S.D.N.Y. 1969); *aff'd* 431 F.2d 779 (2d Cir. 1970).

[13]15 C.F.R. § 400.2(b).

(c) Subzones

A subzone, which can be established only after a general purpose zone is established, can meet the adjacency requirement for the zone if it complies with the following requirements as to Customs' supervision:

1. Proper Customs oversight can be accomplished with physical and electronic means;
2. All electronically produced records are maintained in a format compatible with the requirement of the U.S. Customs Service; and
3. The grantee/operator agrees to present merchandise for examination at a customs site selected by Customs when requested and also agrees to present all necessary documents directly to the customs oversight office.[14]

(d) Zone Grantees

Public or private corporations may apply for a grant of authority to operate a zone project. Preference is given to public corporations.[15] The zone grantee may enter into agreements with others who actually may operate and use the zone.[16]

8.4 The Application for a Zone Grant

(a) Contents and Format

The FTZ regulations prescribe detailed procedures that must be followed when applying to the FTZ Board for a zone grant.[17] The application consists of a letter of transmittal, an executive summary, and five exhibits.

(b) Executive Summary

The executive summary must describe, among other things:

1. The corporation's legal authority to apply;
2. The type of authority requested from the Board (e.g., authority to store, manipulate, or manufacture);
3. The proposed zone site and facilities and the larger facilities of which the zone is a part;
4. The project background, including surveys and studies;

---

[14] *Id.*

[15] 15 C.F.R. § 400.22(a).

[16] See 15 C.F.R. § 400.2(r), (s), (v).

[17] 15 C.F.R. § 400.24.

5. The relationship of the project to the state's overall economic development plans and objectives;
6. The plans for operating and financing the project; and
7. Any additional information needed for a complete summary description of the proposal.

(c) Exhibits

The five exhibits must provide the following details:

1. The legal authority for the application (including, for example, corporate resolution authorizing the application);
2. Detailed description of zone site and facilities, including location, size, security, and access to transportation services;
3. Description of operation and financing;
4. Description of economic justification, including the economic impact of the zone project on public costs, employment, U.S. international trade, environment, and, in the case of zones where manufacturing will occur, a description of the manufacturing operations, anticipated zone benefits, how they will affect the firm, and the economic impact on the community and on related domestic operations; and
5. Maps, surveys, and blueprints showing location of the zone, related transportation network, zone boundaries, structures, etc.[18]

(d) Subzone Application

An application for a subzone, as part of an existing zone, should follow the filing format of the general purpose zone application. However, in the case of the subzone, the exhibit describing the economic justification should describe the specific activity of the proposed subzone and its economic effects, and other details required by the regulations.[19] The subzone applicant must demonstrate significant public benefits and that the application is in the public interest.

(e) Review Process

The zone regulations specifically allow a zone applicant to submit a draft application to the Board for review. A draft filing, together with follow-up with the Office of the Executive Secretary of the FTZ Board, is highly advisable. The draft application enables the zone applicant to learn of deficiencies in the application or concerns the Board may have that could otherwise hinder or delay approval. Correcting such deficiencies and addressing potential concerns will improve the likelihood that the zone grant will be issued.

---

[18] 15 C.F.R. § 400.24.

[19] *See* 15 C.F.R. § 400.25.

(f) Processing the Application

The period for processing zone applications is approximately 10 months, except where the zone involves manufacturing or processing, which generally takes about 12 months. Once the application is reviewed and found to be procedurally sufficient, a notice is published in the *Federal Register*, inviting public comments.[20] The public may support or oppose the zone. The zone applicant or others directly affected by the application may request a public hearing.[21] Hearings are customary when the zone will conduct manufacturing or processing operations. The applicant has an opportunity to file rebuttal comments following comments by the public. After considering the entire record, the Board publishes a determination in the *Federal Register*.

In the course of considering the zone application, reviews are conducted by local Customs officers and the District Engineer of the Department of the Army. The purpose of their review is to ensure that the zone application and operations conform to the regulations and purpose of the FTZ Act. If the examiners' report is unfavorable to the applicant, the applicant is given an opportunity to respond and submit additional evidence.

In the case of zone applicants seeking to conduct manufacturing or processing operations, the examiners will give particular attention to economic factors. The factors include the economic impact on the domestic industry producing like products, and producers of components and materials used in manufacturing, processing, or assembling the products. The evaluation by the examiners takes into account such factors as market conditions, price sensitivity, degree and nature of foreign competition, effect on exports and imports, and the net effect on U.S. employment.[22]

8.5 Conditions, Prohibitions, and Restrictions

The FTZ Act provides that the Board may order the exclusion from the zone of any merchandise or process that "in its judgment is detrimental to the public interest, health, or safety."[23] In evaluating zone applications, the Board draws upon this provision if it concludes that it should attach conditions, prohibitions, or restrictions (collectively referred to herein as "restrictions") to a zone grant. Zones with restrictions have grown as the number of zones have increased, particularly in the case of zones handling import-sensitive commodities such as textiles, steel, motor vehicles, and petroleum.[24] In general, restrictions will be determined on a case-by-case basis, but once established for a particular zone, generally apply to other zones in the same industry. The restrictions may result from the Board's

[20] 15 C.F.R. § 400.27.

[21] 15 C.F.R. § 400.51.

[22] 15 C.F.R. § 400.27.

[23] 19 U.S.C. § 81o(c).

[24] *See generally, U.S. Customs Foreign-Trade Zone Manual* (*FTZ Manual*) (undated), at 145–160.

own initiative or from opposition by members of the industry competing with the zone user.

(a) Industry-Wide Restrictions

An example of an industry-wide zone restriction is a restriction placed on zone grants to petroleum refineries. The restriction was the result of Customs inability to collect duty on certain zone products used in a zone by the Hawaiian Independent Refinery (HIRI). HIRI received a subzone grant covering its petroleum refinery. HIRI imported crude oil, which it refined into various products, including fuel oil. HIRI kept some of the fuel oil in the zone and used it as fuel for its refinery operation.

Customs took the position that the fuel consumed in the zone was subject to duty, while HIRI claimed it was not dutiable because it never left the zone and was never entered for consumption in the United States. The FTZ Act provides that when merchandise is sent from a zone into the customs territory of the United States, it becomes subject to the laws of the United States affecting imported merchandise.[25]

The U.S. Customs Court held Customs' assessment of duty to be unlawful because the fuel had not been removed from the zone for consumption.[26] In its decision, however, the Court noted that the Board had the right to impose conditions on zone operations, including conditions on the use of fuel produced in a zone, if it considers such conditions to be in the public interest, health, or safety. Thereafter, in a series of subzones granted to petroleum refineries, the FTZ Board, cognizant of the position of Customs in the case of the HIRI zone, specifically conditioned the zone grants upon the payment of duty on foreign crude oil used in producing fuel for the refinery.[27]

CITGO Petroleum Corporation, one of the grantees on whom the conditions were imposed, challenged the Board's decision in court. The Board explained that its reason for imposing the "fuel-consumed" condition was to prevent CITGO from obtaining an unfair competitive advantage over other domestic refineries, which it considered to be contrary to the public interest. The Court upheld the restriction as authorized under the public interest provision of the Act.[28]

(b) Denial of Grant

The Board may also decline to issue a zone grant as a matter of public interest. For example, it denied a subzone to Hill Petroleum Company (later known as Phibro Energy, Inc.) in Texas City, Texas, on public interest grounds as a result of

---

[25] 19 U.S.C. § 81oc.

[26] Hawaiian Independent Refinery v. United States, 81 Cust. Ct. 117, 460 F. Supp. 1249 (1978).

[27] *See* FTZ Board orders for Conoco Inc. (53 Fed. Reg. 52,455), Valero Refining Company (53 Fed. Reg. 53,041), Chevron U.S.A. Inc. (53 Fed. Reg. 53,040), and CITGO Petroleum Corporation (54, Fed. Reg. 27,660).

[28] CITGO Petroleum Corporation v. United States Foreign-Trade Zones Board, 83 F.3d 397 (Fed. Cir. May 3, 1996).

opposition from local taxing authorities and community officials projecting a loss of ad valorem tax revenues of approximately $600,000 per year.[29]

(c) Statutory and Regulatory Restrictions

In some cases, restrictions are imposed by statute or regulations. For example, the FTZ Act has provided that bicycle parts in zones would be exempt from customs laws only if they are re-exported.[30] The FTZ regulations require that goods subject to antidumping (AD) or countervailing duty (CVD) orders be placed in "privileged foreign status"[31] upon admission to the zone or subzone, and upon entry for consumption, such items will be subject to the assessment of duties in accordance with the pertinent AD/CVD order.[32]

(d) Revocation

The Board may revoke a grant of authority for a zone whenever it determines that the zone grantee or, in the case of subzones, the subzone operator, has repeatedly and willfully violated the FTZ Act.[33]

8.6 Manufacturing and Processing Activities

When evaluating manufacturing and processing activity to be conducted in a zone, the FTZ Board applies a two-step review process:

1. The FTZ Board must determine that certain "threshold factors" are not present, or the application will be denied or restricted.
2. If the zone passes the threshold test, the zone will then be considered from the standpoint of various economic factors.

(a) Threshold Factors

Threshold factors that would lead the Board to deny or restrict the application for zone manufacturing are as follows:

---

[29]*See* 56 Fed. Reg. 67,058 (1991). The zone applicant challenged the denial in the U.S. Court of International Trade (CIT), and the court dismissed for lack of subject matter jurisdiction, Phibro Energy, Inc. v. Barbara H. Franklin, 822 F. Supp. 759, 17 CIT 383 (Ct. Int'l Trade, 1993). The dismissal was reversed without opinion on appeal, *sub nom.* Phibro Energy, Inc. v. Brown, 33 F.3d 65 (1994 U.S. App. Lexis 31425) (Fed. Cir. 1994), reported in full in Phibro Energy, Inc. v. Brown, 1994 U.S. App. Lexis 12432 (Fed. Cir. May 19, 1994). The CIT remanded back to the FTZ Board with instructions that the Board give a full explanation of the rationale for disapproving the zone application and an explanation of whether, and in what manner, approval of the zone application would not serve the public interest. Phibro Energy, Inc. v. Brown, 886 F. Supp. 863. Following filing of the remand results with the Court, the parties apparently voluntarily agreed to dismiss the action. Therefore, the Court did not rule on the ultimate question of whether the Board's denial of the zone grant was contrary to law.

[30]19 U.S.C. § 81c(b).

[31]Merchandise in a zone may be given one of four "statuses." A later section of this chapter.

[32]15 C.F.R. § 400.33.

[33]15 C.F.R. § 400.28(c).

1. The zone activity is inconsistent with U.S. trade or tariff laws or policy.
2. Board approval of the activity under review would seriously prejudice U.S. tariff and trade negotiations or other initiatives.
3. The activity involves items subject to quantitative import controls or inverted tariffs. An inverted tariff exists when the duty rate on a finished product produced in the zone is lower than the duty rate on the material used to produce it.[34]
4. The use of zone procedures would be the direct and sole cause of imports that, but for such procedures, would not likely otherwise have occurred.[35]

(b) Economic Factors

If the FTZ Board determines not to deny the application due to the threshold factors, the Board will then consider the following economic factors to determine the net economic effect of the proposed zone activity:

1. Overall employment impact;
2. Exports and re-exports;
3. Retention or creation of manufacturing or processing activity;
4. Extent of value-added activity;
5. Overall effect on import levels of relevant products, including import displacement;
6. Extent and nature of foreign competition in relevant products;
7. Impact on related domestic industry; and
8. Other relevant information relating to public interest and net economic impact considerations.[36]

In considering the economic factors, the FTZ Board will seek to take into account their relative weight and significance under the circumstances and to balance the negative and positive factors in arriving at a net economic effect. Thus, the presence of only one or two negative economic factors may not necessarily lead to the denial or restriction of zone activity. The Board also may consider the contributing effect zone savings have as a part of a company's program to improve its international competitiveness.[37] For example in an application filed by Mercedes Benz for a subzone, the FTZ Board found that the savings from zone procedures would help improve the plant's international competitiveness. Applicants for subzones have the

---

[34] For example, the duty rate on automobiles is 2.5% (Subheading 8703.23.00, Harmonized Tariff Schedule (HTS)), whereas automobile bumpers (Subheading 8708.10.30) and brakes (Subheading 8708.39.50) are dutiable at 2.9%.

[35] 15 C.F.R. § 400.31(b)(1).

[36] 15 C.F.R. § 400.31(b)(2).

[37] 15 C.F.R. § 400.31(c)(2). *See, e.g.*, Notice of Application for Subzone of Mercedes Benz, 60 Fed. Reg. 11,070 (1995).

burden of submitting evidence that the activity will result in a "significant public benefit" when considered from the standpoint of the various economic factors to be considered by the Board.[38]

8.7 Activation

A grant of authority for a zone or subzone will lapse unless the zone project is activated and in operation not later than five years from the date of Board authorization. The project may not be activated until approved by the local Port Director of Customs and the Board's Executive Secretary reviews the proposed manufacturing or processing activity and zone schedule containing information prescribed by regulation, as well as rates to be charged by the grantee to zone users.[39]

8.8 Operations of the Zone

(a) Role of Customs

In general, the operation of the zone includes the following activities:

1. Entry of materials into the zone;
2. Storage;
3. Manipulation;
4. Manufacture or other use as provided by law; and
5. Transfer from the zone either for exportation or for consumption.

While the zone is considered to be outside the customs territory of the United States, Customs oversees and regulates zone activities. Customs seeks to ensure that all customs formalities related to the zone operation are followed and that the proper duty applicable to the merchandise entered into the zone is ultimately paid on merchandise that is removed from the zone.

Until 1986, Customs personnel generally had offices at the zone site, or would regularly visit the zones to physically supervise zone operations. In 1986, the customs regulations were amended to replace physical supervision with supervision by audit, inspection, and spot checks.[40] The zone operator is responsible for physical supervision, security, recordkeeping, storage conditions, and processing of zone merchandise. Failure to properly meet these responsibilities can subject the operator to liquidated damages and possible suspension or revocation of the zone operation.[41]

---

[38] 15 C.F.R. § 400.31(c)(3).

[39] 15 C.F.R. § 400.42.

[40] Treasury Decision T.D. 86-16.

[41] 19 C.F.R. § 146, Subpart G.

(b) Inventory Control and Recordkeeping System

Customs has the right to physically inspect goods in a zone. In actuality, however, much of its supervision is through reliance on company records:

1. The zone operator must maintain an inventory control and recordkeeping system that can satisfactorily track inventory to meet Customs' requirements.
2. The zone operator must be able to account for all merchandise, including domestic merchandise, admitted into the zone, stored or processed there, and removed.[42]
3. The zone operator must be able to identify shortages and overages, and provide an audit trail to customs documents from admission through manipulation, manufacture, destruction, or transfer from the zone.[43]

Merchandise entered into a zone must generally be identified by a zone lot number or "unique identifier," which will be used to identify and trace the merchandise. Fungible merchandise may be identified by an inventory method authorized by Customs other than lot number as long as it is consistently applied, such as First-In, First-Out (FIFO), Foreign-First or some type of a unique identifier.[44]

Under the FIFO method, any merchandise withdrawn from stock is assumed to be withdrawn from the oldest stock first. In applying FIFO procedures, each admission is considered a layer. The zone operator is responsible for identifying the appropriate sequence of transfers from the zone to assure the proper layer was used and transferred from the zone. This procedure becomes critical where different costs or values and/or different zone statuses are involved in the fungible merchandise. Since fungible merchandise is commercially interchangeable, it must be stored together and treated in practice as being fungible. Identification must be maintained in the inventory control system records, generally, by description and part or stock number. A history file, reflecting the layers by time of admission, should be maintained by the zone operator to provide the necessary details for Customs spot checks and audits. Under the Foreign-First method, any merchandise withdrawn from stock of mixed foreign and domestic status merchandise is assumed to be withdrawn from the foreign status stock until there is no longer any foreign status merchandise in stock. This method is used by some zones to avoid the need for establishing inventory category layers under FIFO.[45]

The inventory control and recordkeeping system must be capable of accounting for all merchandise in the zone, including domestic merchandise. If Customs cannot positively identify merchandise as domestic, it will be treated as foreign.[46]

---

[42] *See generally* 19 C.F.R. § 146, Subpart B.

[43] 19 C.F.R. § 146.21 (a).

[44] 19 C.F.R. § 146.23 (a).

[45] *FTZ Manual,* at 78–79.

[46] 19 C.F.R. § 146.42 (c).

(c) Admission of Merchandise into a Zone

Any merchandise, other than prohibited merchandise, may be entered into a zone upon filing a Customs Form 214 (Application for Foreign-Trade Zone Admission and/or Status Designation) accompanied by a commercial invoice, and receiving a permit from Customs.[47] Direct delivery is permitted without first filing CF 214 for low-risk merchandise involving a large number of transactions if the zone operations are known in advance, are predictable, and permission is requested in advance. The operator must first file an application with the port director, describing the merchandise to be handled or processed, and specifying the kind of operation that will take place in the zone. If the requisite criteria are met,[48] the application is generally approved. Appropriate records of receipt must be kept, and the operator must file the CF 214 after the entire contents of the shipment have been admitted.[49]

(d) Status of Zone Merchandise

Merchandise admitted into a zone may be given one of the following statuses:

1. Privileged foreign
2. Non-privileged foreign
3. Domestic
4. Zone-restricted

The status is requested on Customs Form 214 either at the time of admission or sometime thereafter. Zone status is discussed in the following paragraphs.

(e) Privileged Foreign Status

Privileged foreign status effectively freezes the classification and valuation of the merchandise to which it applies, based on its condition at the time such status is granted. A request for privileged foreign status may be made anytime prior to the manipulation, processing, manufacture, or other use of the merchandise that would result in changing it into an article with a different tariff classification. A zone user who will import materials for use in manufacture generally will request privileged foreign status for any materials that are subject to a lower duty rate than the finished product.

The following example illustrates privileged foreign status. Airbags for automobiles are dutiable at 1.3% ad valorem under HTS subheading 8708.93.34, while automobiles are dutiable at 2.5% ad valorem under HTS subheading 8703.23.00. An auto producer operating in a zone generally applies for privileged foreign status for the airbag to ensure it will be assessed at the airbag rate rather than at the automobile rate upon removal of the auto from the zone.

---

[47] 19 C.F.R. § 146.32(a); *see also* 19 C.F.R. §§ 146.41–146.44.

[48] *See* 19 C.F.R. § 146.39 (c).

[49] *See generally* 19 C.F.R. § 146.39–40 for procedures related to direct delivery.

Privileged foreign merchandise is treated as if an entry were filed and the merchandise were classified and appraised, and the entry liquidated, upon the filing of the application for privileged foreign status, even though the merchandise continues to remain in the zone. The duties are not deposited, however, until the article is removed from the zone. Privileged foreign status may not be abandoned.[50] Nor may privileged foreign merchandise be withdrawn from a zone and entered for warehouse or under a temporary importation bond.[51]

In some cases, conditions imposed on a zone grant by the FTZ Board or by regulation may require the selection of privileged foreign status. For example, merchandise subject to a dumping or countervailing duty order must be placed in privileged foreign status upon admission into a zone.[52] This process ensures that the imported merchandise will not escape any applicable dumping or countervailing duties if it is later used in the manufacture of an article that is not subject to a dumping or countervailing duty order.

(f) Non-Privileged Foreign Status

The following merchandise is given non-privileged foreign (NPF) status:

1. Foreign merchandise in a zone that does not have privileged foreign or zone-restricted status (described below);
2. Waste recovered from the manufacture or manipulation of privileged foreign merchandise in a zone;
3. Domestic merchandise which, by reason of noncompliance with the regulations, has lost its identity as domestic merchandise.[53]

Non-privileged foreign merchandise that is used in producing another article in the zone will be classified and subject to duty in its condition at the time the finished product is withdrawn from the zone. For example, auto parts having non-privileged foreign status that are used in producing an automobile in a zone will be assessed duty at the rate applicable to automobiles, namely 2.5%. The value of being able to claim non-privileged foreign status for material used in manufacture is demonstrated by a zone application filed by Mercedes Benz for a subzone grant covering its vehicle manufacturing facility in Alabama. The application disclosed that foreign-sourced parts and materials would represent up to 50% of the finished vehicles' material value and that the duty rate for those materials and components ranged from 2.5% to 13.6%. The zone would allow the company to claim non-privileged foreign status for the parts and materials, paying duty at the automobile rate of 2.5%, thus assisting its international competitiveness.[54]

---

[50]*FTZ Manual,* § 5.6 (c).

[51]19 C.F.R. § 146.64(a); C.S.D. 81–213.

[52]15 C.F.R. § 400.33.

[53]19 C.F.R. § 146.42.

[54]*See* Application for Subzone of Mercedes Benz, 60 Fed. Reg. 11,070 (1995); *see also* FTZ Order No. 803, granting subzone status, 61 Fed. Reg. 8,237 (1996).

In view of the "inverted tariff"[55] applicable to so many automobile components, operating in a zone allows automobile producers using foreign components to pay duty at the vehicle rate of 2.5% and achieve considerable cost savings. However, inverted tariff rate savings are not limited to automobile producers. For example, an application seeking subzone status for a producer of in-line skates revealed that the duty rate on finished skates is free, whereas the duty on parts used in production range from free to 10.6%.[56] Zone status would enable the producer to select non-privileged foreign status for its components and materials. The producer would pay no duty because the finished skates are duty-free. Given the volume and variety of parts used by many manufacturers, a zone may offer substantial duty savings to those whose materials are subject to duty rates higher than the rate for the finished product.

(g) Domestic Status

Domestic status applies to three types of merchandise:

1. Merchandise which is the growth, product, or manufacture of the United States and on which all Internal Revenue taxes, if applicable, have been paid;
2. Merchandise that has been previously imported and on which duty and tax have been paid; and
3. Merchandise previously entered free of duty and tax.[57]

Customs will consider domestic status identity to be maintained when it can be established through inventory control and accounting procedures approved by Customs.[58] Domestic status merchandise will not be subject to duty, quotas, or taxes when removed from the zone, whether in its original condition or after manipulation, manufacture, or processing.

(h) Zone Restricted Status

Zone restricted status is given to merchandise that is taken into a zone for the sole purpose of exportation, destruction, or storage pending exportation. Such status may not be abandoned. The merchandise may not be removed to the Customs territory for domestic consumption except when the FTZ Board determines that its return would be in the public interest.

Zone restricted status frequently is used as a basis to satisfy the exportation requirement for drawback purposes or cancellation of a temporary importation bond. In such cases, all pertinent customs requirements relating to an actual exportation

---

[55]*See* ¶ 8.6(a) above.

[56]Application for Subzone Status of Plastic Products Company Inc., 61 Fed. Reg. 9,675 (1996).

[57]19 C.F.R. § 146.43.

[58]*See, e.g.*, footnote 47.

must be met as though the admission of the merchandise admitted into the zone constituted a lading on an exporting carrier. Any form required for actual exportation should be modified to indicate that the merchandise was sent into a zone in lieu of actual exportation.[59]

At one time, Customs ruled that duty-paid merchandise could be sent into a zone for use in manufacture and it would be treated as "exported" for purposes of drawback and to cancel a temporary importation bond, even though the product resulting from manufacture was later withdrawn from the zone for consumption.[60] Customs later revoked its position and ruled that goods sent into a zone for manufacture would not be considered exported.[61] The U.S. Court of International Trade has sustained the Customs position, thus making it clear that drawback will be paid only on duty-paid merchandise sent into a zone under zone restricted status for exportation.[62]

(i) Handling of Merchandise in a Zone

An application (Customs Form 216) must be filed with the appropriate Customs officer requesting permission to manufacture, process, manipulate, or destroy merchandise in a zone. In the case of a repetitive operation, Customs is authorized to approve a blanket application for a period of one year.[63]

The zone operator must advise Customs in writing of theft, shortages, and merchandise not properly admitted into the zone. The operator is liable for duties and taxes on merchandise that is missing or otherwise not accounted for.[64]

8.9 Transfer of Merchandise from a Zone

Foreign status (privileged or non-privileged) merchandise or merchandise composed in part of domestic and in part of foreign status may be entered for consumption from a zone. The entry or entry summary (Customs Form 7501) must be accompanied by the type of entry documentation routinely required for any importation, including invoices and any other documents required by law or regulations that relate to the transferred merchandise. Customs may waive presentation of an invoice and supporting documentation if satisfied that the presentation of those documents would be impractical and the person making entry either files the invoices and supporting documentation at a later date or maintains them and makes them available for Customs examination.[65]

---

[59] *See* 19 C.F.R. § 146.44(c) (1).

[60] *See* C.S.D. 84-97 (republished as C.S.D. 85-10); *see also* Headquarters Ruling Letter 218551 (1986).

[61] T.D. 89-4.

[62] Chrysler Motors Corp. v. United States, 14 Ct. Int'l Trade 807, 755 F. Supp. 388 (1990), *aff'd,* 945 F.2d 1187 (Fed. Cir. 1991).

[63] 19 C.F.R. § 146.52.

[64] 19 C.F.R. § 146.53.

[65] 19 C.F.R. § 146.62.

Domestic status merchandise that has not been combined with or made part of merchandise having another zone status generally may be transferred from the zone without a Customs permit.[66]

(a) Entry for Consumption

In general, the entry for consumption from a zone should be made in accordance with the procedures applicable to any imported merchandise being entered for consumption. However, Customs may allow a weekly entry to be filed showing the estimated removals of merchandise expected during the week, followed by individual transfers of the merchandise after the entry has been accepted.[67] Before transferring merchandise from a zone to the customs territory, the importer must file with Customs a single transaction or continuous bond.[68]

(b) Entry for Warehouse

Privileged foreign status merchandise or merchandise in part of privileged foreign status may not be entered for warehouse from a zone.[69] Non-privileged foreign merchandise containing no privileged foreign components or material may be entered for warehouse. Zone restricted merchandise may be entered for warehouse only for storage pending exportation. Merchandise may not be placed in, or remain in, a customs bonded warehouse after five years from the date of importation of the merchandise.[70] Domestic status merchandise may not be transferred from a zone to a bonded warehouse.[71]

(c) Classification—Privileged Foreign Merchandise

Privileged foreign merchandise is subject to tariff classification according to its character, condition, and quantity, and at the rate of duty and tax in force on the date the application for privilege foreign status is filed. Merchandise subject to a tariff rate import quota[72] is transferred from the zone only at the higher non-quota duty rate in effect on the date privileged foreign status was granted.[73] Even if the quota has not been reached at the time privileged foreign status is requested or at the time the merchandise is actually transferred from the zone, the higher non-quota rate will be imposed.[74]

---

[66] 19 C.F.R. § 146.43(b).

[67] 19 C.F.R. Parts 141, 142, 143; 19 C.F.R. § 146.63(c).

[68] C.F. 301; 19 C.F.R. § 113.62.

[69] C.S.D. 81-8.

[70] 19 C.F.R. § 146.64.

[71] *See* 19 U.S.C. §§ 1555, 1557.

[72] 19 C.F.R. § 132.1(b).

[73] 19 C.F.R. § 146.65(a).

[74] Inter-Maritime Forwarding Co., Inc. v. United States, 46 Cust. Ct. 106 (1961).

Where two or more products result from the manipulation or manufacture of privileged foreign merchandise in a zone, the duties and taxes applicable upon entry for consumption are distributed to the several products produced in accordance with their relative values at the time of separation.[75]

(d) Classification—Non-Privileged Foreign Merchandise

Non-privileged foreign merchandise is subject to classification in accordance with its character, condition, and quantity at the time the entry or entry summary is filed with Customs.[76] If this merchandise has been combined with merchandise of privileged foreign or domestic status, the character and condition of the merchandise are determined based on the entire article being entered and not based only on the non-privileged foreign status portion.[77] For example, various components of non-privileged foreign status used in manufacturing automobiles are classified under the provision for automobiles and assessed duty at the automobile rate, rather than under the provision for the specific component, even if some of the other components used in manufacture receive privileged foreign status. Waste from the manufacture or manipulation of privileged foreign merchandise is treated as non-privileged foreign merchandise.[78]

(e) Valuation

The dutiable value for both privileged foreign and non-privileged foreign merchandise is the price paid or payable for the merchandise in the transaction that caused it to be admitted into the zone. Additional amounts are included for the following items if they are paid separately from the price: (1) packing, (2) selling commission, (3) assists, (4) royalty, or (5) license fee.

If there is no price actually paid or payable when the merchandise is brought into the zone, or no reasonable representation of the cost available, the dutiable value may be determined by taking the value of the merchandise at the time it comes out of the zone (known as "total zone value") and making deductions:

1. Costs of processing or fabrication
2. Costs of any U.S. materials
3. General expenses
4. Profit
5. International freight and insurance
6. U.S. inland freight

---

[75] 19 U.S.C. § 81c(a) (first proviso).

[76] 19 C.F.R. § 146.65(a) (2).

[77] C.S.D. 82-29.

[78] 19 C.F.R. § 146.42(b), (c).

The dutiable value of recoverable scrap will be the price paid or payable to the zone seller in the transaction that caused the recoverable waste or scrap to be transferred from the zone.[79]

8.10 Transfer from a Zone for Exportation

Merchandise may be withdrawn from a zone for exportation without payment of duty.[80] Customs may allow a weekly permit to enter and release merchandise for exportation, transportation, or transportation and exportation, similar to the weekly consumption entries.[81]

Articles exported from a zone and reimported will be subject to the import laws applicable to like foreign articles unless there is proof that the merchandise was produced exclusively with domestic merchandise. Thus, both the domestic and foreign content of zone-manufactured articles will be subject to duty and tax to the same extent as like articles manufactured in a foreign country upon reimportation into the United States unless wholly manufactured from domestic status merchandise.[82]

8.11 Transfer of Zone Restricted Merchandise into Customs Territory

Zone restricted merchandise may be transferred to customs territory only for limited purposes for:

1. Entry for exportation;
2. Entry for transportation and exportation;
3. Warehousing pending exportation;
4. Destruction;
5. Transfer from one zone to another; or
6. Delivery as supplies or equipment to a qualified vessel or aircraft.

However, the Board can rule that the return of the merchandise to the customs territory for domestic consumption is in the public interest.[83]

8.12 Equipment to Be Used in a Zone

Production equipment and similar articles brought into a zone for use in the zone are not entitled to zone status. Such equipment is subject to duty. However,

---

[79] 19 C.F.R. § 146.65 (b) (2).

[80] 19 C.F.R. § 146.67.

[81] 19 C.F.R. § 146.68.

[82] 19 C.F.R. § 146.67 (e); *see also* C.S.D. 84–73.

[83] 19 C.F.R. § 146.70.

duty will not be assessed until the equipment is assembled, installed, tested and used in production.[84]

The equipment rule was challenged in court by Nissan Motor Manufacturing Corporation, U.S.A., in a case involving capital equipment valued at over $100,000,000, which Nissan brought into its motor vehicle subzone assembly plant in Tennessee for use on its assembly line. Nissan claimed that, since the equipment remained in the zone and did not enter into U.S. Customs territory, it was not subject to duty under the FTZ Act. The court held, however, that installation and operation of equipment in a zone is not among the specific activities to which merchandise may be subjected under the FTZ Act (such as storage, assembly, manipulation, and manufacture) without being subject to the customs laws. Consequently, since the equipment was not exempt under the FTZ Act, it was subject to duty.[85]

8.13 NAFTA Effect on Zones

The North American Free Trade Agreement (NAFTA) has special rules affecting foreign trade zones and other duty-deferral programs. Goods that are produced or otherwise changed in condition in a zone in the United States and then removed from the zone for exportation to Canada or Mexico are subject to duty upon removal from the zone. However, rather than assessing the duty at the time of removal, Customs will allow the party responsible for duty 60 days to show the amount of duties, if any, imposed when the goods were imported into Canada or Mexico. Upon showing proof of payment of such duties, U.S. Customs will waive or reduce the U.S. duties in an amount equal to the lesser of the duties due upon removal from the zone or the duties paid on importation into Canada or Mexico.[86]

For example, if the duties due on removal from the zone are $100 and duties paid on entry into Canada are $125, U.S. Customs will waive the U.S. duties entirely. If the duties due upon removal from the zone are $100 and the duties paid upon import into Canada are $75, U.S. Customs will assess duty of $25. These rules apply to goods exported from the United States to Canada on or after January 1, 1996, and to Mexico on or after January 1, 2001.

8.14 Comparison of Zones with Other Duty-Deferral Programs

Some of the benefits available through the use of foreign trade zones are also available through drawback, bonded warehouses, and temporary importation bonds.[87] These programs are simpler to undertake and do not involve the time-consuming and costly application process attendant to a zone application.

---

[84]19 U.S.C. § 81 c (e).

[85]Nissan Motor Mfg. Corp., U.S.A. v. United States, 884 F.2d 1375 (Fed. Cir. 1989).

[86]T.D. 96-14 (interim regulation 19 C.F.R. § 181.53 (b) (4) effective January 1, 1996).

[87]Drawback, bonded warehouses, and temporary importation bonds are treated in depth in other chapters of *The Import Handbook.*

However, as discussed in the following sections, they generally do not offer the flexibility offered by zones.

(a) Drawback

Drawback is the refund of duties paid on merchandise that is exported or is used to produce other articles that are exported.[88] The principal advantage of a zone over drawback is that goods entered into a zone are not subject to duties unless they are withdrawn for consumption in the United States. In contrast, goods entitled to drawback have had the duty paid upon importation.

Drawback is subject to certain time requirements. In the case of imported merchandise used in manufacture, the imported material must be used in production within three years of receipt by the manufacturer. The finished articles must be exported within five years after importation of the imported merchandise.[89] In the case of unused merchandise, the goods must be exported within three years after importation.[90] No such time periods apply to goods in a zone.

The exemption from state and local ad valorem taxation available to zone merchandise[91] would not apply to the same goods held in a plant that is not a zone.

By statute, antidumping duties and countervailing duties are not treated as "regular customs duties" and are not recoverable as drawback.[92] The FTZ Act, on the other hand, contains no such prohibition.

The FTZ regulations require goods covered by an antidumping or countervailing duty order to be designated privileged foreign status.[93] This process ensures the assessment of antidumping or countervailing duties when zone merchandised covered by an antidumping or countervailing duty order is withdrawn for consumption. However, neither the law nor the regulations requires dumping duties to be paid on such merchandise when withdrawn for exportation. Thus, from the standpoint of cash flow, time restrictions, state and local tax savings exports, and avoidance of dumping and countervailing duties on exports, a zone program is preferable to a drawback program.

A benefit afforded by the drawback law but not by the FTZ Act is the ability to substitute domestic for foreign materials. A drawback claimant who uses imported material and domestic material of the same kind and quality can substitute the domestic for the imported merchandise. Such a drawback claim can qualify for a refund of duty paid on the imported material when the exported product is made from the domestic material. Substitution of materials is not permitted under the FTZ law. Duty will be assessed, notwithstanding that domestic material of the

[88] 19 U.S.C. § 1313; 19 C.F.R. Pt. 191.

[89] 19 U.S.C. § 1313 (i).

[90] 19 U.S.C. § 1313(j).

[91] 19 U.S.C. § 81o(e).

[92] 19 U.S.C. § 1677h.

[93] 15 C.F.R. § 400.33 (b) (2).

same kind and quality was used in the exported product, if the zone user's records show that the merchandise withdrawn for consumption in the United States was produced from foreign materials.

(b) Bonded Warehouses

Bonded warehouses may be used to carry out some of the same functions as a zone—namely, storage, manipulation, and manufacturing. Entry into warehouse, like admission into a zone, may be done without depositing duties. In contrast to the FTZ Act, the bonded warehouse statutes do not exempt goods therein from state and local ad valorem taxes. However, judicial decisions have held that goods in a bonded warehouse intended for exportation are in foreign commerce and are not subject to local taxation.[94] Where the goods are not destined for export, they are not free from local taxation.[95]

Bonded warehouses have certain statutory limitations. Goods produced in a manufacturing warehouse (class 6)[96] must be exported and may not be entered for consumption.[97] A storage warehouse (class 2, 3, 4, or 5)[98] may be used only for storage.[99] A manipulating warehouse (class 8)[100] may be used to clean, sort, repack, or otherwise change merchandise in condition, but not to manufacture.[101] Moreover, goods may not remain in a bonded warehouse for more than five years. Thus, no one class of warehouse allows the range of operational flexibility of a single zone.

(c) Temporary Importation Under Bond

Goods may be imported temporarily under bond for repair, alteration, or processing.[102] Such goods, however, may not be sold in the United States and must be exported within a year after importation, with extensions allowed for an additional two years.[103] Failure to export results in liquidated damages equal to double the duties that would otherwise have been due upon importation.[104] The same limitations on sale and duration in the United States do not exist in the case of zones.

---

[94]*See* Xerox Corporation v. County of Harris, Texas, and City of Houston, Texas, 459 U.S. 145 (1982); *See also* McGoldrick v. Gulf Oil Corp., 309 U.S. 414 (1939).

[95]*See* R.J. Reynolds Tobacco Co. v. Durham County, North Carolina, 479 U.S. 130 (1986).

[96]19 C.F.R. § 19.1(a)(6).

[97]19 U.S.C. § 1311.

[98]19 C.F.R. § 19.1(a)(2)–(5).

[99]19 U.S.C. § 1555.

[100]19 C.F.R. § 191.1(a)(8).

[101]19 U.S.C. § 1562.

[102]HTSUS, Subheading 9813.00.05.

[103]HTSUS, Ch. 98, Subchapter XII, U.S. Note 1(a).

[104]19 C.F.R. § 10.39(d)(1).

8.15 Conclusion

Foreign trade zones offer opportunities to reduce costs by the deferral, reduction, and/or elimination of duties and certain taxes. Qualifying for these benefits requires an investment of time, personnel, and money. Whether the investment is warranted can be determined only by a careful evaluation of a company's operations from the perspective of the FTZ laws and regulations. If the benefits are there, a company should not be deterred from going forward by the cost and effort incidental to the zone application.

CHAPTER 9

Duty Drawback and Exportation of Imported Goods

Ronald C. Glowzinski

9.1 Introduction
- (a) Statutory Provisions
- (b) NAFTA
- (c) Historical Background
- (d) Why Import
- (e) Reform

9.2 Drawback Revitalization
- (a) View of Customs
- (b) Views of the Drawback Community

9.3 Major Changes to Statute and Regulations
- (a) Major Administrative Changes
- (b) Electronic Data

9.4 Penalties and Protections
- (a) Conflict
- (b) Penalty Procedures
- (c) Penalty Rates

9.5 Privileges
- (a) Accelerated Payment
- (b) Waiver of Notice of Intent to Export or Destroy
- (c) Exporter's Summary Procedure

9.6 Other Technical Changes
- (a) Fungible Versus Commercially Interchangeable
- (b) Completion of Drawback Claim
- (c) Restructuring Claims
- (d) Claims Filed Under the Wrong Provision
- (e) Unused Merchandise Substitution Drawback
- (f) Successorship
- (g) Accounting Methods

9.7 Drawback Compliance Program
(a) Requirements
(b) Application Procedures
9.8 Drawback Under NAFTA
(a) Two Changes to Drawback
(b) Finished Manufactured Product
9.9 Computerization of Drawback Claims
(a) Diskettes
(b) Automated Broker Interface
9.10 Drawback on Lump Sum Duty Payments for Assists, Direct and Indirect Payments
(a) Proration Issues
(b) Proration Techniques
9.11 Conclusion

9.1 Introduction

Drawback regulations are in a state of flux. The proposed drawback regulations developed by the Drawback Regulations Team[1] are under final review by the lawyers in each of the federal government agencies involved with new Customs regulations. This chapter discusses the proposed and current regulations.

(a) Statutory Provisions

The drawback regulations are found at 19 C.F.R. § 191 of the current regulations. The four most common types of drawback used in most businesses are:

1. Same Condition Drawback (§ 1313 (j) (1))[2], now referred to as Unused Drawback;
2. Same Condition Substitution Drawback (§ 1313 (j) (2)), now Unused Substitution Drawback;
3. Manufacturer's Drawback § (1313 (a), (b)), and
4. Rejected Merchandise Drawback § (1313 (c)).

Drawback is available on a whole series of specific taxes and merchandise, and while they will be briefly mentioned here, they will not be further discussed in this chapter.

[1]See Membership in Exhibit 9.1.

[2]The terminology "Same Condition" Drawback remains in the North American Free Trade Agreement (NAFTA) and in § 181 of regulation covering NAFTA. All 1313 references relate to the sections of the Customs Act of 1930 as amended.

Exhibit 9.1

MEMBERS OF THE DRAWBACK REGULATIONS TEAM

Facilitator	
Hinda Sterling	Sterling & Selesnick, Inc.—Salem, MA
U.S. Customs Service (USC)	
Nancy McTiernan	Director, Technical Programs—Washington, DC
Mary Anne Carney	Chief, Drawback Branch—New York
Bruce Friedman	Chief, Drawback—Washington, DC
Greg Pence	Director, Financial Policy—Washington, DC
Regulatory Audit Division	
Mark Hanson	Supervisory Auditor—Washington, DC
Office of Rulings and Regulations (OR&R)	
Russ Berger	Regulations Branch—Washington, DC
Paul Hegland	Entry Rulings Branch—Washington, DC
Office of the Inspector General (OIG)	
Successor to General Accounting Office (GAO)	
Nan Lyon	Department of Treasury—Washington, DC
American Petroleum Institute	
Bobby Waid	Gulf Coast Drawback Services, Inc.—Katy, TX
Eddie Aquino	A.P.I. Director—Washington, DC
National Customs Brokers and Forwarders Association (NCBFA)	
Alfred D'Amico	Duty Drawback Service, Inc. *Now* Sandler and Travis, Trade Consultants Farmington Hills, MI
Frank McCarthy	J.M. Rodgers, Inc.—Sparta, NJ
David Simcox	Comstock & Theakston, Inc.—Oradell, NJ
National Council on International Trade Development (NCITD)	
Ronald Glowzinski	General Motors Corporation—Detroit, MI
Sandra Hale-Sisto	Expeditors International, Inc.—Bensenville, IL
William Hagedorn	Comstock & Theakston, Inc.—Oradell, NJ
American Association of Exporters and Importers (AAEI)	
J. Lamar Murphree	Monsanto Agricultural Products—St. Louis, MO
Ed Van Ek	C.J. Holt, Inc.—Oradell, NJ
Steve Leahy	Leahy & Ward—Boston, MA

- Internal Revenue tax on flavoring extracts and medicinal or toilet preparations (including perfumery) manufactured from domestic tax-paid alcohol (19 U.S.C. § 1313 (d))
- Supplies for certain vessels and aircraft (19 U.S.C. § 1309)
- Meats cured with imported salts (19 U.S.C. § 1313 (f))

- Materials for construction and equipment of vessels and aircraft built for foreign ownership and account (19 U.S.C. § 1313 (g))
- Foreign-built jet aircraft engines processed in the United States (19 U.S.C. § 1313 (h))
- Merchandise exported from continuous Customs custody (19 U.S.C. § 1557 (a))
- Distilled spirits, wines, or beer that are unmerchantable or do not conform to sample or specifications (26 U.S.C. § 5062 (c))
- Substitution of finished petroleum derivatives (19 U.S.C. § 1313 (p))
- Merchandise transferred to a Foreign Trade Zone from Customs custody. Provision to obtain drawback on merchandise is deemed exported when admitted to a zone in zone restricted status (FTZ Act, § 3, Fourth Provision, and 19 U.S.C. § 81 (c))

(b) NAFTA

Entirely unique drawback procedures apply only to imports and exports between the United States, Canada, and Mexico under the North American Free Trade Agreement (NAFTA). The Customs regulations for NAFTA in 19 C.F.R. § 181 offer unique and, at times, conflicting directions with the drawback programs presented in the Customs Modernization Act (CMA) and 19 C.F.R. § 191. For example, "some condition drawback" continues to exist under NAFTA Regulation 181 whereas it has been replaced by "unused drawback" for all other purposes. The Customs Modernization Act was being developed quite independently by U.S. Customs, the trade associations, and the broker association while the NAFTA trade agreement was being negotiated by the United States, Canada, and Mexico. How the conflicts between the drawback programs will be resolved will remain a mystery until some experience is gained and case law is developed for the NAFTA drawback provisions.

(c) Historical Background

In 1789, the United States decided that if products were taxed by way of a customs duty when they were imported, the tax should be refunded if the products were exported. Duties on components used to make U.S. products should be removed to be competitive in foreign markets. U.S. exports would increase if U.S. products were competitive in foreign markets. Hence, more export sales provided an economic stimulus to the U.S. economy. International trade agreements, with their subtle protections and convoluted objectives, along with massive budget overruns, have become more important than the goals of duty drawback.

While businesses struggle to comply with the laws, regulations, and rulings to obtain their refunds, the Treasury Department and U.S. Customs struggle to "protect the revenue." Honest businesses, recognizing the rewards of obtaining drawback refunds, too often view the eligibility as "so obvious" that they overlook the technical requirements to prove eligibility. Just as a store will not accept the return of a product for a refund without a sales slip, the government has a right and a duty to assure that a drawback claim is valid, accurate, and supported by documented evidence. The crucial facets are the refund of customs duties through duty drawback, the "duty" of the U.S. Customs Service to carry out its mission and "protect the revenue," and the duty of business to follow the drawback laws and regulations to their fullest extent.

(d) Why Import

In 1986, Customs refunded $346 million in drawback. By 1991 drawback grew to $468 million and by 1995, $528 million was refunded. It is estimated that less than half of all eligible drawback is claimed. Business discovered the rewards of the program as drawback brokers began massive sales campaigns and trade associations tried to make drawback provisions more user-friendly. Drawback can be claimed for exports taking place over the past three years, and imports, under certain drawback provisions, can take five years before the export date.

(e) Reform

The Customs Modernization Act of 1993 (CMA), passed as part of the North American Free Trade Agreement Implementation Act,[3] had many objectives, including putting into law customs' practices that previously had little support in the statute. These pilot programs had proved effective, in some cases, for 20 or more years. One area that was in need of reform was the drawback provisions of both the statute and the regulations. Many practical arrangements had been developed between claimants and the U.S. Customs drawback branches. The arrangements served both parties well, but were criticized in a U.S. Customs compliance review. The original *Drawback Revitalization Study Summary,*[4] published by U.S. Customs in February 1990, contained a plethora of observations, criticisms, and recommendations on the state of the drawback program in place at that time.

Customs proposed a civil penalty on drawback. Trade associations fought to prevent penalties and, later, to limit penalties for clerical errors on contracts[5] and claims.

9.2 Drawback Revitalization

Customs needed major revisions to its internal structure, including training for its drawback personnel, better claim verification procedures prior to liquidation,

---

[3]Pub. L. No. 103-182, 103d Congress (8 December 1993), North American Free Trade Agreement Implementation Act, H. R. 3450 Title VI, Customs Modernization.

[4]*Drawback Revitalization Study Summary,* Department of Treasury, U.S. Customs Service, Office of Trade Operations, February 1990.

[5]Manufacturer's drawback claims require approval of formal written drawback contracts (or rates) by U.S. Customs.

and a strong effort to increase uniformity between its drawback liquidation branches. The Government Accounting Office (GAO) and the Office of the Inspector General (OIG) took an interest in the problems of Customs and vigorously pursued the lack of controls that existed. While the reports of the OIG[6] were highly critical of Customs' controls over the drawback program, the reports brought a high level of visibility to Customs' need to computerize, train staff, and audit drawback activities.

Customs, the OIG, and the GAO were never able to convince the CMA negotiators working on the new drawback provisions that major fraud existed. It was obvious that Customs believed that unless changes were made, it was possible that widespread fraud could take place. Any good auditor knows that a control weakness that allows fraud is as serious as one that has led to actual fraud.

Both U.S. Customs and the drawback community recognized that statutory and regulatory changes were needed to address many of the drawback issues causing concerns to both parties. While U.S. Customs' emphasis remained on compliance and penalties, the drawback community searched out methods to secure the privileges they had enjoyed for many years and to expand drawback into areas not previously covered.

(a) View of Customs

Customs identified its statutory and regulatory recommendations as follows:

- Pursue a civil penalty to enhance drawback enforcement.
- Provide statutory language on handling contract amendments, including those relating to corporate takeovers and successorships.
- Reduce the drawback eligible time period for export.
- Reduce the drawback eligible time period for filing claims after export.
- Eliminate unnecessary paperwork by not requiring the filing of Certificates of Delivery (CD) prior to the submission of the pertinent drawback claim.

(b) Views of the Drawback Community

The drawback community wanted statutory and regulatory changes which would:

- Codify the time periods for drawback eligibility and filing claims.
- Eliminate the fungibility standard for same-condition substitution.
- Change the concept of same-condition drawback to the concept of unused material drawback.

---

[6]U.S. Government Accounting Office Audit of Customs' Principal Statements For Fiscal Years 1992 and 1993, *October 1993,* Chapter 4—"Controls over drawback payments were weak." GAO/AIMD-94-38 Customs' Revenue at Risk. The Office of the Inspector General (OIG) is the successor to the General Accounting Office (GAO). The fiscal year chief financial office audit results were originally published October 1993 and followed for corrective action during fiscal year 1994.

- Prevent any new civil penalties from being used in an arbitrary and capricious manner.
- Allow drawback on imports subjected to destruction rather than export.
- Allow drawback on defective material for up to three years (was 90 days).
- Allow drawback on packaging material based on its own status, not that of the product it holds.
- Allow recovery of lump sum assist costs in proportion to exported quantities.

9.3 Major Changes to Statute and Regulations

Tremendous strides were made by both Customs and the drawback community. A brief synopsis of the major changes made under the CMA and reflected in the new regulations will illustrate this point. While some of the issues will be discussed at length others will not, primarily because they are self-explanatory or are too technically complex to adequately address in a handbook designed for general knowledge.

Major Changes	**Reference**
Civil penalties applicable to drawback claims.	19 U.S.C. § 1593 A
Rejected merchandise eligible for drawback for up to three years and when destroyed.	19 U.S.C. § 1313 (c), 19 C.F.R. Subpart D
Direct identification of unused merchandise eligible for drawback when destroyed under Customs' supervision.	19 U.S.C. § 1313 (j) (1), 19 C.F.R. Subpart C
Unused merchandise substitution drawback: • Eligible for drawback when destroyed under Customs' supervision • Defined as "not used" versus "same condition" • May undergo more operations without becoming "used" • May be paid to precisely defined eligible party • Possession requirements clearly defined	19 U.S.C. § 1313 (j) (2), 19 C.F.R. Subpart C
Finished petroleum derivatives. Methods are defined to determine drawback eligibility requirements for articles and claimants.	19 U.S.C. § 1313 (p), 19 C.F.R. Subpart Q
Packaging material eligible for drawback under provision of exported goods contained therein.	19 U.S.C. § 1313 (j) (4), 19 C.F.R. § 191.13
Filing under wrong subsection does not preclude drawback eligibility.	CMA § 632, 19 C.F.R. § 191.12
Successors eligible for substitution drawback on material obtained from predecessors.	CMA § 632, 19 C.F.R. §§ 191.22, 191.32
Agricultural drawback on tariff-rate quota articles clarified.	19 U.S.C. § 1313 (w) (1)

(a) Major Administrative Changes

Customs proposed a series of administrative improvements in the drawback program, which received strong support from the drawback community. A brief synopsis of the major changes follows.

Major Changes	Reference
Definition of what documents are needed to consider a filed claim as "complete"	19 C.F.R. Subpart E
Requirements defined for accelerated payment and waiver of notice of intent to export or destroy	19 C.F.R. Subpart I
Evidence of exportation or destruction defined	19 C.F.R. Subpart G
Drawback compliance program defined	19 C.F.R. Subpart S

(b) Electronic Data

The CMA authorized Customs to use electronic data in lieu of paper documents to fulfill the information requirements. This change carried over into drawback requirements, where the use of diskettes and an ABI drawback module were considered positive changes for both Customs and the claimants. Initially, Customs requested a list of mandatory data elements that far exceeded the detail previously required to file a claim.

Exhibit 9.2 illustrates data needed to submit a claim on diskette. When the new regulations become effective, the harmonized code of products imported after that date will be required on a drawback claim. The harmonized code of the exported product will have to appear on claims filed one year after the effective date of the drawback regulations. Export HTS (Harmonized Tariff Schedule) codes will also be required on the claim. The staggered effective dates will allow Customs, the brokers, and the business community time to reprogram their computers and retain this data. Development of drawback manuals, assignment of Customs drawback professionals, including a Washington headquarters drawback position, planned training programs, expeditious processing of legal rulings, and manufacturers' drawback contracts were all recognized as changes serving both Customs and the drawback community.

Customs offered a bypass system whereby drawback claims would be subjected to selectivity criteria and would be immediately paid and liquidated if not selected for more intensive review. The price for this, of course, was high. Civil penalties amounting to anywhere from 20 to 300% became part of the new legislation.[7] The amounts of these penalties and how they would be applied and the legal protections demanded by the drawback community led to the most difficult discussions in the CMA drawback negotiation sessions.

---

[7]Pub. L. No. 103-182, 103d Congress (8 December 1993), Title VI § 662.

Exhibit 9.2

DRAWBACK CLAIM DISKETTE DATA

DEPARTMENT OF TREASURY

U.S. CUSTOMS SERVICE—CHICAGO REGION

DRAWBACK CODING SHEET

Drawback Entry No:_______/_______ Or Cert. of Mfr. No._______

Drawback Type Code: _______

Claimant Name: _______
(on CM show Mfr. name)

IRS No. and Suffix: _______

Approved Special Privileges: Accelerated Payment _______

Exporter's Summary_______ Waiver of Prior Notice _______

CM/CDs Filed: Yes _______ No _______

INFORMATION ON DESIGNATED IMPORT ENTRIES

Filer/Document Number (import entry no.)	Port	Liq. Date (if known)	Duty Claimed (99% figure)	Status
Grand Total				

Indicate in Status column if protested or paperless.

9.4 Penalties and Protections

(a) Conflict

Penalties on drawback claims were vigorously fought by the trade organizations and the broker association. The fear was not that fair penalties, reasonably administered, would create major problems for most claimants. The concern revolved around a lack of trust in the application of the penalties.

U.S. Customs and the Treasury Department had often shown their displeasure with the drawback "giveaway" program. Many drawback rulings were harsh interpretations of the law and displayed little sensitivity in protecting the intent of drawback in the scheme of international trade. Adding to this attitude was the fact that drawback refunds were a half-billion dollar annual drain on the Treasury, at a time when deficits were criticized and the national debt was front page news.

The Canadian Free Trade Agreement eliminated manufacturer's drawback for shipments to Canada in 1994, with NAFTA extending that date to 1996. The lesser of two duties manufacturer's drawback program that replaced the expired program was so complex that most practitioners are suggesting that manufacturer's drawback for products shipped to Canada (Mexico in 2001) is simply too much trouble and risk for the refunds involved. Many felt that penalties would be used as a tool to scare away new claimants and force experienced claimants to reevaluate the rewards versus the risks involved in filing valid claims, but drawback penalties were included in the CMA and only time will tell the effect they will have on the drawback program.

(b) Penalty Procedures

Section 593A, Penalties for False Drawback Claims[8] provides procedures similar to those in place for other Customs penalties.

1. Clerical errors and mistakes in facts are not violations subject to penalty, unless they are part of a pattern of negligent conduct;
2. A prepenalty notice will be issued, stating all of the relevant facts at issue (if the penalty is $1,000 or less, the prepenalty notice need not be issued);
3. Prepenalty notices claiming fraud require prior approval of Customs headquarters;
4. The penalized party may seek to mitigate or dismiss the penalty by oral or written representations;
5. Customs will issue a written determination and state the amount of the penalty, if any;
6. The claimant can seek relief through the Court of International Trade, as with other Customs issues; and
7. Customs may commence a formal investigation if deemed appropriate.

(c) Penalty Rates

The penalty amounts are 20% of the actual or potential loss of revenue for the first violation, 50% for the second negligent repetitive violation, and 100% for subsequent negligent violations of the same issue. Fraud is penalized by three times

[8]Pub. L. No. 103-182, 103rd Congress (8 December 1993).

the loss of revenue. For prior disclosures relating to fraudulent representations, the penalty is 100%, and for negligence the penalty is interest due on the revenue. In all cases, the original amount of the revenue is refunded.

Certification by Customs that the claimant was a participant in the Drawback Compliance Program allows the claimant an exemption from a negligence penalty for a first violation of an issue. Penalties will apply to all claims filed on or after the nationwide implementation of an automated drawback selectivity program by Customs Service.

The selectivity program in ACS (Automated Commercial Service) is already being used by Customs to select import entries retrieved by the drawback liquidators. However, Customs has not yet published the effective date of the selectivity program in the *Customs Bulletin.* It is not clear if Customs will wait for publication of the new drawback regulations before announcing the drawback selectivity program, but most drawback practitioners believe it is only practical to communicate the rules first. The penalty regulations must be published in the *Federal Register* as a notice of proposed rule making before penalty procedures can be activated.

9.5 Privileges

Drawback is not a privilege granted by Customs. The right to claim drawback when all the requirements of the drawback laws and regulations have been met is provided by the law itself.[9] Drawback is no more of a privilege than is filing for a refund on your income tax. Provisions in the current drawback regulations and new drawback regulations allow special drawback privileges to claimants who comply with all the regulatory requirements.

(a) Accelerated Payment

Accelerated payment is considered a privilege since it allows a claimant to obtain all or a portion of the proceeds in approximately three to five weeks from the filing date of the claim. The current regulations require that an adequate bond be posted and the claimant be in good standing with Customs. The new regulations continue this theme, but are much more specific as to what information must be presented to obtain approval for accelerated payment. The following information is required:

1. Detailed information about the applicant
2. The drawback bond
3. Types of merchandise
4. The estimated dollar value of the claims
5. A written description of the claimant's drawback program.

---

[9]Tariff Act of 1930, 19 U.S.C. § 1313.

The types of controls the claimant has in place to assure the accuracy and validity of the claim and a commitment to retain records and meet all statutory and regulatory requirements round out the application. For all practical purposes, this is a mini-drawback compliance program. The regulation allows Customs to revoke this privilege for good cause, such as noncompliance with the law and/or regulations, but it provides for an appeal process for either denied applications or revoked privileges.

(b) Waiver of Notice of Intent to Export or Destroy

The waiver of notice of intent to export or destroy privilege continues to be available in the new draft regulations, with virtually the same application information requirements as contained in the accelerated payment application. Application for this privilege on a retroactive basis, however, requires that documentary evidence be presented by the claimant. The evidence must prove, among other things, that exported merchandise subject to unused drawback (same condition) or unused substitution drawback was not used prior to export. Evidence must also be provided to prove that the exported merchandise was the same as or commercially interchangeable with the imported merchandise.

Since Customs is unable to inspect the merchandise prior to export, the new regulations demand solid proof regarding the eligibility of the previously exported merchandise.[10] Customs can approve the application after Customs verifies that the applicant is in good standing and has not failed to present merchandise for inspection when requested in the past. Customs was strongly criticized by the Inspector General's Office for allowing the waiver to be used retroactively. For this reason, an applicant can request retroactive application only one time for specified items, assuming all other requirements can be met.[11] This provision is a "failure to file a notice of intent to export or destroy."

(c) Exporter's Summary Procedure

Exporter's summary procedure was a privilege approved by Customs under the current regulations, but it became a procedure available to any claimant under the new draft drawback regulations.[12] The claimant must show, when audited or upon request, that the export summary used to support drawback claims is in compliance with all of the regulatory requirements.

The exporter's summary procedure has undergone some subtle changes. For example, the format of the chronological export summary now includes a column for the Harmonized Tariff Schedule (HTS) number of the export. Documentary evidence proving export, such as bills of lading, manifests, and invoices, must be available upon request and retained for three years after payment of the related claim.

---

[10] § 191.91, Proposed Drawback Regulations RP95-13.

[11] § 191.36 (a) (2), Proposed Drawback Regulations RP95-13.

[12] § 191.73, Proposed Drawback Regulations RP95-13.

9.6 Other Technical Changes

(a) Fungible Versus Commercially Interchangeable

The standard used to measure substitutability for unused substitution drawback was changed under CMA from fungible to commercially interchangeable. Criteria were established to help both Customs and claimants determine if such materials were, in fact, substitutable.[13] "Fungible" was a nebulous standard, but will continue to be used for identifying drawback eligible materials using accounting methods. The factors to be considered in determining commercial interchangeability include governmental and recognized industrial standards, part numbers, and tariff classification and values. In order to assure acceptance of a substitution 1313 (j) (2) claim:

1. A formal ruling on commercial interchangeability can be requested
2. Nonbinding predetermination can be requested from the appropriate drawback office; or
3. All documentation needed to support commercial interchangeability can be submitted with the drawback claim.

(b) Completion of Drawback Claim

Customs was highly motivated to develop procedures that held the claimant responsible for the accuracy, completeness, and timeliness of drawback claims. Claimants were frustrated with Customs because claims were returned unpaid, or held for more information, for what the claimant perceived as unjustified reasons. In some cases, claim filing deadlines expired before the claim was acceptable to Customs, and the claim was then rejected because it was untimely. Under the proposed regulation, the claim must contain six items to be a completed claim:

1. Drawback entry form CF-331
2. Certificate of Manufacturer and Delivery (if applicable)
3. Notices of intent to export or destroy (if applicable)
4. A listing of import entry numbers
5. Coding sheet if not filed electronically (see Exhibit 9.2)
6. Evidence of exportation or destruction

Customs will accept the claim if these documents are complete. Adjustments for accuracy or requests for additional information will not put the time eligibility in jeopardy. Customs will allow the claimant 30 days (plus extensions if permitted) to respond to requests for information or to make corrections to clerical errors before the claim is rejected and the time clock starts again.

---

[13] § 191.32, Proposed Drawback Regulations RP95-13.

Customs was often responsible for determining the amount to be refunded on claims. This responsibility was forced on Customs because the claimants did not know how much duty was paid on an entry unless they were the importer of record. The importer of record was not required to provide the amount of duty paid when drawback rights were passed on a Certificate of Delivery (CD) or Certificate of Manufacture and Delivery (CMD) to the claimant. In other words, Customs was in the business of perfecting the claimants' drawback claims after entries were liquidated and final duties were determined.

The original proposed regulations stated that the claimant will receive the amount claimed if it does not exceed the amount eligible on the entry. The claimant could still amend the claim if additional refunds were due. This proposal was overruled by customs legal counsel during review and Customs continues to be responsible for "perfecting" claims. The amount of duty paid and the harmonized code number of the import will be required on CDs and CMDs in the future. The inclusion of the duty paid amount on these documents should eliminate the amount of estimating a claimant does when filing a claim.

Obtaining this information from the importer may lead to problems. The importer of record may consider the import information to be proprietary and insist that the claimant employ an interim party to file claims to protect the confidentiality of the import information. A properly worded purchase order clause may protect the claimants' rights to obtain this information and help reduce costs in filing claims.

(c) Restructuring Claims

Customs can require that claims be restructured. Issues causing the restructuring include:

1. The number of transactions of the claimants (imports and exports)
2. The value of the claims
3. The frequency of the claims
4. The product or products being claimed
5. The contract provisions for manufacturing drawback, direct identification, and substitution

Customs needed some claims to be larger and filed less often, while other claims needed to be divided into smaller, more manageable pieces. Claims with multiple issues involving several contracts could become so complex that they were nearly impossible to decipher.

(d) Claims Filed Under the Wrong Provision

Claimants who filed under the wrong drawback provision, when disclosed in an audit, found themselves unable to refile under the correct provision because the claim was barred by time. This situation is addressed in the statute, however, if the type of claim is changed, the new claim must comply with all provisions of the newly elected type of claim. For example, if a claimant files an unused drawback claim and, upon audit, Customs proves that the claim would qualify only as a rejected merchandise claim, the merchandise was probably not returned to Customs, or subject to Customs inspection prior to export or destruction, and therefore would not be eligible for drawback as rejected merchandise. Hence, the claim would be unable to receive a refund under the other provision.

(e) Unused Merchandise Substitution Drawback

Unused merchandise substitution drawback often is not understandable; 1313 (j) (2) was never adequately addressed in the current regulations, and claims were often challenged by U.S. Customs. The primary reasons for these challenges were as follows:

1. The term "fungible merchandise" was not clearly defined and therefore was subject to varying interpretations.
2. There was a question as to the drawback eligibility of domestically produced merchandise substituted for imported merchandise and then substituted again and again until exported.
3. The issue of who had to possess the imported and/or domestic merchandise prior to export was resolved only after a long and expensive court battle.
4. In Customs' opinion, a transfer of drawback rights did not occur when a Certificate of Delivery was issued for the merchandise.
5. Substituted merchandise being transferred to a manufacturer on a Certificate of Delivery for use in filing an unused substitution drawback claim was being improperly substituted under the provisions of manufacturer's substitution drawback (19 U.S.C. § 1313 (b)).

This subject is too technically complex to cover in detail in a general presentation of drawback. Sections 191.32, 33, and 34 address each of the issues that have plagued this type of drawback in the past. Eligibility requirements for drawback, under the provisions of unused drawback, are now properly illustrated and documented in the proposed regulations.

(f) Successorship

The substitution provisions of the drawback law for imported products require that the imported product be used in production by the manufacturer (for § 1313 (b)) to be substitutable with domestic products or other foreign products. The exported product is then eligible for drawback, whether it contains domestic or foreign merchandise. When one company purchases another, drawback eligible products may be:

1. Exported and awaiting claims to be filed;
2. Sitting in purchased inventory waiting to be exported; or

3. Used before the sale of the company, but able to be designated in products built in the future.

In all three cases the successor does not use the material to produce the product in inventory and technically may not be eligible for drawback. This interpretation of use needs to be reexamined because of a plethora of acquisitions, consolidations, and spin-offs.

The successor provision provides that as long as the value of the acquired assets exceeds the drawback value acquired, the drawback rights would transfer to the successor. While the initial issue arose with manufacturer's substitution drawback, the same issue existed for unused substitution drawback and it too was included in the successorship provision C.F.R. § 191.32(f).

(g) Accounting Methods

The use of accounting methods for direct identification of drawback on materials ineligible for substitution was significantly liberalized. Previously, materials had to be commingled in the same inventory location to directly identify materials using LIFO, FIFO, low-to-high, or weighted average accounting methods. Under the new regulations, commingling is still permitted, but it is not required, in order to use these accounting methods to identify material.

An inventory turnover rate may still be used to prove that material produced under 1313 (b) was, in fact, used in production. The turnover rate is especially useful in directly identifying materials in finished goods inventory because, even under manufacturer's substitution drawback, Section 1313 (b), once the goods produced reach the finished goods inventory they cannot be further substituted and must be directly identified.

As most drawback practitioners know, the use of accounting methods for identifying drawback eligible materials has created confusion. For example, a high-to-low accounting method was permitted at one time, whereby the highest duty paid imports could be claimed until they were exhausted, and then the next highest, and so forth. Since this did not "protect the revenue," it was concluded by Customs that it was not a valid accounting method and it was eliminated from the list of approved accounting methods.

It will be interesting to see if the weighted average method, which assigns an average amount of duty to all units of the same product in inventory, will withstand an audit review. The fact that the amount of duty drawback claimed for a single part is an amount that was most likely never paid, being an average of all duties over all imports of the same part, might raise questions. Business people deal with this situation constantly, with their budgeted or standard costs and weighted average inventory values, and find no problem in assigning the duty cost on a weighted average basis. NAFTA Schedule X is identified as an acceptable weighted average accounting method under C.F.R. § 181. U.S. Customs has never explained the interrelationship of Schedule X which determines the origin of material for NAFTA, to the designation of imported merchandise for drawback purposes.

9.7 Drawback Compliance Program

The themes of the Customs Modernization Act are informed compliance and reasonable care. These two concepts will take some time to completely understand and apply. However, they are both based on good business practices and common sense.

The Drawback Compliance Program[14] is a direct outgrowth of CMA concepts. Customs had originally planned to allow special privileges only to participants in the drawback compliance program. Customs felt that along with a one-time exemption from the drawback penalties, making accelerated payment and waiver of notice of intent to export available only to participants would assure widespread success for the program. The proposal moved the program from being voluntary to being mandatory in most claimants' minds. However, since claimants were already under closer scrutiny than ever before, with random on-site visits by drawback liquidators and ever increasing numbers of regulatory audits, the final requirements of the drawback compliance program appeared to offer some relief. This was especially true since individual applications for special privileges were as difficult to prepare as the application for the Drawback Compliance Program.

Originally, the proposed compliance program would have scared away most participants. Customs drawback specialists were notified of every change in procedure, documentation, or personnel in the claimant's organization. However, reason prevailed, and the fundamentals of the program were patterned after the recordkeeping compliance program.

(a) Requirements

Customs will certify a drawback claimant, a broker or a party that provides data and documentation for drawback, if the claimant can meet the core requirements. Applicants must demonstrate that:

1. They understand the legal requirements for filing claims.
2. They have in place procedures to explain Customs' requirements to employees involved in preparing claims.
3. They have procedures describing the claim preparation itself.
4. They have designated a dependable individual(s) to be responsible for compliance with the drawback requirements.
5. They have a record maintenance program approved by Customs and communicated to all individuals, employees, and agents involved in preparation of their claims.
6. Finally, when violations occur, and claimants become aware of them, they will correct the situation and notify Customs of their corrective action.

---

[14] § 191.191–.195 and Appendices A, B, C.

(b) Application Procedures

A broker can become certified only on behalf of a given claimant. The procedures and records of each and every claimant will be held up to scrutiny, even if the claimant's program is handled by a broker.

The application process includes the procedures for approval, rejection, and follow-up. Originally, the primary benefit for participating in the program was the one-time exemption from a penalty, as long as there was no fraud or history of repeated violations. This concept was not unlike the exemption from penalties offered in other parts of the CMA for participation in compliance programs.

It was originally proposed that special privileges be tied to participation in the drawback program, which moved the program from voluntary to mandatory in most claimants' minds. An application process for special privileges was designed and, a grandfather clause was developed to prevent immediate loss of special privileges. Customs insisted that all claimants eventually be approved under the same rules with the same criteria. The grandfather clause provides that claimants currently enjoying special privileges must reapply using the current procedures in the proposed regulations within one year of the effective date of the new regulations. Further, the participants will retain the privileges enjoyed prior to new regulation requirements while Customs reviews the application. Unless Customs denies the privileges for cause, there should be no break in the availability of accelerated payment and waiver of prior notice of intent to export or destroy privileges. If no application is presented, the privileges expire one year after the effective date of the regulations.

9.8 Drawback Under NAFTA

NAFTA regulations under 19 C.F.R. § 181 offer a different perspective on drawback than presented in the new drawback regulations. The brokers association, trade organizations, and many U.S. companies were fighting diligently during the NAFTA negotiations to prevent drawback from being eliminated. The complexity of these negotiations and the use of drawback as a negotiating tool was so convoluted that only a few negotiators can actually explain what happened. Suffice it to say, the final NAFTA package offered so many more advantages than disadvantages that it received the support of a large segment of the business community, in spite of the loss of drawback that would result.

(a) Two Changes to Drawback

Manufacturer's drawback to Canada and Mexico changed significantly under NAFTA. While same condition drawback continued under NAFTA the CMA changed same condition to unused drawback for all but NAFTA-related drawback. Other changes to same condition drawback and manufacturer's drawback, both direct identification and substitution, were scheduled. The first change had NAFTA manufacturer's drawback becoming subject to a lesser of two duties concept. The second change had same condition substitution to Canada and Mexico eliminated on the date the agreement was signed.

In principle, the lesser of two duties concept provides that if duty is paid for non-NAFTA (i.e., non-originating) merchandise (assume import to the United States for illustrative purposes) and the merchandise is used to manufacture a product exported to Canada (again for illustrative purposes), a certain amount of duty may be recovered through drawback if the Canadian importer also pays duty on the import to Canada. The amount eligible for refund and the amount of paperwork needed to validate the claim is what makes this drawback program unique.

(b) Finished Manufactured Product

First, the amount of drawback eligible for refund is the lesser of two duties: the duty paid to U.S. Customs on the imported components or the duty paid to Revenue Canada on the finished manufactured product when imported into Canada. Determining both of these amounts with certainty will be a challenge unless the claimant happens to be both the U.S. importer and the Canadian importer.

Second, details about entries into both the United States and Canada must be available to the claimant to assure submission of accurate and complete claims. The currency conversion problems could become difficult because Canadian entries will be in Canadian dollars and U.S. entries will be in U.S. dollars. Imagine importing into Mexico from Japan, with yen converted to pesos, then exporting to the United States with pesos converted to U.S. dollars, and finally exporting to Canada with U.S. dollars converted to Canadian dollars. Determining the lesser of two duties with all these currency conversions will take a considerable amount of effort. Supporting that determination with entry documentation that is subject to change may make claimants less willing to file a claim that could be subject to drawback penalties.

Another interesting complexity is added by Section 181.50(b), which requires that liquidation of the drawback claim must be held until all entries into the NAFTA countries are finalized. If, due to subsequent claims for preferential tariff treatment, any changes in the entries occur reducing the eligible drawback amount, Customs will reliquidate the drawback claim and obtain a refund.[15] This approach does not square well with the CMA drawback program, which allows a claimant to file a claim, cover it with a bond, and, if not selected for review under the selectivity criteria, have payment made and the claim immediately liquidated.

NAFTA originating goods are eligible for drawback if shipped between NAFTA countries. Therefore, if a Mexican or Canadian product is dutiable as entered into the United States, full duty can be recovered if it is further manufactured and shipped to Canada or Mexico. The imported NAFTA good has to be either the directly identified NAFTA good or a good of the same kind and quality as the good appearing in the exported product. C.F.R. 19 U.S.C. § 181.45 provides examples of how this process works.

[15] § 181.52, North American Free Trade Agreement Regulations (T.D. 94-1).

The general consensus is that total drawback will decrease as a result of NAFTA, primarily because Canada is our largest trading partner. New and expanding markets throughout the world should offset the loss of drawback available to many companies.

9.9 Computerization of Drawback Claims

Customs made a commitment early in the development of the drawback revitalization plan to utilize electronic data to the fullest extent practical to control all aspects of duty drawback. Since most import entries cited in drawback claims were processed electronically, the theory was that claims could be verified electronically prior to payment. For several years, the New York drawback branch required claimants to file a drawback coding sheet that concisely listed the entry number, port, liquidation date, and amount of duty claimed against the entry. The sheet made data entry easier and allowed the branch to check on whether the entry was valid and if duty of at least the claimed amount was paid on entry. While not perfect, it was a starting point in the development of the drawback diskette program.

(a) Diskettes

Drawback branches began accepting diskettes with drawback claims on October 1, 1994. The program to process the diskettes needed correction, the instructions for preparing the diskettes needed revision, and the Customs personnel processing the diskettes needed both computer equipment and training, but the implementation date was met. The diskette program was functioning reasonably well within six months of introduction. To this day there are still problems relating to some issues, such as Certificates of Manufacture and Delivery, which do not appear in the Customs computer database.

Customs programming personnel involved with the diskette program recognized the limitations of using electronic data, which was not in the same format as the drawback claim data. For example, an entry often summarizes all imports of the same Harmonized Tariff System (HTS) number into a single value, and duty is assessed on the total. A drawback claim may designate or cite only one of the many products included in the total duty payment for that HTS number.

Until entries are created with invoice line item detail, drawback claims will never be able to be electronically verified for complete accuracy. The need for invoice line item detail will always remain the biggest problem Customs faces in the computerization of any Customs process. One of the benefits of the diskette program was that it identified many clerical errors made by the claimant, which may have gone undetected in a manual verification process. Incorrect entry numbers, entries liquidated at lesser amounts than originally filed, entries cancelled and replaced by other entries, all came to the surface. Phase one served a useful purpose for both Customs and the claimant. Instructions for use of the diskette program can be obtained through any drawback branch of Customs or through Customs Headquarters in Washington, D.C.

(b) Automated Broker Interface

Customs set a due date of October 1, 1995, to introduce the ABI (Automated Broker Interface) drawback module. This goal seemed nearly impossible with all of the major changes taking place at Customs, such as reorganization, NAFTA implementation, and CMA revisions to Customs' processes and procedures. In October of 1995, the first ABI drawback entry was filed by a drawback broker and accepted by U.S. Customs in San Francisco. The paper document remains the lawful entry. Instructions for applying for access to the ABI drawback module are included in Exhibit 9.3.

Electronic data has never been available to Customs for comparison to any export information supplied on a drawback claim. While drawback was certainly not the driving force behind the project, Customs started developing the Automated Export System (AES). If, or when, AES is implemented, drawback claims will most likely be required to show the electronic export data on the claim.

9.10 Drawback on Lump Sum Duty Payments for Assists, Direct and Indirect Payments

Duty payments for items such as assists[16] (e.g., tooling or foreign engineering) and additional direct or indirect payments made to the foreign manufacturer may be paid in a lump sum on a single entry or may be paid in increments as imports occur, thereby spreading the total amount due over all applicable entries. The drawback law allows recovery of duty on assists and direct and indirect payments when the product imported (or a legally substituted product) on which these duties are paid is exported.

The issue is whether lump sums applicable to a large quantity of imports can be protected from drawback recovery. For example, a single entry for only a few imports may contain a lump sum duty payment recoverable when those few imported items or substituted items are exported. Legally Customs couldn't prevent it. Customs therefore issued a position paper in May of 1988 and a pipeline in November of 1988[17] alerting the ports that this problem was occurring and asked that claimants making lump sum payments on a single entry sign an agreement not to drawback against that entry. Customs protected revenue, but it eliminated recovery by the claimant of a proportionate amount of the lump sum payment applicable to the actual exports.

(a) Proration Issues

In some cases, the importer was planning to export the full imported quantity and, unless each entry carried a proportionate share of these added duties, none of the duties could be recovered. The problem became more acute when the Customs

[16]Assists as defined in § 402 (h) (1) (A) of the Trade Agreements Act of 1979.

[17]Pipeline 46 (15 November 1988), Apportionment or Assists Position (23 May 1988).

Exhibit 9.3

LETTER OF INTENT OUTLINE—FOR PARTICIPATION IN THE AUTOMATED BROKER INTERFACE (ABI) DRAWBACK CLAIM SUMMARY MODULE

I. Statement of intent to participate in ABI
II. Company specifics
   A. Company name
   B. Location
   C. Contact person's name, telephone and fax numbers
      1. Customs operational issues
      2. Data processing (technical) issues, including communications
III. Business profile
   A. Type of business: customshouse broker, importer, exporter, manufacturer, etc. (or any combination)
   B. Port where licensed, if a customshouse broker
   C. Commodities involved in the drawback claims (general description)
   D. Filer code (include any filer codes that will be transmitted in addition to that of the ABI participant)
IV. Drawback claims
   A. Drawback filing location
   B. Estimated number of claims and anticipated dollar amount broken down by type of drawback
      1. Manufacturing
         a. Direct identification
         b. Substitution
      2. Unused merchandise
         a. Direct identification
         b. Substitution
      3. All other types
V. System configuration
   A. Software provider
      1. Provider's company name
      2. Provider's contact person's name, telephone and fax numbers
   B. Hardware specifications
VI. Target dates for implementation at each location

The letter of intent should be directed to the drawback filing location (or any of the drawback filing locations) that you plan to use. The letter should be presented on company letterhead.

The addresses for the drawback brand filing locations follow:

U.S. Customs Service
Drawback Branch
10 Causeway Street, Room 801
Boston, MA 02222-1059

U.S. Customs Service
Drawback Branch
6 World Trade Center, Room 762
New York, NY 10048

U.S. Customs Service
Drawback Branch
423 Canal Street, Room 303
New Orleans, LA 70130

U.S. Customs Service
Drawback Branch
610 S. Canal, Room 602
Chicago, IL 60607

U.S. Customs Service
Drawback Branch
909 SE 1st Avenue, Room 710
Miami, FL 33131

U.S. Customs Service
Drawback Branch
2323 S. Shepherd, Suite 1200
Houston, TX 77019-7019

U.S. Customs Service
Drawback Branch
One World Trade Center, Suite 534
Long Beach, CA 90831-0700

U.S. Customs Service
Drawback Branch
33 New Montgomery, Room 414
San Francisco, CA 94105-4510

To ensure that your letter gets prompt attention, please forward a copy to Customs Headquarters:

U.S. Customs Service
User Support Services, Customer Assistance
Trade Support Division
1301 Constitution Avenue NW, Room 2413
Washington, DC 20029

A sample letter is shown on the following page. The italicized, bracketed information should be supplied by you. Feel free to include any additional information that you feel may be helpful.

regulatory auditors began to take exception to recovery of the lump sum payments, but had no alternative solution to offer the claimant. The Customs pipeline was not likely to stand up in court, and denying drawback against an entry with a lump sum payment, properly paid in accordance with the law, would likely not be defensible in litigation. Customs permitted proration in other areas, and it made sense to propose that a regulation be written to prorate the lump sum amount in accordance with the Generally Accepted Accounting Principles (GAAP). Drawback refunds could then include a prorated portion of the lump sum payment applicable to the quantity of product exported.

(b) Proration Techniques

The background statement prepared by the Drawback Regulations Team provided an example of how to prorate a lump sum duty payment amount and how to cite the entry for future recovery.[18] A per unit amount was calculated by dividing

[18]Exhibit 9.4 shows the initial proposed wording.

Exhibit 9.3 ***(Continued)***

THE GENERIC COMPANY, INC.
123 Main Street, Anytown, ST 00000-0000

Today, 1999

U.S. Customs Service
Drawback Unit
[6 World Trade Center, Room 762]
[New York City, NY 10048]

Drawback Specialist:

The Generic Company, Inc., wishes to participate in the Automated Broker Interface (ABI).

The company name is: *[The Generic Company, Inc.]*
The company location is: *[123 Main Street]*
[Anytown, ST 00000-0000]
Principal contacts are: Management: *[Big Boss, 999-888-7777, FAX 999-888-7776]*
Technical operations: *[T. Techie, 999-888-6666, FAX 999-888-6665]*
ADP and communications: *[T. Techie, as above]*

The Generic Company is a [*manufacturer as well as an exporter*]. Our main business is [*the manufacture and export of generic goods*]. Our filer code is *[YP2]*.

The drawback filing locations we use are *[New York and San Francisco]*. The drawback volume estimated by year is as follows:
[New York]
[Manufacturing, Substitution, *25 claims, combined value of $525,000]*
[Unused Merchandise, Direct Identification, *75 claims, combined value of $100,000]*
[San Francisco]
[Unused Merchandise, Substitution, *100 claims, combined value of $75,000]*

The software provider we are going to use: *[The Software Company]*
Contact person at [*The Software Company*]: *[V. Vendor, 999-888-5555, FAX 999-888-5554]*

Computer hardware: *[PC]*

Target dates for full system installation and program utilization for each location are as follows:
[New York *January 7, 1999]*
[San Francisco *March 4, 1999]*

Sincerely,
[R. U. Ready]
[President, The Generic Company]

cc: *[San Francisco]*

Exhibit 9.4

DRAWBACK ON LUMP SUM ASSISTS

Frequently, companies import merchandise that have higher actual dutiable values than the invoices that accompany the shipment. The two primary instances that cause this disparity are assists (as defined in Section 402 (h) (1) (A) of the Trade Agreements Act of 1979) and additional direct and indirect payments made to the manufacturer. Foreign manufacturers invoice the importer on a per unit basis; however, this per unit price does not include assists from the importer or additional direct and indirect payments received from non-merchandise invoicing. For example:

1. A foreign manufacturer contracts with the importer to produce 20,000 ski boots at $50.00 per *boot.* The importer agrees to provide the foreign manufacturer a $50,000 machine to form plastic into the components used to make the ski boots. The invoice accompanying the shipment would be for $50.00 per ski boot and would not include the cost of the machine provided by the importer.
2. A foreign manufacturer contracts with the importer to produce 20,000 ski boots at $50.00 per *boot.* The foreign manufacturer purchases a $50,000 machine to form plastic into the components used to make ski boots. The manufacturer invoices the importer separately for the $50,000 relating to the machine. The invoice accompanying the shipment would be for $50.00 per ski boot and would not include the cost of the machine provided by the importer.

In order to declare the assists or additional direct and indirect payments, the importer has the option to declare the entire value on the initial importation or prorate the value over the import shipments containing products manufactured by the asset. Any prorations used must be in accordance with the Generally Accepted Accounting Principles (GAAP).

If a portion of the imported merchandise is designated for drawback and the importer had declared the entire value of the assist or direct or indirect payment on one consumption entry, while the merchandise was imported on several consumption entries, Customs and the trade have experienced problems in refunding drawback on the lump sum duty payments.

The following illustrates this situation:

A $50,000 assist relates to the production and importation of each boot. The estimated useful life of the assist is 2 years or 20,000 boots. The importer imports boots on the following 10 consumption entries:

Entry Number	Entry Date	Quantity
1	1/94	10
2	3/94	2,500
3	5/94	500
4	5/94	2,490
5	7/94	2,500
6	10/94	2,500

Exhibit 9.4 (*Continued*)

Entry Number	Entry Date	Quantity
7	1/95	2,500
8	4/95	2,500
9	7/95	2,500
10	10/95	2,000

The importer declares the $50,000 assists on entry number 1. The duty applicable to the assist is $5,000. During 1/96, the importer exports 10 boots and designates entry number 1. The drawback paid would be $4,950 for the assist and 99% of the duty paid on the 10 boots.

In an effort to achieve an equitable refund, the following proposal is made:

A $50,000 assist relates to the production and importation of boots. The estimated useful life of the assist is two years or 20,000 units. The importer imports boots on the same consumption entries.

The importer declares the $50,000 assist on entry number 1. The duty applicable to the assist is $5,000. During 1/96, the importer exports 10,000 boots and claims drawback. The entry numbers designated were 1, 2, 4, 5, and 6. It is proposed that assist drawback should be payable from entry number 1 in proportion to the quantity imported divided by the quantity exported. In this example, the drawback paid would be $2,475.00 [(10,000/20,000) × $5,000 × .99].

This methodology would appear equitable since it allows drawback on assists and direct and indirect payments only in proportion to the exported quantities to which the payments apply. Therefore, drawback claimants, filing drawback on assist and additional direct and indirect payments, would be required to establish a per unit assist and direct and indirect payment based on the total units produced. For the preceding examples, the $5,000 in assist duty would be prorated over the 20,000 boots imported to give a duty paid per unit of $.25. When drawback is calculated, the duty on the assist/direct/indirect payment per unit ($.25) is multiplied by the total units exported to get total duty paid. Drawback is 99% of the total duty paid.

The drawback claim designations should include consumption entry (s) covering quantities of imported merchandise that equal the quantity exported, as well as the entry on which the lump sum payment was deposited. The drawback claim should also include a schedule of imports and expected imports in adequate detail to allow Customs to evaluate the methodology used to allocate duty paid on assists to the products exported and subject to a drawback claim. Customs may request additional information, if needed, to complete the evaluation. Examples of additional information requested include a list of consumption entries to date, date of importation, port of importation and quantity imported; contracts; purchase orders and anticipated total production quantities to which the assist payment, direct or indirect payment, applies.

the total duty paid on the assist or payment by the anticipated import quantity. That per unit amount was multiplied by the export quantity and added to the drawback amount on the exported product itself.

A schedule of imports and expected exports is sent with the drawback claim to support the calculation. The entry on which the lump sum duty payment was made would be eligible for drawback only for the length of time that the material on the entry itself was eligible. For example, for an unused drawback claim, the assist proration entry was eligible for drawback only for a period of three years after import.

This issue was not attached to the regulations but processed simultaneously with the regulation package. If objections were raised during the approval process, this proposal could be set aside without derailing the balance of the drawback regulations. At last report, this proposal had passed through all reviews and should be added to the regulations at a later date.

9.11 Conclusion

The process used by the Drawback Regulations Team in resolving controversial issues was called Interest Based Problem Solving. Each problem was defined (framing the issue), the concerns about the issue were outlined by the team (interests), and the criteria were established. Pieces of the various proposed solutions were combined into a solution that met all, or nearly all, of the criteria. All decisions were made by consensus, and it was agreed that unless a solution was illegal, the group's consensus decisions would be final. By using a trained facilitator, the long hours needed to resolve the 21 major issues were productive, although tedious at times. Twenty additional changes will appear in the regulations when they are published in the *Federal Register.*

CHAPTER 10

U.S. Customs Bonded Warehouses and Temporary Importation Bonds

Jill D. Murray

10.1 Establishing a Bonded Warehouse
(a) Construction
(b) Eligibility
10.2 Advantages of Storing in Bonded Warehouses
(a) Liability
(b) Disposition of Merchandise in Customs Beyond Time Fixed by Law
10.3 Classes of Customs Warehouses
10.4 General Order Merchandise
10.5 Requirements and Procedures for Warehouse Entry
10.6 Manipulation
10.7 Transfers
10.8 Withdrawal of Merchandise from a Bonded Warehouse
10.9 Withdrawal for Exportation
10.10 Withdrawal for Consumption
10.11 Rewarehouse Entries
10.12 Recordkeeping
10.13 Materials for Use in Manufacturing Warehouses
10.14 Withdrawal for Exportation of Articles Manufactured in Bond; Waste or Byproducts for Consumption
10.15 Duty-free Stores
10.16 Introduction to Temporary Importation Bonds
10.17 Entry
10.18 Exportation
10.19 Entry Under Bond
10.20 Bond
10.21 Models of Women's Wearing Apparel
10.22 Theatrical Effects and Other Articles

10.23 Vehicles, Pleasure Boats, and Aircraft
10.24 Default on Bond/Cancellation of Bond
(a) Canceling Liability
(i) Export
(ii) Destruction
(iii) Extend Time
(iv) Liquidation
(b) Ending the Bond

10.1 Establishing a Bonded Warehouse

There are many types of bonded warehouses. Merchandise may be stored in a bonded warehouse for up to five years without the payment of duties. This section will discuss establishing a bonded warehouse, advantages of storing merchandise in a bonded warehouse, requirements for warehouse entries, and recordkeeping and withdrawals from the warehouse.

(a) Construction

A bonded section of a warehouse must be separate from the unbonded portion. A blueprint showing measurements, openings, security systems, and so forth, of the building to be bonded shall be submitted to Customs. Materials used to construct this separation must be substantial and only allow for authorized personnel to enter this area. An application to bond must be filed by the owner or lessee to the director of the port closest to the intended bonding site. The application shall advise whether the warehouse is to be operated for storage only, for treatment of merchandise, or treated as a publicly bonded warehouse. This is true for all warehouse classes except a class 2 or a class 7 warehouse.

A bond for the warehouse, excluding a class 1 warehouse, will be executed on Customs Form 301. If a warehouse is substantially altered or rebuilt, the port director may require the proprietor of the warehouse to furnish a new bond. The proprietor is given 10 days to do so. If the bond is not furnished, all the merchandise shall be removed at the expense of the proprietor and no more merchandise will be sent to the warehouse.

Information concerning the applicants qualification, character, and experience can be required for approval to bond as well as information as to the security, suitability, and fitness of the facility. Customs will investigate the applicant as well as the security and suitability of the facility to be bonded. A set of fingerprints may be required on Standard Form 87 at the time of application from an individual and from the officers and managing officials of a business entity. The port director will notify in writing whether the application to bond the warehouse has been approved or denied. In the case of the application being denied, the proprietor of the warehouse can provide reasons why the bonded status should not be revoked or suspended. The port director will consider the responses unless the proprietor has requested a hearing. The Commissioner of Customs or his designee shall designate a hearing officer within 30 days following the proprietor's request. Legal counsel is allowed for the proprietor at the hearing and a stenographic record is maintained with a copy submitted to the Assistant Commissioner Office of Field Operations. Additional views or arguments may be presented to this office by the proprietor within 10 days after the stenographic record is received. The decision is rendered in writing by the Assistant Commissioner, Office of Field Operations or designee stating the decision. This decision is rendered to the proprietor and considered the final administrative action. If the proprietor is adversely affected by the decision of the Assistant Commissioner, Office of Field Operations or designee, an appeal can be made in the Court of International Trade.

(b) Eligibility

Not all merchandise may be stored in warehouses. Perishable and explosive substances (other than firecrackers) are exempt from being stored in warehouses. Other articles such as dangerous and highly flammable merchandise require the written consent of the insurance company in order for the merchandise to be accepted for warehousing.

Merchandise entered under an entry other than a warehouse entry remaining in continuous customs custody may be changed to a warehouse entry. The copies of the warehouse entry shall be marked with the following:

This entry is in substitution of ______________________ entry No. _______, dated ________________ .

If estimated duties have already been tendered, the entry is liquidated for refund of these duties prior to the liquidation of the warehouse entry.

10.2 Advantages of Storing in Bonded Warehouses

Storing merchandise in bonded warehouses can be advantageous for the following reasons:

- Avoid paying duty on selling merchandise to a foreign buyer
- Avoid paying higher duty for merchandise expected to attain a lower duty rate or Generalized System of Preferences (GSP) status
- Merchandise for domestic use is exempt from state and local ad valorem personal property taxes on inventory
- Avoid return or destruction of merchandise for which a quota has closed (when the quota opens, merchandise stored in a bonded warehouse may be withdrawn)
- Defer payment of duties until the articles are withdrawn for actual use
- Store unsold merchandise until a buyer is found

(a) Liability

The importer is liable for the merchandise entered into the warehouse and for the payment of all unpaid duties. The sureties on the bond are liable for the payment of duties and Customs charges not paid by the principal on the bond. The liability may be transferred as well as the right to withdraw the merchandise. Any damage, loss or deterioration of the merchandise while in the warehouse shall not be exempt from duties due unless provided for by law. Allowances in duty will be made by the port director under the conditions above. Any discrepancies will be referred to the Commissioner of Customs. Allowances are made for merchandise abandoned or destroyed while still in bond under the following conditions:

- An application on Customs Form 3499 (modified to read "Application and Permit to Abandon, or Destroy Goods in Bond"). The port directory shall approve the method of destruction filed by the importer for destruction of the merchandise in bond with the method of destruction stated in the application.
- The warehouse proprietor must concur with the application in order to be accepted.
- Any applicable costs must be covered either through government sale of the merchandise or by a sum deposited by the importer in an amount sufficient to save the government from any additional charges should the merchandise be abandoned.

Merchandise can be abandoned voluntarily by the importer to the government within three years from the date of importation. Destruction may take place within five years from the date of importation at the expense of the importer. No merchandise shall remain in a bonded warehouse beyond the period of five years from the date of importation. The port director may authorize a Customs officer to supervise any transaction or procedure at the bonded warehouse facility independent of any need to appraise or classify merchandise. The warehouse proprietor's records; quantity counts of goods in warehouse inventories; spot checks of selected warehouse transactions or procedures; reviews of conditions for recordkeeping, security or storage in warehouse facilities may be reviewed through periodic audits. Access to the warehouse by any Customs officer shall be permitted by the warehouse proprietor.

(b) Disposition of Merchandise in Customs Beyond Time Fixed by Law

Merchandise remaining in a warehouse beyond the period of five years is subject to sale by the U.S. government. Merchandise subject to sale which duties have not been paid or after the expiration of the general order period of one year after the date of importation, even if duties are paid, shall be sold unless entered or withdrawn for consumption. This merchandise may be withdrawn prior to the sale with the payment of duty and any internal revenue tax as well as all charges which may have accrued. Exportation of the merchandise can not take place without payment of duty due. Merchandise may be released to the warehouse proprietor if all duties and charges have been paid or merchandise that remains in a bonded warehouse for more than the general order period that remains in the bonded warehouse.

10.3 Classes of Customs Warehouses

There are several classes of customs warehouses. Customs designates the warehouse according to the following classifications as stated in section 19.1 of the Customs Regulations of the United States:

Class 1—The warehouse premises is owned or leased by the government and used for the storage of merchandise undergoing examination by the Customs officer, under seizure, or pending final release from Customs custody. Unclaimed merchandise stored in such premises shall be held under "general order."

When such premises are not sufficient or available for the storage of seized and unclaimed goods, such goods may be stored in a warehouse of class 3, 4, or 5. When warehouses are used for this purpose, they shall be designated "bonded stores." The port director may rent suitable premises for the storage of seized and unclaimed goods if there are not warehouses with the above classes available. Approval must be obtained from the U.S. Customs Service headquarters.

Class 2—Importers' private bonded warehouses used exclusively for the storage of merchandise belonging or consigned to the proprietor. A warehouse of class 4 or 5 may be bonded exclusively for the storage of goods imported by the proprietor thereof, in which case it shall be known as a private bonded warehouse.

Class 3—Public bonded warehouses used exclusively for the storage of imported merchandise.

Class 4—Bonded yards or sheds for the storage of heavy and bulky imported merchandise; stables, feeding pens, corrals, or other similar buildings or limited enclosures for the storage of imported animals; and tanks for the storage of imported liquid merchandise in bulk. If the port director deems it necessary, the yards shall be enclosed by substantial fences with entrances and exit gates capable of being secured by the proprietor's locks. The inlets and outlets to tanks shall be secured by means of seals or the proprietors' locks.

Class 5—Bonded bins or parts of buildings or of elevators to be used for the storage of grain. The bonded portions shall be effectively separated from the rest of the building.

Class 6—Warehouses for the manufacture in bond, solely for exportation of articles made in whole or in part of imported materials or of materials subject to internal-revenue tax; and for the manufacture for home consumption or exportation of cigars in whole of tobacco imported from one country.

Class 7—Warehouses bonded for smelting and refining imported metal-bearing materials for exportation or domestic consumption.

Class 8—Bonded warehouses established for the purpose of cleaning, sorting, repacking, or otherwise changing in condition but not manufacturing, imported merchandise, under Customs supervision and at the expense of the proprietor.

Class 9—Bonded warehouses, known as "duty-free stores," used for selling, for use outside the Customs territory, conditionally duty-free merchandise owned or sold by the proprietor and delivered from the class 9 warehouse to an airport or other exit point for exportation by, or on behalf of, individuals departing from the Customs territory for destinations other than foreign trade zones. "Customs territory" for the purposes of duty-free stores means the Customs territory of the United States and foreign trade zones.

Class 1 through 7 may in whole or part be designated a constructive manipulation (class 8) warehouse when the exigencies of the service so require.

10.4 General Order Merchandise

By order of the port director on a delivery ticket (CF6043), general order, abandoned, or seized goods and articles are accepted by the proprietor of a general order warehouse. The CF6043 is presented by the cartman or lighterman and the quantity and condition of the goods are determined jointly with the warehouse proprietor. Any discrepancies between the actual quantity and condition of the goods than that reported on the CF6043 shall be reported within two days to the port director. Release of the general order merchandise to the person named in the release order is orchestrated by the proprietor after Customs inspection or examination as ordered by the port director. A permit to release or delivery authorization signed by the appropriate Customs officer on Customs Forms 3461, 7501, 368 or 368A or other Customs forms as designated by the port director is presented and the proprietor may release the goods. Unclaimed general order merchandise which is voluntarily abandoned, seized or forfeited may be released for transfer to the place of sale upon presentation of an approved copy of Customs Form 5251 (order to transfer merchandise for public auction (sale)) and an approved copy of Customs Form 6043 (delivery ticket) to the warehouse proprietor. The proprietor and the cartman or lighterman picking up the goods for delivery to the place of sale shall jointly decide on the quantity and condition of the goods. Discrepancies are to be noted on the delivery ticket. A copy of the delivery ticket is sent to the port director within two business days of the agreement.

Merchandise taken into custody of the port director and placed in public stores or general order warehouses are considered general order merchandise for the following reasons:

- Entry of the merchandise was not made within the time provided by law
- Duties have not been paid on the merchandise rendering the entry incomplete

- Proper documentation is missing to make the entry
- Incorrect or illegally invoiced merchandise deemed by the port director
- Merchandise taken into possession by the port director one day after the vessel arrives at the request of the consignee or owner or master of the vessel

The period of time that the merchandise is not subject to sale is the general order period. This period expires one year from the date of importation.

10.5 Requirements and Procedures for Warehouse Entry

The required documentation or entry into a bonded warehouse is:

- The CF7501 (entry summary)
- Complete set of CF3461s that indicate in box 5 the facility and firms code where the merchandise is presently located
- Commercial invoices
- Packing lists
- Other government agency requirements if applicable

The entry summary (CF7501) shows the value, classification, and rate of duty as approved by the port director at the time the entry summary is filed. However, no duty is owed until the merchandise is withdrawn for consumption from the warehouse. The duty rate on withdrawal is the rate used for duty payment.

The port director may waive the need for Customs supervision on deposit into a bonded warehouse. The inspection or examination shall occur at the place of unloading, bonded warehouse, or other location as ordered by the port director. The proprietor is responsible for the quantity, condition, and any allowances or discrepancies on a discrepancy report on accepting the merchandise into the warehouse. Any joint discrepancy report between the cartman or lighterman and the proprietor is due within two business days and provided to the port director. No report is necessary if the proprietor of the bonded warehouse transports the goods to the warehouse.

With proper authority from the port director the proprietor may break the Customs in bond seals or affix Customs in bond seals to withdrawn or in bond movement of merchandise. The application or removal of any seals shall be deemed to have been done under Customs supervision. Any seals found on arrival to be broken, missing, or improperly affixed shall be reported by the proprietor to the port director. The merchandise shall be held pending instruction from the port director.

The liability of the proprietor after merchandise has been entered into a warehouse may change. Adjustments may be made due to concealed shortages, casualty loss, destruction, or manipulation. The merchandise is subject to expenses of labor and storage, chargeable at the customary rates, as well as other expenses that may accrue while the goods are stored. Rates are agreed on by the importer and the warehouse proprietor and the charges for storage due the government shall be paid prior to delivery of the merchandise. Charges are based on the existing bonded warehouse tariff of the port for storage and labor.

10.6 Manipulation

One of the uses of a bonded warehouse can be for manipulation. By manipulating merchandise, a lower duty rate for the withdrawal can occur. Application to manipulate is filed on Customs Form 3499 with the port director. Description of the manipulation in detail such as merchandise to be cleaned, sorted, repacked or otherwise changed in condition but not manufactured shall be stated. If the port director is satisfied with the information a permit is issued.

A blanket application to manipulate may also be issued by the port director on Customs Form 3499 for a one year period of continuous or repetitive manipulation. Blanket permits may be revoked by the port director and require the proprietor to file individual manipulation applications if necessary to protect the revenue, administer any law, or both.

Manipulation performed under a blanket permit also has a running record of manipulation maintained by the proprietor indicating the quantities before and after each manipulation. These records shall describe marks, numbers of packages, location within the facility, quantities, description of the goods before and after each manipulation, and what took place at each manipulation. Further manipulation may take place if the port director feels that it will not endanger the revenue or interfere with Customs business.

After each manipulation, the merchandise remaining in the warehouse shall be properly repacked. A summary statement of the quantity in the warehouse account after manipulation and immediately before withdrawal, the quantity withdrawn and the quantity remaining in the warehouse after withdrawal shall accompany each withdrawal filed. Merchandise manipulated other than in a bonded warehouse and later withdrawn for consumption shall be covered by a consumption entry on Customs Form 7505.

Duty-free store merchandise or class 9 merchandise may be unpacked into salable units without the port director issuing a permit. Merchandise less than $100.00 per entry, in undamaged condition, found to be nonsalable, may be destroyed for a period of up to one year. The port director will issue a blanket permit to a duty-free store for this task. The permit may be revoked in order to assure proper destruction and protection of the revenue. Records of unpacking merchandise into salable units and destruction of nonsalable merchandise shall be kept by the proprietor in its inventory and accounting records.

10.7 Transfers

The right to withdraw merchandise from a bonded warehouse in part or in whole may be transferred by appropriate endorsement on the withdrawal form.

The person signing the form is primarily liable for payment of duties prior to the completion of the transfer. A bond on Customs Form 301 needs to be filed by the transferee. The transferee may at any time after establishing his right to withdraw merchandise withdraw all or part of the merchandise. Endorsement is made on the applicable withdrawal forms that follow:

- Customs Form 7506 for merchandise to be withdrawn as vessel or aircraft supplies and other conditionally free merchandise;
- Customs Form 7506 for merchandise to be withdrawn for transportation, exportation, or transportation and exportation; or
- Customs Form 7505 for warehouse withdrawals for consumption with duty paid or withdrawal with no duty paid (diplomatic use).

The transferor may blank endorse the withdrawal papers and leave the name of the transferee blank. With the transferee's bond, the holder of a blank endorsed withdrawal fully executed may establish his right to withdraw the merchandise by inserting his own name. Further transfer may occur by the transferee retransferring the right to withdraw the merchandise. The transferor may not revoke the transferee's right of withdrawal.

10.8 Withdrawal of Merchandise from a Bonded Warehouse

Merchandise to be withdrawn from a warehouse may be transferred to another warehouse, withdrawn for transportation, withdrawn for exportation, or withdrawn for consumption.

The person primarily liable for the payment of duties such as the importer of record on the warehouse entry, the actual owner with proper bond filed, or the transferee may withdraw merchandise from a bonded warehouse. A new declaration of the consignee or agent is not required. Each withdrawal shall have a summary statement of the account to which it relates preferably in the lower left-hand part of the margin. The statement indicates:

- The quantity (number of outer containers, or tons, etc.) in the warehouse before withdrawal
- The quantity being withdrawn
- The quantity remaining in the warehouse after withdrawal

In each instance, the quantity may be shown as cumulative even though it may include different commodities and different units such as boxes, cases, or cartons. For cases in which the merchandise has been transferred, the quantity on hand in the transferee's name before the withdrawal is shown as well as the quantity being withdrawn and the quantity remaining in the warehouse after withdrawal. The application to withdraw merchandise will be approved if the Customs officer determines that there are no cartage, storage, labor, or other charges due the government and no notice of lien filed by the carrier. Withdrawals shall not be in amounts less than an entire bale, cask, box, or other package. If the merchandise is in bulk, not less than one ton in weight or the entire quantity imported, whichever is smaller, shall be withdrawn. Any exceptions need to be approved by the special authority of the Commissioner of Customs.

The warehouse proprietor is relieved of responsibility for merchandise withdrawn without Customs supervision for merchandise in the condition and quantity as shown on the application for withdrawal or removal. For merchandise transported in bond from the warehouse, the proprietor must receive the signed receipt on the withdrawal or removal document from the carrier named in the document in order to relieve him of responsibility.

The proprietor's responsibility may change due to any discrepancy report made jointly by the warehouse proprietor and the licensed cartman or lighterman, bonded carrier, weigher, gauger, or measurer and signed by the authorized parties above within 15 calendar days after removal from a warehouse. Any adjustments shall be noted on the permit copy of the withdrawal or removal document and a copy shall be forwarded immediately to the port director.

Merchandise may remain in a warehouse after a permit for withdrawal is approved but must be segregated or physically marked to maintain its identity as merchandise with a withdrawal permit issued. Duty-paid or unconditionally-free merchandise will be deemed no longer in Customs custody if a permit to withdraw has been approved and the merchandise remains in the warehouse.

Other merchandise is in Customs custody for the five year warehouse entry bonded period even though withdrawn but not removed from the warehouse. The presentation of the supplementary withdrawal must be presented prior to removal of any merchandise. If merchandise is removed prior to this time, the proprietor is subject to liquidated damages as if removed without Customs permit. For Customs purposes, when merchandise is deposited or withdrawn from the warehouse, the Customs officer's report of the merchandise received or removed determines the quantity and condition of merchandise received or removed.

Blanket permits for removal of merchandise in small quantities are used for the following:

- Delivery to individuals departing directly from the Customs territory for exportation under sales tickets which serve as a supplementary withdrawal
- Aircraft or vessel supplies
- Personal or official use of personnel of foreign governments and international organizations
- A combination of the above

Blanket permits for withdrawal may only be used at the port where withdrawn and not for transport in bond, transfer to another port, retention, or splitting of shipments. No further Customs approval is necessary for withdrawals under a blanket permit. A copy of the withdrawal document is placed in the proprietor's permit file folder. The withdrawals are on Customs Form 7506 or 7505 and consecutively numbered, prefixed with the letter "B," and specify the quantity and value of each type of merchandise. Additionally, the blanket permit shall state in capital letters on the warehouse entry or on the warehouse entry/entry summary:

SOME OR ALL OF THE MERCHANDISE WILL BE WITHDRAWN UNDER BLANKET PERMIT PER SECTION 19.6(d), C.R.

Customs acceptance of the blanket permit will be approval to remove some or all of the merchandise. The permit may be revoked if found that it is being used improperly or in order to protect the revenue or properly enforce the laws and regulations Customs is in charge of enforcing. The proprietor shall prepare a report on Customs Form 7506, or on the proprietor's letterhead when all of the merchandise is withdrawn under a blanket permit to withdraw. The disposition of the merchandise covered by the blanket permit is stated and bears

BLANKET PERMIT SUMMARY

at the top margin. The proprietor accounts for all the merchandise withdrawn under blanket permit, the tariff number, the quantity and value where applicable. If necessary, a separate list identifying merchandise withdrawn for duty-free store exportation, vessel or aircraft supply use, or personal or official use of persons and organizations is noted. If all items were withdrawn using the sales ticket method, the blanket permit summary is replaced with the sales ticket register.

Transfers to another warehouse may be executed at the same port the merchandise arrived or at another port. Under Customs supervision and with the concurrence of the proprietors of the delivering and receiving warehouse, an order to transfer on Customs Form 6043 by the importer transfers merchandise from one bonded warehouse to another. If the port director determines that proper control of the merchandise is necessary, a rewarehouse entry may be required. Prior to the merchandise being transferred from a class 1 warehouse, all charges must be paid.

Withdrawals for transportation to another port of entry or exportation is allowed as long as the transaction can be executed prior to the expiration of the warehouse period. Physical deposit in a warehouse may not be needed if withdraw for transportation and the merchandise is covered by an entry summary. The merchandise may remain on the vessel or other vehicle or on the pier in a constructive warehouse status pending examination.

The importer shall be required to withdraw the merchandise immediately for consumption or exportation or designate a warehouse to which it may be sent if the merchandise is not forwarded under the withdrawal for transportation on account of damage or other cause. Upon failure to do so, the merchandise will be treated as unclaimed. Withdrawals for transportation are executed on Customs Form 7512 in five copies accompanied by Customs Form 7512-C. An additional copy or copies may be required for delivery of the merchandise to the bonded carrier and two extra copies are required for alcoholic beverages for use in furnishing the duty statement to the port director at destination. For merchandise being withdrawn, Customs Form 7512 shall show the following:

- Original entry number, date of entry, date of entry summary, and port at which filed
- Name of consignee at the port of destination
- Ascertained weight, gauge, or measure
- Entered value of the merchandise
- Estimated duties, if any
- A statement that the merchandise is or is not admissible for consumption and the reason for nonadmissibility if applicable

This information is provided with the statement of quantity. In the case of a withdrawal of rewarehoused merchandise, the rewarehouse entry number, date, and port at which filed should also appear. All legal and regulatory requirements must be met in order for the Customs officer to approve the application to transfer or withdraw merchandise from a bonded warehouse by endorsing the permit copy and returning it to the applicant. The approved permit presented to the warehouse proprietor is evidence of Customs authorization to transfer or withdraw the merchandise. The approved permit is then kept in the warehouse entry file of the proprietor. The proprietor has the option to allow goods covered by permit to be retained in the bonded warehouse.

10.9 Withdrawal for Exportation

There are two types of withdrawals for exportation, direct and indirect. Both types are filed on Customs Form 7512 (transportation entry and manifest of goods subject to Customs inspection and permit) in five copies or on Customs Form 7506 (warehouse withdrawal conditionally free of duty and permit) in three copies if exported merchandise is covered by a TIR (Transport International Routier) carnet accompanied by Customs Form 7512-C (transportation entry and manifest of goods). An extra copy of Customs Form 7512 or 7506 may be required for delivery of the merchandise to the carrier.

Merchandise being transferred to another port for exportation shall be considered an indirect exportation. The cargo moves to the port under a Customs Form 7512, transportation and exportation. Any part of the shipment that is not exported shall be divided at the port of exportation. Extracts in duplicate shall be made on Customs Form 7512 for each portion when the shipment is split as above. One copy of the Customs Form 7512 is forwarded to the discharging inspector and the other to the lading inspector to be used as report of exportation. The splitting of shipments for exportation arriving under warehouse withdrawals for indirect exportation is permitted when various portions of a shipment are destined to different overseas ports or when the exporting vessel cannot properly accommodate the entire quantity of merchandise.

If another similar situation exists as above, the splitting of shipments shall also be allowed. Merchandise covered under a TIR carnet shall not be split if exportation requires splitting the merchandise. An appropriate entry is required and the carnet discharged. Conversion from a withdrawal for indirect exportation to a withdrawal for consumption may occur with approval from the director of the port where the withdrawal for indirect exportation was made. Merchandise may also be withdrawn from a warehouse for exportation by mail. All exportations shall be made under the original marks of importation. By authority of the port director, port marks may be added under Customs supervision but must be marked on all export documentation. Except as otherwise provided for by law, exportation of merchandise in bulk shall be at the same weight, gauge, or measure ascertained at the time of the original entry for warehouse. The port director may require a special report of weight, gauge, or measure of the merchandise being exported if he deems necessary.

Merchandise not laden on board a vessel which is withdrawn from a warehouse for exportation shall be sent to general order unless the port director advises differently. Merchandise exported at a foreign trade zone is considered exported on admission to a zone in zone-restricted status. The withdrawal for exportation can be made at a foreign trade zone in the same or at a different port. Class 9 (duty-free store) merchandise may be withdrawn for exportation. However, only conditionally duty-free merchandise in a class 9 warehouse may be withdrawn for exportation or for delivery to persons and organizations using the sales ticket procedure.

Sales ticket withdrawals are made under a blanket permit to withdraw and the sales ticket serves as the equivalent of the supplementary withdrawal. A sales ticket is the proprietor's design of an invoice to include:

- Serial number and date of preparation of each ticket
- Warehouse entry number or specific identifier if approved by the port director
- Quantity of goods sold
- Brief description of the articles including the size of bottles
- Full name, address, and signature of the purchaser

The address and signature requirement may be waived by the port director for alcoholic beverages in quantities of four liters or less and cigarettes in quantities of three cartons or less. The name requirement is still mandatory. At the time of purchase, the sales ticket is made out in triplicate in the name of the purchaser. One of these copies is retained by the proprietor and a permit copy is attached to the parcel containing the merchandise while the original is given to the purchaser. A statement on the purchaser's copy of the sales ticket shall state that if merchandise purchased in a duty-free store is returned to the United States, duty and/or tax may be assessed. Class 9 warehouse proprietors shall maintain a sales ticket register in addition to the other records required for a bonded warehouse. A similar accounting record for each warehouse entry may be maintained in lieu of the sales ticket register. Either method should include:

- Warehouse entry number
- Specific identifier, if applicable

- Sales ticket date and number
- Description
- Quantity
- Current Balance

The sales ticket register total is verified with the amount withdrawn as each warehouse entry is closed out. This will account for all the merchandise withdrawn and certify that goods have been exported or sold to qualifying persons and organizations. In lieu of the blanket permit summary, the sales ticket register shall be included in the permit file folder. The proprietor shall retain a copy of all sales tickets for at least five years from the date of the last sales ticket entry. Sales tickets may be kept in separate files in numerical sequence by warehouse entry number in lieu of being placed in each permit file folder.

10.10 Withdrawal for Consumption

Customs Form 7505 (Warehouse Withdrawal for Consumption-Duty Paid) in triplicate is used for bonded warehouse withdrawals for consumption. The required documents for a warehouse withdrawal for consumption are:

- A permit copy of CF7507A annotated by the broker as the permit to be used in delivery.
- Original annotated broker's copy of CF7501 (or a "certified true and correct") copy signed by the broker containing the annotated codes for the team.
- Duty check which must match the amount payable on the withdrawal, including user's fees. (The harmonized numbers and rates are the numbers in effect when the merchandise is withdrawn rather than when the warehouse entry was made.)
- Include any required documentation such as visas, textile declarations, and so on which were not included with the warehouse entry.
- If the country demands a visa, make sure that the visa number and the category number are on the CF7505 withdrawal.
- The importer number on CF7501 must be legible.
- Bottom right corner of CF7505 must have the signature of the withdrawer or the person with power of attorney.

Each withdrawal shall state the separate value of each package and the total dutiable value of the merchandise being withdrawn. Packages that are uniform in kind are not subject to listing the quantity, value and duty for each package, but show the lowest and highest numbers in the number series of such packages. Merchandise subject to quota or textiles and textile products subject to levels of restraint shall reflect any correction thereof reported after the filing of the warehouse entry. Items subject to internal revenue tax such as cigars, cigarettes or cigarette papers or tubes shall require the statement for tax purposes on the withdrawal form.

Estimated duties will be deposited on the withdrawal on the duty rate in effect at the time of withdrawal of the merchandise. The port director may increase or decrease the duty amount of estimated duties deposited on the final withdrawal to bring the aggregate amount of duties deposited into balance with the amount which he estimates will be due upon liquidation.

A permit for release of merchandise on Customs Form 7505-A is issued when the duties and other charges have been paid and all other requirement and regulations have been met. The Customs Form 7505-A is delivered to the person making the warehouse withdrawal. During the warehouse period, if there has been a manipulation to textiles and textile products subject to quota, visa, or export license requirements to alter the country of origin, exempt them from quota or visa or export license requirements other than a change brought about by statute, treaty executive order or presidential proclamation or from one textile category to another textile category, they may not be withdrawn from the warehouse for consumption.

10.11 Rewarehouse Entries

Merchandise that has been withdrawn and transferred from one port to another port may be entered for rewarehouse by the consignee stated in the withdrawal. The rewarehouse entry is on Customs Form 7501 in duplicate. An extra copy of the Customs Form 7501 annotated PERMIT may be required by the port director for use in the delivery of the merchandise to the warehouse. No declaration is required on the entry. Separate shipments consigned to the same consignee arriving at the same port may not be combined into one rewarehouse entry unless the warehouse withdrawals are from the same original warehouse entry.

A bond is needed on Customs Form 301 before a permit is issued on Customs Form 7501 for storage of merchandise in a bonded warehouse. No bond is needed if the merchandise is entered by the consignee on the original bond filed or if it is entered by a transferee who has rights to withdraw the merchandise and has already filed a bond. The duty in effect will be the duty chargeable under the rewarehouse entry except in cases that pertain to certain classes of merchandise excluded from liquidation of the original warehouse entry and merchandise on which rates of duty or tax are changed by an act of congress or by a proclamation by the president.

Examinations shall be made if necessary to identify the merchandise to determine shortages or for other purposes if deemed necessary. Rewarehouse entries not filed before the five day period after its arrival or any authorized extension shall be sent to the general order warehouse as unclaimed freight but will not be sold until the expiration of the original five year period which the merchandise is allowed to remain in the warehouse under bond. A protest may be filed against a liquidation at a rewarehouse entry port or against a refusal of the port director to liquidate the entry. A protest shall be filed against the original warehouse entry in all other cases.

In the case that a consignee wishes to enter for consumption merchandise withdrawn and transported to another port under bond, he may rewarehouse the merchandise and make an immediate withdrawal for consumption. This combined entry follows regular entry procedures with the following exceptions:

- Entry is made on Customs Form 7501 in four copies with one copy used as the permit. No declaration is required on the entry.
- Cigars, cigarettes or cigarette papers or tubes require an additional copy of the Customs Form 7501 marked "For Internal Revenue Purposes" when articles are subject to the Internal Revenue Service and tax is payable to Customs.
- Estimated duties, taxes, and other charges are deposited on presentation of the combined entry with the port director issuing a permit for release on Customs Form 7501.

10.12 Recordkeeping

The proprietor records all merchandise in a bonded warehouse in the inventory records using a bonded lot number. The annual reporting to the regional director within 45 days of the proprietor's end of business year.

The warehouse proprietor is expected to adhere to certain recordkeeping requirements. Automated operating and inventory control systems may be implemented by the proprietor if they are in support of Customs procedural requirements and do not adversely affect Customs supervision and control of warehouse activities and transactions. Records are to be kept in sufficient detail to enable Customs to easily determine the proprietor's compliance with these regulations and the correctness of the annual submission.

Recorded in the warehouse proprietor's accounting inventory records by bond lot number is all merchandise entered, manipulated, manufactured, smelted, refined, or removed from the bonded warehouse. All receipts, damage or shortage reports, manipulation requests, withdrawals, removals and blanket permit summaries are to be reported within two business days after the event occurs and stored in the permit file folder. Theft, suspected theft, overages, extraordinary shortages or damages (one percent or more of the value of the merchandise in an entry) after brought to the attention of the port director shall be reported within two business days. The responsible party for duties and taxes owed on thefts and shortages reported shall pay. Customs within 10 working days after discovery. Duties for multiple shortages may be consolidated and paid in one payment.

The permit file should be reviewed by the proprietor when final withdrawal of merchandise occurs relating to a specific warehouse entry, general order, or seizure. Review of the permit file is done to:

- Ensure that all necessary documentation is in the file folder accounting for the merchandise covered by the entry.
- Enable the proprietor to notify Customs of any merchandise covered by the entry which is not removed.
- File the final permit file folder with Customs in 30 business days after final withdrawal.

Except in the cases of a manufacturer involved in refining and smelting, a Customs Form 300 shall be filed by the warehouse proprietor with the Field Director, Regulatory Audit, within 45 days from the end of the business year. Records pertaining to merchandise not withdrawn during the general order period shall be kept in the permit file folder and submitted to the port director on receipt from Customs of the Customs Form 6043. The documents in the permit file folder may contain proprietary information which the proprietor or his employees shall not disclose. The information in the file shall be safeguarded and not disclosed to anyone other than the importer, importer's transferee, owner of the merchandise or the authorized agent. The proprietor's status as a bonded warehouse operator may be suspended or revoked if such unauthorized disclosure of proprietary information should occur.

Security and storage of the records and warehouse are:

- Supervision of all receipts, deliveries, sampling, recordkeeping, repacking, or manipulation of merchandise in a bonded warehouse shall be done by the proprietor.
- Permit file folders shall be maintained by the warehouse proprietor and kept in a secure place. These records shall be made available for inspection by Customs at reasonable hours.
- Adequate procedures to ensure security of the warehouse and the merchandise located within the bonded area must be established by the warehouse proprietor. The specific standard specifications should be met as long as they do not conflict with any local, state, or federal standard for the safe and sanitary storage of merchandise. If there are conflicting standards, the Federal standard shall prevail.

Damage to the merchandise should be minimized by safe and sanitary storage procedures. Storage of merchandise should not pose any hazards to persons and meet local, state, and federal requirements applicable to specific kinds of goods. Trash and waste shall be removed from the bonded area. Fires are not permitted except in the case of class 6, 7, or 8 warehouses where manipulation or processing is taking place. All aisles, doors, and entrances shall be left unblocked for access by Customs officers and warehouse personnel.

Storage of merchandise is recorded in the proprietor's inventory and accounting records according to their marks and numbers. Packages not identical in quantity or quality due to damage or loss shall be stored separately. The general order or warehouse entry number or seizure number and the date of general order or seizure shall be marked on all shipments for identification by the warehouse proprietor. Exception to this requirement is given in writing by the port director. Upon request by a Customs officer, the port director must provide a record balance of goods covered by any warehouse entry, general order or seizure in order to take a physical count to verify the accuracy of the record balance.

The proprietor of a manufacturing warehouse shall comply with all of the above. Additionally, the proprietor shall record all transfers from any storage area to a manufacturing area and record all transfers from a manufacturing area to a finished product storage area in the proprietor's inventory control and accounting records.

10.13 Materials for Use in Manufacturing Warehouses

Customs Form 7501 prepared in five copies is used for importing merchandise to be used in a bonded manufacturing warehouse. The entry is prepared at the port where such warehouse is located. Importations at a different port other than the location of the warehouse may be transferred under an immediate transportation without appraisement entry or warehouse withdrawal for transportation, whichever is applicable. A bond on file is necessary before the transfer of the merchandise can take place. Domestic merchandise for use in the manufacturing process is permitted in the bonded warehouse upon application to the port director in the following form:

APPLICATION TO RECEIVE FREE MATERIALS

Port of ________________________________, 19 _____ .

To the Port Director:

Application is hereby made to receive into the bonded manufacturing warehouse known as ______________, situated at ______________ the following described articles and materials:

Marks	Nos.	Description	Quantity	Value

____
(Signature)

To the warehouse proprietor in charge of the bonded manufacturing warehouse specified above:

The above described articles and materials are hereby permitted to be received into the warehouse in your charge, to be used therein in connection with the manufacture of articles as authorized by law.

____
Port Director

Merchandise subject to internal revenue tax is not used in connection with this form. Domestic spirits transferred from the bonded premises of a distilled spirits plant to a bonded manufacturing warehouse or for the transfer of domestic wines from a bonded wine cellar to a bonded manufacturing warehouse require a bond on Customs Form 301. All merchandise that internal revenue tax has not been paid used in the manufacture of articles shall be reported monthly to the port director by the proprietor of the warehouse. This statement shall represent each warehouse entry in the manufacturing process.

10.14 Withdrawal for Exportation of Articles Manufactured in Bond; Waste or Byproducts for Consumption

Articles received into a bonded manufacturing warehouse or articles manufactured therefrom shall not be withdrawn or removed except for direct exportation or transportation and exportation in bond to a foreign country. The only exception to the above are cigars manufactured in bond and supplies for vessels. Exportation is under Customs supervision in every case. Coverings or containers of imported articles or materials need not be exported but may be withdrawn from the warehouse for consumption on Customs Form 7505 upon payment of applicable duties for such coverings or containers in their conditions as withdrawn.

However, labels, coverings, or empty containers imported to be used in putting up the manufactured articles constitute articles or materials if subject to duty or tax and may be withdrawn for consumption with payment of all applicable duties and taxes. Wastes or byproducts are withdrawn for consumption on Customs Form 7505 modified as necessary and describing which imported material the waste and byproduct was produced.

The wholesale value of the waste or byproduct shall be appraised at the time of withdrawal in the principal markets of the country from which the material was imported. The withdrawal permit is issued on payment of the duty and proper credit given on the manufacturer's bond. A statement summary accompanies each withdrawal covering the items permitted for withdrawal showing each class of merchandise, quantity on hand in the account, quantity covered by the withdrawal presented, and the quantity remaining in the warehouse account. Articles withdrawn for exportation from a bonded manufacturing warehouse follow the same procedure for articles for exportation covering warehouse withdrawals except in the case of flour. Each copy of the Customs Form 7512 covering flour shall state:

> Produced from wheat imported after September 15, 1930, without payment of duty thereon. Must not be exported to Cuba without permission from the director of the port withdrawal.

For the sole purpose of immediate export, articles may be withdrawn for transportation and delivered to a bonded storage warehouse at an exterior port except for distilled spirits which may be withdrawn for transportation and delivery to any bonded storage warehouse for immediate export or withdrawal only. Withdrawals are executed on Customs Form 7512.

Rewarehouse entries may be made as long as supported by a bond on Customs Form 301. Transfers of domestic distilled spirits from a Customs bonded manufacturing warehouse, class 6, to a Customs bonded storage warehouse class 2 or 3 shall be rewarehoused. The manufacturer is the only person to withdraw merchandise manufactured in a bonded manufacturing warehouse or from a warehouse where the merchandise is stored awaiting direct exportation. The manufacturer may endorse on the face of the withdrawal thus transferring the right of withdrawal to another party. Within six months from the date of demand by the port director, proof of manufacture and exportation shall be filed in the case of each transaction or period of manufacture, a statement certified by the warehouse proprietor showing the date and number of the bond, the quantity and identity of the dutiable or taxable merchandise used, and the quantity and description of the articles into which it has been manufactured.

Quantities of any byproducts and waste produced must accompany the proof of manufacture. Articles manufactured with the use of distilled spirits shall have a statement verified by the foreman or chemist of the factory showing the number of packages of spirits used, the marks and numbers, the number of wine, proof and taxable gallons, and the degree of proof. The bond given by the manufacturer shall be canceled when all of the products, waste, and byproducts have been exported or released for consumption. Shortages, irregular delivery, and nondelivery of merchandise while in transit under bond withdrawn from a bonded manufacturing warehouse shall be charged against the bonded carrier.

10.15 Duty-free Stores

Merchandise that is conditionally duty-free to be exported by individuals departing the Customs territory may be stored in a class 9 warehouse (duty-free store). Conditionally duty-free merchandise in duty-free stores means that no duty and/or internal revenue tax (when applicable) is paid on articles sold. Such articles shall accompany the person in the same vehicle which they are departing the country. Class 9 warehouses are located within the same port of entry from which a purchaser of duty-free merchandise departs the Customs territory or within 25 miles from the exit point through which the purchaser departs the Customs territory. The exit point refers to an area in close proximity to an actual exit for departing from Customs territory. This includes the gate holding area in the case of an airport only if there is reasonable assurance that the merchandise purchased from duty-free store will be exported from the Customs territory. Exit points by land or sea are the points at which a departing individual has no practical alternative to depart the Customs territory or return to the Customs territory by passing through a U.S. Customs inspection facility. A duty-free store or class 9 warehouse with multiple locations will be treated as one location if:

- The proper on-hand balance of each inventory item in each storage location, delivery cart or other conveyance or noncontiguous location can be provided by the proprietor to Customs upon demand
- The recordkeeping system is centralized so that a sale from any location automatically reduces the sale quantity by location from centralized inventory

Proprietors of class 9 warehouses shall display in a prominent place signs that state clearly that any conditionally duty-free merchandise purchased from the store has not been subjected to any U.S. federal duty or tax, must be declared and is subject to U.S. federal duty and tax if brought back into the United States and is subject to customs laws and regulations of any foreign country to which it is taken. If state, local, or other governmental authority decides that another form of approval is necessary for export or transfer of duty free merchandise, the operator of a duty-free store must demonstrate to the port director that the concession or approval required has been obtained.

10.16 Introduction to Temporary Importation Bonds

Importers can enter certain goods duty free through the Temporary Importation under Bond program. The importation must be deemed "temporary" and the importer must be willing to submit a bond to U.S. Customs to ensure its compliance with the Temporary Importation Bond (TIB) rules. Articles imported temporarily into the United States are exempt from duty under Chapter 98, Subchapter XIII. This tariff provision is routinely used by companies temporarily importing items such as theatrical effects, tools of the trade, samples, motion picture films, and items brought into the United States for repair or alteration.

10.17 Entry

The importer must carefully comply with the TIB entry requirements. First, the importer needs to include the particular product, the Harmonized Tariff Schedule of the United States (HTSUS) subheading number for the merchandise, and the HTSUS number from Chapter 98. The importer must submit both a declaration stating that the items imported will not be put up for sale in the United States and a statement to the customs port director of the actual use for the merchandise.

The TIB can be renewed for two consecutive periods of one year each if merchandise is to remain in the United States for a longer period of time. Extensions are granted by the port director on Customs Form 3173. Merchandise for which no extension is filed must be exported or destroyed within the one-year period. The importer needs to meet certain criteria to apply for special tariff treatment under this provision.

10.18 Exportation

Articles entered free of duty under Chapter 98, Subchapter XIII, can be exported at the port of entry or another port. Application to export the merchandise is made on Customs Form 3495, allowing sufficient time for inspection of the merchandise if deemed necessary. In such an event, the applicant will be notified on Customs Form 3495 of the location to move the merchandise if inspection is necessary prior to export. Export from a port other than the port of entry requires Customs Form 3495 to be filed in triplicate along with a certified copy of the import entry or a certified copy of the invoice used on entry. The merchandise is transported to another port using a transportation and exportation entry.

Customs must supervise the export if the merchandise is exported by mail or parcel post. Exportation is suspended for articles that cannot be exported due to seizure, other than by private persons, for the duration of the seizure. Exportation takes place promptly after release of the merchandise. Merchandise exported without complying with U.S. Customs regulations is subject to liquidated damages.

10.19 Entry Under Bond

Entry is made for TIB merchandise on Customs Form 3461 or on Form 7533. Customs Form 7501 is filed within ten days of the date of entry. The entry invoice describes each article in detail, includes any marks, numbers, or distinguishing characteristics, and provides the value of the merchandise. In the case of vehicles, aircraft, or pleasure boats, the registration number, engine or motor number, and the body number must also be included.

10.20 Bond

The importer provides a bond on Customs Form 301 for the import. The bond is equal to double the amount of duties that would be due if a regular consumption entry were filed. A bond for 110% of the estimated duties is put forth for samples solely for use in order taking entered under Subheading 9813.00.20, motion picture advertising films entered under Subheading 9813.00.25, and professional equipment, tools of the trade, and repair components for equipment or tools entered under 9813.00.50.

Surety or cash deposit for surety is waived if the merchandise is entered without a formal entry or if the amount of the bond is less than $25.00. No bond or security is required for entry under Chapter 98, Subheading XIII. Such articles are tools of the trade, equipment for the press or for sound or television broadcasting, cinematographic equipment, or articles for sports purposes or display or demonstration purposes, imported into the United States by a resident of Canada or Mexico, and are goods of Canadian or Mexican origin. The articles are released to the importer after the acceptance of the entry and the bond. The entry is not liquidated.

10.21 Models of Women's Wearing Apparel

Women's wearing apparel imported under a TIB cannot be removed from the importer's premises and can be used solely for order taking. Invoices for such merchandise include a detailed description of the articles, including information about the lining and the application of the trim, as well as the total value of the garments.

10.22 Theatrical Effects and Other Articles

Motion picture advertising films under Subheading 9813.00.20 and equipment or tools under 9813.00.50 HTSUS do not require formal entry and can be entered on the importer's baggage statement. However, a bond is still necessary for the merchandise to protect the revenue of the United States if any merchandise is not exported or destroyed in the allotted one-year time period or a renewal is filed. If the articles imported exceed $500.00 in value, a separate invoice describing the merchandise is required upon entry and clearance of the merchandise as passenger's baggage.

Scenery, properties, and apparel of the proprietor or manager of a theatrical exhibit traveling to contiguous countries is permitted as long as the travel is executed within the time period during which the merchandise is approved to be in the U.S. Customs Territory under bond, including any extensions. A copy of the entry for the merchandise is deemed as permission to reenter the merchandise into the U.S. Customs territory upon return.

10.23 Vehicles, Pleasure Boats, and Aircraft

Vehicles such as boats, automobiles, and motorcycles may be entered as passenger baggage as long as only one is imported. If two or more are imported at the same time, a formal entry must be filed, as well as a bond with surety or cash deposit in lieu of surety, in case the importer defaults on the bond conditions.

10.24 Default on Bond/Cancellation of Bond

Large and small bonds are handled in different manners. The Fines, Penalties and Forfeiture office handles claims that do not exceed $100,000. The Director, International Trade Compliance Division, Office of Regulations and Rulings, handles claims that exceed $100,000.

(a) Canceling Liability

The liability of payment of liquidated damages may be canceled under a TIB under one of three circumstances.

(i) Export. The Fines, Penalties and Forfeitures group is furnished with evidence that the article would have been entered free of duty as a domestic product exported and returned.

(ii) Destruction. Export or destruction of the merchandise has taken place under Customs' supervision, but not within the period of time the merchandise was in the United States under bond. A lesser penalty may be imposed if deemed appropriate under the law and in view of the circumstances. The Fines, Penalties and Forfeiture Officer may decide to eliminate the collection of liquidated damages if the officer finds that the delay for destruction of the merchandise was for the benefit of the United States or due to circumstances reasonably beyond the control of the importer that could not have been anticipated.

(iii) Extend Time. Export or destruction of the merchandise without Customs' supervision past the period allowed by law for the merchandise to be in the United States should be supported with satisfactory documentation, such as a foreign landing certificate, along with a complete explanation by the importer of the failure to obtain Customs' supervision. Payment of a lesser amount, as deemed appropriate by the Fines, Penalties and Forfeiture Officer is permitted if the officer is convinced that the merchandise was exported or destroyed under circumstances that precluded any arrangement of Customs' supervision.

(iv) Liquidation. Payment of liquidated damages in the amount of double the duty is taken into account if the merchandise has been entered under a consumption entry or is equal to 110% of the duties. The liquidation provision applies to motion picture films, tools of the trade, professional equipment, and repair components if this amount is considered to be less than the full amount of the bond.

(b) Ending the Bond

For an importer that complies with part of the bond conditions, a petition for relief of liquidated damages may be executed. If double the duty or 110% of the duty does not exceed $100,000, the Fines, Penalties and Forfeitures Officer has the power to cancel the liability. The Officer may cancel the liability for the payment upon the payment of an amount equal to double the duty or 110% of the duty. This provision applies as long as there was no intent to defraud the revenue or delay the payment of duty.

An importer anticipating default on a temporary importation bond should notify Customs in writing before the bond period has expired. At the time of written notification, the importer should pay to Customs the full amount of liquidated damages that would be assessed at the time of default of the bond. The entry is then considered closed. The importer should notify the surety in writing of the default and the payment.

Cash deposits made in lieu of a surety are refunded to the person whose name is on the entry upon exportation in compliance with the Customs regulations. If the merchandise is to remain in the United States under an extension permissible by law, or if the merchandise is not exported or destroyed within the applicable time period, the cash deposit is transferred to liquidated damages unless a written application for relief from payment of the full liquidated damages is filed with the port director within 60 days after the date of the notice.

CHAPTER 11

Import Quotas

Peter W. Klestadt
David M. Murphy

11.1 Introduction
11.2 Entitlement to Entry
11.3 Quota Status Information
11.4 Miscellaneous Quotas
 (a) Safeguards
 (b) Import Licenses
11.5 Textiles and Apparel
 (a) Background
 (b) Special Access Program/Guaranteed Access Levels
 (c) Mexico Quotas
  (i) Quota Elimination
  (ii) Special Regime Goods
  (iii) Safeguards
 (d) Tariff Preference Levels (TPLs): Canada and Mexico
 (e) Administration
 (f) Cotton Fiber
 (g) Quota Status and Specific Information

11.1 Introduction

Quotas have been explicitly renounced by most trading nations in international trade agreements. Despite these lofty aspirations, the United States and most of its trading partners have clung to use of quotas for a number of economic and political reasons. There is a trend to simplify, reduce, and eliminate certain quotas; however, the use of quotas and import licenses is likely to continue through the next century. Generally, as a result of the North American Free Trade Agreement (NAFTA), import quotas applicable to originating goods from Canada and Mexico are not subject to the quotas discussed in this chapter.

The U.S. Customs Service administers a broad array of quota restrictions and import licensing requirements established under a number of specific statutes and international agreements, primarily designed to protect domestic industry from import competition. These quotas, as to produce and agricultural products, sugar, beef, and apparel, are generally reflected in the Chapter Notes or headings of the Harmonized Tariff Schedule of the United States (HTSUS) applicable to the product, or in Chapter 99 of the HTSUS. Chapter 99 also contains additional duties, agricultural safeguards under the Uruguay Round, and other import restrictions under miscellaneous trade legislation.[1]

Some quota limits are omitted from the Harmonized Tariff Schedule (HTS), such as for apparel and textiles. While the relevant textile category is reflected in HTSUS, the quantities under quota are omitted.

Quotas fall into two classes: absolute or tariff-rate. Absolute quotas are those that impose a specific annual quantitative limit on importations. Once that quota limit amount has been imported, no further merchandise can be imported during the relevant quota period. Quotas may be global or country-specific allocations or a combination of both. Absolute quotas exist for the importation of certain apparel and textiles.[2]

In keeping with the lofty ideas of removal of quotas, the Uruguay Round of the General Agreements on Tariffs and Trade (GATT, 1994) provided for the "tariffication" of quotas. Thus, many formerly absolute quotas on agricultural products were supplanted by tariff-rate quotas (TRQ).[3] Tariff-rate quotas provide a specific quantitative limit on importations at the normal or Most Favored Nation duty rate (i.e., the in-quota rate).[4]

Once the specified quantity has been imported, all additional quantities are subject to a higher over-quota duty rate. This over-quota duty rate may vary with the value or quantities imported. While in theory the tariff-rate quota allows imports above an absolute level, the over-quota duty rates are almost uniformly prohibitive, effectively precluding importation of merchandise above the specified in-quota amounts.

11.2 Entitlement to Entry

Quota allocations are charged at the time of entry. Thus, at the time of entry, the available quota amount is reduced by the quantity entered. The time of presentation of the consumption entry establishes the entry's quota priority[5] for allocation of a portion of the available quota allotment.

---

[1] 7 U.S.C. § 624 (Agricultural Adjustment Act).

[2] 19 C.F.R. § 132.1(a).

[3] Pub. L. No. 103-465.

[4] 19 C.F.R. § 132.1(b).

[5] 19 C.F.R. § 132.1(f).

Presentation is a term of art as it pertains to quota merchandise.[6] Generally, presentation occurs when the withdrawal for consumption from the bonded warehouse or consumption entry is filed in proper form with estimated duties attached.[7] If the entry is presented prior to the filling of the quota, the entry attains quota status, allowing entry of the merchandise within the absolute quota or entry at the in-quota rate for a tariff-rate quota.[8] If an absolute quota fills prior to the presentation of the entry in the United States, the shipment will not be released to the importer until the next quota period opens.[9] If a tariff-rate quota fills prior to the presentation of the entry in the United States, the shipment will be released to the importer subject to the higher duty rate.[10]

A consumption entry of quota merchandise may be submitted for review, without estimated duties, before the merchandise arrives within the port limit.[11] For prefiled entries, official presentation occurs upon the deposit of estimated duties after the merchandise arrives within the port.

If a number of entries that will fill the quota are deemed to be presented simultaneously prior to the close of a quota, those entries will receive the same quota priority and a proration of the available quota.[12] Thus, a portion of the merchandise under each of the entries will be permitted entry under the quota.

Where a quota will immediately fill upon opening of the quota period, all consumption entries, with estimated duties attached, may not be presented prior to 12 noon, Eastern Standard Time, in all ports on the days of opening of the quota period.[13] This provides all importers an equal opportunity to enter the merchandise. In some cases, all entries of merchandise for this quota may be filed prior to that time and will be deemed to be presented simultaneously with the opening of the quota.[14] Where the entries are presented simultaneously, Customs will prorate the quota allocation applicable to the entries if necessary.[15]

When a quota fills prior to presentation of an entry, the merchandise under that entry may be held in a Customs bonded warehouse or foreign trade zone pending the reopening of quota, reexported, or destroyed under Customs' supervision.[16] In addition, where the quota is a tariff-rate quota and the quota closes prior to presentation of the entry, the merchandise may be entered at the higher rate of duty.

---

[6] 19 C.F.R. §§ 134.1(d), 132.11(a), (d).

[7] *Id.*

[8] 19 C.F.R. § 132.1(g).

[9] 19 C.F.R. § 132.13(a)(1)(ii).

[10] 19 C.F.R. § 132.13(a)(1)(i).

[11] 19 C.F.R. §§ 132.11(a), (b); 132.12(a).

[12] 19 C.F.R. § 132.13(1)(iii).

[13] 19 C.F.R. § 132.12(a).

[14] 19 C.F.R. § 132.12(b).

[15] 19 C.F.R. § 132.12(c).

[16] 19 C.F.R. § 132.5(c).

11.3 Quota Status Information

Generally, information on the status or fill rates of most quotas may be obtained from the United States Customs Service. U.S. Customs issues a weekly quota status report for commodities, other than textiles, covering agricultural commodities and sugar. The report may be obtained through the Customs' Electronic Bulletin Board (BBS:703-440-6155; Voice: 703-440-6236), and it is anticipated that the report ultimately will be available on U.S. Customs' Web site (http://www.ustreas.gov/treasury/bureaus/customs/). In addition, inquiries may be directed to the local port of importation or to Customs Headquarters Quota Branch (202-927-5850). This information is also reprinted by a number of private sources and trade associations and is available for a fee.

11.4 Miscellaneous Quotas

The quotas employed under the U.S. trade laws are numerous and diverse. These quotas are sprinkled throughout the HTSUS Chapter and Section Notes. Exhibit 11.1 provides a listing of those quotas that appear in the HTSUS and references to where they appear. The specific restrictions are also set forth in Chapter 99 of the HTSUS. These quotas are all tariff-rate quotas and generally do not apply to products of Canada and Mexico. Some provide for simple global in-quota quantities; others are specifically allocated to specific countries. In the latter situation, imports of the products from countries without a quota allocation will subject them to the over-quota duty rates given if the quota has not or will not be fully utilized. Review the specific chapter and heading of the imported article to assure the quota is or is not applicable.

(a) Safeguards

The United States and other World Trade Organization (WTO) members adopted certain safeguards as tariff-rate quotas under GATT 1994 in the form of duties that are in addition to the high over-quota duty rates. There are two types of safeguards: trigger volume and trigger price.

A trigger volume safeguard may be applied whenever the imports of a commodity exceed a given quantity, that is, the trigger volume. A trigger volume safeguard is an additional duty that does not exceed one-third the ordinary Customs duty applicable to the merchandise. The trigger volume quantity is to be reset annually.

A trigger price safeguard may be applied whenever the imported commodity is imported at a price below a given price threshold, that is, the trigger price. The trigger price is fixed and is not adjusted annually. The additional trigger price safeguard duties increase as the difference between the trigger price and the import price increases.

For some products, Chapter 99 of the HTSUS provides for both trigger volume and trigger price safeguards. However, a single product may not be subject to both safeguards during the same period.[17]

---

[17]HTSUS 9904.18.09-18 (chocolate).

Exhibit 11.1

HTSUS QUOTAS AND SOURCES

Agricultural Products Subject to Quota	Primary Harmonized Tariff Classification
Beef, described in Additional U.S. Note 3 to Chapter 2	Various Subheadings under Headings 0201 and 0202
Milk and cream, fluid or frozen, fresh or sour, containing over 6% but not over 45% butterfat, described in Additional U.S. Note 5 to Chapter 4	0401.30.05, 0403.90.04
Butter and fresh or sour cream containing over 45 percent butterfat, described in Additional U.S. Note 6 to Chapter 4	0401.30.50, .75, 0403.90.74, 0405.00.20
Dried milk, whether or not sweetened, described in Additional U.S. Notes 7–9 to Chapter 4	0402.10.10, 0402.21.05, 0402.21.30, 0403.90.51, 0402.21.75, 0403.90.61
Dairy products, described in Additional U.S. Note 1 to Chapter 4 and as described in Additional U.S. Note 10 to Chapter 4 (including malted milk, margarine, and other articles)	Various Subheadings under Headings 0402, 0403, 0404, 1517, 1704, 1806, 1901, 2105, 2106, and 2202
Milk and cream, condensed or evaporated, described in Additional U.S. Note 11 to Chapter 4	0402.91.10, 0402.91.30, 0402.99.10, 0402.99.30
Dried milk, dried cream, and dried whey, whether or not sweetened, described in Additional U.S. Note 12 to Chapter 4	0403.90.41, 0404.10.50
Butter substitutes containing over 45% butterfat, described in Additional U.S. Note 14 to Chapter 4, and butter oil	0405.00.60, 2106.90.34, and other subheadings
Cheese and cheese substitutes, described in Additional U.S. Note 16 to Chapter 4	0406.10.04, 0406.10.84, 0406.20.89, 0406.3089, 0406.90.95
Blue-mold cheese, described in Additional U.S. Note 17 to Chapter 4	0406.10.14, 0406.20.24, 0406.20.61, 0406.30.14, 0406.40.54, 0406.4058, 0406.90.72
Cheddar cheese and cheese and cheese substitutes containing or processed from Cheddar cheese, described in Additional U.S. Note 18 to Chapter 4	0406.10.24, 0406.20.31, 0406.20.65, 0406.30.24, 0406.30.65, 0406.90.08, 0406.90.76
American-type cheese, including Colby, described in Additional U.S. Note 19 to Chapter 4	0406.10.34, 0406.20.36, 0406.20.69, 0406.30.34, 0406.30.69, 0406.90.52, 0406.90.82

Exhibit 11.1 (*Continued*)

HTSUS QUOTAS AND SOURCES

Agricultural Products Subject to Quota	Primary Harmonized Tariff Classification
Edam and Gouda cheese and cheese and substitutes for cheese containing or processed therefrom, described in Additional U.S. Note 20	0406.10.44, 0406.20.44, 0406.20.73, 0406.30.44, 0406.30.73, 0406.90.16, 0406.90.86
Italian-type cheeses, described in Additional U.S. Note 21 to Chapter 4	0406.10.54, 0406.20.51, 0406.20.77, 0406.30.77, 0406.90.31, 0406.90.36, 0406.90.41, 0406.90.66
Swiss and Emmentaler cheese other than with eye formation, Gruyere cheese, and cheese and substitutes for cheese containing or processed from such cheeses, described in Additional U.S. Note 22 to Chapter 4	0406.10.64, 0406.20.81, 0406.30.51, 0406.30.81, 0406.90.34
Cheese and substitutes for cheese containing 0.5% or less butterfat (except Note 25 to Chapter 4), described in Additional U.S. Note 22 to Chapter 4	0406.10.64, 0406.20.81, 0406.30.51, 0406.30.81, 0406.90.90
Stilton cheese, the product of the U.K., described in Additional U.S. Note 24 to Chapter 4	0406.20.15, 0406.30.05, 0406.40.44, 0406.40.48
Swiss and Emmentaler cheese with eye formation, described in Additional U.S. Note 25 to Chapter 4	0406.90.46
Green olives	0711.20.18.28, 200.70.102-23
Peanuts, described in Additional U.S. Note 2(b) to Chapter 12	1202.10.40, 1202.20.40, 2008.11.25, 2008.11.45
Tuna and skipjack (not in oil)	1604.14.30
Anchovies	1604.16.10.30
Raw cane sugar, described in Additional U.S. Note 5 to Chapter 17	1701.11.10
Sugars, syrups, and molasses other than raw cane sugar, described in Additional U.S. Note 5 to Chapter 17	1701.12.10, 1701.91.10, 1701.99.10, 1702.90.10, 2106.90.44
Blended syrups containing sugars, described in Additional U.S. Notes 4 and 9 to Chapter 17	Various Subheadings under Headings 1701, 1702, 2106
Articles containing over 65% sugar, described in Additional U.S. Notes 2 and 7(b) to Chapter 17	Various Subheadings under Headings 1701, 1702, 1704, 1806, 1901, 2101, and 2106
Articles containing over 10% sugar, described in Additional U.S. Notes 3 and 8 to Chapter 17	Various Subheadings under Headings 1701, 1702, 1704, 1806, 1901, 2101, 2103, and 2106

Exhibit 11.1 (*Continued*)

HTSUS QUOTAS AND SOURCES

Agricultural Products Subject to Quota	Primary Harmonized Tariff Classification
Cocoa powder containing over 10% sugar, described in Additional U.S. Note 1 to Chapter 18	1806.10.10, 1806.10.34, 1806.10.15
Chocolate containing over 5.5% butterfat, described in Additional U.S. Note 2 to Chapter 18	1806.20.24, 1806.32.04, 1806.90.15
Chocolate and low-fat chocolate crumb containing 5.5% or less butterfat, described in Additional U.S. Note 3 to Chapter 18	1806.0.34, 1806.20.85, 1806.32.14, 1806.90.25
Infant formula, described in Additional U.S. Note 2 to Chapter 19	1901.10.15, 1901.10.60
Mixes and doughs, described in Additional U.S. Note 2 to Chapter 19	1901.20.30, 1901.20.65
Peanut butter and paste, described in Additional U.S. Note 5 to Chapter 20	2008.11.05
Satsumas	2008.30.42-55
Mixed condiments and seasonings, described in Additional U.S. Notes 3 and 4 to Chapter 23	2103.90.74
Ice cream, described in Additional U.S. Notes 5 to Chapter 21	2105.00.10
Animal feed containing milk or milk derivatives, described in Additional U.S. Note 2 to Chapter 23	2309.90.24, 2309.90.44
Tobacco, described in Additional U.S. Note 5 to Chapter 24	2401.10.63, 2401.20.33, 2401.20.85, 2401.30.33, 2401.30.35, 2401.30.57, 2403.10.60, 2403.91.45, 2403.99.60

Only over-quota entries are subject to additional safeguards duties. Thus, the safeguard duties have the effect of increasing the over-quota duty rate. The safeguard additional duties are set forth in Subchapter IV of Chapter 99 of the HTS and are also referenced in the subheadings applicable to particular products or the primary chapters providing for the articles. Quota products subject to safeguards are highlighted.

(b) Import Licenses

Several dairy quotas (primarily for cheese) are administered through import licenses issued by the U.S. Department of Agriculture. In these situations, no person may enter certain dairy products at the low in-quota duty rate without an import license.[18] These licenses are specific as to type and quantity of merchandise that may be imported. Requests for information concerning dairy licensing can be directed to U.S. Department of Agriculture, Import Policies and Program Division, Foreign Agricultural Service, 14th and Independence S.W., Washington, D.C. 20250 (202-720-2916).[19]

11.5 Textiles and Apparel

(a) Background

Textiles and apparel are subject to absolute quota limits, which are country of origin-specific. The specific country quota allocations do not appear in the HTSUS. Prior to January 1, 1995, nearly 90% of the U.S. imports of textiles and apparel were subject to quotas imposed under the Multi-fiber Arrangement with over 45 countries. Imports of apparel and textiles "originating" from Canada and Mexico are not subject to these quotas but are subject to a number of different restraints.

The HTSUS classification applicable to a textile or apparel product carries a three-digit textile category designation if it is subject to quota. The category designations represent the grouping of the hundreds of textile and apparel products classified under the HTSUS into a more limited set of approximately 167 categories. These categories were developed by an interagency committee consisting of members from the Departments of Commerce, State, Labor, Treasury and Office of the Trade Representative. The Committee on the Implementation of Textile Agreements (CITA) monitors and enforces the various existing bilateral and multilateral agreements relating to the importation of textiles and apparel into the United States. CITA directs U.S. Customs to take actions under these agreements.

Many textiles categories are defined in *Guidelines for Reporting of Imported Products in Various Textile and Apparel Categories*[20] and subsequent updates issued by Customs and CITA. Each exporting country, through a bilateral agreement, may have some of all of the 167 textile categories subdivided into parts or subparts covering more specific classes of merchandise, and each having a specific quality limitation. In addition, the bilateral agreement may merge a number of categories into a group covering a wider class of merchandise subject to a broad overall limitation.

These quotas originate from the Multi-fiber Arrangement Regarding International Trade in Textiles (MFA). The MFA created an international system between textile and apparel importing and exporting countries. Under the MFA umbrella, a series of bilateral agreements were executed by the United States and the major

---

[18]7 C.F.R. § 6.23

[19]7 C.F.R. Pt. 6.

[20]CIE 13/88, November 23, 1988.

textile exporting countries, which set quantitative limits (absolute quotas) on textile and apparel exports to the United States. The terms and conditions of the agreements with specific countries vary. Most agreements are comprehensive, covering all commercial shipments of textiles or textile products of cotton, wool, silk blend, man-made, or vegetable fibers. However, several agreements, in particular those with newer textile source countries, are limited in the products they cover.

In addition, in the absence of a bilateral textile agreement on the specific merchandise from a specific country, the United States may unilaterally impose a quota where imports are causing, or there is an actual threat to cause, serious disruption to the U.S. industry. These "calls" are usually followed by negotiation and adoption of a bilateral textile agreement setting the new quota.

As part of the Uruguay Round of the GATT, the Agreement on Trade in Textiles and Clothing (ATTC) was concluded. Beginning January 1, 1995, the MFA will be gradually superseded. For members of the new World Trade Organization (WTO), bilateral agreements will expire and will be subject to new restraints under the ATTC. Restraints on MFA-covered products will be integrated into the ATTC.

Two major textile and apparel exporting countries, Taiwan and China, are not members of the WTO as of January 1, 1997. As a result, with respect to imports from these countries, and all other non-WTO members, quotas will administered pursuant to bilateral agreements as they were under the MFA. If and/or when these countries accede to the WTO, the ATTC restraints will be phased-in, generally over a longer period of time.

Fifty-one percent of all textile quotas established pursuant to the MFA will be phased out over ten years in three consecutive stages. Sixteen % of textile and apparel imports were integrated on January 1, 1995; an additional 17% will be integrated on January 1, 1998; and on January 1, 2002, an additional 18% must be integrated. Products were selected from the ATTC's four required groups: clothing, fabric, made-up textile products, and yarn. At the end of the ten-year period, the remaining 49% must be integrated. The United States' list of products to be integrated under the ATTC in the first stage of the integration process did not contain any items that were currently subject to MFA quotas.[21] It appears that approximately 88% of quota merchandise will not be integrated until the final phase of integration, which will begin on January 1, 2005.

Once integrated into the ATTC, products cannot be subjected to quotas with respect to WTO member countries except in accordance with WTO rules. These rules generally forbid bilateral quota agreements and other discriminatory, country-specific restraints. However, some form of global quota is still possible after completion of the ten-year phase-out period.

The ATTC establishes a supranational body known as the Textile Monitoring Body (TMB) to supervise implementation of the Agreement. This body replaces the Textile Surveillance Body (TSB). The TMB will hear any disputes on the implementation of the ATTC. For example, the TMB and WTO reviewed and issued

[21]This list was published on October 13, 1994 (59 Fed. Reg. 51,942). The balance of products to be integrated at the various stages was published on May, 1, 1995 (60 Fed. Reg. 21,075).

a report on the United States' imposition of cotton and man-made fiber quotas on goods from Costa Rica. In addition, the newly established Council for Trade in Goods will review the implementation of the ATTC before the end of each stage of the phase-out.

(b) Special Access Program/Guaranteed Access Levels

Beginning in 1986, under the auspices of the Caribbean Basin Initiative (CBI), Caribbean beneficiary countries entered into agreements with the United States, creating guaranteed access levels (GALs) for apparel products in specialized quota categories. The GAL is separate from any applicable Specific Limit (SL) imposed with respect to the category.

GALs are subject to two unique rules. First, a GAL can be increased at the request of the exporting country upon a showing of production capacity sufficient to serve the increase. Second, articles eligible for a GAL will not be embargoed. Even if shipments of eligible products exceed the GAL, the United States will not take any action to restrict further importations.

The United States reserves the technical right to impose restrictions in the event of actual or threatened market disruption. As a practical matter, however, the GALs are a complicated fiction; they are really not limits at all. Customs does not even monitor quantities imported under GALs. The program therefore affords virtually unlimited access to the United States market for products meeting its requirements. Importers must nevertheless obtain visa documentation in the country of exportation and are subject to the jurisdiction of CITA, which monitors the quota agreements under which the GALs are created.

To qualify for the Special Access Program, a garment must be assembled from U.S. cut and formed fabric. The fabric itself must be woven or knitted in the United States (but it can be woven or knitted from foreign yarn). It does not suffice merely to cut the fabric in the United States, as is otherwise the case for the allowance in an ordinary 9802 assembly program.

Findings and trim incorporated in the garment do not have to be of U.S. origin, provided they do not exceed 25% of the cost of the components of the assembled product. However, findings and trim are narrowly defined to include only sewing thread, hooks and eyes, snaps, buttons, bow buds, decorative lace trim, elastic strips, zippers (including zipper tapes), and labels. Significantly, the definition has been defined so as to exclude fabric interlinings or pocketing.

The U.S. bona fides of the fabric must be certified through use of Form ITA-370P. The first part of the form, entitled "Shipper's Declaration," requires the importer to certify (on pain of civil and criminal penalties, forfeiture, seizure and sale, and prohibition from further participation in the program) that the fabric parts were cut in the United States from fabric formed in the United States. This Shipper's Declaration must be filed with Customs and verified by a Customs officer prior to the loading of the cut parts on an exporting carrier for shipment to the country of assembly. Documents supporting the information shown on the form, such as invoices, cutting documents, or signed affidavits by suppliers, must be retained in the U.S. company's files.

The second part of Form ITA-370P is an Assembler's Declaration, on which the foreign assembler certifies that he performed assembling, manufacturing, or processing operations. The third part of the form is an Importer's Declaration. The importer is required to certify, subject to serious consequences, that the imported finished goods were assembled from the qualifying components and otherwise meet the requirements of the program.

The completed Form ITA-370P is filed with Customs as part of the importer's entry package. The information as to the description and quantities of the finished goods must correspond with the description of the parts. The importer signing the Importer's Declaration and the shipper signing the Shipper's Declaration must be the same firm.

Seven countries presently participate with the United States in the Special Access program: Costa Rica, the Dominican Republic, El Salvador, Guatemala, Haiti, Honduras, and Jamaica. Other eligible countries can be expected to participate when and as the United States seeks to impose quota restraints with respect to their products.

(c) Mexico Quotas

The North American Free Trade Agreement (NAFTA) formally established a free trade area comprising Canada, Mexico, and the United States. NAFTA immediately eliminated quotas on textile and apparel from Mexico to the extent that they are considered originating goods under NAFTA's origin rules; however, non-originating apparel from Mexico remains subject to textile and apparel quotas for the meantime.

Nevertheless, exemptions from quota are presently available for Special Regime and 9802 production, as well as certain other non-originating goods. Indeed, the greatest preferential treatment (i.e., immediate elimination of all duties and quotas) is available to Special Regime goods, which need not necessarily qualify as originating goods.

Articles assembled abroad from U.S. components are entitled to a duty exemption on the value of the U.S. components under heading 9802.00.80 of the Harmonized Tariff Schedule of the United States (HTSUS). Production utilizing this exemption is popularly referred to as "807 production," after the item number for the exemption under the prior tariff schedules. Mexico is the source of significant 807 apparel production involving the assembly by sewing U.S. cut garment parts. The Special Regime is a program similar to the Special Access Program under which, prior to NAFTA, certain 807 merchandise assembled in Mexico from U.S.-formed and cut fabric (i.e., fabric of U.S. origin that is cut into garment parts in the United States) was afforded almost unlimited access to the U.S. market under U.S. textile quotas. NAFTA significantly expands the coverage and benefits of the Special Regime.

(i) Quota Elimination. Effective January 1, 1994, quotas were eliminated on all originating goods. Between Mexico and the United States, quotas on non-originating goods are eliminated in each of three staging categories, as follows:[22]

---

[22]Numbers in parentheses are quota category numbers.

- *Staging Category 1.* Quotas were eliminated, effective January 1, 1994, on cotton and man-made fiber men's and boys' coats (334/634), women's and girls' cotton coats (335), cotton and man-made fiber dresses (336/636), cotton and man-made fiber woven blouses (341/641), cotton and man-made fiber skirts (342/642), cotton and man-made fiber pajamas and nightwear (351/651), cotton and man-made fiber underwear (352/652), cotton and man-made fiber coveralls (359-C/659-C), women's and girls' wool coats (435), and women's and girls' man-made fiber coats (635).
- *Staging Category 2.* Quotas will be eliminated, effective January 1, 2001, on cotton and man-made fiber knit shirts and blouses (338/339/638/639), cotton and man-made fiber woven shirts (340/640), cotton and man-made fiber trousers and pants (347/348/647/648), men's and boys' man-made fiber suit-type coats (633), and men's and boys man-made fiber suits (643).
- *Staging Category 3.* Quotas will be eliminated, effective January 1, 2004, on men's and boys' wool suit-type coats (433) and men's and boys' wool suits (443).

The United States has not established or maintained any quotas on apparel products from Canada, except for Tariff Preference Levels (TPLs) established under the CFTA and increased under NAFTA.

(ii) Special Regime Goods. NAFTA provided that all duties and quotas on Special Regime goods were eliminated effective January 1, 1994. Special Regime goods are those articles assembled in Mexico as 807 production from fabric wholly formed and cut in the United States. A new HTSUS subheading 9802.00.90 was added, effective January 1, 1994, for articles covered by this program.

Prior to NAFTA, the Special Regime was merely a quota preference program, and the preference was afforded only to selected quota categories. Qualifying garments enjoyed special quota status (i.e., they were guaranteed access), but were dutiable to the same extent as other 807 production on their full value less the value of the qualifying U.S. components. NAFTA provides that the duty-free treatment and exemption from quota under NAFTA are now available not only to goods afforded the Special Regime quota preference prior to NAFTA, but to *all* apparel made under the Special Regime's requirements. Now, any garment assembled in Mexico from U.S.-formed and cut fabric is both duty and quota free.

(iii) Safeguards. A NAFTA safeguard provision allows any NAFTA country either to suspend further duty reductions for originating goods, or to reinstate pre-NAFTA duty rates, for up to three years, if originating apparel products are being imported in such increased quantities as to cause serious damage, or actual threat thereof, to a domestic industry producing similar merchandise. A similar safeguard provision allows Canada or the United States to reinstate quotas on non-originating goods from Mexico. The ultimate safeguard is a provision allowing any NAFTA country to withdraw from NAFTA on six months notice to the other parties.

(d) Tariff Preference Levels (TPLs): Canada and Mexico

Under NAFTA, non-originating goods will generally be dutiable at MFN rates. MFN rates are rates generally applicable to products of countries determined to enjoy Most Favored Nation status. However, the tariff eliminations under NAFTA applicable to originating goods also apply to limited annual quantities of non-originating goods that are cut (or knit to shape) and sewn or otherwise assembled in Canada or Mexico from fabric produced in a non-NAFTA country. This treatment would be available for a garment cut and sewn in Mexico, for example, from fabric manufactured in the Far East. These limited annual quantities are called tariff preference levels (TPLs). For each country, one TPL covers all cotton and man-made fiber apparel, and another covers all wool apparel. The TPLs can be viewed as providing exceptions to the strict yarn forward standard in the origin rules. Once a TPL is "filled" for any year, articles covered by the TPL will revert to their MFN rates.

A separate TPL for Mexico exists for 807 production that fails to meet the origin rules (or, presumably, the special exception for Special Regime goods discussed earlier). One TPL covers all such 807 production, regardless of constituent fibers. This TPL would be available, for example, for the dutiable portion of 807 garments assembled by sewing in Mexico of parts cut in the United States from fabric produced in the Far East. This TPL for 807 production will go out of existence when quotas under the Multifiber Arrangement (MFA) are terminated. The MFA is an international agreement under which the United States and other developed countries negotiate bilateral quota agreements with textile-producing countries. The MFA has been phased out over a period of ten years as a result of the Uruguay Round Agreement adopted by the United States in late 1994.

The NAFTA drafters determined that some fibers, yarns, and fabrics are in such abundant supply in the NAFTA countries that garments made from those materials should be ineligible for coverage by the TPLs. Thus, the exception to the origin rules furnished by the TPLs is itself subject to a further exception. This exception-to-the-exception tends to be incomprehensible. The following garments are those that never enjoy the benefit of the TPLs:

- All apparel made from oxford cloth or blue denim.
- T-shirts and men's and women's underwear made from cotton or man-made fiber circular knit fabric under 100 metric count. However, women's cotton briefs and panties made from this type of fabric are covered by the TPL for 807 production.
- Man-made fiber sweaters.

(e) Administration

Textiles and apparel products subject to quota restraints must be accompanied by a textile visa and/or export license. A visa is an endorsement in the form of a stamp on an invoice or export control license. The visa is issued by a governmental organization in the exporting country. The export control organization can thus monitor the exports of merchandise in the various categories.

Upon importation into the United States, the visas are checked for authenticity and accuracy by U.S. Customs. Under a pilot program, the United States and number of countries are electronically exchanging visa information in a program known as ELVIS (Electronic Visa Interface System). Under ELVIS, visa information is transmitted to the United States electronically. When a visa is presented for the entry of merchandise into the United States, this entry is checked against the electronic information from the foreign country. If the information does not match, the visa is rejected. This system is still under construction, and full implementation was projected for January 1, 1997. However, the pilot program with a number of countries has encountered a number of technical problems hampering its full-scale implementation.

A visa does not guarantee entry of merchandise into the United States. Quota allocations are charged at the time of entry. "Quota status" or "quota priority" attaches only upon presentation of an entry in proper form, with duties attached prior to the filling or close of the quota. If the quota closes between the time the visa is issued and the shipment's arrival in the United States, the shipment will not be released to the importer until the quota reopens. Simply because a visa is issued, it cannot be assumed that the merchandise can enter at any time. If an entry is submitted prior to the close of the quota, the textile entries may be subject to proration, as discussed earlier. Merchandise entered at or after the close of quota may be reexported, destroyed under Customs' supervision, or stored in a bonded warehouse or foreign trade zone until the next quota period.

(f) Cotton Fiber

Cotton fibers are subject to a number of tariff-rate quotas. These include:

- Cotton, not carded or combed, having a staple length under 28.75 mm (Subheading 5201.00.14; Additional U.S. Note 5(b) to Chapter 52)
- Cotton, not carded or combed, having a staple length between 28.755 and 29.36875 mm (Subheading 5201.00.24; Additional U.S. Note 5(b) to Chapter 52)
- Cotton, not carded or combed, having a staple length between 29.36875 mm and 34.925 mm (Subheading 5201.00.34; Additional U.S. Note 5(b) to Chapter 52)
- Cotton, not carded or combed, having a staple length of 34.925 mm or more (Subheading 5201.00.60; Additional U.S. Note 5(b) to Chapter 52)
- Card strips made from cotton having a staple length of 30.1625 mm, lap waste, silver waste, and roving waste of cotton (Subheading 5202.99.10; Additional U.S. Note 9(b) to Chapter 52)
- Fibers of cotton, processed but not spun (Subheading 5203.00.10; Additional U.S. Note 10(b) to Chapter 52)

In addition, a 180-day quota on upland cotton based on its spot price may also be imposed under U.S. Note 6 to Subchapter III, Chapter 99, and Subheading

9903.52.13. This quota is based on the Secretary of Agriculture's determination of the spot price for certain upland cotton fiber.

(g) Quota Status and Specific Information

Textile and apparel quota status information may be obtained from a number of sources. The Customs broker can obtain up-to-date status information through Customs' Automated Commercial System (ACS) and the Automated Broker Interface (ABI).

A weekly status report is provided by the U.S. Customs Service (Report: QS9120-01). The report may be obtained through the Customs Electronic Bulletin Board (BBS:703-440-6155; Voice: 703-440-6236), and it is anticipated that the report ultimately will be available on U.S. Customs' Web site (http://www.ustreas.gov/treasury/bureaus/customs/). Information on closed categories and opening information may be obtained from CITA at 202-482-3715. Information on individual countries or concerning specific visa or quota requirements may be obtained by calling the following:

China	202-927-6703
Hong Kong	202-927-6711
Indonesia	202-927-6704
India	202-927-6705
Japan	202-927-6706
Korea	202-927-6707
Sri Lanka	202-927-6708
Macau	202-927-6709
Malaysia	202-927-6712
Philippines	202-927-6713
Pakistan	202-927-6714
Romania	202-927-6715
Singapore	202-927-6716
Thailand	202-927-6717
Turkey	202-927-6718
Taiwan	202-927-6719

Other countries subject to textile quotas include Bangladesh, Bulgaria, Bahrain, Brazil, Columbia, Costa Rica, the Czech Republic, the Dominican Republic, Egypt, Fiji, Guatemala, Honduras, Haiti, Hungary, Jamaica, Kenya, Kuwait, Laos, Macedonia, Burma (Myanmar), Mauritius, Mexico, Nepal, Oman, Poland, Qatar, Slovakia, El Salvador, Ukraine, the United Arab Emirates, and Uruguay.

Information concerning other countries, except visa requirements, and those listed above, may be obtained at 202-927-5850. Questions regarding visa requirements may be directed to the Customs Commercial Enforcement Branch at

202-927-1959. In addition, inquiries may be directed to the local port of importation or Customs Headquarters Quota Branch at 202-927-5850. This information is reprinted by a number of private sources. For example, VIAX^{sm} provides this and other information on international trade via electronic bulletin board for a per-use fee. The board may be accessed by dialing 718-341-3606. Hard copies of the information are republished by trade organizations for their members such as the American Association of Importers and Exporters (212-944-2230).

CHAPTER 12

Import and Export Documentation and Recordkeeping Compliance

Frank Chioccola
Harry L. Isacoff
Richard P. Wulwick

12.1 Introduction
12.2 Import Documentation
- (a) Evidence of Right to Make Entry
- (b) Commercial Invoice
- (c) Packing Lists
- (d) Entry Summary Form
- (e) Entry/Immediate Delivery
- (f) Purchase Order
- (g) Customs Power of Attorney
- (h) Bond Information

12.3 Other Import Documents
- (a) Export License (Visa)
- (b) Textile and Textile Products
- (c) Single Country Declaration
- (d) Multiple Country Declaration
- (e) Quota Charge Statement
- (f) GSP Declarations
- (g) Caribbean Basin Initiative
- (h) NAFTA Certificate of Origin
- (i) Special Footwear Invoice

12.4 Import Recordkeeping
- (a) Records

(b) Record Retention Period
(c) Recordkeeping Penalties
12.5 Export Documents
(a) Shipper's Export Declaration
(b) Export License
(c) Determining Merchandise Export Requirements
12.6 Export Recordkeeping
(a) Export Record Retention Period
(b) Export Records to Be Maintained
(c) Exempt Documents
(d) Enforcement
(e) Prohibitions
(f) Penalties
(g) Criminal Sanctions
12.7 Conclusion

12.1 Introduction

United States import and export transactions increased dramatically because of the global liberalization of trade, as evidenced by agreements such as the Uruguay Round of the General Agreement on Tariffs and Trade (GATT) and the North American Free Trade Agreement (NAFTA). The United States Customs Service and other government agencies have found it difficult to oversee and regulate transactions on an entry-by-entry basis because of the volume of trade and budget-related government downsizing. Customs focuses its attention on post-entry reviews of import transactions and documentation.

The form and maintenance of import and export documents are fundamental to the international movement of merchandise and the ability of the exporter and importer to withstand government scrutiny. The Customs Modernization and Informed Compliance Act, or Mod Act, enacted as part of NAFTA, contains a detailed list of documents and specific recordkeeping requirements for the storage and retrieval of documents.

The Mod Act contains specific penalties for recordkeeping violations, and the U.S. government promulgated rules for regulating export transactions. Requiring importers and exporters to maintain specific records for a statutorily required time will allow Customs and the Commerce Department to effectively police more transactions with fewer personnel and smaller budgets.

The types of import and export documentation vary, depending on the transaction. For example, some documents need to be generated and saved because of government regulations (such as NAFTA Certificates of Origin), while others are essential to conduct the transaction (such as purchase orders). Customs has specifically listed the documents that must be saved and made available to Customs, upon request, for all import transactions. This comprehensive list contains almost every document involved in the import transaction.

12.2 Import Documentation

Importers must present certain documents and pay estimated duties to obtain the release of merchandise from Customs.[1] The documents determine final duty assessments and provide statistical information. Entry information can be filed electronically by qualified companies or individuals and must generally be presented to Customs within five working days of the arrival of merchandise at a United States port of entry. This information may be submitted before the merchandise arrives in the United States.[2] The following documents must be presented at the time of merchandise arrival:

1. Entry manifest (Customs Form 7533), on Application and Special Permit for Immediate Delivery (Customs Form 3461)
2. Evidence of right to make entry
3. Commercial invoice, or a pro forma invoice when a commercial invoice is not available
4. Packing lists, when applicable
5. Other documents necessary to determine the admissibility of imported merchandise, as described in the Customs regulations

Parties wishing to import merchandise to the United States are advised to consult a Customs broker or qualified Customs consultant or attorney before importing merchandise to ensure that all documents are present and properly completed for the importation. A more detailed description of these documents and information follows.

(a) Evidence of Right to Make Entry

Imported merchandise may be entered only by its owner, purchaser, or agent, the latter of which is typically a Customs broker. When merchandise is shipped by a common carrier, the Customs regulations may require some evidence of the right to make entry to obtain release of the articles from Customs' custody.[3] If merchandise is not entered by a common carrier, possession of the merchandise at time of arrival is sufficient evidence for the importer to make entry.[4]

The treatment of merchandise transported by a common carrier varies, depending on the entity to which the merchandise is released. No official evidence of the right to make entry is required if the merchandise is released from Customs' custody directly to the carrier bringing the merchandise to the report.[5] For merchandise not released directly to the carrier, one of the following types of evidence must be filed with entry:[6]

---

[1] 19 C.F.R. pt. 142.

[2] 19 C.F.R. §142.2 (b).

[3] 19 C.F.R. §142.3 (a)(2).

[4] 19 C.F.R. §141.12.

[5] 19 C.F.R. §141.11(b).

[6] 19 C.F.R. §141.11(a)(1)–(6) contains a detailed description of the evidence of the right to make entry.

1. A properly endorsed bill of lading or air waybill
2. A genuine extract from a bill of lading or air waybill certified by the carrier
3. A certified duplicate bill of lading or air waybill prepared by the carrier
4. A carrier's certificate executed on the official entry form or, where appropriate, by use of a properly signed rubber-stamped or typewritten combined carrier's certificate and release order
5. A blanket carrier's release order on an appropriately modified bill of lading or air waybill for the relevant time period
6. Under certain circumstances, a properly certified shipping receipt or other document presented in lieu of a bill of lading or air waybill

(b) Commercial Invoice

Customs requires the filing of a commercial invoice contemporaneously with the entry, entry summary, or withdrawal document for most imports.[7] A commercial invoice is a statement from the seller to the buyer for payment and must itemize the merchandise sold and payment due. The documents must be in English or have attached to them an accurate English translation[8] and must be prepared in a manner customary in the trade.[9]

A commercial invoice is not required for certain transactions, including the following:

1. Entered merchandise having an aggregate purchase price or value of $500 or less
2. Merchandise not intended for sale or other commercial use
3. Merchandise returned to the United States after having been exported for repairs or alterations, under Harmonized Tariff Schedule Subheadings 9802.00.40 and 9802.00.60
4. Merchandise shipped abroad, not delivered to the consignee, and returned to the United States

Instead of a commercial invoice, importers in the transactions described in the preceding list must present any invoice, memorandum invoice, or bill pertaining to the merchandise or available to them. If such documentation is unavailable, the importer must file a pro forma invoice (see 19 C.F.R. §141.85) or substitute documentation to allow for an adequate examination of the merchandise and assessment of duties.[10]

Commercial invoices must contain certain specified information about the transaction, including the following:[11]

---

[7] 19 C.F.R. §141.83.

[8] 19 C.F.R. §141.86 (d).

[9] 19 C.F.R. §141.83 (c)(1).

[10] 19 C.F.R. §141.83(d).

[11] 19 C.F.R. §§141.86, 142.6.

1. The port of entry through which the merchandise has been, or will be, imported.
2. The quantities imported in weights and measures.
3. A detailed description of the imported merchandise, including the commercial name by which it is known, its grade or quality, and the marks, number, or symbols under which it is sold by the seller or manufacturer.
4. All rebates, drawbacks, and bounties, separately itemized, allowed upon the exportation.
5. The purchase price in the currency where the merchandise was purchased. This amount is generally the basis for determining the merchandise's dutiable value.
6. The country of origin of the merchandise.
7. A statement of all goods or services the buyer furnished to the manufacturer for producing the merchandise, the cost of which is not included in the invoice price (known as "assists").
8. If known, the appropriate eight-digit Harmonized Tariff Schedule classification designation for the merchandise.
9. The name and complete address of the overseas individual or firm responsible for invoicing the merchandise.

The Customs regulations contain a complete list of invoice requirements,[12] in addition to special requirements for textiles, apparel, and footwear. When in doubt, importers should consult with their customs consultant, broker, or attorney before preparing and filing the invoice. Importers should reference invoice numbers on all import documents to ensure easy tracking and guard against problems during post-entry audits.

(c) Packing Lists

A packing list should contain a detailed description of the merchandise in a shipment and a description of how the goods were packed. Packing lists are especially important for shipments that may contain defects or shortages and will require an insurance claim. Customs does not require packing lists, but if they exist, they must be filed with the other import documentation.

(d) Entry Summary Form

The entry summary Customs Form 7501, is the principal import document and is used for most formal entries.[13] Customs will not release imported merchandise from its custody without an entry summary or an entry/immediate delivery form.

The entry summary consolidates the pertinent information of an import transaction, including the following information:

---

[12] 19 C.F.R. §§141.86(a), 142.6.

[13] 19 C.F.R. §142.11.

1. Entry number and date
2. Bond number
3. Port code
4. Ultimate consignee's name, address, and identification number
5. Importer of record's name, address, and identification number
6. Date and country of export
7. Country of origin of the imported merchandise
8. Bill of lading or air waybill number
9. Importing carrier
10. Date of import

The entry summary includes a detailed description of the merchandise, including the following:

1. Harmonized Tariff Schedule classification number
2. Gross weight
3. Net quantity
4. Entered value
5. Duty rate
6. Amount of duty owed

The entry summary must also show calculations for determining the Merchandise Processing Fee (currently 0.19%) and the Harbor Maintenance Fee (currently 0.125%). These amounts, plus any customs duties owed, must be paid at the time of entry.

The importer must also affirm on the entry summary that all of the information presented to Customs, including the prices, values, quantities, rebates, drawbacks, fees, commission, and royalties, are true and correct and that all assist have been fully disclosed.[14] An assist is something supplied directly or indirectly, at reduced cost or free of charge, by the buyer to the seller for use in the production or sale for export to the United States of merchandise. The value of an assist must be included in the dutiable value of imported merchandise. Ensuring the accuracy of this information is extremely important because incorrect and false statements can result in civil monetary penalties and criminal penalties, even if any errors are unintentional.

(e) Entry/Immediate Delivery

Instead of an entry summary, and before merchandise arrives, the importer may submit a Customs Form 3461, Entry/Immediate Delivery form in conjunction with a customs bond to apply for the immediate release of merchandise.[15] Obtaining im-

[14]Customs Form 7501.

[15]19 C.F.R. §§142.24, 142.25.

mediate delivery rights is at the discretion of the Port Director and is not available to importers in default of payments to the Customs Service. Even for immediate deliveries, importers must file a properly completed Entry Summary (Form 7501) within ten working days after entry, or face penalties. Use of immediate delivery is limited to the following situations:

1. For merchandise arriving from Canada or Mexico, with proper approval and the appropriate bond
2. For certain fresh fruits and vegetables for human consumption arriving from Canada and Mexico
3. For merchandise destined for any United States government agency or officer
4. For articles destined for a trade fair
5. For certain quota merchandise
6. For merchandise released from a warehouse, followed within ten days by a warehouse withdrawal for consumption
7. For merchandise that has received prior approval from U.S. Customs Headquarters

(f) Purchase Order

A purchase order is a commercial document describing the merchandise purchased from the seller and typically prepared by the buyer in a sales transaction. Purchase orders may take various forms, as they are not required by any government agency. Purchase orders may contain any additional terms and conditions a buyer wishes to include for the transaction. Often, purchase orders are self-serving to the buyer, and sellers should ensure they are not bound by any terms without their express consent.

(g) Customs Power of Attorney

A customs power of attorney gives the importer's customs broker, or other qualified individual, the authority to conduct customs business on the principal's (that is, the importer's) behalf. Typically, power of attorney is granted through Customs Form 5291. If not granted in this way, power of attorney can either be a general power with unlimited authority, or limited, as explicitly stated in its terms and executed as Form 5291.[16] A copy of the power of attorney should be presented with the entry documents.

(h) Bond Information

To import merchandise to the United States, importers or their agents must generally obtain a bond[17] executed by an approved corporate surety or secured by cash

[16] 19 C.F.R. §141.32.

[17] 19 C.F.R. §§142.4(a), 113.11.

deposits. The bond guarantees that all customs fees, charges, penalties, and expenses will be properly paid. Customs Form 301, evidencing the bond, must be filed with Customs along with the entry documents.

The cost of a bond, which can cover a single transaction or a continuing series of transactions, varies, depending on the kind of bond. Customs brokers possess their own bonds. Importers may, with a broker's permission, import merchandise under this bond authority.

Bonds must be filed with the District Director of Customs at the location of merchandise entry in the United States. Evidence of the bond's existence must be filed with the entry documents, as demonstrated by a Customs Form 301.

12.3 Other Import Documents

Depending on the particular facts and circumstances of an importation, the following documents may also be required upon entry.

(a) Export License (Visa)

An export license/visa is official permission for an exporter to transport certain restricted merchandise from the country of origin. Export licenses are not required for most merchandise, but it is wise business practice for the buyer (importer) to require the seller (exporter) to warrant that no export license is required, or if one is required, that the seller will obtain or promise to timely obtain one. If the seller is required to possess an export license, the buyer is usually required to obtain an International Import Certificate from the United States Department of Commerce.

(b) Textile and Textile Products

Customs scrutinizes Single and Multiple Country Declarations to determine the country of origin of certain textile products. These declarations must be prepared by either the textile manufacturer, producer, exporter, or importer. A separate declaration can be prepared and filed by each party when multiple parties are involved. Customs will deny entry of appropriate merchandise not accompanied by properly executed declarations. The date of exportation for quota, visa, export license, and statistical purposes is the date the vessel or carrier leaves the last port in the country of origin.[18]

Declaration requirements apply to imported textile products subject to Section 204 of the Agricultural Act of 1956, as amended (7 U.S.C. 1854) and include products governed by the International Arrangement Regarding Trade in Textiles, more often known as the Multi-Fiber Arrangement. This includes the following:

1. Textiles whose chief value is of cotton, wool, or man-made fibers, or any textile fibers subject to the terms of any textile trade agreement, or any combination thereof; or

[18] 19 C.F.R. 12.130(f)(i). See 19 C.F.R. §12.130(f)(1), (2) for sample forms.

2. Textiles that contain 50% or more by weight of cotton or man-made fibers, or any textile fibers subject to the terms of any textile trade agreement; or
3. Articles containing 17% or more by weight of wool; or
4. Articles, if in chief value of textile fibers or textile materials, containing a blend of cotton, wool, or man-made fibers subject to the terms of any textile trade agreement, or any combination thereof, which fibers, in the aggregate amount to 50% or more by weight of all component fibers.[19]

(c) Single Country Declaration

The Single Country Declaration is required for imported textile articles wholly grown, manufactured, or assembled from components originating in a single country or United States insular possession.[20] The declaration attests to the product's origin. A completed form must identify any marks or numbers on the article, describe it, state the quantities imported, list the single country of origin, and state the date exported.

(d) Multiple Country Declaration

The Multiple Country Declaration must be used for imported textile and textile articles produced in, or containing components made in, more than one country, territory, or United States insular possession.[21] Merchandise containing U.S. and non-U.S. origin components must be accompanied by Multiple Country Declaration forms.

A completed Multiple Country Declaration must identify any marks or numbers on the article, describe the merchandise, list the quantities imported, state the date of manufacture and/or processing and the country in which it occurred, and state the component materials, country of production, and date of exportation to the country of assembly.

(e) Quota Charge Statement

The United States government imposes quotas on various imported items, such as textiles and apparel. The quotas may be absolute (that is, quantitative),[22] or tariff-rate (increased duty as volume increases).[23]

Absolute quotas limit the number of units that can be entered or withdrawn for consumption during a specified period. Once an absolute quota is filled, no further imports of that merchandise are permitted in that year.

Tariff-rate quotas do not limit the amount of product that can be imported to the United States but, rather, alter the duty rate for such product. Tariff-rate quotas permit a specified quantity of merchandise to be entered or withdrawn for consumption

[19] 19 C.F.R. 12.130(a)(1)–(4).

[20] 19 C.F.R. 12.130(f)(1).

[21] 19 C.F.R. 12.130(f)(2).

[22] 19 C.F.R. §132.1(a).

[23] 19 C.F.R. §132.1(b).

at a reduced duty rate. Once the quota is filled, the merchandise can be imported, but at a higher duty rate.

A Quota Charge Statement contains information about the quota treatment of imported merchandise. This form is either a free-standing form or an addendum to the invoice; it should state whether there are quota costs associated with the importation, or whether all quota costs are included in the price of the relevant merchandise.

(f) GSP Declarations

The Generalized System of Preferences (GSP) is a tariff preference program designed to promote economic revitalization in, and develop trade from, lesser developed nations. The GSP program provides duty-free treatment to eligible articles upon United States importation.

Importers claiming GSP preferential tariff treatment must meet certain documentary requirements. Merchandise for which GSP benefits are claimed, and that originate in more than one GSP eligible country, must be accompanied by a GSP Declaration.[24] If merchandise is wholly the growth, product, or manufacture of a single GSP eligible country, the accompanying commercial invoice must contain a statement attesting to this fact.[25] No GSP Declaration is required in these cases. This form contains relevant production details and must be completed by the exporter or any other appropriate party having knowledge of the transaction. In particular, a GSP Declaration must include a detailed description of the finished article's components, their country of origin and cost, and all processing operations and costs involving the components.

Significantly, the importer must *claim* GSP treatment. To do this, the symbol "A" must appear on the entry document (Form 7501) as a prefix to the tariff classification subheading for each GSP eligible product.[26]

Though a Customs Form is not required by law, the importer should nonetheless obtain and submit to United States Customs with other entry documentation a Form A—Country of Origin Certification. This form is generated in the country of export and signed by a qualified government official, and the importer typically obtains it from the exporter. To obtain GSP benefits, the importer must demonstrate that the merchandise was directly imported to the United States from the GSP country. The primary evidence for direct importation includes invoices, bills of lading, and other shipping documentation.

(g) Caribbean Basin Initiative

The Caribbean Basin Initiative (CBI) is a United States government program under which qualifying products from most Caribbean nations are given preferential tariff treatment (lower duty) on United States import. CBI is similar to the GSP program, but its requirements are less stringent.

---

[24] 19 C.F.R. 10.173(a)(1)(i).

[25] 19 C.F.R. 10.173(a)(2).

[26] 19 C.F.R. 10.172.

As with GSP, to claim preferential tariff treatment under CBI, importers must meet certain documentary requirements. For example, merchandise for which CBI benefits are claimed, and not originating in a single CBI eligible country, must be accompanied by a CBI Declaration.[27] Where merchandise is wholly the growth, product, or manufacture of a single CBI eligible country, its commercial invoice must contain a statement attesting to this fact.[28] This declaration describes production of the merchandise and must be completed by the exporter or another appropriate party having knowledge of the transaction's pertinent facts.

A CBI Declaration must include a detailed description of all of the finished article's components, their country of origin and cost, and all processing operations and their cost. The importer must *claim* preferential CBI treatment by including a written claim on the entry document. To do this, the symbol "E" must appear on the entry document (Form 7501) as a prefix to the tariff classification subheading for each CBI eligible product.

In addition, although not required, it is prudent for importers to obtain a Form A—Country of Origin Certification to verify country of origin. The CBI Form A is the same as that for GSP, except for CBI purposes the form need not be signed by a government official in the country of export.

To claim CBI benefits, the importer must demonstrate that the merchandise was directly imported to the United States from the CBI eligible country. The primary evidence demonstrating direct importation includes invoices, bills of lading, and other shipping documentation. For CBI purposes, direct shipment can include merchandise passing through another CBI country.

(h) NAFTA Certificate of Origin

Merchandise originating in Mexico or Canada may be entitled to preferential U.S. tariff treatment under the North American Free Trade Agreement, or NAFTA. To qualify for NAFTA benefits, the imported merchandise must be a product of either Mexico or Canada under an applicable eligibility rule. For example, products for which NAFTA benefits are claimed must be supported by an exporter's Certificate of Origin attesting to the merchandise's origin.[29]

(i) Special Footwear Invoice

Invoices for imported footwear must be accompanied by special addenda that thoroughly identify the footwear and include the following information:[30]

1. Manufacturer's style number
2. Importer's style and stock number

---

[27] 19 C.F.R. §10.198(a)(1)(i).

[28] 19 C.F.R. §10.198(a)(2).

[29] This form is required by 19 C.F.R. 12.132.

[30] 19 C.F.R. 141.89.

3. Composition, by percentage of surface area, of the shoe's upper portion, excluding reinforcements and accessories
4. Composition, by percentage of surface area, of the shoe's outer sole, excluding reinforcements and accessories
5. Statement as to whether the footwear is waterproof
6. Description of how high on the wearer's leg the footwear will reach
7. Statement concerning how the shoe will be worn and by whom

12.4 Import Recordkeeping

The Mod Act has established detailed and explicit recordkeeping regulations requiring all persons involved in import transactions to maintain, store, and produce, when lawfully requested, all import-related records they have generated. The Mod Act permits Customs to examine these records to ascertain the accuracy of an entry, determine fine and penalty liability, and ensure general compliance. Failure to follow the recordkeeping requirements can result in recordkeeping penalties, as well as general customs penalties.

(a) Records

In particular, the Mod Act requires any owner, importer, consignee, or their agent, who imports, or knowingly causes any merchandise to be imported to the United States customs territory, to keep specific records, including statements, declarations, books, papers, correspondence, accounts, technical data, automated record storage devices (i.e., magnetic discs and tapes), computer programs necessary to retrieve information in usable form, and other documents that:

1. Pertain to any importation, or to the information contained in the documents required by law or regulation under the Tariff Act of 1930, as amended, in connection with the entry of merchandise;
2. Are of the type normally kept in the ordinary course of business; and
3. Are sufficiently detailed.

The detail should be sufficient to

1. Establish the right to make entry;
2. Establish the correctness of any entry;
3. Determine the liability of any person for duties and taxes due, or which may be due, in the United States;
4. Determine the liability of any person for fines, penalties, and forfeitures; and
5. Determine whether the person has complied with the laws and regulations administered by the Customs Service.

Any other documents required under laws or regulations administered by the Customs Service may be required under the Mod Act.

(b) Record Retention Period

All import-related records must be kept for five years from the date merchandise enters the United States, unless expressly stated otherwise in the Customs regulations.

(c) Recordkeeping Penalties

Failure to maintain customs records as required by law can result in specific recordkeeping penalties. These penalties can be assessed in addition to other penalties for customs violations, as follows:

1. For the willful failure to maintain, store, or retrieve information Customs demands, penalties can be assessed in an amount up to $100,000, or equal to 75% of the merchandise's appraised value, per entry.
2. For the negligent failure to maintain, store, or retrieve information Customs demands, penalties can be assessed in an amount up to $10,000, or equal to 40% of the merchandise's appraised value.

The severity of these penalties, which can be assessed in addition to the standard penalties, demonstrates the vital importance of strict recordkeeping practices and record retrieval capabilities.

12.5 Export Documents

Specific documents must be filed with the United States government for export transactions. Many export documents exist, but this section focuses on two of the most significant: (1) the Shipper's Export Declaration and (2) the Export License.

(a) Shipper's Export Declaration

The Shipper's Export Declaration, or SED (Form 7525-V), must be filed with the United States government for most export shipments valued over $2,500, or for any shipment requiring a validated export license. Exporters must give a completed SED to the exporting carrier prior to clearing the port of exportation.

An SED serves the following purposes:

1. *Provides information on exports to the Bureau of Census.* A SED must list the merchandise's Schedule B number, the quantities shipped, the FOB value, and destination. The Census Bureau uses this information to publish monthly reports listing commodities exported and countries for which they are destined.

2. *Serves as an export control document.* Since the SED must state the type of license under which a product is shipped, it helps to ensure that the shipment is authorized for export.
3. *Serves as an enforcement mechanism.* U.S. Customs and the Commerce Department's Bureau of Export Administration use SEDs to monitor United States exports for enforcement actions against violators of export control laws.

The SED must contain accurate and detailed information, including the following:

1. Name and address of the principal party making the export
2. Statement as to whether the transaction involves related parties
3. Exportation date
4. Bill of lading or air waybill number
5. Names of any consignees involved in the transaction
6. Country of ultimate destination
7. Name of the carrier transporting the merchandise from the United States
8. Value of exported merchandise

Since SEDs must be filed with the government, false statements, intentional or not, subject the exporter to serious civil and criminal penalties. The penalty may be a $10,000 fine per false statement, five years imprisonment, or both. Consequently, exporters should ensure that any agent, such as a freight forwarder, properly prepares the SED and that all information submitted is accurate and complete.

(b) Export License

Virtually all exports are subject to one or more licensing requirements. The laws enabling and regulating export licensing requirements include the Export Administration Act, the Arms Export Control Act, the Atomic Energy Act of 1954, and the Trading with the Enemy Act. Export licensing is administered by the United States Commerce Department's Bureau of Export Administration (BXA). The export licensing system furthers the overseas policy objectives and national security interests of the federal government and limits the proliferation of technology and weapons that may harm the United States or its interests.

The BXA has established two specific product categories, controlled and noncontrolled products, to facilitate exports. All merchandise must be designated in one of these categories. This distinction is significant, because noncontrolled items may usually be exported under a general license, exempting the items from BXA approval for export. Alternatively, exporters of controlled items must typically obtain prior written authorization from the BXA through an Individual Validated License (IVL).

There are 22 general license categories. The more significant of these categories, and their respective abbreviations, are as follows:

1. G-DEST Exports to noncontrolled destinations
2. GLV Shipments of limited value
3. GLR Returns, replacements, or repairs of certain commodities

The rules governing eligibility for classification under a specific general license are contained in the Commerce Department's Commodities Control List (CCL) and the General License regulations.

If a commodity's classification permits shipments to a designated country under a general license, then merchandise may be exported by merely filing a Shipper's Export Declaration describing the commodity(ies) with the United States Customs Service at the port of export, or with the postmaster at the post office, and placing the general license symbol (for example, G-DEST) on the SED.

(c) Determining Merchandise Export Requirements

Exporters must take the following steps to determine exporting requirements for their merchandise:

1. *Review the Table of Denial Orders* to determine whether any of the parties to the transaction are prohibited from receiving merchandise exported from the United States. The transaction cannot be legally completed if a party appears on the list. Tables of Denial Orders are published by the Office of Export Licensing.
2. *Determine the destination of merchandise.* The United States affords certain countries distinct treatment for U.S. exports destined there. For export purposes, the world is divided into seven groups, ranging from those receiving the most restrictive treatment to those receiving the most favorable. The most restrictive treatment is reserved for embargoed countries (Group Z), such as Libya and Iraq. All trade is prohibited with these countries. The most liberal is afforded Group T countries (located in North and South America) and Group V countries (all countries not expressly mentioned elsewhere on the list). Different licensing requirements exist, depending on ultimate destination.
3. *Review the Commerce Control List.* As in the tariff schedule, all merchandise is classified in the Commerce Control List. The CCL is divided into ten commodity group classifications, which are further subdivided to provide more specific descriptions. Products with military or similar potential are listed by name and described in detail. In addition, each classification contains a "basket" provision for products not more specifically described elsewhere. An article's classification within the CCL, as represented by an Export Control Classification Number (ECCN), determines its designation. Exporters should seek advice from the Office of Export Licensing where uncertainty exists regarding a merchandise's classification within the CCL.

By following these steps, exporters can determine the specific requirements that apply to their merchandise and transaction, and whether any other limitations or conditions exist.

12.6 Export Recordkeeping

Significant export recordkeeping requirements are located in the Bureau of Export Administration's Export Administration Regulations. These requirements apply to all commodity and technical data exports and cover all records kept in connection with the export, as well as all records pertaining to the negotiations of an export transaction. *Negotiations* is a technical term. Preliminary inquiries or mere offers to do business do not constitute negotiations unless the inquiry or offer proposes a transaction that a reasonably prudent exporter would believe is likely to lead to a transaction.

The recordkeeping requirements discussed in this section apply to all persons subject to United States jurisdiction who participate in an export transaction. The recordkeeping requirements apply to exports to Canada if, at any stage in the transaction, it appears that a person in a country other than the United States or Canada has an interest in the export, or if the commodity or technical data involved is to be reexported, transshipped, or diverted from Canada to another country.

(a) Export Record Retention Period

All required export documents must be kept for a period of *two years* from the latest of the following:

1. Export from the United States; or
2. Any known reexport, transshipment, or diversion; or
3. Any other termination of the transaction, whether formally in writing or by any other means.

Exporters are wise to maintain records longer than two years because the statute of limitations for criminal actions brought under the Export Administration Act of 1979, and its predecessor acts, is five years.[31]

(b) Export Records to Be Maintained

The following is a partial list of the records that *must be maintained* for U.S. export transactions:

1. Validated export licenses
2. Applications for export licenses

[31] 18 U.S.C. §3282.

3. Requests for authorization to reexport
4. Documents submitted in support of an export license
5. Application or request for reexport authorization
6. Shipper's export declarations
7. Powers of attorney
8. Dock receipts
9. Bills of lading or air waybills
10. Memoranda and notes
11. Correspondence
12. Contracts
13. Invitations to bid
14. Books of account
15. Financial records
16. Other written items relating to the export that the exporter made or obtained

(c) Exempt Documents

The following documents are *exempt* from the export recordkeeping requirements:

1. Export information pages
2. Special export price lists
3. Vessel logs from freight forwarders
4. Inspection certificates
5. Warranty certificates
6. Guarantee certificates
7. Packing material certificates
8. Goods quality certificates
9. Notifications to customers of advance mailings
10. Letters of indemnity
11. Financial release forms
12. Financial hold forms
13. Export parts shipment problem forms
14. Draft number logs
15. Expense invoice mailing logs
16. Financial status reports
17. Bank release of guarantees
18. Cash sheets
19. Commission payment backups
20. Commissions payable worksheets
21. Commissions payable controls

22. Check request forms
23. Accounts receivable correction forms
24. Check request registers
25. Commission payment printouts
26. Engineering fee invoices
27. Overseas tax receipts
28. Individual customer credit status reports
29. Requests for export customer code forms
30. Acknowledgments for receipt of funds escalation
31. Development forms
32. Summary quotes
33. Purchase order review forms
34. Proposal extensions
35. Financial proposals to export customers' sales summaries

(d) Enforcement

All Customs, Postal Service, and Office of Export Enforcement officials are authorized to take appropriate action to detect violations and ensure compliance with the Export Administration Regulations. This includes, but is not limited to, examining all commodities and technical data declared for export, and an inspection of all pertinent documents.

(e) Prohibitions

United States law forbids exporters to do any of the following:

1. Without written approval of the Office of Export Licensing, permit any person, other than the person to whom the export license is granted or that person's agent, to expedite or in any way assist the export of any commodity or technical data described in the license
2. Alter or modify an export license or allow its unauthorized use
3. Possess merchandise with intent to export illegally
4. Transact business with persons subject to a denial order
5. Misrepresent or make false or misleading representations, statements, or certifications, or falsify or conceal any material fact involving an export, for the purpose of facilitating an export from the United States
6. Cause, aid, abet, solicit, attempt, or conspire to violate the Export Administration Regulations
7. Fail to comply with reporting requirements

Such violations can trigger severe civil and criminal penalties, as discussed in the following paragraphs.

(f) Penalties

Violations of the export regulations may result in civil, administrative, and criminal sanctions and the seizure or forfeiture of property. The Commerce Department may compromise and settle any administrative proceeding brought with respect to such violations. Civil sanctions include the following:

1. *Prohibiting lading.* U.S. Customs can prevent the lading of commodities or technical data on an exporting carrier whenever there is reasonable cause to believe the export is contrary to the Export Administration Regulations.
2. *Merchandise seizure and detention.* U.S. Customs can seize and detain any commodities or technical data if an attempt is made to export them in violation of the Export Administration Regulations, or whenever probable cause exists to believe that commodities or technical data are intended to be, in the process of being, or have been exported in violation of the Export Administration Regulations.
3. *Denial of export privileges.* Export privileges will be denied by placing the offending exporter on a "denial list," officially known as the Table of Denial Orders (available from the Office of Export Administration). This table names those who may not apply for, obtain, or use any license, Shipper's Export Declaration, bill of lading, or other export control document. Every exporter must verify that the party with whom he or she is dealing is not included on the Table of Denial Orders.
4. *Civil monetary sanctions.* The head of any department or agency exercising any power under the Export Administration Act may impose monetary penalties of up to $10,000 for each general violation, or $100,000 for violations involving national security controls. The payment of a penalty may be made a condition for restoring export privileges.

(g) Criminal Sanctions

Criminal penalties are imposed in addition to civil sanctions for intentional violations of any provision of the Export Administration Act. The penalties vary, depending on whether the violation occurred knowingly, willfully, or involves national security or military technology.

Criminal sanctions include the following:

1. For violations that establish knowledge or willfulness, criminal penalties reach up to five times the value of the export or $50,000, whichever is greater, and/or imprisonment for a period of not more than five years. If merchandise is intended for a country to which such exports are controlled for policy concerns, criminal penalties amount to five times the value of the export involved, or $1,000,000, whichever is greater. In the case of an individual, a fine of not more than $250,000 may be imposed, or imprisonment for not more than ten years, or both.

2. For violations involving national security, criminal penalties can reach up to five times the value of the exports involved, or $1,000,000, whichever is greater. If the violating exporter is an individual, the fine will be not more than $250,000, or imprisonment for not more than five years, or both.
3. For submitting false or misleading information, or for concealing material facts—whether in connection with license applications, boycott reports, investigations, compliance proceedings, appeals, or otherwise—criminal penalties can reach $10,000 or imprisonment for not more than five years, or both, for each violation.[32]

12.7 Conclusion

Import and export record preparation and maintenance are fundamental to international transactions. More important, international traders are obligated under various laws and regulations to use reasonable care regarding such records. Increased governmental scrutiny has become commonplace to ensure compliance.

As part of this increased scrutiny, U.S. Customs now has expansive power to compel parties to produce records for examination. Accordingly, record preparation, storage, and retrieval mechanisms have never been more important, and parties not in compliance, or lacking adequate retrieval mechanisms, may be subjected to significant penalties.

Parties wishing to import or export merchandise must exercise reasonable care before completing a transaction, and in maintaining all required documentation contemporaneously and following the deal. To do so, they may wish to consult a customs consultant, broker, or attorney for assistance.

[32] 18 U.S.C. §101

CHAPTER 13

Unfair Trade Remedies

Joseph S. Kaplan

13.1 Introduction
- (a) Administration
- (b) Legislative Background

13.2 Subsidies and Countervailing Duties
- (a) Subsidies
- (b) Specific Subsidies
- (c) Congressional Intent
- (d) Material Injury
- (e) Countervailing Duties

13.3 Dumping and Antidumping Duties
- (a) Fair Value
- (b) Normal Value
- (c) Constructed Value
- (d) Adjustments
- (e) Factors of Production
- (f) Definitions
- (g) Comparisons
- (h) Additional Adjustments

13.4 Injury to Domestic Industry
- (a) Industry
- (b) Special Industry Rules
- (c) Regional Industries
- (d) Segments
- (e) Material Injury
- (f) Impact on the Relevant Domestic Industry
- (g) Special Situations
- (h) Cumulation
- (i) Threat of Material Injury
- (j) Applying the Cumulation Rule

13.5 Investigations and Enforcement
13.6 Procedures for Initiating Investigations
(a) Initiating the Investigation
(b) The Petition
(c) Filing the Petition
(d) Interested Parties
(e) Timing
(f) Issuance and Monitoring
13.7 Preliminary Determinations
(a) Waiver of Verification
(b) *De Minimis* Rule
(c) Timing Issues
(d) Complicated Cases
(e) Countervailing Duty Investigation
(f) Antidumping Investigation
13.8 Termination or Suspension of Investigations
(a) Withdrawal
(b) Suspension
(c) Prohibition
13.9 Final Determinations
(a) Final Determination of Injury
(b) Affirmative Determination
(c) Finalization Process
(d) Procedural Issues
13.10 The Duty Assessment Order
13.11 Miscellaneous
13.12 Administrative Review of Duty Determinations
(a) Duty Determination
(b) Review of Injury Determinations
(c) Sunset Provisions
(d) Special Reviews
13.13 Practice and Procedure
(a) Mandatory Hearings
(b) Best Information Available
(c) Access to Information
13.14 Judicial Review and Dispute Settlement
(a) Judicial Review
(b) Dispute Settlement

13.1 Introduction

Federal law protects domestic producers against unfair import competition. This chapter is concerned with protection from unfair price competition through the countervailing duty and antidumping laws.

The U.S. countervailing duty and antidumping laws are the domestic statutory embodiments of the corresponding codes of the 1994 General Agreement on Tariffs and Trade (GATT), which created the World Trade Organization (WTO). The codes are annexed to the WTO Agreement. The WTO codes provide mandatory guidelines governing domestic legislation. However, the domestic legislation contains many refinements unique to the United States.

(a) Administration

The countervailing duty and antidumping laws are detailed and complex. Three governmental agencies are involved in their administration within the Import Administration of the Department of Commerce:

1. The International Trade Administration (ITA);

2. The United States International Trade Commission (ITC); and

3. The United States Customs Service (Customs).

The ITA and the ITC conduct investigations and issue countervailing duty and antidumping determinations and orders. The Customs Service monitors traffic in goods subject to countervailing duty and antidumping orders and collects countervailing and antidumping duties.

Countervailing duties compensate for the effect of subsidies. Antidumping duties compensate for the effects of dumping, that is, the selling of goods for export at a price less than their fair value. As required by the WTO, countervailing and antidumping duties may not be imposed unless the affected domestic industry in the United States has demonstrated that it has been or is likely to have been injured by reason of the existence of the subsidy or the dumped price. However, this rule does apply to subsidized products of countries do not provide the same protection to United States exports.

Although often referred to in the media as penalties, countervailing and antidumping duties are compensating duties. These duties are not penalties, although viewed as such by the media. Compensating duties are accorded the same tax treatment as ordinary customs duties.

(b) Legislative Background

Countervailing and antidumping laws are provided for in Subtitle IV of the Tariff Act of 1930 as amended by Public Law 103–465, December 8, 1994, 108 Stat 4809, the Uruguay Round Agreements Act. The Uruguay Round Agreements Act amendments are comprehensive. In many respects these provisions supersede or clarify judicial decisions and have required a reexamination and rewriting of the regulations at 19 Code of Federal Regulation Parts 353 and 355. The reader must consult the regulations and judicial decisions before coming to any conclusions about the state and application of these laws.

This chapter deals with: subsidies and countervailing duties, dumping and antidumping duties, injury to domestic industry, investigations and enforcement, suspension and termination of investigations, reviews of countervailing and antidumping orders, and judicial review and dispute settlement.

13.2 Subsidies and Countervailing Duties

The imposition of countervailing duties against subsidies is provided for by statute.[1] The section provides for the imposition of a countervailing duty if a government or any public entity within the territory provides a "countervailable subsidy" tied to the manufacture, production, or export of a "class or kind" of merchandise. A countervailing duty equal to the amount of the "net countervailable subsidy" is imposed upon such merchandise, provided that the ITC has determined that an "industry" in the United States has been materially injured or threatened with material injury, or that the establishment of such an industry has been materially retarded. Leased goods are also subject to the imposition of countervailing duties.

(a) Subsidies

The test of whether a subsidy is countervailable depends on whether it is (1) described as a subsidy,[2] and (2) is "specific."[3]

Specific subsidies are countervailable, but nonspecific, or generally available, subsidies are not. Three types of benefits provided by a government or public entity are deemed subsidies. These are:

1. The provision of a financial contribution;
2. The provision of any form of income or price support within the meeting of Article XVI of the 1994 GATT; or
3. The making of a payment to a funding mechanism to permit it to provide a financial contribution would normally be made by a government.[4]

A financial contribution may be direct or indirect. The contribution may encompass the direct transfer of funds, loan guarantees, tax-free infusions, tax deferrals, credits or deductions, the provision of goods or services, and the purchasing of goods.[5]

(b) Specific Subsidies

Not all such transactions confer a benefit. If each transaction is conducted on a normal commercial basis, it is likely that the transaction will not be considered to confer a benefit.

---

[1] 19 U.S.C. §1671-1671 h.

[2] 19 U.S.C. §1677 (5).

[3] As described in 19 U.S.C. §1677 (5a).

[4] 19 U.S.C. §1677 (5)(b).

[5] 19 U.S.C. §1677 (5)(e).

Subsidies are specific if they are export subsidies, import substitution subsidies (subsidies contingent on the use of domestic rather than imported goods), or domestic subsidies available to a limited class of manufacturers, producers, or exporters.[6]

(c) Congressional Intent

Trade statutes are extremely detailed, reflecting an ongoing congressional preoccupation with the special economic problems of international trade. The original countervailable duty law was a single paragraph in length. The current definition of countervailable subsidy and the associated definitions of specific and noncountervailable subsidies alone take up five pages of print in the *United States Code Annotated.* The extreme detail of the statute is ultimately an expression by Congress of its intentions in myriad situations that have been the subject of lengthy and difficult litigation.

(d) Material Injury

Material injury to the domestic producer must be demonstrated before a countervailing duty may be imposed. However, there are exceptions to the rule.

The material injury test depends upon the identity of the country in which the goods are manufactured and the status of that country. The country is usually a member of WTO or a country that assumed obligations toward the United States. The assumed obligations must be substantially equivalent to those of the GATT Subsidies Agreement. Countries entitled prior to December 8, 1994, to unconditional most favored nation treatment for articles imported into the United States and could meet certain additional specifications are included.

Most of the world's nations meet one or more of the criteria mentioned. The handful of countries that do not are not entitled to a material injury determination, and their goods become subject to the imposition of countervailing duties based upon proof of the existence of a countervailable subsidy alone. In fact, this rule is rarely utilized because most countries whose goods are not entitled to an injury determination in a countervailing duties case are countries with whom the United States has restricted trade relationships.

(e) Countervailing Duties

Ordinarily, countervailing duties are based on the countervailable subsidy received by the manufacturer, producer, or exporter of the subject merchandise. However, in two instances the receipt of subsidies by other parties is taken into account.

1. If the subject merchandise is produced by an international consortium, any subsidy relative to the production in any country in which the consortium manufactures or produces may be taken into account.[7]

---

[6] 19 U.S.C. §1677 (5a).

[7] 19 U.S.C. §1671 (d).

2. If the subject merchandise is produced with the benefit of an "upstream" subsidy (a countervailable subsidy other than an export subsidy)[8] bestowed on an "input product," that subsidy may be taken into account in determining the countervailing duty to be imposed.[9]

Regulations implementing the countervailing duty law are found in 19 C.F.R. Part 355.

Judicial decisions issued recently include measurement of the impact of a subsidy following change of ownership, or time and benefit, and the effect of privatization on wholly or partly owned state enterprises.

13.3 Dumping and Antidumping Duties

The antidumping law[10] provides for the imposition of a compensating duty to equalize the difference between the selling price of the merchandise when exported to the United States and its "fair value" if the latter is higher. As in the case of countervailable subsidies, leasing arrangements that are equivalent to sales are subject to antidumping law.

(a) Fair Value

Antidumping duties may be imposed if an industry in the United States has been materially injured or threatened with material injury, or the establishment of an industry has been materially retarded. Antidumping duties are imposed upon the entire class or kind of merchandise exported from the country of origin to the United States.

The term "*fair value*" is found in the statute, but is not found in the GATT Subsidies Code. The term that appears there is "*normal value.*" The latter term does find its place in U.S. legislation. "Normal value" is a provision of the antidumping law that must be kept clearly in mind in understanding how the antidumping law works.[11]

The statute provides in determining under this subtitle whether subject merchandise is being, or is likely to be, sold at less than fair value, a fair comparison shall be made between export price or constructed export price and normal value.[12]

(b) Normal Value

Normal value is equal the price in the exporting country or other foreign market at a time reasonably corresponding to the time of the sale used to determine the ex-

---

[8]19 U.S.C. §1677-1.

[9]19 U.S.C. §1677 (e).

[10]19 U.S.C. §§1673-1673 (h).

[11]19 U.S.C. §1677 (b).

[12]19 U.S.C. §1677b (a).

port price or constructed export price.[13] "Price" is further defined to mean either the price at which a "foreign like product" is first sold or offered for sale for consumption in the exporting country. Price is determined in the "usual commercial quantities," in the "ordinary course of trade," and, to the extent practicable, at the "same level of trade" as the exported product.[14]

This pricing rule applies where the normal value is based on sales for consumption in the home market of the exporting country. At times, such sales, or even offers to sell, are nonexistent in the market, or their aggregate quantity is insufficient to permit a proper comparison with sales to the United States, or the particular market situation in the exporting country does not permit a proper comparison. Third country sales come into play at such times.[15]

Home market sales are normally considered as insufficient if the quantity or value of sales in the home market is less than 5% of the aggregate quantity or value of sales from that country to the United States. In insufficient quantity situations normal value is ascertained by reference to the price at which the foreign like product is sold or offered for sale for consumption in a country other than the exporting country and other than the United States. If the price in that sale is representative, the quantity or value of sales to the third country is sufficient (5% or more of the quantity or value sold in or to the United States), and the market situation in the third country permits a proper comparison with the export price to the United States.[16]

(c) Constructed Value

Notwithstanding the availability of a comparison based on third country sales, the export price may be compared with the constructed value of the merchandise.[17] Constructed value is equal to the cost of the materials, fabrication, and other processing of any kind employed in producing the merchandise.[18] The time period is time that would ordinarily permit production in the ordinary course of business. Costs include the actual amounts of selling, general and administrative expenses, and profits incurred by the exporter or producer in connection with the production and sale of the foreign like product in the ordinary course of trade for consumption in the foreign country. If this data is not available, the statute provides several alternative means to determine constructed value.

(d) Adjustments

Several adjustments are considered when the determination of normal value is based on a price.[19] The price is increased by the cost of containers and coverings

[13] 19 U.S.C. §1677b (1).

[14] 19 U.S.C. §1677b (a)(1)(B)(i).

[15] 19 U.S.C. §1677b (a)(1)(C).

[16] 19 U.S.C. §1677b (a)(1)(B)(ii).

[17] 19 U.S.C. §1677b (a)(4).

[18] 19 U.S.C. §1677b (e).

[19] 19 U.S.C. §1677.

and other costs incident to placing the merchandise in condition packed ready for shipment to the United States.[20] The price is reduced by the corresponding home market charges if included in the price and by any taxes included in the price of the foreign market product if such taxes are not included in the price of the export product. The price is increased or decreased in the amount of any difference attributable to differences in quantities sold or other differences in circumstances of sale.

Additional adjustments may be recognized for differences in level of trade. Also, adjustments may be made for differences in indirect selling expenses incurred in the home markets (or third country markets). The limit is indirect expenses that are not greater than indirect expenses in sales to the United States importers, or to unrelated customers in circumstances in which the importers are related to the exporters.

Sales at less than cost of production are disregarded.[21] Normal prices, are based in the case of goods manufactured in a non-market economy country, on the factors of production utilized in producing the merchandise, plus an amount for general expenses and profit plus the cost of containers, coverings, and other expenses.

(e) Factors of Production

Evaluation of the "factors of production" is based on the best available information, including the values of such factors in a market economy country considered appropriate by the ITA. However, if the ITA finds that the available information is inadequate for the purpose, the normal price may be based on the price of comparable merchandise produced in a market economy country at a level of economic development comparable to that of the non-market economy country, even including the United States.[22] The reference to "factors of production" is defined to include hours of labor required, quantities of raw materials employed, amounts of energy and other utilities consumed, and representative capital costs including depreciation.[23]

(f) Definitions

Important definitions are applicable to the determination of normal value:[24]

1. "Domestic like product" means a product that is like or most similar in characteristics and uses to the article subject to an antidumping investigation.[25]
2. "Ordinary course of trade" means the conditions and practices which, for a reasonable time prior to the exportation of the subject merchandise, have

---

[20] 19 U.S.C. §1677b (a)(6).

[21] 19 U.S.C. §1677b (b).

[22] 19 U.S.C. §1677b (c).

[23] 19 U.S.C. §1677b (c)(3).

[24] 19 U.S.C. §1677.

[25] 19 U.S.C. §1677(10).

been normal in the trade under consideration as to merchandise of the same class or kind.[26]

3. "Foreign like product" provides a declining order of similarity between the product exported to the United States and its foreign counterpart and requires that the most similar product be selected.[27]
4. "Usual commercial quantities" means the price or prices for one quantity in an aggregate volume that is greater than the aggregate volume sold at the price or prices for any other quantity.[28]
5. "Non-market economy country" means a foreign country that does not operate on market principles of cost or pricing, taking into account the following: convertability of the currency, whether wage rates are determined by free bargaining, the extent to which joint ventures are permitted by the country in question, the extent of government ownership or control over the means of production, the extent of government control over the allocation of resources and over the price and output decisions of enterprises, and such other factors as the ITA may consider appropriate.[29]

(g) Comparisons

The normal price is to be compared with the export price or the constructed export price.[30] Export price is the price at which the merchandise is first sold or agreed to be sold before the date of importation by the producer or exporter of the subject merchandise outside of the United States. Such transaction takes place with an unaffiliated purchaser in the United States or an unaffiliated purchaser for exportation to the United States.

Constructed export price is the price at which the subject merchandise is sold in the United States by a seller affiliated with the producer or exporter to a non-affiliated purchaser. In general, constructed export price is applicable when the U.S. importer is affiliated with or related to its vendor. In such cases, the relevant price is that at which the first sale to an unaffiliated customer occurs. The export price and constructed export price are subject to the following adjustments:

The prices are increased by:

1. The cost of containers, coverings, and all else necessary to place the merchandise in condition packed ready for shipment to the United States, or uncollected foreign customs duties; plus
2. The amount of customs duties imposed by the country of exportation applicable to the product that have been rebated or the collection of which has

[26] 19 U.S.C. §1677(15).

[27] 19 U.S.C. §1677(16).

[28] 19 U.S.C. §1677(17).

[29] 19 U.S.C. §1677(18).

[30] 19 U.S.C. §1677a.

been deferred by reason of the exportation of the subject merchandise to the United States; and

3. The amount of any countervailing duty imposed on the subject merchandise under United States law.

The export price or constructed export price is to be reduced by:

1. United States import duties;
2. The cost of bringing the merchandise from the original place of shipment in the exporting country to the place of delivery in the United States; and
3. The amount of any export tax to which the subject merchandise has been subjected by the exporting country.

(h) Additional Adjustments

Additional adjustments may be required for merchandise to which constructed export price applies. The constructed export price is subject to various reductions:

1. The amount of commissions for selling the merchandise in the United States;
2. Expenses that result from or bear a direct relationship to sales such as credit expenses, guarantees, and warranties;
3. Selling expenses paid by the seller on behalf of the purchaser;
4. Any other selling expenses;
5. The costs of any further manufacture or assembly; and
6. The profit allocated to any of the foregoing expenses.

Further special rules apply where the value added in the United States by the affiliated importer substantially exceeds the value of the subject merchandise and with regard to determining the profit earned by the affiliated importer.

The proposed suspension is provided to the petitioner. Parties have the opportunity to comment. Once the suspension agreement becomes effective, the investigation can be terminated and the liquidation of entries can resume. If cash deposits of anticipated duties have been made or bonds posted, the cash deposits are to be returned and the bonds canceled. The resumption of the investigation can be requested within 20 days after the date of publication of the notice of suspension and for resumption if the agreement upon which the suspension is based is violated.

13.4 Injury to Domestic Industry

Most countervailing duty cases and all antidumping cases require a showing of material injury before a countervailing or antidumping duty may be imposed. The language of the two statutes is identical. If the ITC determines that an industry in the United States is materially injured or is threatened with material injury, or the establishment of an industry in the United States is materially retarded by reason of imports of that merchandise or by reason of sales (or the likelihood of sales) of that merchandise for importation, a countervailing duty or antidumping duty is to be imposed. Definitional standards and rules guide the determination as to whether the injury requirement has been met.[31]

(a) Industry

The statute requires that injury be suffered by an industry.[32] In general, "industry" means the producers as a whole of a domestic like product, or those producers whose collective output of a domestic like product constitutes a major proportion of the total domestic production of the product.

"A domestic like product" means a product that is like, or in the absence of a like product, one that is most similar in characteristics and uses to the article subject to an antidumping or countervailing duty investigation.[33]

The requirement that injury be sustained by producers representing at least "a major proportion" of the total domestic production of the product has practical implications. An individual producer to whom only a minor proportion of domestic production is attributable may apply for the institution of a countervailing or antidumping investigation. However, it would be necessary for that producer to demonstrate that the injury is sufficiently widespread to affect a major proportion of production. Relief is not granted no matter the extent of injury to that individual producer.

(b) Special Industry Rules

Two special rules apply to the definition of "industry." The first special rule applies "in appropriate circumstances." The special rule applies to a domestic producer that directly or indirectly controls the exporter or importer, or is controlled by the exporter or importer, or when the exporter or importer and the producer control or are controlled by a third party. In such cases, the production of that producer may be excluded from the calculation of the total domestic production and from the determination as to whether a major proportion of the total domestic production has been or is subject to injury.[34] "In appropriate circumstances" is not defined or explained in the statute. It is necessary to examine the regulations and the case law to determine whether the related party exclusion is likely to apply in any given case.

(c) Regional Industries

The second special rule modifies the requirement that the production of all producers in the United States be taken into account. The statute recognizes the existence of regional industries. When a regional industry exists, the producers and

---

[31] 19 U.S.C. §1677.

[32] 19 U.S.C. §1677(4).

[33] 19 U.S.C. §1677(10).

[34] 19 U.S.C. §1677(4)(B).

production to be taken into account are those within the region rather than within the United States as a whole. If injury is determined to exist on this basis, and a countervailing or antidumping duty order results, the duty is nevertheless applicable to all imports into the United States from the affected exporting country, not just imports destined for the target regional market.

The criteria that determined the existence of a regional industry,[35] are that:

1. The producers within such market sell all or almost all of their production of the domestic like product in question in that market; and
2. The demand in that market is not supplied, to any substantial degree, by producers of the product in question located elsewhere in the United States.

Injury may be found to exist when a regional market exists and there is a concentration of dumped in or subsidized imports into such an "isolated" market, thereby injuring producers of all or "almost all" production within that market. An example of a regional industry is the cement industry. In cases against exports from Mexico, a regional market consisting of southern border states extending from Arizona to Florida was found to exist.

(d) Segments

Another special rule[36] permits proof of injury to be focused on individual product lines or narrow groups or ranges of products. The scope of a countervailing or antidumping order may encompass merchandise that has not been demonstrated to be a source of injury to a domestic industry, provided that injury to a product line within the scope of the investigation has been ascertained. In such cases all merchandise within the scope of the investigation, including merchandise outside the product line, may be subjected to the imposition of countervailing or antidumping duties.

Another special rule[37] lumps together both producers and processors of agricultural products. This combination rule applies if two requirements are met:

1. The processed product must be produced from the raw agricultural product through a single continuous line of production.
2. There is a "substantial coincidence" of economic interests between the producers of the raw product and the processors of the processed product.

(e) Material Injury

We turn now to the statutory concept of material injury. The threshold of "materiality" is low. The term "*material injury*" means harm that is not inconsequential, immaterial, or unimportant.[38]

---

[35] 19 U.S.C. §1677(4)(C).

[36] 19 U.S.C. §1677(4)(D).

[37] 19 U.S.C. §1677(4)(E).

[38] 19 U.S.C. §1677(7)(A).

The materiality definition is accompanied by several important special rules. The ITC must consider the following:[39]

1. The volume of imports of the subject merchandise;
2. The effect on prices in the United States for domestic like products; and
3. The impact on domestic producers of domestic like products in the context of production operations within the United States.

The ITC may, and routinely does, take into account other economic factors it considers important in evaluating whether the material injury requirement has been met. Concerning the volume and impact, the statute mandates additional analysis on the part of the ITC.[40] With regard to volume, the ITC must consider whether the volume of imports of the merchandise or any increase, either absolutely or relative to United States production or consumption, is significant.

With regard to price, the ITC is required to consider "underselling." The ITC is to determine whether the price of the imported product is lower than that of the domestic like product. The ITC is to consider whether the pricing of the imported product to a significant degree either depresses prices of domestic products or prevents increases that otherwise would have occurred.

(f) Impact on the Relevant Domestic Industry

In considering the impact on the relevant domestic industry, the ITC is mandated to evaluate all relevant economic factors having a bearing on the state of the United States industry, including actual and potential decline in output, sales, market share, profits, productivity, return on investment and utilization of capacity,

The ITC is to consider factors affecting domestic prices:

1. Actual and potential negative effects on cash flow, inventory, employment, wages, growth, ability to raise capital, and investments;
2. Actual and potential negative effects on the existing development and production efforts of the domestic industry, including efforts to develop a derivative or more advanced version of the domestic like product; and
3. In antidumping cases, the magnitude of the margin or dumping.

(g) Special Situations

The ITC is required to examine the question of whether domestic producers sell the domestic like product to captive producers of downstream articles as well as to the "merchant" market. In such cases, the ITC is required to separate domestic production into two streams and consider only the stream of production destined for the merchant market.[41]

---

[39] 19 U.S.C. §1677(7)(B).

[40] 19 U.S.C. §1677(7)(C).

[41] 19 U.S.C. §1677(7)(C)(iv).

A special rule is provided for agricultural products. The ITC must determine the prevailing market price or minimum support price of the product in the United States.[42] The ITC also must consider whether an increased burden on government income or price support programs results from the dumping or the subsidy.

(h) Cumulation

Not infrequently, countervailing duty and antidumping investigations are commenced simultaneously against the same class or kind of goods from multiple countries. The law requires the "cumulation" of such imports in determining material injury. The ITC is required to cumulate injury findings with regard to all petitions filed or investigations commenced on the same day, of imports that compete with each other and with domestic like products in the United States market.[43]

There are limited exceptions to the cumulation rule. Exemptions apply to:

1. Goods that are determined by the ITA not to have benefited from subsidies or to have been dumped.
2. Goods from countries in regard to which the investigation has been terminated.
3. Goods from Caribbean Basin beneficiary countries.

Goods from Canada are exempt in limited circumstances. The cumulation rule applies to all Caribbean Basin goods for exports from several Caribbean Basin beneficiary countries.[44]

(i) Threat of Material Injury

An affirmative material injury determination may be made when material injury exists or is likely. In addition, a material injury determination may be made if material injury is threatened. However, in the case of threatened injury, the standards that the ITC is required to consider in ascertaining whether such a threat exists are different from actual injury determination. Threat of material injury[45] mandates nine analyses and permits the ITC to consider other economic factors that it deems relevant. The nine mandatory factors are:

1. In a countervailing duty, the likelihood of increases in imports of subsidized merchandise;
2. The likelihood that imports into the United States will increase substantially because of existing unused production capacity or imminent substantial increase in such capacity in the exporting country;

---

[42] 19 U.S.C. §1677(7)(D).

[43] 19 U.S.C. §1677(7)(G).

[44] 19 U.S.C. §1677(7)(G)(ii).

[45] 19 U.S.C. §1677(7)(F).

3. Increases in the level of market penetration achieved by the subject imports and the likelihood of substantial increases in market penetration;
4. Whether the prices at which the subject imports are entering the United States market are likely to significantly depress or supress the prices of like domestic products or to increase the level of demand for imports;
5. Inventories of the imported merchandise;
6. The potential for product shifting in the exporting country from other products to the subject imports;
7. The potential for product shifting as between raw and processed agricultural products;
8. The negative effect (actual and potential) on existing development and production efforts of the United States industry, including efforts to develop derivative or more advanced versions of the domestic like product; and
9. Other demonstrable adverse trends indicating the probability that material injury is likely by reason of imports or contracts to import the subject merchandise.

The ITC is required to consider the foregoing nine factors as a whole.

(j) Applying the Cumulation Rule

A special rule on cumulation has been provided for application in cases in which threatened material injury is claimed. The rule is noteworthy, chiefly because it is applicable only "to the extent practicable." It follows the general cumulation rule in that its application is limited to cases in which the petitions were filed or investigations commenced on the same day. The ITC may consider changes in conditions pertinent to injury investigations that occur after the filing of the petition.[46]

13.5 Investigations and Enforcement

Countervailing and antidumping duty cases are extremely document-intensive. The statute itself identifies the petition and various notices required to be published, as well as determinations and orders. These documents are described in greater detail in the regulations. The regulations provide for exporter, producer, importer, and domestic producer questionnaires. These documents, along with their responses and the exhibits required to be submitted, lie at the heart of every countervailing and antidumping duty case.

The volume of information required is extensive. Each transaction in each relevant market during the period of investigation must be documented in a computerized format acceptable to the ITA. Information pertaining to the corporate structure and financial statements of the parties must be submitted and examined. Details of cost, pricing, and competitiveness are examined.

---

[46] 19 U.S.C. §1677(7)(I).

Following the submission of the questionnaire responses, verifications of the responses are conducted. Verifications take place at the premises of the producer and the exporter. Almost invariably, deficiency letters are issued at the conclusion of the verification, which require very prompt responses. In addition, the parties are given, and take, the opportunity to comment on submissions of other parties.

All of this verification activity takes place within a fairly short time frame. The administrative burden on parties to countervailing and antidumping duty cases is heavy. It is of great importance that adequate resources be devoted by petitioners to the preparation of a case, and by respondents to their replies. Parties must be prepared to select both legal counsel and economic experts to assist in the preparation of the legal and economic aspects of the cases.

13.6 Procedures for Initiating Investigations

The rules for the prosecution of countervailing duty and antidumping cases are similar but not identical. We consider them together, pointing out applicable differences. Initiation of countervailing duty cases is provided in 19 *United States Code* Section 1671(a) and for antidumping cases in Section 1673(a). Either type of case may be commenced by the ITA upon its determination from available information that a formal investigation is warranted. In practice, this authority is rarely utilized.[47]

The ITA is authorized to monitor merchandise that is not the subject of an investigation if two requirements are met:

1. Two antidumping orders as to the same class or kind of merchandise from other countries are in effect.
2. The ITA has reason to suspect the existence of an extraordinary pattern of persistent injurious dumping from one or more additional supplier countries.

The ITA is required to immediately initiate a formal investigation if the ITA determines that sufficient information exists to justify the initiation of a formal investigation.

(a) Initiating the Investigation

More commonly, and in fact almost universally, investigations are initiated by petition.[48] An interested party may initiate an investigation by petitioning the ITA on behalf of an industry. The petition must allege the elements necessary for the imposition of a countervailing or antidumping duty, as the case may be.

Petitions may be filed simultaneously under the antidumping and the countervailing duty laws, but separate petitions must be filed. Leave is given to amend the

---

[47] 19 U.S.C. §1671(a), §1673(a).

[48] 19 U.S.C. §§1671a(b), 1673a(b).

petition within the discretion of the ITA or the ITC. The law requires simultaneous filing with the ITC when a petition is filed with the ITA.

(b) The Petition

The petition is an important document that requires careful preparation. The petition must allege each element necessary to success and to make out what is equivalent to a *prima facie* case. In practice, this means careful research of markets and of any available data pertinent to both the domestic industry and the competing industry in the country of exportation.

Usually this analysis entails visiting the country of exportation to gather information. The analysis includes reliance on local experts, the gathering and analysis of information available from public resources, and preparation under proper legal supervision of information pertinent to the condition of the domestic industry as a whole.

A special provision, applicable to the countervailing duty law only, provides for the filing of a petition based on the derogation of an international undertaking on official export credits.[49] If this undertaking occurs, the ITA is required to notify the Secretary of the Treasury, who, within five days after the date on which the investigation is initiated, must determine the existence and estimated value of the derogation and publish its determination in the *Federal Register.*

(c) Filing the Petition

Under both statutes,[50] the following rules apply upon the filing of a petition:

1. *Notice.* Notice must be given to the government of any exporting country named in the petition by providing that government with a copy of the public version of the petition. The reference to "public version" reflects the fact that petitions usually contain confidential information subject to protective order. Whenever confidential information is filed with either the ITA or the ITC, a public version with confidential information deleted must be filed simultaneously.
2. *Consultation.* Under the countervailing duty law, if the exporting country is a party to the GATT Subsidies Agreement, the ITA is required to provide that country with the opportunity for consultations as to the petition.
3. *Non-interference.* After a petition is filed, the ITA is forbidden to accept any unsolicited oral or written communication from any person, other than an interested party, until a decision as to whether to initiate an investigation has been made. Inquiries regarding the status of consideration of a petition are permissible.

---

[49] 19 U.S.C. §1671(b)(3).

[50] 19 U.S.C. §§1671(b)(4), 1673(b)(4).

4. *Nondisclosure.* If a petition is submitted to the ITA or the ITC for review prior to its filing, neither the ITA nor the ITC may disclose any information with respect to it.

(d) Interested Parties

The phrase "interested party" is defined to include:[51]

1. A foreign manufacturer, producer, or exporter of the subject merchandise, the United States importer, and a trade or business association of which a majority of the members are producers, exporters, or importers
2. The government of the country of exportation
3. A United States manufacturer, producer, or wholesaler of a domestic like product
4. A labor union or group of workers that is representative of a United States industry engaged in the manufacture, production, or wholesaling of a like product
5. A trade or business association, the majority of whose members manufacture, produce, or wholesale a domestic like product in the United States
6. An association, the majority of whose members is composed of "interested parties"
7. With regard to agricultural products, processors, producers, and growers of such products in the United States

(e) Timing

Various time constraints apply to the petition. In general, the ITA must reply within 20 days of the filing of a petition. If exceptional circumstances exist, the ITA must reply within 40 days after filing. If practicable, the ITA must reply within less than 20 days if the petition is filed for merchandise that was the subject of a revoked or suspended countervailing or antidumping duty order.

The ITA must determine whether the petition sufficiently alleges the elements necessary for the imposition of a countervailing or antidumping duty. In addition, the ITA must determine whether the petition has been filed on behalf of a domestic industry. If the ITA determines that elements and parties are satisfied, the ITA must make an affirmative determination and commence an investigation as to the existence of a countervailable subsidy or sales at less than fair value. If the determination is negative, the ITA must dismiss the petition.

A 25% test and a 50% test apply. For the purpose of initiating a petition, the ITA must determine that the domestic producers or workers who support the petition account for at least 25% of total domestic production of the like product and more than 50% of the production of the domestic like product produced by the portion

[51] 19 U.S.C. §1677(9).

of the industry expressing support or opposition to the petition. In making this calculation, the production of domestic producers related to foreign suppliers is to be disregarded unless such domestic producers demonstrate that their interests would be adversely affected by the imposition of a countervailing or antidumping duty order. Also, the ITA is authorized to disregard the position of domestic producers who are also importers.

Interested parties are permitted to comment on the petition before the determination is issued.[52] The phrase "domestic producers or workers" means those interested parties who are elegible to file a petition.

(f) Issuance and Monitoring

The ITA is required to immediately give notice to the ITC upon the issuance of a determination. If the determination is affirmative, the ITA is required to make available to the ITC information in its possession relating to the matter. This procedure is designed to protect the confidentiality of the information.

A subsection provides for the monitoring of current import information by Customs. A subsection provides for transmission to the ITA of such information at least monthly if, in a countervailing duty case, the subsidy is inconsistent with the GATT Subsidies Agreement. A subsection provides for transmission to the ITA in an antidumping duty case if there is a history of dumping of the subject merchandise or the importer should have known that the merchandise was sold at a dumped price.

13.7 Preliminary Determinations

The first step which follows after an investigation is officially commenced is the preliminary determination.[53] Preliminary determinations are made both on injury and on subsidization or dumping. The injury determination does not establish the existence of injury, only whether there is reasonable indication of injury. This determination is made by the ITC within 45 days after the date on which the petition is filed or self-initiated by the ITA. Alternatively, the determination is made within 25 days from the commencement of the investigation if the time within which the ITA is required to commence an investigation has been extended.

The ITC is required to determine whether a reasonable indication of injury exists, and whether imports of the subject merchandise are not negligible. If the ITC is unable to make either of these findings, the investigation must be terminated.[54]

A "reasonable basis" standard applies to countervailing duty investigations. The ITA must determine if the ITC has made an affirmative determination of reasonable indication of injury. The time period is within 65 days after the initiation of the investigation. The determination specifies whether there is a reasonable basis to believe or suspect that a countervailable subsidy is being provided as to the subject

---

[52] 19 U.S.C. §§1671A(c), 1673a(c)(4)(E).

[53] 19 U.S.C. §§1671d, 1673b.

[54] 19 U.S.C. §§1671b(a), 1673b(a).

merchandise.[55] An expedited determination may be required. If so, it must be made within 65 days after the date of initiation of the investigation unless the case is determined to be extraordinarily complicated.

(a) Waiver of Verification

A procedure known as waiver of verification may be applicable. The procedure applies if the interested party to the investigation has filed an irrevocable written waiver of verification of information provided to the ITA in the course of the investigation. In that event the ITA is authorized to issue a preliminary determination on an expedited basis.[56]

The expedited preliminary determination must be based on the facts gathered in the first 50 days after the investigation was initiated. The ITA must disclose that information to the interested parties within 5 days thereafter. The waiver of verification must be filed within 3 days from that date.

(b) *De Minimis* Rule

A net countervailable subsidy that is less than 1% of the value of the subject merchandise is *de minimis* and must be disregarded.[57] If the subject merchandise is the produce of a developing country, the *de minimis* level rises to 2%. The applicable percentage rises to 3% if the developing country is a least developed country or has notified the ITA that it has eliminated export subsides on an expedited basis. The 3% rule lapses on January 1, 2003.

(c) Timing Issues

In an antidumping investigation, the ITA is required to make its preliminary determination within 140 days after the date of initiation of the investigation. A prerequisite is an affirmative determination of reasonable indication of injury by the ITC. In second offender cases, the 140-day period is shortened to 100 days; in multiple offender cases, the period is shortened to 80 days.[58]

The waiver of verification rule applies to antidumping investigations. The time period for the receipt of information is 60 days rather than 50 days. The ITA must determine that sufficient information to make the decision exists. The ITA must disclose this information to the petitioner and any interested parties within 75 days. The preliminary determination must be made within 90 days from the date of initiation of the investigation.[59] The *de minimis* dumping margin under the antidumping law is less than 2% of the value of the merchandise.

---

[55] 19 U.S.C. §1671b(b).

[56] 19 U.S.C. §1671b(b)(2).

[57] 19 U.S.C. §1671b(d)(4).

[58] 19 U.S.C. §1673b(b)(1).

[59] 19 U.S.C. §1673b(b)(2).

(d) Complicated Cases

The period of the investigation may be extended in complicated cases upon the request of the petitioner. The extension may be granted if the ITA concludes that the parties concerned are cooperating and determines that the case is extraordinarily complicated because of:

1. The number and complexity of the alleged countervailable subsidy practices or, in an antidumping case, the number and complexity of the transactions or adjustments in issue
2. The novelty of the issues presented
3. The number of firms whose activities must be investigated
4. In the case of a countervailing duty investigation, the need to determine the extent to which particular countervailable subsidies are used by individual manufacturers, producers, and exporters

The ITA is authorized to extend the date if the ITA concludes that additional time is necessary to make the preliminary determinations. The time period within which the preliminary determination must be made can be not more than 130 days after the date a countervailing duty investigation is initiated or 190 days after the date an antidumping investigation is initiated.

(e) Countervailing Duty Investigation

The ITA must determine the estimated individual countervailable subsidy rate if the preliminary determination is affirmative in a countervailing duty investigation. The countervailable subsidy rate is determined for each exporter and producer individually investigated. An estimated "all-others" countervailable subsidy rate is determined for all exporters and producers not individually investigated or for new exporters and producers. The ITA should order the posting of a cash deposit or other security to be applied to each importation of the subject merchandise. The amount is based on either the individual countervailable subsidy rate or the all-others rate or, if applicable, the countrywide rate. The ITA orders the suspension of liquidation of all entries of subject merchandise from the date on which the notice of determination is published in the *Federal Register* or, if later, a date that is 60 days from the day the notice of determination to initiate the investigation is published in the *Federal Register*.[60]

(f) Antidumping Investigation

The ITA must determine an estimated weighted average dumping margin in the case of an antidumping investigation when an affirmative determination is made. The average dumping margin applies for each exporter and producer individually

[60] 19 U.S.C. §1671b(d).

investigated. An all-others rate applies for all exporters and producers not individually investigated. The ITA must require the posting of a cash deposit or other security for each entry of the subject merchandise based on the estimated weighted average dumping margin, or all-others rate, as may be applicable. The ITA must also order the suspension of liquidation of all entries under the same rules as apply to an affirmative countervailing duty preliminary determination.[61]

If a critical circumstances determination has been made, the dates for the suspension of the liquidation are rolled back. The rollback is the later of 90 days before the date the suspension order is entered, or from the date on which the notice of the determination to initiate the investigation was published in the *Federal Register*.[62] The ITA must provide notice of its determination to the ITC, and vice versa.

Producer, exporter, and importer questionnaires are issued upon the commencement of an investigation. These questionnaires are multisection forms that require respondents in countervailing and antidumping duty investigations to expose every fact relevant to the investigation.

The framework of the questionnaires corresponds to the requirements of United States law. Culturally, conceptually, and linguistically, the questionnaire respondents are usually unprepared and unable to cope readily with the questionnaires. Recipients require assistance to permit them to understand the completeness of what is required, the unyielding time frame within which the information must be produced, and the detail required. The respondents must be educated about verification procedures and the necessity to have available all underlying documentation to support questionnaire responses.

13.8 Termination or Suspension of Investigations

An investigation may be terminated if the petitioner withdraws its petition.[63] If a withdrawn petition is refiled within three months after the date of withdrawal, the investigative record of the previous investigation may be used.

(a) Withdrawal

If the withdrawl of a petition results from an agreement to limit imports, the withdrawl may not be accepted by the ITA unless it is in the public interest. The public interest factors that may be taken into account are:

1. Whether the agreement will have a greater adverse impact on United States consumers than the imposition of antidumping duties, based on the relative impact on consumer prices and the availability of the supplies of the merchandise

---

[61] 19 U.S.C. §1673b(d).

[62] 19 U.S.C. §§1671(b)(e), 1673(b)(e).

[63] 19 U.S.C. §§1671c, 1673c.

2. The relevant impact on the international economic interests of the United States
3. The relative impact on competitiveness of the domestic industry producing the like merchandise

A decision to terminate may not be made without prior consultations with potentially affected consuming industries and potentially affected producers and workers in the domestic industry producing the like merchandise. A decision to terminate may not be made before an affirmative preliminary determination has been made.

(b) Suspension

Both statutes also permit the suspension of an investigation if the countervailable subsidy has been eliminated or offset, or if sales at less than fair value have been eliminated or exports of the subject merchandise have ceased. The statutes permit suspension of an investigation if agreements to eliminate the injurious effects of the countervailable subsidies or dumped prices are concluded. Suspension of an investigation, based on an agreement to eliminate injurious effects, require a determination that ordinary circumstances are present. The extraordinary circumstances contemplated by the statute are, in the case of the countervailing duty law, that suspension of the investigation will be more beneficial to the domestic industry than its continuation, and that the investigation is complex. The statute ascribes the same meaning to "complex" as it does to "extraordinarily complicated."[64]

(c) Prohibition

The ITA is prohibited from accepting a suspension agreement unless the ITA is satisfied that the suspension is in the public interest and that effective monitoring of the agreement by the United States is practicable. Under the countervailing duty law, if a period of time is provided for elimination or offset of the countervailable subsidy, a mechanism to monitor imports to assure that the subsidy does not increase during that interim period must be established.

Example

A recent case highlights the use of the suspension power. A countervailing duty case was instituted against imports of softwood lumber from Canada. The government of Canada and the provincial governments opposed the imposition of countervailing duties. Ultimately, an agreement was entered into imposing the countervailing export tax on producers and exporters to the extent that countervailable subsidies continued to be granted to producers or exporters by the provincial authorities. Thus, the benefit of the countervailable subsidy was eliminated; as was the fallout resulting from the imposition of a countervailing duty by the United States perceived by the Canadian government, the provincial governments, and many citizens of Canada, to be unfair, was avoided.

---

[64] 19 U.S.C. §1671b.

13.9 Final Determinations

Following a preliminary determination, if the investigation has not been terminated or suspended,[65] the investigation must proceed to separate final determinations by the ITA and ITC.[66] The final determination is required to be made within 75 days after the date of the preliminary determination. The final determination in an antidumping duty investigation may be postponed until the 135th day after the date of publication of the preliminary determination.

The postponement can be requested by exporters who account for a significant proportion of exports of the subject merchandise if the preliminary determination was affirmative. The postponement can be requested by the petitioner if the preliminary determination was negative.

The final determination must incorporate the finding of the ITA in its investigation of critical circumstances if the petitioner sought to designate the case as involving such circumstances. The ITA must disregard any *de minimis* countervailable subsidy or dumping margin.[67]

(a) Final Determination of Injury

The ITC makes a final determination of injury if the ITA has made a final affirmative determination of net countervailable subsidies or sales at less than fair value that are more than negligible.[68] In other cases, the injury investigation is to be terminated. The ITC is required to make its final injury determination 120 days after the date of the ITA's affirmative preliminary determination or 45 days after its final affirmative determination, whichever is later. If the ITA's preliminary determination was negative, but its final determination was affirmative, the ITC must make its final determination within 75 days of the date of the ITA's final affirmative determination.

In its final determination, in cases in which retroactive application of the final order is required to be taken into account, the ITC must consider whether the imports that are the subject of the affirmative determination are likely to undermine seriously the remedial effect of the countervailing or antidumping duty order intended to be issued. In making this determination, the ITC is required to consider the timing and the volume of the imports, whether there has been a rapid increase in inventories, and any other circumstances apparent to the ITC indicating that the remedial effect of the order will be seriously undermined. If the ITC determines that there is no material injury, but that a threat of material injury exists, the ITC must take account of whether the threat would have been actualized but for the suspension of liquidation.

---

[65] 19 U.S.C. §1671c or §1673c.

[66] 19 U.S.C. §1671d.

[67] 19 U.S.C. §§1671d(a), 1673d(a).

[68] 19 U.S.C. §§1671d(b), 1673d(b).

(b) Affirmative Determination

Subsection (c)(1) of both statutes requires that the ITA, upon making an affirmative determination, make available to the ITC all information upon which its determination was based and which the ITC considers relevant to the injury determination. Procedures prevent disclosure of confidential information to unauthorized parties.

The ITA is required in a countervailing duty case to estimate the individual countervailable subsidy rates. Countervailable subsidy rates apply each exporter and producer individually investigated. The "all-others" rate applies for all other exporters and producers, including new exporters and producers, or if applicable to determine the estimated countrywide subsidy rate. In an antidumping case, the ITA must determine the estimated weighted average dumping margin for each exporter and producer individually investigated, and the "all-others" rate for all exporters and producers not individually investigated.

(c) Finalization Process

The ITA must also order the posting of a cash deposit, bond, or other security for each entry of the subject merchandise, based on its estimated determination of the countervailing or antidumping duty applicable. If the preliminary determination was negative, the ITA must order the suspension of the liquidation of unliquidated entries at the time of the final determination. A duty assessment order is required in the event of affirmative final determinations of the ITA and ITC. If either final determination is negative, a notice of the negative determination must be published. The ITA must then terminate the suspension of liquidation and release any other bond or security or refund any cash deposits.

The method for establishing the "all-others" rate and the countrywide subsidy rate in countervailing duty cases is set forth by statute.[69] In general, the all-others rate is equal to the weighted average of the net countervailing duty rates or average dumping margins of individually investigated exporters and producers. Zero and *de minimis* rates established individually in the investigation are excluded.

(d) Procedural Issues

Subsection (d) of both sections of the statute provides for publication in the *Federal Register* of any determination made under these sections of the statute. Subsection (d) requires notice to the petitioner, the other parties to the investigation, and the ITA in the case of an ITC decision, and vice versa. The decision must set forth the facts and conclusions of law upon which the determination is based.

Judicial review of countervailing and antidumping duty cases is based on the agency record, so that the facts and law discussed in the determinations have great significance. Because the final determination has such significance, and in contemplation of the exceeding complexity of the countervailing duty and antidumping

[69] 19 U.S.C. §§1671d(c)(5), and 1673d(c)(5).

analyses, Congress has provided for the correction of ministerial errors in the final determination in subsection (e) of both statutes. These are defined as errors in addition, subtraction, or other arithmetic function, clerical errors resulting from inaccurate copying, duplication, or the like, and any other type of unintentional error that the ITA considers ministerial.

13.10 The Duty Assessment Order

Customs takes over once it is finally determined that a United States producer is suffering some injury from foreign competitors that are dumping or that enjoy a net countervailable subsidy. The ITA must issue an order describing the subject merchandise in sufficient detail as it deems necessary, requiring the deposit along with any normal applicable customs duties or estimated countervailing or antidumping duties. The ITA must issue the order within seven days of a final injury determination by the ITC. These deposits are to be made with Customs not later than ten days from the date of each importation.

The duty assessment order must direct Customs officers to assess a countervailing duty equal to the amount of the net countervailable subsidy or the amount by which the normal value of the merchandise exceeds its export price. This duty assessment is to be made within six months after the date on which the ITA receives satisfactory information to permit it to make this calculation. In any event, the assessment order is to take place no later than twelve months after the end of the annual accounting period of the manufacturer or exporter in a countervailing duty case or an antidumping case in which the merchandise is sold prior to importation. The time period in an antidumping case in which the merchandise is so sold is within twelve months after the end of the annual accounting period of the manufacturer or exporter in which the merchandise is sold in the United States.[70]

Special rules are provided in both statutes to deal with situations in which material injury is not actual, but threatened. Other provisions apply when the establishment of an industry has been materially retarded. These provisions limit, to the extent possible, the imposition of countervailing or antidumping duties to manufacturers or exporters doing business in the region that has suffered injury in a regional industry case. They apply to the treatment of new exporters and producers. These rules are necessary to assure that remedies provided by domestic law do not exceed the scope of what is permissible under the GATT Agreement. The provisions apply to unfairly traded merchandise when the injurious effects are established.

13.11 Miscellaneous

Each statute provides several rules that, although important, are too narrow in their focus and application to be discussed fully in this chapter. However, to be

[70] 19 U.S.C. §§1671e(a), 1673e(a).

sure, the reader should be aware of their existence. Differences between estimated duty deposits required pursuant to a preliminary affirmative determination and the final estimated duty provided in the final determination are reconciled.[71]

Export-Import Bank financing is not superseded based on the existence of a preliminary countervailing duty determination.[72] Instead, the Secretary of the Treasury may not authorize the Export-Import Bank to provide guarantees, insurance, and credits to competing United States sellers.

Customs enforces countervailing and antidumping duty orders through the following measures:

1. Requiring the cash deposit of the duties assessed
2. Requiring the maintaining and producing of records containing necessary information to customs officers to permit a proper assessment, and payment on demand of the amount of duty imposed[73]

Special rules apply for short life cycle merchandise.[74] Short life cycle merchandise is any product that the ITC determines is likely to become outmoded within four years, by reason of technological advances, after the product is commercially available. For purposes of this paragraph, the term "outmoded" refers to a kind of style that is no longer state-of-the-art.[75]

Prior antidumping duties were subject to the application of the drawback laws upon exportation. This is no longer the case. Consequently, refunds of antidumping duties paid on reexported goods subject to an antidumping order are not allowable.

13.12 Administrative Review of Duty Determinations

(a) Duty Determination

Once a countervailing or antidumping duty order is issued, the order does not readily disappear. The order remains in force for a minimum of several years. During that time, foreign producers and exporters may find that the amount of the countervailing or antidumping duty may be sufficiently high to render imports noncompetitive.

The duty order results in the disappearance of the producer's or exporter's goods in the United States market. The producer or exporter may continue to sell into the United States market. If they do, the goods are subject to ongoing scrutiny and annual adjustment of the rate of the countervailing duty or the dumping margin.

---

[71] 19 U.S.C. §§1671f, 1673f.

[72] 19 U.S.C. §1671g.

[73] 19 U.S.C. §§1671h, 1673g.

[74] 19 U.S.C. §1673h.

[75] 19 U.S.C. §1673h(b)(4).

The ongoing scrutiny takes the form of an administrative review[76] of the countervailing or antidumping duty order at least once within each 12-month period following the anniversary date of the original order. These reviews are not automatic; they take place at the request of either the petitioner or another interested party. If no review is requested, the estimated duties deposited are accepted as final.

Until these reviews are completed, the countervailing or antidumping duty remains tentative; the duty is subject to revision based on the outcome of the review. Accordingly, the importer remains at risk that the final assessed countervailing or antidumping duty will be higher than estimated at the time of importation. The costs of the increase may not be recoverable.

Administrative reviews serve to bring current the amount of any net countervailable subsidy or antidumping duty. Administrative reviews may also inquire into the current status of and compliance with suspension agreements whereby countervailing duty investigations were suspended. Administrative reviews may also be utilized to establish specific rates for new exporters and producers otherwise subject to all-others rates.

Although the statute provides time limits for the completion of administrative reviews of the amounts of countervailing and antidumping duties, the time for completion may and often does extend to 18 months. Accordingly, the importer remains at risk for an extended period of time.

The process of review usually includes a verification of the date submitted by the producer and the exporter in questionnaire responses. Since verification takes place at the premises of the producer and exporter, the process is expensive as well as time-consuming.

(b) Review of Injury Determinations

Injury determinations of the ITC are subject to review. The question considered in an injury determination review is whether changed circumstances warrant a review of the determination. In the case of an accepted suspension agreement, that agreement is subject to review.

In "changed circumstances" reviews, the burden of persuasion rests upon the party seeking the change. Thus, if a party subject to an antidumping or countervailing duty order believes that changed circumstances have eliminated the likelihood of material injury, it is incumbent upon that party to carry the burden of persuasion. Similarly, a party seeking to set aside a suspension agreement must show that continuance of the suspension agreement will not completely eliminate the injurious effects of imports of the subject merchandise or lead to the continuation or recurrence of material injury.

(c) Sunset Provisions

Five years after the date of publication of a countervailing or antidumping duty order or notice of suspension, the ITC must give notice and conduct a review to de-

---

[76] 19 U.S.C. §1675.

termine whether revocation of the order or termination of the suspension agreement would be likely to lead to continuation or recurrence of dumping, countervailable subsidization, or material injury.[77] The order may be revoked or the suspended investigation terminated if the order does not meet this objective. The statute does not make revocation the obvious outcome. The ITA and ITC are required to give full consideration to all the circumstances and to issue an order supported by substantial evidence.

(d) Special Reviews

Special rules apply to changed circumstances reviews[78] and five year reviews.[79] The special rules are similar in subject matter, but different in detail from the special rules applicable to preliminary and final investigations of countervailing and antidumping duty petitions. These rules must be consulted in the event a party wishes to make use of these procedures or is subject to them. Other special rules are provided to deal with the review of countervailing duty determinations as to with no injury determination is required.[80]

Special rules apply to the review of countervailing duty cases that have been disposed of through the imposition of quantitative restrictions rather than countervailing duties.[81]

13.13 Practice and Procedure

Several rules of practice and procedure, mostly governed by detailed regulations, must be mentioned.

(a) Mandatory Hearings

Mandatory hearings take place prior to the issuance of final determinations.[82] However, the statute provides many more opportunities for hearings, and it is only rarely that the opportunity is not utilized.

Both the ITA and the ITC act as investigating agencies, not as judicial tribunals. The staffs of the agencies participate very significantly in the investigations and provide testimony, as well as reporting in writing to the decision makers. Also, since the hearings are not quasi-judicial, there is no right of cross-examination and the judicial rules of evidence do not apply.

---

[77] 19 U.S.C. §1675(c).

[78] 19 U.S.C. §1675(b).

[79] 19 U.S.C. §1675(c).

[80] 19 U.S.C. §1675b.

[81] 19 U.S.C. §1676.

[82] 19 U.S.C. §1677c.

(b) Best Information Available

The best information available (BIA) rule permits the ITA and the ITC to infer critical facts that an exporter or producer fails to provide.[83] The BIA rule significantly relaxes the substantial evidence rule when the circumstances described in the statute apply. Because BIA is frequently utilized and its liberal use generally approved by the courts, note must be taken of it.

BIA may generally be utilized if necessary information is not available on the record, or an interested party:

1. Withholds information that has been requested
2. Fails to provide such information by deadlines for the submission of information or in the form and manner requested
3. Significantly impedes any type of countervailing duty or antidumping proceeding
4. Provides such information but the information is not verifiable

In making use of BIA, the statute provides a mighty cudgel. Unless the party who has failed to cooperate has acted to the best of its ability to comply, the ITA or the ITC may use an inference that is adverse to the interests of that party in selecting from among the facts otherwise unavailable. The information that the statute permits the ITA or ITC to rely on includes:

1. The date provided by the petitioner in the petition;
2. Information gleaned from other investigations; and
3. "Any other information placed on the record."

The ITA or ITC is required to corroborate secondary information when relying on it. The agency is required to rely on this information only to the extend practicable and with the use of independent sources reasonably at its disposal.

(c) Access to Information

Very sensitive, confidential information must be provided by all parties to the ITA and the ITC. As a result, the statute contains an extensive law governing the protection of sensitive information.[84] All documents containing confidential information must be accompanied by nonconfidential public versions. Protective orders are strictly enforced and carry severe sanctions. The forms of protective orders are provided in the regulations. They cover not only disclosure pursuant to the orders, but disposition of documents containing confidential information upon the windup of a proceeding.

---

[83] 19 U.S.C. §1677e.

[84] 19 U.S.C. §1677f.

13.14 Judicial Review and Dispute Settlement

(a) Judicial Review

Determinations of the ITA and ITC are subject to judicial review. Review is vested exclusively in the United States Court of International Trade, and appellate review is conducted by the United States Court of Appeals for the Federal Circuit. In general, the scope of review is limited to the agency record and the standard of review is the substantial evidence standard.

The courts have had considerable experience in reviewing the statutes. The courts are mindful not only of the complexity of the statutes but also of the time and personnel constraints under which the ITA and the ITC operate. They have therefore developed very clear and broad rules of deference. When there is a gap in the statute, the determination of the ITA or ITC as to how to fill it is generally respected. Moreover, the courts have been careful not to interfere with the factual determinations of the agencies when there is evidence of record to support those determinations. The courts routinely abstain from weighing competing evidence, holding that it is the prerogative and duty of the agencies to carry out that function.

(b) Dispute Settlement

"Dispute settlement" refers to intergovernmental disputes among members of the World Trade Organization or between the United States and countries with whom treaties providing for dispute settlement exist. Private parties do not participate directly in dispute settlement.

Dispute settlement exists because the countervailing and antidumping duty laws are the domestic embodiments of treaty obligations of the United States. These treaties define the scope of rights and remedies permissible to WTO members. Dispute settlement is utilized when one member state believes that another nation has exceeded the scope of its treaty rights or deprived another nation of the rights expected by that other nation. The outcome of dispute settlement usually is not the setting aside of a disputed determination. Typically, it leads to a right to compensation, and sometimes to a conforming change in domestic law or regulation.

CHAPTER 14

Dumping and Transfer Pricing

Edward L. Farrell, Jr.
Seth T. Kaplan
Beril J. Lapson
Kenneth C. Stanhagen

14.1 Introduction
14.2 Antidumping Laws and Regulations
(a) Administrative Framework and Definitions
(b) Relationship to GATT
14.3 Antidumping Procedures
(a) Time Frame for Investigation
(b) Administrative Reviews
14.4 Injury Determination
14.5 Dumping Analysis
(a) Analysis of U.S. Sales
(b) Calculation of Normal Value
(c) Average Ex-Factory Price
(d) Using Constructed Value and Cost of Production
(e) Test for Sales below Cost
14.6 Constructed Value
(a) Transactions with Affiliated Companies
(b) Combining Affiliated Party Data
(c) Research and Development Expenses
(d) Startup Costs
14.7 Determining Dumping Margins
(a) Reporting Companies
(b) Reporting Data
(c) The Dumping Margin Formula
14.8 Relational Topics
14.9 Implementing a Market Share Strategy

14.10 Use of Confidential Data
- (a) Antidumping Procedures
- (b) APO Example
- (c) APO System
- (d) Transfer Pricing

14.11 Use of "Facts Available" Rule
- (a) FA Example
- (b) Transfer Pricing

14.12 I.R.C. Section 6038A Recordkeeping

14.13 Pricing Methodologies

14.14 Summary

14.1 Introduction

With the expansion of international trade and increased competition, two areas relevant to the process of international trade, dumping and transfer pricing, have become more important than ever before. Multinational companies are faced with real world implications and must consider both of these areas for strategic planning and pricing decisions.

Both dumping and transfer pricing deal with goods in international commerce, but differ in scope. Dumping typically refers to sales between unrelated parties, and is deemed to occur when prices charged to third-party customers in the import market are below the prices charged in the manufacturer's home market. Dumping penalties are generally imposed only when dumping has caused "injury" to producers in the import market. In contrast, transfer pricing pertains to pricing of transactions between related parties. Antidumping laws apply only to sales of tangible property, but arm's-length transfer pricing requirements apply to all cross-border transactions between related persons, including sales of tangible property, intellectual property, and services. Because of this crucial difference in focus, the impacts of a dumping investigation and a transfer price audit do not usually conflict or adversely interact.

Given the arcane and specialized nature of each of these areas, they have traditionally been the professional provinces of separate practitioners with little or no regard for overlap and strategic differences. Because of this, Section 14.2 of this chapter provides an overview of the antidumping rules. Although antidumping rules focus on the definitions and procedures under U.S. law, almost all of our major trading partners employ similar definitional rules under multilateral and bilateral antidumping agreements. Exporters can refer to these basic concepts as a frame of reference for the application of the dumping rules of a foreign country applicable to export sales from the United States. In all cases, however, persons engaged in international trade should consult appropriate counsel before taking any specific action.

The remainder of this chapter deals with some areas of strategic importance to the multinational company when planning or defending its policies in these areas. It also addresses certain public policy issues that have arisen in the United States in connection with the revision of the transfer pricing rules under Internal Revenue Code (I.R.C.) Section 482. Commentators and government officials have questioned whether certain procedures used in the antidumping area may be of use in the transfer pricing area. As explained later, the authors urge caution in transposing antidumping procedures to the transfer pricing area.

On December 8, 1994, Congress passed the Uruguay Round Agreements Act (URAA). The URAA became effective on January 1, 1995, and updates the existing antidumping statute, the Tariff Act of 1930 (the Act) to conform with the new General Agreement on Tariffs and Trade (GATT) antidumping agreement (the Agreement) negotiated in the Uruguay Round of multilateral trade negotiation.

Regulations and administrative practice are important elements in the conduct and ultimate outcome of an antidumping case. Thus, until the regulations have been published and cases have been adjudicated dealing with issues in each of the areas affected by the new law, it will not be clear exactly what the effects of the new will be on parties and practitioners. The first cases under the new law, pursuant to petitions filed in early 1995, reached final dumping and injury determinations in mid-1996. The authors were involved in many of these cases. Although the DOC has taken positions on many issues, the application of certain new provisions in the URAA are not entirely clear. We provide a brief summary of the new law, the more significant changes it makes to the legal framework in the antidumping area. Specific administrative practice and implementation, some of which may have a major effect on parties involved, will evolve as the cases currently in process are completed.

In addition to substantive changes, the new legislation made several changes in terminology with the purpose of standardizing the language used in the Agreement and U.S. law. These changes, which are not intended to affect the meaning given to the terms, are shown in the following table:

Old Terminology	**New Terminology**
Purchase price	Export price
Exporter's sales price	Constructed export price
Foreign market value	Normal value
Such or similar	Foreign likc product
Like product	Domestic like product
Class or kind	Subject merchandise

In addition, the concept of "Related Parties" and "Best Information Available" have been replaced by the similar "Affiliated Parties" and "Facts Available."

14.2 Antidumping Laws and Regulations

Dumping is the practice of selling a class of products in the United States at prices that are less than their market values in the countries in which they are made and from which they are exported. U.S. law provides for a penalty if goods from a certain country are sold (or are likely to be sold) in the United States at less than their fair value. The penalty applies if the sale causes an industry in the United States to suffer or to be threatened with material injury, or which materially retards the establishment of an industry in the United States.

(a) Administrative Framework and Definitions

An antidumping petition is filed against a specific country and requires two determinations:

1. Whether the subject goods from that country have been dumped, and if so, by how much, that is, by what amounts below fair value they have been sold in the United States; and
2. Whether a U.S. industry producing the subject goods has been "injured," that is, injured, threatened with injury, or materially retarded from being established.

The two determinations are made after investigations by distinct U.S. government agencies. The U.S. International Trade Commission (ITC), a tribunal of six commissioners appointed by the President of the United States for nine-year terms, is charged with determining whether a U.S. industry has been subject to material injury or retardation due to dumped imports. The International Trade Administration (ITA), a unit of the U.S. Department of Commerce (DOC), is charged with determining whether dumping has actually occurred, and if so, its extent.

(b) Relationship to GATT

The URAA implemented the Agreement with the added elaboration of certain procedural rules and provisions. The Agreement modifies the 1979 Tokyo Round Antidumping Code and adopts higher standards of transparency and procedural fairness. Where these modifications require changes in the U.S. antidumping law, such changes are accomplished through URAA. The GATT agreement does not specify the composition of the government agencies making the determinations in an investigation. In the United States, the DOC is designated as the "administering authority." The ITC determines injury.

The Agreement acknowledges the application of the World Trade Organization (WTO) dispute settlement procedures to antidumping actions. In reviewing the antidumping actions of national authorities, WTO review panels are to rely on "the facts made available in conformity with the appropriate domestic procedures to the authorities of the importing member."[1]

The preamble to Article VI states its intent that "antidumping practices should not constitute an unjustifiable impediment to international trade" and that it is "desirable to provide for equitable and open procedures" in resolving such cases. GATT refers to the "normal" value of the exported goods (GATT Article VI), whereas the U.S.

[1]General Agreement on Tariffs and Trade, 1994, Agreement on Implementation of Article VI art. 17.5(ii).

law refers to "fair value" and to "foreign market" value as the basis for comparison and dumping evaluation of U.S. prices.[2] The GATT agreement does not specify the composition of the government agencies making the determinations in an investigation. In the United States, the DOC is designated as the "administrating authority." The ITC determines injury.

A determination of injury in an antidumping proceeding applies to all countries whether or not they have accepted the obligations of GATT. Other countries, in their own antidumping regulations, generally provide a similar test in proceedings against U.S. products.

14.3 Antidumping Procedures

An antidumping petition begins when the members of a U.S. industry manufacturing a class of products believe they have been injured by dumped imports from a particular country. A complaint, or petition, requesting relief is filed simultaneously with two agencies—the ITC and the Department of Commerce.[3] The "U.S. industry" generally means domestic producers of the subject merchandise,[4] but in certain situations it may include producers of raw materials or inputs. Interested parties that may file a petition include domestic producers, labor unions, trade associations, and, for processed agricultural products, a coalition of processors and producers or growers.[5] U.S. producers that are related to the foreign exporters of the subject goods or that are importers themselves may be excluded from the definition of U.S. industry, with standing to make or protest a petition.[6] The DOC may also initiate an antidumping investigation.[7] Although this is rarely done, the DOC initiated an antidumping investigation of dynamic random access memories of 256 kilobits and above from Japan.[8]

Under the prior practice, the "domestic industry" was presumed to support an antidumping petition if there was no significant opposition from domestic producers or workers. Under the URAA, the general rule is that the petitioners must show either affirmative support on behalf of domestic producers or workers accounting for at least 25% of U.S. production of the domestic like product or affirmative support by producers or workers representing a majority of the production of those expressing positions. The positions of domestic producers that are related to foreign producers and of domestic producers that are importers are to be disregarded.[9]

After an antidumping petition has been filed with both the ITC and the DOC, an investigation is commenced and proceeds on a fairly rigid schedule. The schedule

[2] 19 U.S.C.S. § 1673 (1993).

[3] 19 U.S.C.S. § 1673a(b)(2) (1993).

[4] 19 U.S.C.S. § 1677(4)(A) (1993).

[5] 19 U.S.C.S. § 1673a(b)(1) (1993).

[6] 19 U.S.C.S. § 1677(4)(B) (1993).

[7] 19 U.S.C.S. § 1673a(a) (1993).

[8] 50 Fed. Reg. 51,450 (Dec. 17, 1985).

[9] § 732(c)(4) of the Act.

is prescribed in detail by law.[10] The first two events under this schedule are initiation by the DOC, 20 days after filing, and preliminary determination of injury by the ITC, 45 days after filing. These steps in which the relevant agencies—the DOC and the ITC—determine whether the petition meets a set of basic requirements and whether there is reasonable indication that the U.S. industry has been injured, are the first hurdles. If the petition is flawed, the DOC will refuse to initiate an investigation unless it is corrected and refiled. If the ITC rejects the petitioner's assertion of injury at the preliminary level, then the petition is rejected and the case must be developed afresh.

(a) Time Frame for Investigation

After both of the initial hurdles have been cleared, an antidumping investigation proceeds on a rigid schedule. Under this schedule, which is precisely specified in the antidumping statute,[11] the Customs Service will begin to collect an antidumping duty deposit immediately after a DOC preliminary determination of dumping is published. This determination is made from five to seven months after the filing date of the petition. The statute provides for certain extensions, hence there is a range of dates for the determination. The final disposition of the petition takes place nine to thirteen months after the petition is filed. The disposition can be the imposition of an antidumping order for deposits on all imports of the class of goods from the named country at rates finally determined by the DOC after an extensive investigation, a finding of a zero or *de minimis* (less than 2.0%) dumping by the DOC, or a finding of no injury by the ITC. The statutory schedule has rarely, if ever, been changed by more than a few days. Under the old law, the *de minimis* rate was 0.5%. The *de minimis* rate was changed to 2.0% for investigations by the URAA. It remains 0.5% for administrative reviews.[12]

The parties to an antidumping investigation may achieve a relatively swift resolution. The petitioner will receive its first relief in the form of imposition of antidumping duty deposits five to seven months after its complaint, if the complaint has merit. Respondents will know whether they will be subject to these duties, duty deposits, or to future reviews after nine to thirteen months.

Findings of both agencies can be appealed to the U.S. Court of International Trade (CIT), but only after the final ITC and DOC results have been published and put into effect. CIT decisions can, in turn, be appealed to the Court of Appeals for the Federal Circuit.

(b) Administrative Reviews

The investigation is only the first step of an antidumping proceeding. Its objective is to determine whether the petitioner's complaint is valid, and to set a deposit

[10] 19 U.S.C.S. § 1673a(c), 1673b, and § 1673d (1993).

[11] 19 U.S.C.S. § 1673a, § 1673b, § 1673d (1993), and elsewhere.

[12] §§ 733(b)(31), 735(a)(4) of the Act.

rate of estimated antidumping duties to be collected for all subject imports. Duties are imposed for about two years from implementation of the final determinations, until sales prices and conditions are reviewed and final duty amounts can be calculated and assessed. The review process in each proceeding is conducted by the DOC on an annual basis and generally lasts for one year. The first review period, which normally extends from the date of the DOC preliminary determination until one year after implementation of the ITC final determination, is somewhat longer. The annual review procedure of the DOC is similar to that of the initial investigation, except that the main objective is to assess the actual amount of duty to be paid for each sale made during the review period.

A new deposit rate for each exporter to be collected prospectively is determined as the weighted average of dumping rates found on all sales reviewed in each period. An administrative review of a respondent's sales can be requested by an interested party—the respondent, the petitioner, or an importer. If no review is requested for a company in a particular year, all entries in the period of that company's sales will be liquidated and duties will be collected at the estimated deposit rates already in effect.

Unfortunately, during the 1970s and early 1980s, the U.S. government was not as strict in adhering to its one-year schedule for administrative reviews as it was to the statutory schedule for investigations. In fact, reviews in one case[13] were more than ten years behind schedule as of 1987. In reaction to this, the URAA imposed Statutory deadlines of one year, extendable by six months, are now imposed on the annual review process.[14]

The URAA introduced the procedure of performance reviews for revocation ("sunset" reviews) of antidumping orders at five-year intervals. Under this provision, an existing order would be revoked unless it is determined that dumping would be likely to continue or recur, resulting in injury to the domestic industry.[15]

14.4 Injury Determination

The objective of the ITC injury analysis is to determine whether imports subject to the DOC investigation are injuring or threatening to injure a domestic industry that produces a like product. According to law, the ITC must evaluate several factors in reaching an injury determination. These factors include the volume of imports of the subject merchandise, the effect of imports of such merchandise on prices, and the impact on the affected domestic industry. In turn, the impact on the affected domestic industry is analyzed by considering the following four items:

1. Actual and potential decline in output, sales, market share, profits, productivity, return on investments, and utilization of capacity;

[13]Tapered Roller Bearings Four Inches or Less in Outside Diameter and Certain Components Thereof from Japan.

[14]§ 751(a)(3)(A) of the Act.

[15]§ 751(c) of the Act.

2. Factors affecting domestic prices;
3. Actual and potential negative effects on cash flow, inventories, employment, wages, growth, ability to raise capital, and investments; and
4. Actual and potential negative effects on the existing development and production efforts of the domestic industry, including efforts to develop a derivative or more advanced version of the subject product.

The courts have given the ITC considerable leeway in administering the statute. In particular, the ITC is allowed to reach an injury determination by at least two logically distinct methods. The ITC may evaluate first whether an industry has been injured (i.e., is unhealthy), and second, whether subject imports are a cause of the injury. Alternatively, the ITC may determine whether the domestic industry would be materially better off but for the subject imports. In recent years, particular commissioners have been associated with each approach.

The ITC must reach a preliminary determination 45 days after the petition is filed. If the determination is in the affirmative, the DOC proceeds to a final investigation. The ITC will begin a final injury investigation after an affirmative preliminary finding of dumping by the DOC. The standards for an affirmative determination differ significantly in the preliminary and final stages of an ITC investigation. To reach an affirmative preliminary determination, the ITC must find only a reasonable indication of material injury or threat of material injury by reason of the subject imports.

The courts have interpreted this to be a very low threshold. The ITC must determine whether:

1. The record as a whole contains clear and convincing evidence that there is no material injury or threat of material injury; and
2. No likelihood exists that contrary evidence will arise in a final investigation.

In the final determination, the ITC must find actual injury or an actual threat thereof. The actual determination of injury is made by a majority vote of the commissioners.

The record of evidence in an ITC investigation is compiled by its staff through extensive distribution and analysis of questionnaires to domestic producers, foreign producers, importers, and domestic purchasers. The ITC staff tabulates and analyzes questionnaire responses and prepares a report covering the indicia of statutory injury and threat. In addition to this report, the ITC staff also evaluates in separate memoranda the central arguments presented by petitioner and respondent in their briefs. These memoranda highlight and evaluate issues that the Commission is most likely to find difficult and contentious.

14.5 Dumping Analysis

The DOC analyzes U.S. sales made to the first unaffiliated party. These sales may be made in the following three ways:

1. Directly by the foreign manufacturer to an unaffiliated U.S. customer;
2. By the foreign manufacturer to an affiliated U.S. sales company, and then to an unaffiliated party (known as a constructed expert price (CEP) sale); or
3. The subject goods may be sold to an affiliated U.S. company that transforms (further manufactures) the goods into other products that are then sold to an unaffiliated customer.

(a) Analysis of U.S. Sales

A methodology is applied in each situation to determine the ex-factory price of the goods imported to the United States, based on the price actually charged to the first unaffiliated customer.[16] In the case of a direct sale, adjustments are made for costs incurred in moving the goods from the foreign factory to the delivery point to the customer. In the case of an affiliated U.S. distribution company, additional adjustments may be made to account for selling and distribution expenses incurred in the United States, including the imputed cost of carrying inventory in the United States.

Under the URAA, a deduction to U.S. price is made for the profit, which is allocated to U.S. selling expenses on U.S. sales of imported goods in addition to the expenses themselves.[17] A complicated methodology is applied when the imported goods are transformed before they are sold to the first unaffiliated customer. This procedure removes the effects of the U.S. further manufacturing, including actual costs and actual profit, from the price at which the finished article is sold. This calculation is used to determine an ex-factory price for the imported goods.

This process emphasizes the analysis of sales of imported goods to unaffiliated parties. Inbound sales prices by the foreign manufacturer to its U.S. subsidiary are not significant in determining final assessment amounts. All evaluations are based on prices charged to U.S. customers adjusted back to the loading dock of the foreign factory that made the subject goods. Customs values that are based on transfer prices are used only to calculate deposit amounts.

(b) Calculation of Normal Value

The normal value (NV), which is used as the benchmark for analyzing each U.S. sale, is calculated as one of the following four alternatives:

1. The average ex-factory price of sales of the same product or similar product in the home market (HM);
2. The average ex-factory price of sales of the same or similar product to a third country, if the company's home market unit sales of the class of merchandise is less than five percent of its U.S. sales; (The definition of the "adequacy of

---

[16] 19 U.S.C.S. § 1677a(d), (e) (1993).

[17] § 772(d)(3) of the Act.

the home market" as a viable comparison market to determine normal value (NV)[18] was previously whether home market sales are 5% or more of third country sales.) If the home market is not viable, a third-country market may be viable if the third-country market sales are 5% or more of U.S. sales. Prices to the chosen market must, however, be representative and allow for a proper comparison.

3. An amount known as "constructed value" (CV), if home market or third-country sales are determined not to form an adequate basis for comparison;[19] or
4. Constructed value, if home market or third-country sales have been made at prices below their full ex-factory cost of production (COP).[20]

(c) Average Ex-Factory Price

The average ex-factory price of sales can be calculated for the same product or a similar product in the home market during a specified period. Adjustments are made to calculate NV. These adjustments include the following four items:

1. Removal of all movement expenses from the invoice price;
2. Differences in direct selling expenses between the home and the U.S. markets;
3. Any difference in packing between home market sales and those shipped to the United States;
4. In the case of similar products, the direct costs of any physical differences between the product sold in the United States and its counterpart in the home market.

Adjustments for differences in direct selling expenses between U.S. and home markets include differences in warranty costs, commissions, and the costs of services provided to the customer, as well as any difference in imputed credit expenses for carrying unpaid receivables after shipment from the factory. The latter may result from differences in actual customer payment experience resulting from differences in payment terms, billing date structure, or other causes. Differences between the company's short-term borrowing rates in U.S. dollars and other currencies used to finance sales could also affect credit expense differences. An additional offset may be permitted for indirect selling expenses and the imputed cost of holding inventory for the home market if the U.S. sale was made through an affiliated U.S. distributor (CEP), or if the subject goods were further manufactured by a plant in the United States before they were sold.

---

[18] 19 U.S.C.S. § 1677b(a)(2) (1993).

[19] 19 U.S.C.S. § 1677b(a)(2) (1993).

[20] §§773(a)(1)(B)(ii), 773(a)(1)(C) of the Act.

The additional offset permitted for indirect selling expenses incurred in the comparison market for comparisons involving constructed expert price (CEP) (formerly ESP) sales is not automatic, but must be justified on the basis of a "level of trade" analysis.[21] An adjustment is also made for indirect selling expenses in one market up to the amount of any sales commission paid in the other market.

(d) Using Constructed Value and Cost of Production

Constructed value is used if home market or third-country sales do not provide an adequate basis for the calculation of normal value. Whenever home market or third-country sales were determined to be the primary basis for calculating NV for a company's U.S. sales of the class of goods investigated, those sales may be further evaluated to see whether they were made below the full cost of production of the subject goods.[22] This evaluation is usually made only if the petitioner alleges sales below COP.

If such an allegation is accepted, then the actual full COP must be calculated for each product sold in the home market or third-country market. The data is then submitted for analysis. The COP is the full cost of production, including the following:

1. Actual cost of manufacture (COM); and
2. Allocations of selling, general and administrative, and financial expenses (SGA&F) of the respondent company and of any parent or related companies.

A fairly sophisticated methodology for calculating the COP of individual products includes calculation of the cost of manufacture (COM) of each product, as well as layered approaches for allocating SGA&F expenses. SGA&F expenses may first be calculated on a functional basis, then in the second stage, based on relative COM.

It has been our experience that most companies' cost accounting systems are not sufficiently able to pinpoint the costs of individual products. Responding to a DOC questionnaire requesting COP information can require a significant effort. Transactions with affiliated suppliers of inputs are generally valued at transfer price or actual cost in calculating the COP of the final product. Sales prices are then compared to this COP. Sales below cost of production will be disregarded if they are found to be made over an extended period of time, and in substantial quantities and at prices that do not permit the recovery of all costs over a reasonable period of time.

(e) Test for Sales below Cost

The manner in which the test for sales below COP is performed is subject to some variation. The current approach to the cost test is basically as follows: First, the net price of each sale reported in the home market or third-country market is

---

[21]§773(a)(7) of the Act.

[22]19 U.S.C.S. § 1677b(b) (1993).

tested against the COP of the product sold, and is classified as either above or below COP. The results are then summarized by product. For products for which more than 20% of the sales in the comparison market are below COP, or for which the weighted average price of all sales is below COP, all sales at prices below COP are excluded from the calculation of normal value. Normal value is calculated using only the remaining, above-cost COP sales. If no above-cost sales of a product remain, then normal value for that product is calculated using constructed value.[23] This differs significantly from the test applied prior to the implementation of the URAA.

14.6 Constructed Value

Constructed value (CV)[24] is essentially a cost-based calculation of what the home market price or third-country price of a product would be if it were sold in that market at a normal or fair price. Constructed value is used to calculate NV both for products failing the COP test and for products that were sold in the United States but had no comparable products (whether the same or sufficiently similar for comparison) sold in the comparison market.

Constructed value is calculated based on the actual COM of the product, allocations of SGA&F expenses, and application of a profit factor calculated for the general category of subject products. Rules for calculating CV are very similar to those for COP, except that CV includes an amount for profit. Under the URAA, the minimum ratios formerly applied for SGA&F expenses (10%) and profit (8%) in constructed value were eliminated. Ratios based on actual cost are used to determine amounts for SGA&F expenses and profit for each product. The profit ratio is now calculated only for comparison market sales "in the ordinary course of trade," which is defined to exclude all sales at prices below COP.[25] This can result in unusually high profit ratios even for companies and product lines that are losing money.

(a) Transactions with Affiliated Companies

The antidumping methodology emphasizes using actual costs in calculating adjustments for costs and selling expenses and in calculating cost of production against which to test home market prices. For example, if subject products are manufactured using affiliated subcontractors for portions of the production process, the actual costs incurred by those subcontractors would be compared with the transfer price amounts charged for their services and the higher amount would be used to calculate COP. Similarly, if goods sold in the home market are delivered using a subsidiary transport company, the respondent is expected to use

---

[23]§773(b) of the Act.

[24]As defined in 19 U.S.C.S. § 1677b(e) (1993).

[25]§§ 773(e)(2), (771)(15) of the Act.

only the actual costs incurred by the transport company to calculate the freight adjustment.

It is not always practical to calculate actual costs for minor production operations that are subcontracted, or for ancillary freight services, because the companies providing such services often lack the cost accounting sophistication to be able to calculate and match their costs to the services performed. When a methodology to allocate the costs does not exist and cannot easily be devised based on available company data, the transfer prices charged by the affiliated suppliers are tested in two ways:

1. Against prices actually charged for similar goods or services to other unaffiliated customers—providing that the services were profitable; and
2. Against prices paid by the main company for similar goods or services it purchased from unaffiliated suppliers.

These tests seem to be similar to the comparable uncontrolled price method used in transfer pricing analyses. This analysis does not usually apply to developing the mainstream data used for calculation of U.S. price, home market price, or COP, but is used only to value inputs and adjustments related to the total main transactions.[26]

(b) Combining Affiliated Party Data

Affiliated parties are not combined in only two situations. First, constructed value or home market COP may be calculated using the true costs of any major production inputs from affiliated parties. This computation applies only if the transfer prices of these inputs are less than their true cost or if there is not a market value for the inputs. Otherwise, if transfer prices are above true cost and fairly reflect market values, the transfer prices of such inputs are to be used.[27] If a manufacturer receives ordinary (i.e., non-major) production inputs from a related supplier, the inputs should be valued at market prices, not actual costs. In fact, however, inputs are not commodities whose prices are quoted in most situations. The transfer prices of production inputs from an affiliated supplier should be used if they reflect market prices and are above their actual costs of production.[28] Thus, a two-tier test applies, one against comparable market prices as described earlier in connection with price adjustments, and another against the actual cost of production of the inputs. If there is no regular market as such for the input items, then their actual production costs are used.[29]

---

[26]§§ 773(f)(2), (3) of the Act.

[27]19 U.S.C.S. § 1677b(e)(2), (3) (1993).

[28]G. Kaplan, L. Kamarck, and M. Parker, "Cost Analysis Under the Antidumping Law," 21 *Geo. Wash. J. Int'l. L. and Econ.* 357, 402 (1988).

[29]*See* "Final Determinations of Sales at Less Than Fair Value: Antifriction Bearings (Other Than Tapered Roller Bearings) and Parts Thereof from the Federal Republic of Germany," 54 Fed. Reg. 18,992, 19,074 (May 3, 1989).

A second situation, which occurs frequently, involves home market sales of the subject merchandise to trading companies, distributors, or other customers that are affiliated with, but not controlled by, the respondent company. Sales to such a company may be considered in calculating NV if they are at-arm's-length prices. This fact is usually established by testing such sales against prices charged to unaffiliated buyers. A variety of tests have been used for this purpose on a case-by-case basis in past antidumping investigations. The most recent test required each respondent to establish that 99.5 percent of the sales to each affiliated customer were at or above the weighted average price for each product charged, after adjustments, to third parties.[30]

(c) Research and Development Expenses

Under U.S. GAAP and the GAAP of most other countries, research and development (R&D) costs would normally be expensed as incurred. Under the antidumping methodology, historical product-specific R and D costs are accumulated and amortized over the prospective market life of the product, regardless of their accounting treatment.[31] Only actual costs are included. No account is taken of the prospective benefits or economic value of any discoveries, other than their actual development costs. Costs for R&D activities that are identified as related to a product line, but not to specific products, as well as general R&D are treated the same way as under GAAP. These costs are allocated to products on a multitier basis.

(d) Startup Costs

A new provision in the URAA allows for adjustment of COP and CV to account for startup operations. Under this method, product costs during the startup period are normalized based on the most recent or other product cost data for a regular production period.[32] The residual amount of startup costs will most likely be amortized and taken into account in subsequent periods.

14.7 Determining Dumping Margins

It is the usual practice of the DOC to base an antidumping investigation on events occurring during a one year period of investigation (POI). Exceptions are made in the case of sales of large made-to-order products (for example, offshore platform jackets and piles), which may entail a longer period from the original sale date through construction and delivery. The POI generally ends with the most recently completed quarter at the time the petition is filed.

---

[30] *See* "Preliminary Determination of Sales at Less Than Fair Value: Certain Cold-Rolled Carbon Steel Flat Products From Argentina," 58 Fed. Reg. 7066, 7069 (February 4, 1993).

[31] *See* G. Kaplan, L. Kamarck, and M. Parker, "Cost Analysis Under the Antidumping Law," 21 *Geo. Wash. J. Int'l. L. and Econ.* 357, 389 (1988).

[32] § 773(f)(1)(C) of the Act.

The normal period of investigation was changed by the URAA from six months to one year. Similarly, the normal period used for the evaluation of sales below cost was changed to one year.[33]

For example, if a dumping petition against product X from country Q were filed in April 1996, the POI would normally extend from April 1995 through March 1996. This means that the respondent foreign companies in the investigation would have to report individually all U.S. sales, whether direct or through U.S. affiliates, and all home market or third-country sales during the period April 1995 through March 1996. In addition, any calculation of CV and/or COP would be made using data for this one-year POI. The CIT has found, in *Toho Titanium* and other cases, that in some industries a longer period should be used to calculate COP due to the "extended period of time" required to determine below-cost sales and the "reasonable period of time" needed for cost recovery.[34]

The investigation itself generally lasts for a period of 13 months or less, as noted in Section 14.3(a). Therefore, the data dealt with is fairly fresh.

(a) Reporting Companies

Although an antidumping petition is filed against a country, the DOC requires questionnaire responses from individual companies whose goods are sold in the United States. In each investigation, the DOC selects the respondent companies as the largest-volume companies whose products accounted for a major percentage of imports of the class of products from the subject country in the POI. The number of respondents selected in each investigation is limited by DOC resources. Each company investigated will receive its own dumping margin and deposit rate. Companies not investigated will be subject to a rate for "all others," usually an average of the individual company rates. A company that is not in the selected group may submit information and participate as a voluntary respondent in order to receive its own company-specific margin rate, provided the DOC is willing to devote the resources to reviewing and verifying its submission.

(b) Reporting Data

DOC dumping margin calculations are based on analysis of all of each company's U.S. sales during the POI in comparison with their respective values of NV. Thus, each respondent is required to report individually:

1. All of its U.S. sales of the subject class of merchandise during the POI; and
2. All of its home market or third-country sales of the subject goods during the POI.

In addition, the company may be required to report the COP of each product sold in the home market or third-country market, as well as the CV of some portion of these products.

---

[33] § 773(b)(2)(B) of the Act.

[34] Toho Titanium Co. v. United States, 657 F. Supp. 1280, 1286 (Ct. Int'l. Trade 1987).

Sales are reported to the DOC on magnetic tape (one record for each sale) or diskette with hard copy listings. It is not unusual for a company to report more than 10,000 U.S. sales and 100,000 or more HM sales during a POI. These sales may encompass from a single product up to several thousand distinct products, as did cases involving cement and antifriction bearings. Fewer than ten U.S. sales were reported during a POI in other situations. Dumping margin calculations may require computer computations.

(c) The Dumping Margin Formula

The formulae to be used for calculating weighted average (WAV) dumping margins in investigations were changed by the URAA. The formulae used in annual reviews remain the same as before. Each of these are shown below.

The new margin formulae for use in investigations are product- rather than sale-oriented.[35] The weighted average dumping margin is now calculated as follows:

The unit dumping margin on each Product A sold to the U.S. is

$$\text{Unit margin on Product A} = (\text{NV of Product A} - \text{WAV U.S. price of Product A})$$

where

$$\text{WAV U.S. price of Product A} = \Sigma_{\text{all sales of A}} \frac{(\text{net U.S. price of Sale i})\,(Q_i)}{\Sigma_{\text{all sales of A}}\,(Q_i)}$$

where net U.S. price of Sale i = gross unit price of Sale i
− discounts and rebates on Sale i
− movement costs on Sale i

Q_j = quantity of Sale i of Product A

$$\text{NV of Product A} = \sum_{\text{all sales } Y_j}$$

(gross unit price of Sale Y_j)
− discounts and rebates on Y_j
− movement costs of Y_j
− direct selling expenses and packing of Sale Y_j
+ (WAV direct selling expenses and packing of U.S. sales of A) Q_j
$\div \sum_{\text{all } Y_j}(Q_j)$

where Q_j = the number of units sold of the product comparable to A in the jth home market sale, and

Sale Y_j = each home market sale of the product sold in the home market that is comparable to Product A.

---

[35] § 777A(d)(1) of the Act.

The weighted average margin (WAV margin) for a company is calculated using a similar, somewhat lopsided method, in which only positive dumping margins are counted, but are averaged over all products.

Because a regular weighted average price is first calculated for each product, however, the process is less biased than before. The new formula is:

$$\text{WAV margin} = \frac{\Sigma\ (\text{margin on Product } A_k \geq 0\ (Q_k)\ \text{for all } A_k}{\Sigma\ (\text{WAV U.S. price of Product } A_k)(Q_k)\ \text{for all } A_k}$$

where
A_k = the kth product sold in the United States
Q_k = total quantity sold in the United States of Product A

For annual reviews, the calculation is as follows:

$$\text{Unit margin on Sale X} = (\text{FMV for Sale X} - \text{U.S. price of Sales X})$$

where U.S. price of Sale X = gross unit price of X
− discounts and rebates on X
− movement costs of X

$$\text{FMV for sale X} = \frac{(\Sigma}{\text{all sales}}$$

(gross unit price of Sale Y_j
− discounts and rebates on Y_j
− movement costs of Y_j
− direct selling expenses and packing of sale Y_j
+ direct selling expenses and packing of sale X)Q_j

$$\div \frac{\Sigma\ (Y_j Q_j)}{\text{all } Y_j}$$

where $Q_j Y_j$ = the number of units sold of the product comparable to X in the jth home market sale, and
Sale Y_j = each home market sale of the product sold in the home market which is comparable to product X.

The weighted average margin (WAV) for a company is calculated using a somewhat lopsided method in which only positive dumping margins are counted, but are averaged over all sales.

$$\text{WAV margin} = \frac{\Sigma\ (\text{margin on sale } X_i \geq 0)\ Q_{xi}\ \text{for all } X_i}{\Sigma\ (\text{U.S. price of sale } X_i)\ Q_{xi}\ \text{for all } X_i}$$

where X_i = the ith U.S. sale X, and
Q_{xi} = number of units sold in the ith U.S. sale

14.8 Relational Topics

Despite the fundamental differences in the focus of the dumping rules and the requirements for arm's-length transfer pricing, a number of relational issues warrant attention by those concerned with transfer pricing issues.

In the following section we deal with six topics:

1. The relationship between dumping and transfer pricing;
2. Implementing a market share strategy;
3. The use of confidential data;
4. The best information available (BIA) rule;
5. Recordkeeping requirements; and
6. Pricing methodologies.

There is a fundamental difference between the focus of the antidumping rules and that of transfer pricing.[36] If a foreign manufacturer distributes in the United States through a controlled U.S. sales subsidiary, dumping rules focus on the sales price charged by the U.S. distributor to its first uncontrolled customer. Transfer pricing, however, will focus on the price charged by the foreign manufacturer to the controlled U.S. sales corporation. There have been cases in which transfer prices of products are challenged as too high for income tax purposes, but the third-party resale prices of the same products are too low under the dumping rules.

Any dumping duties imposed are assessed against the importer and would form a part of the acquisition cost of the imported product. Duties reduce the selling profits earned by the controlled sales corporation and increase the possibility that a transfer pricing adjustment might be made for income tax purposes, depending on the size of the dumping margins assessed and the transfer pricing methodology employed.

When imported property is acquired from a related person, the cost of the property for tax purposes is limited to the costs taken into account in determining the customs value.[37] The normal customs value is not changed if dumping duties are assessed. The time period for final liquidation may be altered because of the dumping collection procedures. The agreed customs valuation method might in effect reflect the dumping duties as an adjustment. The impact of such adjustments should be monitored in such cases. Deposits for estimated dumping margins are not finally liquidated until final determinations of the dumping margins are made in an administrative review for the applicable period. As goods are imported, a reasonable estimate of the final liability would appear to be accruable for federal income tax purposes, but in a private letter ruling accrual was not permitted until the end of the review period.[38]

---

[36]*See* M.J. McKee and K.S. Kirwan, "Dumping and Transfer Pricing: Is There a Conflict?" 21 *Tax Mgmt. Int'l. J.* 476 (1992).

[37]I.R.C. § 1059A.

[38]See Priv. Ltr. Rul. 9538001 (May 5, 1995) and I.R.C. § 461(f) and (h).

14.9 Implementing a Market Share Strategy

The new final transfer pricing regulations take into account the special impact on pricing that can result when the controlled transfer is subject to a pricing strategy undertaken to enter a new market, increase market share, or meet competition.[39] A controlled sale can be priced at an amount not otherwise arm's length to achieve a market share only if various requirements are met, including having the controlled distributor make corresponding reductions in the resale price to uncontrolled purchasers, or engage in greater sales promotion activities.

In an antidumping context, direct sales from a foreign manufacturer to an unrelated U.S. customer would usually be found to have been dumped when priced at low levels to establish a market. The motivation for low pricing in the U.S. market is not considered relevant to the dumping margin analysis. Prices could be low in order to build market share, or simply to follow market price levels in the United States and avoid losing market share. If goods are priced below NV, they are dumped.

Sales by a foreign exporter to its U.S. subsidiary for resale or further manufacture are largely irrelevant in a dumping analysis, as only the prices of transactions with unaffiliated buyers are considered. Therefore, if a foreign manufacturer sells goods to its U.S. subsidiary at low transfer prices in order to help the subsidiary build a market, those transactions would be neutral with regard to dumping. As long as the U.S. subsidiary sells the goods to unaffiliated parties at prices that are above NV, after adjustments, there will be no dumping margin.

Under the new law, in certain isolated cases involving parts or components that are imported by the U.S. subsidiary and are "substantially" further manufactured before the resulting final product is sold to an unaffiliated party, transfer prices could be used as a proxy for the net U.S. prices of the imported parts or components that would otherwise be calculated under a complicated procedure, as noted in Section 14.5(a) of this chapter.[40] This approach would be used only when it is impractical to use the normal, cost-based further manufacturing analysis.

Thus, if the motivation for low transfer prices from a foreign parent is to allow the U.S. subsidiary a higher than normal markup so that it can cover operating costs on temporarily low sales volume, this would not necessarily be a dumping situation. If, however, the lower than normal transfer prices are intended to permit the U.S. subsidiary to increase market share by selling to third parties at similarly low prices, those sales will probably be at dumped prices. No special allowance will be made for those sales by the DOC. On the contrary, evidence of such activity would be used by a petitioner in the ITC injury investigation.

The ITC views increases in import penetration as a key factor in determining whether the subject imports have injured the domestic industry. Any transfer pricing methodology that encourages the importer to increase market share will be

---

[39] Treas. Reg. § 1.482.

[40] § 772(e) of the Act.

under scrutiny. Foreign producers who engage in these practices become more susceptible to affirmative injury findings by the ITC.

The only situation in which long-range pricing effects are theoretically taken into account in the antidumping methodology is in determining whether home market sales have been made at less than the cost of production. Home market sales made over an extended period of time, in substantial quantities, and at prices that do not permit recovery of all costs within a reasonable period of time in the normal course of trade, are to be disregarded in determining NV.[41] The DOC has developed an objective test for applying this principle as it relates to the limited period of investigation or period of review in a proceeding. This is described in Section 14.5(e).

In theory, aggressive experience curve pricing or market development pricing in the home market would permit "recovery of all costs within a reasonable period of time in the normal course of trade." However, this provision has not been successfully applied with regard to prospective recovery of costs.[42]

14.10 Use of Confidential Data

Many types of information that must be submitted to the DOC and ITC in an antidumping proceeding are confidential or proprietary by their very nature. This information includes listings of individual sales prices, selling expenses, and actual costs of manufacture of individual products. The confidentiality of this proprietary information is protected by law while in the hands of the respective U.S. government agencies.[43] Information designated by its submitter as proprietary cannot even be released to another U.S. government agency, nor even to a part of the DOC or ITC not directly involved in the proceeding, except to the U.S. Customs Service in connection with a customs fraud investigation.

(a) Antidumping Procedures

A proceeding is more effective when the petitioner can review and comment on submitted data. However, the confidentiality would be compromised if the actual data were accessible to employees of the U.S. companies themselves.

Therefore, the U.S. antidumping statute[44] provides for release of information submitted in each proceeding at two levels. First, a nonproprietary summary of every submission is available to the general public. Second, a version of each submission is made available to all interested parties covered by an administrative protective order (APO), which contains all "business proprietary" information, ex-

[41]19 U.S.C.S. § 1677b(b) (1993).

[42]See B. Lapson, "Determination of Sales Below Cost over Extended Period," in *Comprehensive Issue Review Under the Antidumping and Countervailing Duty Laws* (Georgetown University Law Center, 1988) at 321, 331.

[43]19 U.S.C.S. § 1677f(b) (1993).

[44]19 U.S.C.S. § 1677f (1993).

cept information that is "privileged" or "classified," and information for which there is a "clear and compelling need to withhold from disclosure." The proprietary information released under an APO generally includes sales listings, product costs, profitability calculations, production process descriptions, and operational statistics of each company. Although the petitioner companies, that is, members of the U.S. industry, are the actual interested parties in an antidumping proceeding, usually only their outside attorneys and outside consultants can be approved as their representatives to receive information under an APO.

(b) APO Example

How confidentially submitted data may be released is illustrated by the following example. Suppose a foreign company submits details of all of its home market sales over a six-month period. This data would consist of a narrative explanation and a list of all sales, including for each sale of the product, the customer, date of sale, date of shipment, gross unit price, all discounts and rebates, all movement expenses, credit terms, and applicable direct selling expenses (known as "circumstance of sale adjustments"), which are used to adjust home market prices for differences between home and U.S. markets with respect to such costs as imputed credit expense, warranty costs, and advertising. This data is submitted on either magnetic tape or, for small transaction volumes, on floppy disks, as well as in hard copy.

Normally, the petitioners' counsel that has been included in the APO will receive the entire detailed narrative and sales listings on both magnetic and paper media with only the names of the respondent's customers deleted. At the same time, a nonconfidential or public version of the submission will be made available in a public-reading room. This version includes the same narrative, except that discussions of proprietary material such as special marketing arrangements, rebate programs, and production processes will be deleted. In addition, numerical data will usually be ranged by ten or twenty percent, unless the data is so sensitive that it would not be protected even by ranging. Sales reported in the public version are incomplete; amounts for price and other numerical data would be ranged. Customer identities would, of course, be excluded. Either the public summary must have sufficient detail to permit a reasonable understanding of the substance of the submission, or the submitting party must show that the information cannot be so summarized without compromising its confidential nature.

A similar procedure would be followed for release to respondents and to the public of any information submitted by the petitioner that was based on its own proprietary data. Thus, the APO system followed by the DOC and ITC provides both sides in a proceeding with fairly transparent access to proprietary data. The public versions of submissions allow a petitioner's officials to follow the main issues and arguments in a case that may determine the survival of their company. Using these materials, the petitioner's officials should be able to bring to bear their knowledge of the industry, its markets, and products, even without access to proprietary materials, and can intelligently discuss strategies with the attorneys who represent them, and who do have access to this information.

(c) APO System

The APO system has functioned quite successfully for years. The few known violations have generally been inadvertent and have not involved information of major importance.

Sometimes a dispute arises over where to draw the line between what information is proprietary and what should be disclosed to the public. In such instances, the party submitting the data is required to justify its nondisclosure. Examples of this would be the fact that a respondent is connected with a related freight company that is not disclosed in the respondent's annual report, or the existence of a special pricing or rebate program for selected customers that has made the company the leader in a certain market.

If the DOC does not accept the argument of the respondent for nondisclosure of this information, the respondent has the option either to authorize the DOC to make the disputed information public or to withdraw it, that is, remove the disputed items from its submission entirely, and suffer any consequences. These consequences may be relatively minor (for example, loss of a possible freight expense or rebate adjustment to the home market price when calculating NV), or they may be so significant that the entire submission is rejected. In the latter case, the facts available (FA rule) would be used to calculate the company's dumping margin. Similar disputes arise regarding whether certain data items should be disclosed to counsel as proprietary or are actually "secret," "privileged," or should be withheld under "a clear and compelling need." The options and consequences are the same as in the case of public disclosure.

The consequences of withdrawing information regarding U.S. sales may be more punitive than in the case of home market sales. This is because if support for a home market price adjustment is withdrawn, usually it will merely be set to zero under the FA rule. If there is no support for a U.S. adjustment, the resulting FA could be quite large and damaging, as discussed later.

(d) Transfer Pricing

In determining an arm's-length price in connection with the transfer of tangible property, the availability of information as to price, markups, and profits earned by comparable companies is a crucial factor in choosing the best transfer pricing method.[45]

There is a considerable amount of data available from public databases, filings with the Securities and Exchange Commission, and many other sources. All too often, however, the usefulness of public information is limited, and taxpayers and the government are left to draw conclusions from poor comparables or to utilize pricing methods that rely less explicitly on identified comparable behavior.

The Internal Revenue Service (IRS) files contain nonpublic information from the tax returns of many corporations and businesses. This information must be kept confidential and cannot be disclosed to third parties.[46] Taxpayers are aware of who

---

[45]Treas. Reg. § 1.482.

[46]I.R.C. § 6013.

their competitors are, but have no real way to obtain data on comparable prices or profits earned by these potentially comparable operations, except in rare cases when relevant and useful information can be obtained from public sources, trade organizations, or government filings. On occasion, a comparable company has been willing to voluntarily provide information on prices and profits.

The question to be considered is whether the availability of a limited disclosure procedure under APO would result in the development of more useful and comparable data in the transfer pricing area. The APO antidumping procedures would have the following crucial differences if used in the transfer pricing area. These differences may make this procedure unworkable:

1. The confidential data submitted in the dumping context is obtained voluntarily, from either the U.S. domestic petitioners or the foreign entity accused of dumping. Both have significant incentive to cooperate and to submit relevant and complete data on a prompt basis. An identified comparable third party potentially holding information relevant to a transfer pricing case of a competitor presently lacks the same incentive to cooperate. On this basis, neither the taxpayer nor the IRS would have good reason to have confidence in the process.
2. Assume the issue were access to third-party tax return information already contained in IRS files, and under an APO procedure this information could be disclosed by the IRS to the taxpayer's counsel. This procedure raises many concerns. Would counsel have access to all companies in the overall database, or only to those volunteered by the IRS? If the antidumping model were followed, would the third party whose data is considered comparable have the option to withdraw or block disclosure to the counsel for a competitor?

14.11 Use of "Facts Available" Rule

The respondents that are investigated in antidumping proceedings are foreign companies that manufacture, process, or, in some cases, trade in merchandise goods that are exported to the United States. Usually, most of the transactions involve the purchase of inputs, processing, and sale of the subject merchandise, both in the home market and in the United States.

Past investigations covered the world, including Western Europe, Japan, China, the former Soviet Union, and a vast array of Third-World countries. The U.S. government's power to subpoena data from entities in these countries may be limited. Why, therefore, should a foreign widget maker cooperate with a DOC antidumping investigation of widgets from his country and truthfully answer a rather lengthy and intrusive questionnaire from the U.S. DOC? The answer is the use of "facts available," or FA. Under the antidumping regulations of the DOC,[47] the DOC is directed to use FA, which may include data submitted by the petitioner, if a respondent refuses to provide requested factual information. In actual practice,

[47] 19 C.F.R. § 353.37 (1989).

such petitioner-originated FA data is often structured so that, if used, the data would result in an average dumping margin for a company of well over 100%. The prospect of receiving such a high punitive dumping margin is usually enough to encourage companies investigated to submit reasonably timely, complete, and accurate information in response to the DOC's questionnaires.

(a) FA Example

For example, assume that a foreign company has been selling in the United States at dumped prices that are 15 to 20 percent below NV, including all adjustments. The company refuses to cooperate in the DOC investigation and could find itself faced with a dumping margin of 150%. In many industries, a 15 to 20% antidumping duty deposit rate will still allow a company to do business in the United States, partly due to a shift in price levels. A deposit rate of 150%, however, would effectively exclude a company's imported products from the U.S. market, as the cash flow needed to support such deposits would be crippling. Thus, the threat that the DOC will apply punitive FA is a potent incentive to cooperate in its investigation. This cooperation includes permitting on-site verification of company-submitted data by a team of DOC personnel.

Nonpunitive FA or less punitive, FA is also used by the DOC when single elements in a company's submission cannot be verified, either because of missing documents or because of incorrect calculations that are not of a significant enough magnitude to undermine the credibility of the entire response. In the first situation, FA might be drawn from verified data in the submissions of other companies, from calculations using the respondent's own unfavorable data, or from other sources. In the latter case, petitioner's FA would be used.

It is not unusual that a company's records are not organized in a manner that facilitates precise and accurate calculation of certain sales price adjustments in the limited time permitted for response preparation—generally 4 to 6 weeks, or 12 to 15 weeks if a company starts work when the petition is filed. This situation applies to packing costs. The dumping law provides for an adjustment to NV for the difference in packing costs between the home market and the United States. Many manufacturers consider packing to be a minor part of plant operations, especially for high-value products. Packing materials are often included in factory overhead as indirect materials, and packing operations are often handled by indirect workers whose activities are not standardized or measured. The mandated adjustment for differences in packing costs between the home and U.S. markets for each product often cannot be calculated directly. This analysis may require extensive specific analysis based on secondary records. Such an analysis is usually acceptable if properly made. On occasion, however, a calculation of this type may be rejected; some form of FA would then be used for that item. The FA might ignore the packing cost for home market sales as part of the packing adjustment. The company might include packing cost for U.S. sales only, resulting in double counting and increasing NV and the dumping margin. A more punitive approach would be to include a different, higher, U.S. packing cost and to ignore the cost for the home market.

(b) Transfer Pricing

In the transfer pricing area, the lack of detailed taxpayer data regarding transfer pricing policies has been a consistent complaint by IRS examining agents.[48] In response to this lack of data over the years, a number of legislative and regulatory initiatives have been taken. Foreign-controlled taxpayers are subject to arbitrary assessments and/or penalties if the recordkeeping requirements of I.R.C. Section 6038A are not met in connection with transactions with related persons. The transfer pricing regulations,[49] proved use of profit splits as I.R.C. Section 482 pricing method,[50] as well as proposed rules and legislation on valuation misstatement penalties[51] all place new emphasis on more contemporaneous documentation.

Under the 1992 proposed transfer pricing regulations (now withdrawn),[52] most taxpayers would have been forced to conform their pricing to a comparative profit interval (CPI). Under the CPI, profit level indicators would be utilized for comparable firms in the tested party's applicable business classification. The mandatory use of this method, regardless of the availability of comparable data, resembles the application of a FA rule to the transfer pricing area. New rules have backed away from this approach.

In antidumping, FA is often the result of actions taken or not taken. Its penalty aspects seem harsh, but they at least have a rational basis. There is no place for this approach in the transfer pricing area. As mentioned earlier, the IRS now has sufficient powers to impose sanctions against taxpayers who do not supply background information, even when such data is originally maintained outside the United States. Arbitrary pricing methods do not have to be imposed in addition to these sanctions.

14.12 I.R.C. Section 6038A Recordkeeping

Before the enactment of I.R.C. Section 6038A in 1989,[53] the IRS had experienced difficulties in enforcing summonses for information from foreign persons engaging in transactions with related persons in the United States.[54] In regulations issued in June 1991 pursuant to I.R.C. Section 6038A,[55] U.S. businesses (reporting corporations) with 25% or more foreign ownership are subject to specific requirements for reporting and record maintenance in connection with transactions with

[48] *See* U.S. Department of the Treasury and Internal Revenue Service, "A Study of Intercompany Pricing," Discussion Draft, Notice 88-123, 1988-2 CB 458, Chapter 3.

[49] Regs. § 1.482, INTL-0401-88, 58 Fed. Reg. 5310.

[50] Reg. § 1.482. *See* Feinschreiber, *Tax Reporting for Foreign-Owned U.S. Corporations* (New York: John Wiley & Sons, 1992).

[51] Prior Prop. Reg. § 1.6662-5(e), (j).

[52] Prop. Reg. 1.482, INTL-0372-88; INTL-0401-88, 57 Fed. Reg. 3571.

[53] For a complete discussion of this area, *see* R. Feinschreiber, *Tax Reporting for Foreign-Owned U.S. Corporations* (New York: John Wiley & Sons, 1992).

[54] United States v. Toyota Motor Corp., 561 F. Supp. (1983); 83-1 U.S.T.C. 9302. United States v. Toyota Motor Corp., 1158 F. Supp. (1983); 83-2 U.S.T.C. 9468.

[55] T.D. 8353, 56 FR 28056 (June 19, 1991).

25% or more related foreign persons. Although the required records will be generated by the foreign related person, the U.S. reporting corporation will be subject to penalties if it does not comply with the requirements, including production of the documents when requested by the IRS.

One of the main features of these rules is the mandatory requirement that the foreign related party appoint the U.S. subsidiary as its limited agent solely for purpose of requests by the Secretary of the Treasury to examine records or produce testimony related to reportable transactions and to related summonses for such records and testimony.[56] This limited agency is not intended to apply for any other purpose under federal law, including antidumping.[57]

In an antidumping proceeding, most records and documents supporting information submitted by respondents are lodged outside the United States. The DOC does not require foreign company records and documents, other than samples, to be produced in the United States. A respondent is required to submit detailed information derived from records in response to a questionnaire, along with a description and supporting worksheets, if applicable, showing how the submission data was derived from the company's normal records. At one point during each proceeding, DOC personnel, accompanied by a translator and sometimes a product expert, visit the foreign company to verify the submission against company records. This verification of submitted data is required by law in all investigations.[58] Administrative review data must be verified at least once in three years.[59] The penalty is usually use of FA if data verification cannot be accommodated by the respondent or if records are not produced.

All claims are required to be supported by company records—either directly or through a calculation methodology—and not simply estimated.[60] Except for differences in methodologies and issues regarding what types of data are recorded and retained by each company, whatever supporting documentation exists has usually been found to be accessible when needed, as investigations generally occur within a short time of the events being measured.

In past annual administrative reviews, the DOC has encountered problems with destroyed documents. During the late 1970s and the 1980s, the DOC allowed the administrative review schedules for many cases to slip drastically from the normal 12-month schedule. In one case, as noted earlier, the agency was more than ten years behind in 1987. Such a situation, which the DOC has taken steps to correct and prevent in the future, can create problems in developing or verifying information. After five or ten years, many supporting documents may have been destroyed in a company's normal legal document retention cycle. The result for a company caught in this situation could be disastrous if FA were used to calculate margins for years for which supporting documentation was no longer available. The prospec-

---

[56]Reg. § 1.6038A-5(a).

[57]*See* Feinschreiber, *supra*, note 38, at 151. *See* Feinschreiber, *The Transfer Pricing Handbook* (John Wiley & Sons).

[58]*See* 19 U.S.C.S. § 1677e(b)(1).

[59]*See* 19 U.S.C.S. § 1677e(b)(3)(B).

[60]*See*, e.g., G. Kaplan, L. Kamarck, and M. Parker, "Cost Analysis Under the Antidumping Law," 21 *Geo. Wash. J. Int'l. L. and Econ.* 357, 375 (1988).

tive solution for such a company is to include the need to support its dumping submissions in its normal document retention program.

14.13 Pricing Methodologies

In connection with pricing tangible property, the rules under I.R.C. Section 482 contain a variety of sophisticated techniques and alternatives available for determining an arm's-length price: the comparable uncontrolled price (CUP), the resale price method, the cost plus method, the comparable profits method, and other methods, including several profit split alternatives. A detailed functional analysis[61] generally needs to be performed so as to appropriately identify the risks, functions, and related assets of each member of the related group involved in the cross-border transaction. The impact of intangibles also presents unique analytic problems in valuation and in identifying their profit contribution.[62] The search for comparables (whether of actual sales transactions for third parties, or the profits and other profit-level indicators for comparable benchmark companies) is a challenging task in and of itself.

By contrast, the methodologies and procedures used in the antidumping area seem to be more rudimentary and more narrowly defined. The comparisons to be made require details of sales of a product to third parties, both in the home market and in the United States, to be identified. Actual cost-based adjustments must be made for transportation and selling expenses, to make the appropriate comparisons of selling prices. The cost of manufacture of each of a company's products must be determined. This often requires a level of cost analysis and development of special methodologies that may not otherwise be performed or created. All of these computations must be prepared within a fairly narrow time frame in order to abide by the investigation timetable.

14.14 Summary

The tasks of the two disciplines (transfer pricing and dumping) are partially related and overlapping. A market share strategy might make good sense as a transfer pricing defense, yet have important antidumping ramifications. A challenge by competitor-producers in the import market may bring on a dumping investigation that could serve to highlight exposure areas in the transfer pricing area. Recordkeeping designed for one area must also be viewed in terms of its impact in the other area. Some of the procedures and practices in the dumping area may be adopted in the transfer pricing area as the tax authorities continue to struggle with effective means to enforce arm's-length pricing by multinational groups.

---

[61]Treas. Reg. § 1.482.

[62]Prop. Reg. § 1.482-6T.

CHAPTER 15

Country of Origin Marking Requirements

Peter W. Klestadt
David M. Murphy

15.1 Introduction
15.2 Marking Statute
(a) Location of Marking
(b) Legibility, Indelibility, and Permanence
(c) English-Language Name of the Country of Origin
(d) Exceptions to Individual Marking
(e) Ultimate Purchaser
(f) Repackaging Requirements
15.3 Substantial Transformation
15.4 Liability for Failure to Properly Mark
15.5 Proposed Simplification: Tariff Shift Rules of Origin
15.6 Textiles and Apparel
(a) Application of Tariff Shift Rules
(b) Exceptions to the New Rules of Origin
(c) Quota and Marking Ramifications
15.7 Conclusion

15.1 Introduction

Country of origin determinations can have wide-reaching effects on importers. The origin of the product determines if the product is, or is not, subject to quotas for apparel, textiles, or commodities and for punitive tariffs as well as for the proper marking of imported merchandise at the wholesale and retail levels. The standards developed under the marking statute generally dictate if an article is the "product of" a beneficiary country under other customs rules.

15.2 Marking Statute

Determination of origin is the key fact under the marking statute, Section 304 of the Tariff Act of 1930, as amended.[1] This statute provides that every article of foreign origin imported into the United States must be marked, in the English language, in a conspicuous place as legibly, indelibly, and permanently as the nature of the article (or its container) will permit, unless excepted. The marking must be made in a manner as to indicate the name of the country of origin of the article to the ultimate purchaser in the United States. The purpose of the statute, as explained by the courts, is to require importers to "mark the goods so that at the time of purchase the ultimate purchaser may, by knowing where the goods were produced, be able to buy or refuse to buy them, if such marking should influence his will."[2]

The origin for marking purposes dictates the application of quota and duty rates (with the exception of duty preference programs). The statute charged U.S. Customs with the responsibility to establish regulations to prevent deception, authorize exemptions, and instruct on how to mark. These complex regulations, set forth in Title 19, Code of Federal Regulations, Part 134[3] are explained in the following sections.

(a) Location of Marking

The "ultimate purchaser" (as defined *infra*) in the United States must be able to find the marking easily and read it without strain.[4] There are no specific requirements as to color, location, or type size of the marking except as discussed in the following paragraphs.

In addition, the regulations provide that in any case in which the words "United States" or "America," the letters "U.S.A.," any variation of such words or letters, or the name of any city or locality in the United States (i.e., a U.S. address), appear on the article or its container, there should appear, legibly and permanently, in close proximity to such words, letters, or name, and in at least a comparable size, the name of the country of origin preceded by "Made in," "Product of," or other words of similar meaning.[5] "Close proximity" means on the same side or panel of a box; "comparable size" means reasonably proportional.

This rule is subject to exception. Where the words "United States" or "America," the letters "U.S.A.," or other designations of origin ("London," "Paris," etc.) are part of a trademark, the marking must be either in close proximity or in some other conspicuous location.[6] Thus, the trademark "Perry Ellis America" on garments has been held to fall under this exception.[7] Pursuant to the "trademark" ex-

[1]19 U.S.C. § 1304.

[2]United States v. Friedlander & Co., 27 C.C.P.A. 297, C.A.D. 104 (1940).

[3]19 C.F.R. pt. 134.

[4]19 C.F.R. § 134.41(b).

[5]19 C.F.R. § 134.46.

[6]19 C.F.R. § 134.47.

[7]C.S.D. 88-38.

ception, the country of origin preceded by the words "Made in" or "Product of" need only appear in a conspicuous location, not necessarily in close proximity and in comparable size to the trademark, trade name, or souvenir marking (e.g., a T-shirt with the logo "Disneyland, USA"). This regulation has been applied even if the trademark incorporates a foreign location, for example, "Rome 2001".[8]

(b) Legibility, Indelibility, and Permanence

The regulations governing the manner and method of marking are fluidly applied, depending on the circumstances. Customs regulations provide that the degree of permanence should be at least sufficient to ensure that in any reasonably foreseeable circumstance, the marking will remain on the article (or its container) until it reaches the ultimate purchaser unless it is deliberately removed.[9] The regulations suggest certain methods of marking:[10]

- Articles of metal—die-sinking, etching, cast-in-mold lettering
- Earthenware or chinaware—glazing on in the process of firing
- Paper articles—imprinting

The regulations also approve marking by sticker labels and hangtags.[11] The marking must survive normal distribution and store handling.[12]

Certain articles are subject to specific marking requirements. For example, die stamping, cast-in-mold lettering, etching, and engraving are required methods of marking for knives, forks, clippers, shears, scissors, surgical instruments, pliers, and the like.[13] The statute itself requires these methods for iron or steel pipes and pipe fittings, compressed gas cylinders, and manhole covers.[14] Wearing apparel must be marked by means of a permanent sewn-in label under this statute and the Textile Fibers Products Identification Act.[15]

Other statutes and regulations, such as the Textile Fiber Products Identification Act, may require a specific content and/or location of the country of origin marking. For example, the Textile Fiber Products Identification Act require that apparel products must have a label disclosing the country of origin, fiber content, registration number, or other identification, and care instructions inside center of the neck mid-way between the shoulder seams if the garment has a neck (blouses, shirts, jackets, coats, *etc.*).[16] Similar contents and location of marking requirements may

---

[8]C.S.D. 80-20.

[9]19 C.F.R. § 134.41(b).

[10]19 C.F.R. § 134.41(a).

[11]19 C.F.R. § 134.44.

[12]19 C.F.R. § 134.41(b).

[13]19 C.F.R. § 134.43.

[14]19 U.S.C. § 1304(c), (d), (e).

[15]T.D. 54640(6), T.D. 71-264(3).

[16]16 C.F.R. § 303.15(b) (Rule 15(b)).

also be mandated by the Federal Trade Commission or the Food and Drug Administration for certain consumer products, food, drugs, and cosmetics.

(c) English-Language Name of the Country of Origin

Customs defines "country" to mean the political entity known as a nation.[17] Colonies, possessions, and protectorates outside the boundaries of the mother country are considered separate countries for marking purposes. Often the Customs Service confers with the Department of State in order to ascertain the status of a political entity. Once identified, the country's name must be indicated on a product in the English language.

From time to time, Customs issues directives containing recognized English-language names. Two recent examples involve Myannmar and Macedonia. Customs suggests use of the name "Burma" rather than Myannmar; Customs requires marking to state "Former Yugoslav Republic of Macedonia" (or "F.Y.R.O.M.").[18] These are the names politically recognized by the U.S. Department of State.

Variant spellings that clearly indicate the English name, such as "Brasil" for "Brazil" and "Italie" for "Italy," are acceptable.[19] Foreign words used in conjunction with an English name that do not confuse may be acceptable (e.g., "Hecho en Mexico," "Fabrique en France," "Producto de Chile" are acceptable, but "Fabrication Suisse" is not). Abbreviated names that unmistakably indicate the name of a country, such as "U.K." for "United Kingdom," "Gt. Britain" for "Great Britain," or "Luxemb" and "Luxembg" for "Luxembourg," are acceptable. However, "Can." for "Canada" and "Holl." for "Holland" have been disapproved. Adjectival forms have been approved (e.g., "Italian," "Canadian"), provided the adjectival form of the name does not appear with other words so as to refer to a kind or species of product (e.g., "English walnuts" or "Brazil nuts" is unacceptable).[20]

(d) Exceptions to Individual Marking

Articles are exempted from individual marking requirements due to impossibility (e.g., liquid gases, ores, crude substances, precious stones, etc.), impracticality, economic infeasibility, and similar reasons. Exemptions from individual marking (other than "J-list" articles, discussed later) must be applied for in advance of importation from U.S. Customs Headquarters in Washington, D.C.[21] Notwithstanding a binding ruling, Customs officers at the port of entry must be satisfied that the imported articles will be processed as claimed. Customs officials must also be satisfied that the imported articles will be imported in marked containers that will reach the U.S. processor in unopened condition. Local Customs officials have authority to grant exemptions in the absence of a binding ruling, especially where a

---

[17] 19 C.F.R. § 134.1(a).

[18] Notice, T.D. 95-46, 60 Fed. Reg. 28,202 (May 30, 1995).

[19] 19 C.F.R. 134.45(b).

[20] 19 C.F.R. § 134.45(c).

[21] 19 C.F.R. pt. 177.

case is clear-cut. For instance, district directors are specifically authorized to grant exemptions in hardship cases.[22]

Containers of the exempted articles must be marked to indicate the origin of the contents.[23] Customs regulations require the outermost container of exempted articles to bear the country of origin marking.[24] Marking of the container alone may qualify the article for an exemption from being marked itself[25]—for example, a "blister pack" or sealed retail container that will reach the ultimate purchaser unopened.

As permitted in the statute, Customs has listed certain articles (known as the "J-list")[26] that are given a blanket exemption from individual marking.[27] These articles include artworks, nuts, bolts, washers, screws, natural products such as vegetables, fruits, berries, sawed lumber, and so forth. The outermost container of the article that will reach the ultimate purchaser is required to be marked to indicate the origin of its contents. J-list articles are subject to the repackaging requirements discussed in Section 15.2(f).

Articles imported for the importer's own use and not for sale may be exempt from marking of the product and the container.[28] Likewise, merchandise destined for an importer who does his own processing (amounting to a "substantial transformation") and who necessarily knows the origin of the imported articles may also be exempted from marking.[29]

Customs regulations also grant administrative exemptions for articles entered or withdrawn from warehouse for immediate exportation or for transportation and exportation,[30] products of American fisheries that are duty free,[31] products of possessions of the United States,[32] products of the United States exported and returned,[33] and certain small-value articles.[34]

(e) Ultimate Purchaser

Marking is for the benefit of the ultimate purchaser. The Customs regulations define "ultimate purchaser" as the last person in the United States who will receive the article in the form in which it was imported.[35] Only the ultimate purchase is entitled

---

[22] 19 U.S.C. 1304(a)(3)(K).

[23] 19 U.S.C. 1304(b).

[24] 19 C.F.R. § 134.22(a).

[25] 19 U.S.C. § 1304(a)(3)(D); 19 C.F.R. § 134.32(d).

[26] 19 U.S.C. § 1304(a)(3)(J).

[27] 19 C.F.R. § 134.33.

[28] 19 U.S.C. § 1304(a)(3)(F).

[29] 19 U.S.C. § 1304(a)(3)(H).

[30] 19 C.F.R. § 134.32(j).

[31] 19 C.F.R. § 134.32(k).

[32] 19 C.F.R. § 134.32(l).

[33] 19 C.F.R. § 134.32(m).

[34] 19 C.F.R. § 134.32(n).

[35] 19 C.F.R. § 134.1(d).

to country of origin information. A retail customer may not be the ultimate purchaser of an imported product that is changed in form prior to resale or, following importation, has been incorporated into a retail product and lost its identity.

By example, the Customs regulations explain who the ultimate purchaser may be:

1. A person who substantially transforms an imported article is an "ultimate purchaser" even though the imported article is not transformed into a new or different article.
2. If the manufacturing process is merely a minor one that leaves the identity of the imported article intact, the consumer or user of the article who obtains the article after the processing, will be regarded as the ultimate purchaser.
3. If an article is to be sold at retail in its imported form, the purchaser at retail is the ultimate purchaser.
4. If the imported article is distributed as a gift, the recipient is the ultimate purchaser.[36]

The idea of "substantial transformation" is discussed in detail in Section 15.3. A manufacturer or processor in the United States may claim to be the ultimate purchaser and ask that the imported article be exempted from individual marking since the processor will be the last person in the United States to receive the article in the form in which it was imported. In other words, the manufacturer will claim that the importer has "substantially transformed" the imported article.

(f) Repackaging Requirements

The importer of merchandise is under an affirmative obligation to notify Customs about any repacking, manipulation, or processing operation (not resulting in a substantial transformation). The original marking of the foreign article may be concealed, obscured, or obliterated by the activities. The Customs regulations provide rules if imported articles are intended to be repacked in new containers for sale, or otherwise manipulated prior to sale, after release from Customs' custody. The importer must certify that the new container will be properly marked to indicate the country of origin of the article if the importer does the repacking or manipulation.

If the article is intended to be sold or transferred to a subsequent purchaser or repacker, the importer should notify such purchaser or transferee, in writing, at the time of sale or transfer, that any repacking of the article must conform to the marking requirements.[37] The certification, in the form provided by Customs, may be submitted in either of two manners:

1. On an entry-by-entry basis, the certification may appear on the commercial invoice or an attachment to the invoice filed with entry papers at the time of entry; or

---

[36] 19 C.F.R. § 134.2(d).

[37] 19 C.F.R. §§ 134.25, 134.26.

2. In a blanket form to cover all importations of a particular product for a given period (e.g., calendar year) filed in each port where the imported articles will enter.

The certification allows Customs to ensure that the repackaged or manipulated product is conspicuously marked to indicate the foreign origin of the article or non-transformed ingredients contained therein. Customs also must be satisfied that, if any misleading markings are placed on the repackaging (e.g., a marking containing a U.S. reference such as the importer's U.S. address or a U.S. patent number, etc.), a conspicuous country of origin marking preceded by the words "Made in" or "Product of" appears in close proximity and comparable size wherever such misleading reference appears.[38]

15.3 Substantial Transformation

Country of origin is defined as the country of manufacture, production, or growth of a product.[39] A product that was wholly grown, produced, and manufactured in a single country does not present and issue, for example, aluminum ingots formed in Jamaica from smelted bauxite mined in Jamaica.

In all other situations, an imported article is generally considered to be a product of the country where it last underwent a substantial transformation. It may be difficult to determine the country of origin when an article is produced and manufactured in more than one country. An article grown, produced, or manufactured in Country A that is further worked, or has material added to it, in another country must undergo a substantial transformation in Country B to be deemed a product of Country B.[40] The concept of "substantial transformation" has been the subject of contentious debate for several decades. This metaphysical change is not easily defined nor easily explained.

An article used in manufacture that results in a new article having a new name, character, or use differing from that of the imported article is considered substantially transformed.[41] The question of when a substantial transformation occurs for

---

[38] 19 C.F.R. § 134.46.

[39] 19 C.F.R. § 134.2(b).

[40] 19 C.F.R. § 134.2(b).

[41] *See* Anheuser-Busch Brewing Ass'n v. United States, 207 U.S. 556 (1908); United States v. Gibson-Thomsen Co., 27 C.C.P.A. 267 (1940); Texas Instruments Inc. v. United States, 69 C.C.P.A. 152, 681 F.2d 778 (1982). The Customs regulations incorporate this theory at 19 C.F.R. 134.35:

> § 134.35 Articles substantially changed by manufacture.
>
> An article used in the U.S. in manufacture which results in an article having a name, character, or use differing from that of the imported article, will be within the principle of the decision in the case of U.S. v. Gibson-Thomsen Co., Inc., 27 C.C.P.A. 267 (C.A.D. 98). Under this principle, the manufacturer or processor in the U.S. who converts or combines the imported article into the different article will be considered the "ultimate purchaser" of the imported article within the contemplation of § 304(a), Tariff Act of 1930, as amended (19 U.S.C. 1304(a)), and the article shall be excepted from marking. The outermost containers of the imported articles shall be marked in accord with this part.

marking purposes is treated by U.S. Customs as a question of fact, to be addressed on a case-by-case basis.[42]

No comprehensive set of criteria has been created that is used to determine whether a substantial transformation has occurred. A two-prong test has been developed for substantial transformation determinations.[43] In *Uniroyal,* the court considered the complexity and cost of the processing operations *in addition to* whether the essence of the article had been changed by the processing. The court denied a marking exemption to imported shoes uppers that were processed in the United States by the attachment of an outsole. The operation in the United States was deemed insubstantial in completing the shoe when compared to the foreign processing that resulted in the imported uppers (the essence of the shoe). The final product was therefore required to indicate the foreign origin of the uppers.

The two-prong test used to determine whether a "substantial transformation" is whether:

1. A new and different article of commerce emerges—
2. As the result of a substantial manufacturing or processing operation.

In the first part of the test, a new and different article is considered to be one with a new name, character, or use. In the second part of the test, Customs determines whether merchandise has been subjected to substantial manufacturing operations by considering the:

1. Physical change in the article;
2. Time involved in the processing;
3. Complexity of the processing;
4. Level or degree of skill and/or technology required; and
5. Value added to the article.[44]

If the two-prong test is satisfied, then the U.S. processor is considered the ultimate purchaser and he is the last person to receive the article in the form in which it was imported. The article is thus exempted from marking, and only the containers that reach the processor need be marked.[45]

15.4 Liability for Failure to Properly Mark

An imported product that bears a *false designation of origin* is considered a prohibited importation and is subject to seizure.[46] The statute provides for the imposi-

---

[42]Uniroyal Inc. v. United States, 3 Ct. Int'l Trade 220, 542 F.Supp. 1026 (1982), *aff'd,* 1 Fed. Cir. 21, 702 F.2d 1022 (1983).

[43]Uniroyal, Inc. v. United States, 3 Ct. Int'l Trade 220, 542 F.Supp. 1026 (1982), *aff'd,* 702 F.2d 1022 (Fed. Cir. 1983).

[44]C.S.D. 85-47.

[45]19 U.S.C. § 1304(a)(3)(D).

[46]19 C.F.R. § 11.13.

tion of additional marking duties of 10% ad valorem[47] if the marking requirements are not complied with, either at the time of importation or after importation as required by Customs. The importer does not have the option to pay the 10% additional duties and ship unmarked merchandise into commerce.[48] However, properly remarking the merchandise will avoid these duties.

If unmarked or improperly marked merchandise is imported, then Customs can withhold delivery[49] or release the merchandise subject to a Notice of Redelivery requiring the importer to remedially remark the merchandise. Under Customs' regulations and the Customs bond, the importer undertakes an obligation to redeliver merchandise to Customs' custody within 30 days of a notice from Customs that it has determined that the imported merchandise is not properly marked.[50] Every importer must file a bond with U.S. Customs in order to make entry. The bond is either an annual continuous bond covering all entries by the company for the year or a single entry bond. The terms and conditions of the bond are established by Customs regulations.[51] If the Notice to Redeliver is issued after release of the merchandise, Customs must issue the Notice no later than 30 days after the release of the merchandise (or 30 days following the end of the conditional release period, if applicable). In no event, however, can the Notice to Redeliver be issued after liquidation of the entry has become final.

An importer has 30 days in which to mark the merchandise where specified by Customs (e.g., either in Customs' custody, public stores, or at the importer's premises).[52] Since Customs is permitted by regulation to "spot" check and inspect merchandise subject to a marking notice, an importer must be careful not to return a Notice certified to Customs unless the entire shipment has been remarked.[53] If a request to redeliver is timely issued and the importer fails to redeliver or remark the merchandise, then Customs will issue a claim for liquidated damages equivalent, at least, to the dutiable value of the shipment.[54]

The liquidated damages for failure to redeliver or remark the merchandise is an amount equal to the value of the merchandise plus estimated duties thereon.[55] These liquidated damages are subject to mitigation in accordance with Customs' mitigation guidelines. If an importer returns a Notice to Redeliver to Customs falsely certifying that the merchandise has been remedially marked, failure to file a required certification, concealing marking, false statements concerning marking (on invoices, etc.), or mismarking merchandise, could result in civil penalties against the importer.[56]

---

[47] 19 U.S.C. § 1304(f).

[48] *See* A.N. Dergner v. United States, 51 Cust. Ct. 21, C.D. 2408 (1963).

[49] 19 U.S.C. § 1304(g).

[50] 19 C.F.R. § 113.62(d).

[51] 19 C.F.R. pt. 113.

[52] 19 C.F.R. § 134.3.

[53] 19 C.F.R. § 134.52, § 134.54

[54] 19 C.F.R. § 134.54.

[55] 19 C.F.R. § 134.54(a).

[56] 19 U.S.C. § 1592.

Any person, not only an importer, who intentionally alters or obliterates country of origin marking can also incur criminal penalties.[57] A first violation is punishable by a $100,000 fine and/or a one-year prison term. A second or subsequent violation can result in a $250,000 fine and/or a one-year prison term.

15.5 Proposed Simplification: Tariff Shift Rules of Origin

Customs has adopted a codification of the rules of origin in connection with marking of goods that are subject to NAFTA.[58] Customs had proposed to extend these rules to all origin determinations for marking purpose.[59] If successful, this proposal would codify origin determinations to a large extent.

These rules establish a hierarchy for origin determinations. Generally, the country of origin of a good is the country in which:

1. The good is wholly obtained or produced;
2. The good is produced exclusively from domestic materials; or
3. Each foreign material incorporated into that good undergoes an applicable change in tariff classification and satisfies the applicable requirements of the tariff shift rules.

This last category is known as the "tariff shift" rules of origin. Customs has stated that it sought to codify the existing substantial transformation requirements in the form of tariff-shift rules. Under these rules, all products are listed by 4-digit to 10-digit Harmonized Tariff Schedule (HTS) classifications or groups of classifications in the tariff shift rules.

A tariff shift rule for a specific heading states that, for any given classification, to change the country of origin of a product there must be a shift from one HTS classification to another as listed in the tariff shift rules. Alternatively, the processing must meet any requirements specified in the tariff shift rules in Customs regulations. Customs' codification was recently called into question as abandoning existing statutory interpretations and the substantial transformation rule.[60] Marking rules have created some confusion where marking is different than origin for duty purposes or has changed existing, longstanding practice. These problems generally arise where a good is considered Canadian or Mexican because of the application of a Regional Value Content. Despite being NAFTA-originating for duty purposes, in many cases the marking rules do not consider such goods a product of Mexico or Canada requiring them to be marked with the non-NAFTA origin of their components. As these discrepancies work their way through the administrative and judicial process, these apparent conflicts should be resolved or explained.

---

[57] 19 U.S.C. § 1304(i).

[58] Final Rules: T.D. 96-48, Annex 311, North American Free Trade Agreement, 61 Fed. Reg. 29,932 (June 6, 1996); 19 C.F.R. pt. 120.

[59] Notice of Proposed Rule Making, 59 Fed. Reg. 141 (January 3, 1994).

[60] 19 U.S.C. § 1304. CPC International Inc. v. United States, Slip Op. 96–106 (July 8, 1996).

Customs has implemented other tariff shift rules for textiles and apparel under recent specific legislation. See the discussion in the following section.

In addition, under the Uruguay Round Agreement under the General Agreements on Tariff and Trade, the International Trade Commission has initiated an investigation toward international harmonization of rules of origin.[61] Draft proposals for these rules for several Chapters have published for comment. However, the rules conflict in several instances. As a result, the importer is now subject to a shifting basis for marking. These rules, like Customs proposals, rely on a code based on tariff shift rules.

Whether these tariff shift rules will prevail is yet to be seen. However, even if adopted they will not alleviate all case-by-case origin determinations. These rules are subject to exception and cannot be easily applied to certain articles like sets or composite articles.

The NAFTA marking rules state that, for composite articles, the country of origin is the country or countries of origin of the single material that imparts the *essential character* of the good.[62] If that rule is not effective or the article is a set or a composite good, the country or countries of origin of all the materials are considered co-equally in determining the *essential character* of the good. Essential character, like substantial transformation, is an essentially subjective determination that determines among components of a set or composite good, which component confers the character of the good. The weight, value, visual effect, and functionality are examined in making this determination. Thus, if a composite good with five components from Hong Kong and two components from China, and based on weight, value, etc., the Chinese components confer the essential character of the good, the origin will be China. Finally, if essential character cannot be determined, then the last country where the good underwent production other than simple assembly or minor processing applies.[63]

If the good is simply assembled, the origin will be the country of assembly if the countries of origin of the materials that merit equal consideration in the essential character of the good are different.[64] However, the origin will be the country of origin of the components if (1) the good is simply assembled and (2) all the materials that merit equal consideration in the essential character of the good are from the same country.[65]

15.6 Textiles and Apparel

Unique rules apply to textiles and apparel as a result of Section 334 of the Uruguay Round legislation.[66] The statute wiped away decades of rulings and court

---

[61]Investigation No. 332–360, 60 Fed. Reg. 19,605 (April 19, 1995).

[62]19 C.F.R. § 102.12(b)(1).

[63]19 C.F.R. § 102.12(d)(1).

[64]19 C.F.R. § 102.12(d)(2)(i).

[65]19 C.F.R. § 102.12(d)(2)(ii).

[66]Uruguay Round Agreements Act (the Act), Public Law 103–465, 108 Stat. 4809 (December 8, 1994).

cases concerning the country of origin for apparel and textile products. Previously, the cutting of fabric components determined country of origin for 90% of wearing apparel imports. Under the new rules, assembly of the article, not cutting of the fabric, determines the country of origin. A "subjective" determination under the provisions of former Customs Regulation 12.130 is allegedly replaced by "objective" processing operations expressed in terms of tariff shifts.

Country of origin for textile and apparel products processed, assembled, or manufactured in two or more countries is determined by where the most important processing occurs, and, if that cannot be ascertained, the last country in which an important processing operation occurs.

The statute provides:

1. For purposes of the customs laws and the administration of quantitative restrictions and except as otherwise provided for by statute, general rules for determining when a "textile or apparel product" originates in a country, territory, or insular possession, and is the growth, product, or manufacture of that country, territory, or insular possession;
2. Special origin rules for goods classifiable under certain specified tariff headings and subheadings;
3. A "multicountry rule" for determining origin when the origin of a good cannot be determined;
4. Special rules governing the treatment of components that are cut to shape in the United States from foreign fabric, exported for assembly, and returned to the United States; and
5. An exception to the application of Section 334 that specifically provides for the continued application of the administrative practices that were applied immediately before the enactment of the Act to determine the origin of textile and apparel products from Israel, unless such practices are modified by the mutual consent of the United States and Israel.

These rules became effective for goods entered, or withdrawn from warehouse, for consumption on or after July 1, 1996.

The rules establish a hierarchy for determining the origin of these products. A textile or apparel product is any good classifiable in Chapters 50 through 63, Harmonized Tariff Schedule of the United States (HTSUS), and any good classifiable under certain HTSUS headings or subheadings.[67] The country of origin of a textile or apparel product is determined by sequential application of the following rules.[68]

---

[67] 3005.90, 3921.12.15, 3921.13.15; 3921.90.2550; 4202.12.40–80; 4202.22.40–80; 4202.32.40–95; 4202.92.15–30; 4202.92.60–90; 6405.20.60; 6406.10.77; 6406.10.90; 6406.99.15; 6501; 6502; 6503; 6504; 6505.90; 6601.10–99; 7019.10.15; 7019.10.28; 7019.20; 8708.21; 8804; 9113.90.40; 9404.90.10; 9404.90.80–95; 9502.91; 9612.10.9010. 19 C.F.R. § 102.21(b)(5).

[68] 19 C.F.R. § 102.11.

1. The country of origin of a textile or apparel product is the single country, territory, or insular possession in which the good was wholly obtained or produced.
2. Where the country of origin of a textile or apparel product cannot be determined under the above rule, the country of origin of the good is the single country, territory, or insular possession in which each foreign material incorporated in that good underwent an applicable change in tariff classification, and/or met any other requirement, specified for the good in tariff-shift rules set forth in the regulations.[69]
3. Where the country of origin of a textile or apparel product cannot be determined under paragraph (1) or (2), if the good was "knit to shape," the country of origin of the good is the single country, territory, or insular possession in which the good was knit; or except for goods of heading 5609, 5807, 5811, 6213, 6214, 6301 through 6306, and 6308, and subheadings 6209.20.5040, 6307.10, 6307.90, and 9404.90, if the good was not knit to shape and the good was wholly assembled in a single country, territory, or insular possession, the country of origin of the good is the country, territory, or insular possession in which the good was wholly assembled.
4. Where the country of origin of a textile or apparel product cannot be determined under paragraph (1), (2), or (3), the country of origin of the good is the single country, territory, or insular possession in which the *most important assembly or manufacturing process occurred.*
5. Where the country of origin of a textile or apparel product cannot be determined under paragraph (1), (2), (3), or (4), the country of origin of the good is the last country, territory, or insular possession in which an important assembly or manufacturing process occurred.

The term *knit to shape* applies to any good of which 50% or more of the exterior surface area is formed by major parts that have been knitted or crocheted directly to the shape used in the good, with no consideration being given to patch pockets, appliques, or the like. Minor cutting, trimming, or sewing of those major parts will not affect the determination of whether a good is "knit to shape." The term *major parts* means integral components of a good but does not include collars, cuffs, waistbands, plackets, pockets, linings, paddings, trim, accessories, or similar parts.[70] The country of origin of each component of the set that is a textile or apparel product is determined separately. Where a good classifiable in the HTSUS as a set includes one or more components that are textile or apparel products and a single country of origin for all of the components of the set cannot be determined under the above rules.[71]

[69] 19 C.F.R. § 102.21.

[70] 19 C.F.R. § 102.20(b)(3),(4).

[71] 19 C.F.R. § 102.20(d).

The term *wholly assembled* when used with reference to a good means that all components, of which there must be at least two, preexisted in essentially the same condition as found in the finished good and were combined to form the finished good in a single country, territory, or insular possession. Minor attachments and minor embellishments (for example, appliques, beads, spangles, embroidery, buttons) not appreciably affecting the identity of the good, and minor subassemblies (for example, collars, cuffs, plackets, pockets), will not affect the status of a good as "wholly assembled" in a single country, territory, or insular possession.[72]

(a) Application of Tariff Shift Rules

The key to these rules is the application of the tariff shift rules to specific products. The following are examples of the results of the tariff shift rules:

1. *Yarn, including single and multiple yarns.* The country of origin of yarn, thread, twine, cordage, rope, or braiding is:
   - **a.** Staple yarn—the country in which yarn is spun
   - **b.** Filament yarn—the country in which filament is extruded
   - **c.** Plied, gimped, and cabled yarns—the country in which the fibers or filaments used in the yarn are spun or extruded
2. *Articles produced from yarns.* The country of origin of articles made from yarn, strips, twine, cordage, rope, or cables (classified under HTSUS heading 5609) is the country in which the yarn is produced.
3. *Fabric.* The country of origin of a fabric is the country in which the fabric is woven, knitted, needled, tufted, felted, entangled, or created by any other fabric-making process. A fabric-making process is any manufacturing operation that begins with polymers, fibers, filaments (including strips), yarns, twine, cordage, rope, or fabric strips and results in a textile fabric.[73] By application of a specific exception, the country of origin of quilted fabrics is the country in which the fabrics are produced.
4. *Articles produced from fabric.* The country of origin of certain articles made from fabric in the following Harmonized Tariff Schedule classifications is the country in which the fabric is produced:

   5807—Labels, badges, emblems

   5811—Quilted textile products in the piece, or lengths or rolls of quilted fabrics to be cut and hemmed

   6209.20.5040—Baby diapers

   6213—Handkerchiefs

   6214—Shawls, scarves, mufflers, mantillas, veils

   6301—Blankets, traveling rugs

   6302—Bed linen, table linen, toilet linen, kitchen linen

---

[72] 19 C.F.R. § 102.20(b)(6).

[73] 19 C.F.R. § 102.20(b)(2).

6303—Curtains, drapes, interior blinds, valances

6304—Bedspreads, furnishings

6305—Sacks and bags for packing

6306—Tarpaulins, awnings, sun blinds, tents, sails, camping goods

6307.10—Dust cloths, mop cloths, polishing cloths, shop towels, bar mops, dish cloths

6307.90—Labels, cords, tassels, corset and footwear lacings, toys for pets, wall banners, surgical towels, tufted towels, pillow shells, quilt shells, comforters, national flags, moving pads

6308—Needlecraft sets

9404.90—Pillows, cushions, quilts, comforters

5. *Knit-to-shape garments.* The country of origin of knit-to-shape garments is the single country in which the major parts are knitted or crocheted. The term *knit to shape* applies to any garment of which 50% or more of the exterior surface area is formed by major parts that have been knitted or crocheted directly to the shape used in the garment, with no consideration being given to patch pockets, appliques, or the like. Minor cutting, trimming, or sewing of those major parts does not affect the determination of whether a garment is "knit-to-shape." The term *major parts* means integral components of a garment, but does not include collars, cuffs, waistbands, plackets, pockets, linings, paddings, trim, accessories, or similar parts. A unique quota preference exists for Hong Kong. Under Category 845(2), panels knit in China and assembled in Hong Kong may ship with Hong Kong quota. They must be marked, however, "Made in China, linked in Hong Kong."
6. *All other woven and "cut and sew" knit textile products.* Except for knit-to-shape garments, the country of origin of all other textile and apparel products is the country in which the components of a textile or apparel product are wholly assembled, except for minor attachments such as buttons, beads, spangles, embroidery, etc., or minor subassemblies such as collars, cuffs, pockets, and plackets.
7. *The most important assembly or manufacturing process.* If the garment is not wholly assembled or manufactured (or wholly knit to shape) in one country, then the country of origin is the single country in which the most important assembly or manufacturing process occurred. This decision is made on a case-by-case basis, and a binding ruling is recommended in advance of production and shipment. U.S. Customs has specifically stated that rulings issued to other importers cannot be relied upon unless the exact same factual situation is present.
8. *The last country of important production.* If Customs cannot decide which is the most important assembly or manufacturing process in a multicountry production scenario, e.g., if the assemblies in Country A and Country B are deemed equally important, the country of origin is the *last* country in which an important assembly or manufacturing process occurred.

(b) Exceptions to the New Rules of Origin

Certain exceptions to the assembly rule already have been discussed previously, such as for knit-to-shape products, fabrics, and textile furnishings. Other exceptions exist:

- The new rules of origin do not affect the United States-Israel Free Trade Agreement. That is, garments currently considered to be of Israeli origin because the components are cut in Israel will continue to be considered Israeli products after July 1, 1996.
- For purposes of continuing the duty allowance for U.S. components assembled abroad pursuant to an 807 program (9802.00.80, HTSUS), components cut in the United States from foreign fabric continue to be treated as U.S. components.
- For the purpose of effectuating the Caribbean Basin Initiative (CBI), such U.S.-cut components apply toward the 35% value-added requirement, up to 15%.
- Products of insular possessions continue to have undergone a "double substantial transformation" by virtue of being cut and assembled in the possession from imported fabric.

(c) Quota and Marking Ramifications

Once a country of origin determination is made under the new rules of origin, the determination generally applies for all U.S. Customs purposes, such as quota and marking. For example, a garment cut into components in Country A, but wholly assembled in Country B, will be required to be marked "Made in B." An export license from Country B also will be required upon entry into the United States, and quota restraints in connection with Country B will apply. If the country of origin of an article, such as a textile furnishing, is based on where the fabric was formed, then an export license from that country is required, but in the category for the finished article.

15.7 Conclusion

Customs recent efforts to simplify marking rules of origin have only made matters complex. Together with the unique origin rules for tariff preference, importers are faced with shifting, technical, and often conflicting mandates as to the origin of an article. Importers can only hope that the World Trade Organization's attempt to harmonize rules of origin will clarify rather than further cloud the issue.

CHAPTER 16

U.S. Customs Rulings, Litigation, and Appeals

Patrick D. Gill

16.1 Customs Rulings
- (a) Oral Rulings
- (b) Delegation of Authority
- (c) National Commodity Specialized Division
- (d) Timing Issues
- (e) The "Prospective Transaction" Requirement
- (f) Application for Further Review
- (g) Ruling Request
- (h) Information Requirement
- (i) Pre-Importation Review Program

16.2 Thirty-Day Rulings Versus Interpretive Rulings
- (a) Advantages of the 30-Day Ruling
- (b) Disadvantages of the 30-Day Ruling
- (c) Interpretive Rulings
- (d) Appeals from Interpretive Rulings
- (e) Preparation of an Interpretive Ruling
- (f) Classification Issues

16.3 Modification and Revocation
- (a) Modification
- (b) Evolution of the Ruling Process

16.4 Challenges to an Adverse Ruling
- (a) Remedies
- (b) Protest Procedures
- (c) Application for Further Review

16.5 Litigation and Appeals
- (a) Review and Decisions
- (b) Contestable Actions

(c) Court Procedure
(d) Fact Analysis
(e) Customs Limitation of Unfavorable Decisions
(f) Multiple Protests
(g) Suspension Procedure
(h) Trial Practice
(i) Timing Issues
(j) Interest Recovery
(k) Actions by Other Non-Importers
(l) Classification
(m) Antidumping and Countervailing Duties
(n) Special Proceedings
(o) Advance Determinations
(p) Administration and Enforcement
(q) Parties Subject to Suit
(r) Rejection of Review

16.6 Appeals
(a) Timing
(b) Remand
(c) Supreme Court

16.7 Conclusion

16.1 Customs Rulings

The Customs rulings process is an essential aspect of importing merchandise into the United States.[1] A ruling issued pursuant to those regulations is in writing, signed by an appropriate official, and binding on both the Customs Service and the importer. Ruling can be issued by the Office of Regulations and Rulings, Customs Service Headquarters, Washington, D.C., or by a local port director after review by the Office of the Director of the National Commodity Specialist Division in New York.

(a) Oral Rulings

An importer may often receive advice over the phone or through a visit from an Import Specialist employed by Customs at the port of entry or from the National Import Specialists in New York. However, there is no such thing as an "oral ruling," and such advice is not binding on Customs or the Import Specialist who rendered the advice. For instance, an Import Specialist might advise an importer on a classification over the phone. The Import Specialist could later decide that merchandise subsequently entered has different classification, either because the Import Specialist has changed his or her position or a subsequent ruling on the classification of that type of merchandise has been issued requiring a different result.

[1] 19 C.F.R. pt. 177.

Therefore, a prudent importer will utilize the ruling process to obtain a binding ruling to avoid an unanticipated and adverse Customs decision affecting imports.

(b) Delegation of Authority

In seeking a binding ruling, it is helpful to have an understanding of the various levels within the Customs Service involved in the ruling process and their respective roles. Central control of the ruling process is vested at Customs Service Headquarters in Washington. In the past, only Customs Headquarters could issue binding rulings. Rulings at lower levels, such as the former regional and district levels and at the ports of entry, were not binding even if in writing. In recent years, Customs completely revamped the Customs Regulations, the procedure permits local Customs offices at the district level, now the port level, to issue binding rulings on the classification of merchandise. Local ruling authority at the port level has since been extended to country of origin marking and the North American Free Trade Agreement (NAFTA). By the time of publication, it is expected that this authority will also be extended to the textile rules of origin.

If an importer seeks a ruling on any subject other than previously enumerated, the ruling request must still be directed to the Office of Regulations and Rulings at Customs Headquarters in Washington. Examples of areas where ruling requests must be directed to Customs Headquarters include Customs valuation, entry requirements, drawback, and partial exemptions from duty under Chapter 98. Ruling requests that are made to Customs Headquarters should be addressed as follows:

United States Customs Service Headquarters
1301 Constitution Avenue N.W.
Washington, DC 20229
Attention: Office of Regulations and Rulings

(c) National Commodity Specialized Division

Rulings that may be issued by local Customs offices are issued under the auspices of the Director of the National Commodity Specialist Division in New York. This group is now considered part of the Office of Regulations and Rulings at Customs Service Headquarters. That office may assign the individual ruling request to the National Import Specialist responsible for the commodity in New York or to one of the Field National Import Specialists who are located at ports throughout the United States. Ultimately, the ruling will be signed by the Port Director where the Field National Import Specialist is located or the Area Director in New York.

Currently, an importer may also submit a classification ruling request, or other request within the sphere of the National Commodity Specialist Division, directly to Customs Headquarters. An importer may do this when a complicated question of law is presented and an in-depth legal analysis is sought. Such so-called precedential or interpretive rulings cannot be issued locally. This will change when the Customs Regulations are revised as expected sometime in 1997. When that occurs,

Customs Headquarters will not issue initial decisions on classification, marking, or NAFTA. Such ruling requests will have to be directed to the Customs Information Exchange in New York for assignment through the National Commodity Specialist Division.

The Customs Service office in Washington will issue rulings only in these areas upon appeal from decisions made by the National Commodity Specialist Division. In the case of rulings in other areas such as Customs valuation, Customs Headquarters will continue to issue the initial rulings.

The importer or his representative may submit a request for a binding classification ruling to any Port Director or to the Customs Information Exchange in New York, addressed as follows:

Director
National Commodity Specialist Division
United States Customs Service
6 World Trade Center
New York, NY 10048
Attention: Customs Information Exchange
Binding Rulings Section
Room 437

(d) Timing Issues

The principal advantage of seeking a noninterpretive binding ruling through Customs in New York is time. The rulings will be binding on the date of the ruling letter, at all ports of entry, unless revoked by the Washington Headquarters Office of Regulations and Rulings. Under this program, Customs will issue a written binding ruling on the imported merchandise within 30 days of the date of receipt of the binding ruling request. Some delay may occur if a laboratory report or consultation with another agency, for example, the Food and Drug Administration, is required.

If the National Commodity Specialist Division determines that referral of the question to the Office of Regulations and Rulings in Washington is necessary, then the ruling will be issued within 120 days of receipt of the initial ruling request by Customs. The vast majority of rulings issued under this program have been issued within the 30-day period self-mandated by Customs. When issues have been referred to Customs Headquarters, either by the local offices or at the request of the importer, the 120-day period has often been extended because of the complexity of the issues and the need for the submission of additional information and/or conferences.

(e) The "Prospective Transaction" Requirement

Under the regulations, a ruling request must concern a prospective transaction. This means that the subject matter of the ruling request has not yet been imported. When the local district ruling program was first initiated, a local 30-day ruling would not be issued if the product was already imported and the subject of a "prior or current transaction." Even a single entry was considered a current transaction, precluding the issuance of a local 30-day ruling. However, the procedure has been liberalized so as to permit the filing of a 30-day ruling request so long as there are continuing importations of the product. In that case, Customs' view is that there are "prospective" as well as "current transactions." If only past transactions are involved, then the importer will have to use a different vehicle to obtain a ruling.

Currently, an importer may request "internal advice"[2] at the port where the product has been entered. That request will be referred through the National Commodity Specialist Division to Customs Headquarters for the issuance of a ruling. When the Customs Regulations are revised, the importer will no longer have an option to seek internal advice. In that case, the only way for an importer to obtain a ruling on a current or completed transaction will be to file a Protest and Application for Further Review.[3] The protest will be referred to Customs Service Headquarters for review, and ultimately a ruling will be issued on the protested transaction.

(f) Application for Further Review

An Application for Further Review may be filed on the same Customs Form 19 (C.F. 19) used for filing regular protests (see the section on protests, *infra*). Alternatively, the Application for Further Review may be filed on a separate C.F. 19. The request must be filed in quadruplicate, and if a fifth copy is filed for the purpose of having a recorded receipt date, then the fifth copy will be returned to the party filing the Protest and Application for Further Review. The Application for Further Review must contain the following information:

1. Information identifying a protest to which it applies, the protesting party, and his importer number;
2. Allegation that the protesting party has not previously received an adverse administrative decision from the Commissioner of Customs or his designee nor has presently pending an application for an administrative decision on the same claim with respect to the same category of merchandise;
3. Allegation that the protesting party has not made a prior request for further review of the same claim or to the same or substantially similar merchandise; and
4. Allegation that the protesting party has not received a final adverse decision from the United States Court of International Trade or any other Customs Court on the same claim as to the same category of merchandise and does not have an action involving such a claim pending before the U.S. Court of International Trade or any other court.

---

[2] 19 C.F.R. § 177.11.

[3] 19 C.F.R. § 174.25.

(g) Ruling Request

When a 30-day ruling request is filed, the ruling request must be filed in writing in triplicate. The outside of envelopes and packages should be annotated "Binding Ruling Request." The ruling request must contain a complete statement of all relevant facts relating to the transaction, including:

1. The names, addresses, and other identifying information of all interested parties (if known), and the manufacturer ID code (if known);
2. The name(s) of the port(s) in which the merchandise will be entered;
3. A description of the transaction;
4. A statement that there are, to the importer's knowledge, no issues on the commodity pending before the Customs Service or any court; and
5. A statement as to whether classification advice had previously been sought from a Customs officer; and if so, from whom, and what advice was rendered.

(h) Information Requirement

Ruling requests must also contain sufficient information to determine the proper tariff classification, such as:

1. A full and complete description of the article;
2. The article's principal use in the United States;
3. The commercial, common, or technical designation;
4. For articles composed of two or more materials, the relative quantity by weight of each component;
5. Samples individually packed for mailing, or illustrative literature;
6. Chemical analysis, flow charts, etc.;
7. Inclusion of any special invoicing requirements in Part 141 of the Customs Regulations; and
8. Any other information that may assist in determining the appropriate tariff classification of the article.

The ruling request must contain no more than five items. The items in a single request must be of the same class or kind. Customs will not accept a request concerning textile articles and articles of a different class or kind, such as footwear. If more than five items are involved or different classes or kinds of articles are involved, it is a simple matter to file additional ruling requests.

(i) Pre-Importation Review Program

If an importer has a large number of items for which classification determinations are sought, the importer may qualify for a line review under the Pre-Importation Review Program (PIRP), formerly known as the "preclassification" or "pre-class" program. An importer interested in participating in this program should contact the local Customs field office. An appointment will be scheduled under which one or more of the Field National Import Specialists at the port or the National Import Specialist in New York will review and examine the importer's merchandise and issue a written list of tariff classifications. Those classifications will be reviewed by the National Commodity Specialist Division in New York, and the importer will receive a binding classification on all of the articles reviewed. In some cases, individual classification decisions may be referred to the Customs Service Headquarters Office in Washington if complex, novel, or precedential classification decisions are involved.

Classification decisions issued under the PIRP program are binding on Customs and the importer, as with any other rulings. If an importer is dissatisfied with a classification decision issued under PIRP, that classification decision can be appealed to Customs Headquarters in the same way as any local ruling. However, until Customs Headquarters issues a decision reversing or revoking the PIRP classification, the importer must enter the merchandise at the assigned classification.

16.2 Thirty-Day Rulings Versus Interpretive Rulings

Most importers are familiar with the 30-day ruling procedure. These rulings are not precedential and are binding on Customs only on imports by the importer or party who requested the ruling. The rulings contain no analysis, but merely state the facts and render a decision on the classification, marking, or related facets of the article that is the subject of the ruling request. Customs also issues precedential rulings that are now referred to by statute as "interpretive ruling(s)."[4] Customs may issue an interpretive ruling even when a 30-day ruling request is made if it is determined that the issue is of significant importance to warrant the issuance of an interpretive ruling. In addition, the importer may request that an interpretive ruling be issued. From the importer's perspective, there are advantages and disadvantages in seeking both types of rulings.

(a) Advantages of the 30-Day Ruling

The principal advantage of a 30-day ruling is the speed with which it is issued. Most importers may be reasonably certain of the classification of a product and seek the protection of the binding ruling as extra insurance. An importer whose product is subject to quota that is based on classification may find the need to have a ruling issued promptly, even if the ruling results in a higher rate of duty than anticipated. An erroneous assumption with respect to classification resulting in a different quota category may have the disastrous consequence of the importer's being unable to import the product for lack of quota and/or the appropriate visa for the

---

[4] 19 U.S.C. § 1625.

merchandise. The danger and uncertainty of falling into a different quota category can be quickly avoided by seeking a 30-day ruling.

The importer may also have consulted with the Import Specialist, Field National Import Specialist, or National Import Specialist and received oral advice as to the classification. Since it is unlikely that that advice would be changed upon receipt of a binding ruling request, the importer has little to lose in seeking a 30-day ruling to confirm and bind Customs to that classification. A 30-day ruling request is a quick way to achieve this result.

(b) Disadvantages of the 30-Day Ruling

A much higher percentage of 30-day rulings are subsequently revoked or modified by Customs than interpretive rulings. The latter will have had full consideration of the facts and law by the local and Headquarters offices of the Customs Service. The factual presentation in a 30-day ruling request may be the minimum required by the regulations and may be based on little more than a perfunctory examination of the sample. Subsequent modification or revocation of the ruling is less likely if the importer, in requesting a 30-day ruling, presents Customs with an analysis and recommended classification, based on an examination of the statute, its legislative history, and available precedents, both administrative and judicial.

It is often advisable to seek professional assistance in researching a recommended classification and in making the ruling request presentation to Customs Headquarters. Research and analysis, particularly the citation to earlier pertinent rulings on the classification, will greatly assist the Field National Import Specialist or National Import Specialist in reaching a decision and in ruling in favor of a classification proposed by the importer. Conversely, a skeletal ruling request, consisting of little more than the submission of a sample and a brief description of the merchandise, often paves the way for the issuance of erroneous rulings that are later modified or revoked. Customs welcomes as much information as possible for a ruling request and considers any reference by the importer or the importer's representative to pertinent authorities that will assist in analyzing the issues and reaching a decision on the correct classification.

Because of the time pressures on Customs in connection with the issuance of 30-day rulings, the widest possible input by knowledgeable Customs officials is not likely to occur. A Field National Import Specialist preparing the ruling may not be aware of the fact that other issues pertaining to the commodity have been raised by other Import Specialists at other ports, and those contrasting opinions may not have been registered with either the National Import Specialist or Customs Headquarters. After the 30-day ruling is issued, others within the Customs Service are likely to bring their dissenting views to the attention of the National Commodity Specialist Division in New York and seek a modification or revocation of the ruling. While there are protections to the importer, even in the case of modification or revocation, the long-term effect of a modification or revocation could have a substantial negative impact on the importer.

(c) Interpretive Rulings

There are situations where an importer will be well advised to seek an interpretive ruling, notwithstanding the disadvantage of the time it takes to have such a ruling issued, a minimum of 120 days. The first reason is that the importer that obtains an interpretive ruling will greatly minimize the danger or likelihood of subsequent revocation or modification of that ruling by Customs Headquarters. Currently, the National Commodity Specialist Division does not issue interpretive rulings and automatically refers requests requiring interpretive rulings to Customs Headquarters within 30 days of receipt. Customs Headquarters then issues the interpretive ruling within 120 days from the date the request was filed, unless additional follow-up submissions are made and additional time is requested by the importer to consider the submission of supplemental information and materials.

When the ruling procedures are revised under the new regulations, interpretive ruling requests will not automatically be referred to Customs Service Headquarters. Instead, the ruling request will be issued by the same offices issuing the 30-day rulings, but the rulings will be issued in 60 days rather than 30 days.

(d) Appeals from Interpretive Rulings

If the importer is dissatisfied with the ruling, an appeal to Customs Headquarters may be made. In that case, the National Commodity Specialist Division will have 30 days to respond to the appeal and Customs Headquarters will have an additional 60 days in which to review the appeal. The statute provides that, upon a reasonable showing of business necessities, the appeal will be considered and decided no later than 60 days following the date on which the appeal is filed.

Normally, a minimum of 150 days will have elapsed from the date on which the original ruling request was filed until a ruling after appeal is issued. It is likely that a far greater period of time will be involved in the appeal, if for no other reason than the lag time between the issuance of the initial ruling and the filing of the appeal. If a meeting or conference at Customs Headquarters is requested, or if an additional submission is made by the importer in connection with the appeal or the conference, at the very minimum, an additional 60 days will be added to the process, bringing the total minimum time to 210 days.

(e) Preparation of an Interpretive Ruling

In all cases, a great deal more consideration will be given to the facts and legal issues in the issuance of an interpretive ruling than will be involved in the issuance of a 30-day ruling. Customs is required by statute, under amendments resulting from the Customs Modernization Act, to publish interpretive rulings in the *Customs Bulletin* within 90 days of issuance.[5] The *Customs Bulletin* is a weekly publication of decisions, rulings, regulations, notices, and other related materials issued by the

[5] 19 U.S.C. § 1625(a).

Customs Service, as well as decisions of the United States Court of International Trade and the United States Court of Appeals for the Federal Circuit.

Because of the widespread dissemination of a published ruling, special care will be exercised by Customs in issuing an interpretive opinion. Such a ruling, once issued, is less likely to be disturbed, at least administratively. An importer may desire this additional degree of certainty when the commodity imported is an expensive commodity that will be imported over a long period of time and where potentially higher rates of duty could have disastrous consequences. In that case, the importer will be well advised to seek the assistance of counsel to prepare a detailed legal analysis for presentation to Customs in order to obtain a ruling affirming the classification asserted by the importer.

(f) Classification Issues

Other reasons may exist that would cause an importer to forgo the time benefit of a 30-day ruling in favor of seeking an interpretive ruling. The classification issue presented may be novel or potentially contentious. The importer may already know that the Import Specialists are of an initial opinion that a different classification and higher rate of duty than that contended by the importer may apply. If that is the case, seeking a 30-day ruling may be pointless and even counterproductive. Once the 30-day ruling is issued, the importer will be forced to enter the merchandise under the classification dictated by the 30-day ruling until such time as the ruling is revoked, either on appeal or through litigation in the courts.

By seeking an interpretive ruling, the importer will at least have the opportunity to present alternative views to the National Commodity Specialist Division and to set the stage for a more considered review on appeal by the Office of Regulations and Rulings at Customs Headquarters in Washington. If the issue is resolved after appeal to the Classification Appeals Division at Customs Service Headquarters in Washington, the importer will have been afforded every opportunity to present its views, to have a conference at Customs Headquarters, and to submit any additional information that is helpful to the importer's case after meeting with the attorneys involved at Customs Headquarters.

Ultimately, the importer will have to make a judgment as to which type of ruling is most appropriate to the particular circumstances. In doing so, the importer must consider factors such as the need for speedy issuance of a ruling, the difficulty of the classification issue involved, the need for long-term certainty, and the greater likelihood of receiving a favorable ruling on the basis of which type of ruling is requested.

16.3 Modification and Revocation

The Customs Modernization Act, which was incorporated into the legislation implementing NAFTA, imposed statutory requirements on Customs as to the modification and revocation of rulings. Under these provision, if a ruling has been effective for less than 60 days, then Customs may modify or revoke the ruling without formal notice or an opportunity to be heard by the importer or other interested parties. In many cases, such revocations may occur even at the behest of the importer receiving an adverse 30-day ruling. If the modification or revocation is adverse to the importer, then the initial ruling will be binding as to all entries made from the time of issuance until the time when the ruling is revoked. Under the current regulations, if the importer makes a showing of detrimental reliance, Customs may delay the effective date of such a ruling for a period of up to 90 days from the issuance of the modification or revocation.

(a) Modification

If the ruling was in effect for 60 days or more, the provisions of the Customs Modernization Act supersede the prior regulations as to the procedures for modification or revocation. If modification is contemplated, Customs is required to publish the proposed letter ruling modifying or revoking the earlier ruling in the *Customs Bulletin.* Normally, the importer will receive advance notice of such publication, which should serve as a warning of a possible change in classification.

When the notice is published in the *Customs Bulletin,* the importer and other interested parties will be given at least 30 days in which to submit comments on the proposed ruling or decision. After the comments are considered, Customs must publish a final ruling affirming, modifying, or revoking the original ruling within 30 days of the close of the comment period. A final ruling or decision will then become effective 60 days after publication of the final ruling.

As a practical matter, the importer will have at least 120 days' notice of the potential change in classification or other decision and may be able to adjust its import program accordingly. The importer will have notice of an impending change and will be entitled to receive the original classification until such time as the final ruling modifying or revoking the original ruling becomes effective.

(b) Evolution of the Ruling Process

The ruling process described in the preceding paragraph is currently in a state of evolution. Changes undoubtedly will continue as regulations under the Customs Modernization Act are finalized and revised in the future. Customs considers the ruling process to be a keystone to the administration of the Customs laws because the process serves both Customs and the importing community.

Customs uses the ruling process as a vehicle to inform the public and to establish precedent where necessary on important issues of classification, marking, value, quota, drawback, and other subjects relevant to the administration of the Customs laws. The importer is in a unique position to utilize the ruling process to protect its rights and to ensure the most favorable type of tariff treatment possible from the Customs Service. The ruling process is also an important component of the new standards of reasonable care and informed compliance imposed on importers by the Customs Modernization Act.

As part of the concept of shared responsibility, Customs places upon the importer the initial burden to ensure the correctness of the classification and valuation of imported merchandise. Failure to exercise reasonable care in these areas will potentially subject the importer to penalties for failure to meet minimum standards of reasonable care and due diligence with respect to classification, valuation, and other requirements in importing merchandise.[6] While it is true that an importer may satisfy standards of reasonable care by basing his decisions on expert advice from persons such as Customs brokers or lawyers, there may be considerable difficulty in establishing and proving by documentation or otherwise that such advice was correctly sought and rendered. On doubtful questions, there is no better way for an importer to establish that reasonable care has been exercised than by presenting the question to Customs for the issuance of a binding ruling.

16.4 Challenges to an Adverse Ruling

The issuance of a ruling may satisfy the need for certainty and meet standards of reasonable care and informed compliance, but the importer may disagree with the ruling. Although the importer will be required to follow the ruling until such time as it is overturned, procedures allow an importer to contest an adverse ruling under the law. When a ruling is issued, the Customs Service will liquidate entries of all merchandise subject to the ruling in accordance with the ruling. However, this is not the end of the road for the importer who wishes to challenge the ruling.

(a) Remedies

There are both administrative and judicial remedies available to an importer dissatisfied with a Customs ruling that enable the importer to challenge a Customs Service determination. The protest procedures constitute the principal way in which an importer may challenge a Customs Service determination administratively.[7] The protest is the mechanism by which an importer can make a formal administrative challenge to a Customs decision. In addition, the filing of a protest is the first step that must normally be taken by an importer prior to litigating Customs decisions in the courts.

A protest is a legal document. It is governed not only by the regulatory provisions[8] but also by the statutory provisions.[9]

The types of decisions that may be protested and the time in which a protest may be filed are strictly circumscribed by the statute.[10] Most decisions as to the classification and value of merchandise may be challenged by an importer only by filing a protest[11] after the liquidation of a specific entry of imported merchandise.

[6] 19 U.S.C. § 1592.

[7] 19 C.F.R. pt. 174.

[8] *id.*

[9] 19 U.S.C. § 1514.

[10] *id.*

[11] *id.*

A protest filed before liquidation or more than 90 days after liquidation is invalid. A protest that is filed outside of this 90-day period will not be considered by Customs, and its denial will not form a predicate for the filing of an action in the Court of International Trade.[12] Customs will allow a protest against an adverse ruling to constitute a basis for an appeal to Customs Headquarters: Under the proposed regulations, however, if an importer contemplates challenging in the courts an unfavorable decision resulting from an adverse Customs ruling, a protest will have to be filed, not against the ruling, but against the liquidation of entries made pursuant to that ruling if that liquidation involves decisions as to the appraisement and/or classification of the merchandise.

(b) Protest Procedures

The types of issues that may be protested, the contents of protests, and the manner of filing protests are covered by the regulations.[13] A protest is normally filed on a Customs Form 19. A legally binding protest may be filed in other formats. Nevertheless, an importer is well advised to utilize Customs Form 19 to avoid a perfunctory denial of the protest.

Extreme care should be exercised in the preparation of a protest, and it should be treated as any other legal document that affords a party substantial rights. The failure to include all protestable decisions in a protest filed within 90 days of liquidation will, in most cases, effectively preclude the importer from any further administrative or judicial review of the decisions not challenged by the protest. The language of the protest and the description of the merchandise covered by the protest can therefore be most critical in determining whether the protest is valid and whether the decisions that the importer intends to challenge will effectively be reviewed pursuant to the protest.

(c) Application for Further Review

For decisions encompassed by Customs rulings, the liquidation of any entries covered by a ruling will be, in most cases, the operative event that must be challenged by protest. If a ruling has been issued, the importer should expect that the protest will be denied on the basis of the ruling. However, if by protesting a liquidation the importer still wishes to challenge a ruling administratively before Customs, then the importer can seek further review of the protest by filing an Application for Further Review.[14]

An Application for Further Review is accomplished by checking the appropriate boxes on Customs Form 19 requesting further review. The Application for Further Review and the protest must both be filed within 90 days of liquidation, or no further action will be taken. If an Application for Further Review is filed, then the

---

[12] 28 U.S.C. § 1581(a).

[13] 19 C.F.R. §§ 174.11–174.13.

[14] 19 C.F.R. § 174.25.

issue will be forwarded to Customs Headquarters for review. If there has been no appeal of an initial ruling by Customs, that is, a 30-day ruling, then the Application for Further Review may provide a useful tool to the importer to seek a reconsideration of the issue at Customs Headquarters without the need for judicial review.

A Protest and Application for Further Review can be filed after liquidation even if an appeal from an initial ruling was not taken. When an issue is forwarded to Customs Headquarters on an Application for Further Review, the importer will be afforded, if requested, an opportunity for a conference at Customs Headquarters and may also be given the opportunity to submit additional information in support of the Protest and Application for Further Review. In this way, the importer has one more opportunity at the highest level in the Customs Service before being forced to seek judicial review.

If a protest or a Protest and Application for Further Review is ultimately denied by Customs, then the importer, in most cases, will have exhausted his administrative remedies with respect to challenging a Customs ruling or other decision. At this point, if the importer seeks judicial review of a denied protest, a summons in the Court of International Trade must be filed within 180 days after denial of the protest.[15]

16.5 Litigation and Appeals

Most decisions of the Customs Service that are subject to judicial review are initially reviewable only in the United States Court of International Trade. The Court of International Trade has exclusive jurisdiction of actions commenced to contest the denial of a protest.[16] As a result, virtually all Customs rulings[17] are subject to judicial review only in the Court of International Trade. The Court of International Trade is located in New York City. However, the Court has national jurisdiction and regularly hears cases before single judges at locations throughout the United States. The Court even has authority to take testimony outside the 50 states.

(a) Review and Decisions

Most decisions of the Customs Service that are reviewable by the Court of International Trade are also subject to protest.[18] In order to litigate an issue in the Court of International Trade of a protestable matter,[19] an importer must first file a protest.[20] The importer may file an action in the Court of International Trade[21] only after denial of the protest. Therefore, an importer must understand which matters are pro-

[15]28 U.S.C. § 2636(a)(1).

[16]19 U.S.C. § 1514.

[17]Issued under Part 174.

[18]19 U.S.C. § 1514.

[19]*id.*

[20]*id.*

[21]28 U.S.C. § 1581(a).

testable[22] before filing an action in the Court of International Trade. An action[23] may be commenced against the denial of a protest[24] under the following subjects:

1. The appraised value of merchandise;
2. The classification and rate and amount of duties chargeable;
3. All charges or exactions of whatever character within the jurisdiction of the Secretary of the Treasury;
4. The exclusion of merchandise from entry or delivery or a demand for redelivery to Customs custody under any provisions of the Customs laws;[25]
5. Liquidation or reliquidation of an entry, or reconciliation as to the issues contained in a reconciliation entry, or any modification thereof;
6. The refusal to pay a claim for drawback; or
7. The refusal to reliquidate an entry, which provides for reliquidation of an entry due to clerical error, mistake of fact or other inadvertence not amounting to an error at law.[26]

(b) Contestable Actions

If an action is commenced,[27] it is essential that all liquidated duties and interest thereon be paid prior to the filing of the action in the Court of International Trade.[28] Failure to pay liquidated duties prior to commencement of an action will result in dismissal of the action.[29]

(c) Court Procedure

Once a protested decision is the subject of an action in the Court of International Trade,[30] the matter is subject to a full trial *de novo* before the Court. The case will be tried before a single judge of the Court, or, in special cases upon motion, before a three-judge panel of the Court. All of the rules of evidence and rules of civil procedure that govern proceedings before the district courts apply. The rules of civil procedure in the Court of International Trade are virtually identical in material part to the Federal Rules of Civil Procedure that govern proceedings in the district courts. The Court will hear testimony and weigh the evidence. While there is a presumption of correctness that attends Customs decisions, the Court will consider the evidence and review the law impartially before reaching a decision.

---

[22] 19 U.S.C. § 1514.

[23] 28 U.S.C. § 1581(a).

[24] 19 U.S.C. § 1514.

[25] Except a determination appealable under 19 U.S.C. § 1337.

[26] 19 U.S.C. § 1520(c).

[27] 28 U.S.C. § 1581(a).

[28] 28 U.S.C. § 2637(a).

[29] Glamorize Foundations, Inc. v. United States, 11 CIT 394, 661 F. Supp. 630 (1987).

[30] 28 U.S.C. § 1581(a).

(d) Fact Analysis

In some cases, only a question of law may be involved. It may be possible to proceed in the Court on the basis of stipulated facts or on a motion for judgment on the pleadings or for summary judgment without the necessity of a full-blown trial. If the Court decides in favor of the importer, a decision will be rendered ordering reliquidation of all entries that were subject to the original protests or protest covered by the civil action.

(e) Customs Limitation of Unfavorable Decisions

Customs may ultimately limit the application of an unfavorable decision to the entries before the Court to seek relitigation of an issue. When Customs limits a decision, only the entries that were the subject of the civil actions in court will be reliquidated pursuant to the judgment. Other entries of merchandise will have to be covered by protests and additional civil actions, and the importer will be forced to retry the issue a second time.

Customs may force the litigation by limiting the initial decision because it believes that by producing new evidence or making additional arguments in a retrial of the case, a different decision might be reached. Fortunately, Customs usually follows final decisions of the Court so that the importer receives the benefit of a favorable decision not only on the entries in court but on all future entries. For this reason, an action in court is the most effective way in which to overcome an adverse Customs ruling or decision.

(f) Multiple Protests

All liquidated entries must be protested within 90 days of liquidation, and the subsequent denial of any such protests must be made the subject of a civil action.[31] It is often necessary for importers litigating issues in the Court to continue to file multiple protests and successive summonses in order to protect their right of recovery while the issue is litigated in the Court. Failure to cover all liquidated entries with valid protests and all denied protests with appropriate civil actions will result in an inability to recover the duties on uncovered entries even if a successful judgment is obtained in another action or group of consolidated actions involving the same merchandise or same issues.

(g) Suspension Procedure

Procedures exist for the so-called suspension of subsequent summons in the Court of International Trade pending the outcome of an initial test case initiated by an importer. It is even possible for an importer to file actions and suspend his cases under other actions commenced by other importers involving the same issue. This

[31] *id.*

is a common practice in the Court of International Trade, and, in some cases, thousands of cases have been suspended pending the decision in a test case.

(h) Trial Practice

Litigation before the Court can be costly and time-consuming, particularly if complicated factual issues requiring a lengthy trial are involved. When an action is commenced in court by the filing of a summons,[32] it must be accompanied by a complaint or followed by a complaint within six months. The government has an additional 60 days to file an answer and will often seek additional time. Thereafter, protracted discovery proceedings may take place, including interrogatories, depositions, and other pre-trial procedures.

The case will be tried before a judge of the Court and normally subject to post-trial briefing. In recent years, most judges of the Court have been relatively prompt in rendering decisions after the cases have been submitted and briefs have been filed. However, there have been notable exceptions where cases have remained pending awaiting decision more than a year after submission to the Court.

(i) Timing Issues

Importers have been successful in obtaining decisions very quickly in the Court of International Trade when they have established that any delay in rendering a decision would result in substantial damage or irreparable harm. One such decision, which was rendered in the fastest time possible for a final judgment in the history of the Court of International Trade, was *Manhattan Shirt Co. v. United States.*[33] In that case, a final decision was reached within 30 days after the action was initially commenced.

The importer in *Manhattan Shirt Co.* needed a prompt decision because the Customs classification assigned to its imported shirts prevented the importer from importing the shirts. The importer could not obtain the quota required for that classification and, as a result, could not secure the visas necessary for entry of the merchandise. The Court heard the testimony and issued its decision on proposed findings of fact and conclusions of law on the 30th day after the action was commenced.

In *Hampco Apparel Inc. v. United States,*[34] the Court issued a final decision overturning a Customs classification within 60 days after the date on which the action was commenced. That case also involved an adverse Customs classification and quota category under which the importer could not import its goods.

(j) Interest Recovery

An importer should attempt to exhaust all administrative remedies where possible in order to avoid the difficulties of litigation. Thereafter, judicial review in the

---

[32] 19 U.S.C. § 1581(a).

[33] 2 CIT 332 (1981).

[34] 12 CIT 92 (1988).

Court of International Trade remains a viable and effective means by which an importer can overturn an adverse and unlawful Customs ruling or determination. If an importer successfully challenges a Customs determination, it will receive not only refunds of the duties paid on the entries that are subject to the civil actions, but also interest from the date of payment. In many cases those interest recoveries can be quite substantial. The interest rate is the rate established by the Internal Revenue Service and has ranged between 7 and 10% in recent years.

(k) Actions by Other Non-Importers

Litigation before the Court of International Trade may involve other issues.[35] Importers are not the only ones who may avail themselves of judicial review in the Court of International Trade. An administrative framework permits a domestic interested party to challenge the appraised value or classification of imported merchandise.[36] Domestic interested parties include wholesalers, manufacturers, and producers of similar merchandise, as well as unions or workers groups that are representative of industries engaged in United States production of such goods.

In addition, United States trade or business associations, a majority of whose members are United States manufacturers, producers, or wholesalers, may petition Customs to change its position on imported merchandise. If Customs adheres to its initial determination on the appraisement or classification of the imported merchandise, then the domestic interested parties may challenge the action by Customs.

(l) Classification

The Court of International Trade also has jurisdiction to review challenges by domestic interested parties to Customs decisions involving the classification and value of imported merchandise.[37] Such actions may be commenced by domestic manufacturers, producers, or wholesalers, certified unions, or trade and business associations, a majority of whose members are manufacturers, producers, or wholesalers in the United States of goods of the same class or kind of the imported merchandise. When such an action is commenced after denial of the domestic petition challenging the Customs decision, the importer of the first entry liquidated after denial will automatically become a party-in-interest to that action.

Other importers who may be adversely affected if the Customs ruling or decision is overturned upon motion may appear in Court as *amici curiae.* In the most recent decision of the Court the party-in-interest appeared in defense of the government classification along with several other importers who appeared as amici curiae.[38] The Court ultimately sustained the government's classification and the position taken by the importers.[39]

---

[35] 28 U.S.C. § 1581.

[36] 19 U.S.C. § 1516.

[37] 28 U.S.C. § 1581(b).

[38] 28 U.S.C. § 1581(c).

[39] Amithy Leather Company and Luggage and Leather Goods Manufacturers of America, Inc. v. United States, ________ CIT ______ , slip op. 96–140 (1996).

(m) Antidumping and Countervailing Duties

The Court of International Trade has jurisdiction to review the administration of the antidumping and countervailing duty laws administered primarily by the Department of Commerce and the United States International Trade Commission. Importers may challenge antidumping duty and countervailing duty determinations by the Commerce Department and the International Trade Commission.[40] Even though Customs is the agency that collects the antidumping and countervailing duties, it is actually the determination of the Commerce Department and/or the International Trade Commission that is the subject of judicial review.[41] As a result, antidumping and countervailing duty assessments are not protestable matters[42] or reviewable under traditional protest procedures.[43]

An importer wishing to challenge a Commerce Department or International Trade Commission determination under the antidumping duty and countervailing duty laws must utilize and comply with the unique requirements for bringing an action challenging those determinations.[44] The basic preconditions for review of Commerce Department and International Trade Commission determinations are set forth by statute.[45] Review may be sought by any interested party in the administrative proceedings, including importers, exporters, and domestic manufacturers. The determinations that may be reviewed are as follows:

1. Final affirmative determinations by the Commerce Department and the International Trade Commission, under 19 U.S.C. § 1671d or 19 U.S.C. § 1673d including any negative part of such a determination (other than a part referred to in the next paragraph). An affirmative determination means that grounds exist for the assessment of antidumping or countervailing duties, while a negative determination under the statute means that such grounds do not exist.
2. A final negative determination by the Commerce Department or the International Trade Commission, under 19 U.S.C. § 1671d or 19 U.S.C. § 1673d including any part of a final affirmative determination which specifically excludes any company or product.
3. A final determination, other than a determination reviewable under paragraph (1) above by the Commerce Department or the International Trade Commission under 19 U.S.C. § 1675 which involves review of initial antidumping and countervailing duty determinations.
4. A determination by the Commerce Department under 19 U.S.C. § 1671c or 19 U.S.C. § 1673c to suspend an antidumping duty or countervailing duty investigation, including any final determination resulting from a continued

[40]28 U.S.C. § 1581(c).

[41]*id.*

[42]19 U.S.C. § 1514.

[43]28 U.S.C. § 1581(a).

[44]28 U.S.C. § 1581(c).

[45]19 U.S.C. § 1516(a).

investigation which changes the size of the dumping margin or the net countervailable subsidy calculated, or the reasoning underlying such calculations, at the time the suspension agreement was concluded.

5. An injurious effect determination by the International Trade Commission under 19 U.S.C. § 1671c(h) or 19 U.S.C. § 1673c(h).
6. A determination by the Commerce Department as to whether a particular type of merchandise was within the class or kind of merchandise described in an existing antidumping or countervailing duty order.
7. A determination by the Commerce Department or the International Trade Commission under 19 U.S.C. § 3538 concerning a determination under Title VII of the Tariff Act of 1930 involving subsidies and countervailing duties.
8. A determination under 19 U.S.C. § 1675b(a)(1).

Review of Commerce Department and International Trade Commission determinations under the antidumping duty and countervailing duty laws is limited. The review is based on the agency record and is not a *de novo* review of the type involving challenges to Customs Service decisions.[46] The cases are normally submitted to the Court on motion for summary judgment, and so long as there is substantial evidence to support the agency determination, the decision will be affirmed.[47]

(n) Special Proceedings

There are also special proceedings in the Court of International Trade which provide for:

1. Judicial review of worker adjustment assistance determinations under the Trade Act of 1974;[48]
2. Country of origin determinations affecting government procurement;[49]
3. The issuance of protective orders in countervailing or antidumping duty proceedings;[50] and
4. Revocation and suspension proceeding involving customs broker licensing.[51]

(o) Advance Determinations

One unique provision that provides for judicial review in advance of importation and without the payment of duties is the provision for review of rulings.[52] This

---

[46]28 U.S.C. § 1581(a).

[47]Carlisle Tire & Rubber Co. v. United States, 9 CIT 520, 622 F. Supp. 1071 (1985).

[48]28 U.S.C. § 1581(d).

[49]28 U.S.C. § 1581(e).

[50]28 U.S.C. § 1581(f).

[51]28 U.S.C. § 1581(g).

[52]28 U.S.C. § 1581(h).

provision has rarely been successfully utilized because of the difficulty in establishing the prerequisite irreparable that which must be shown in order to secure judicial review under this section. In *718 Fifth Ave. Corp. v. United States,*[53] the Court refused to grant a declaratory judgment, holding a Customs ruling to be illegal because the importer failed to establish that his monetary losses alone would constitute irreparable harm if it was forced to go the normal protest route in challenging the Customs decision.

Ironically, the Court overturned the Customs ruling and sustained the importer's claim after the more time-consuming channels for relief were pursued.[54] Nevertheless, there have been successful challenges under this section, and it remains a possible avenue for prompt judicial review if the importer can meet the rigorous standard of establishing irreparable harm.[55]

(p) Administration and Enforcement

The last but very significant way in which an importer can seek judicial review of administration and enforcement[56] is under the residual jurisdictional provision of the statute. This unique provision provides for exclusive jurisdiction within the Court of International Trade for review of all other Customs decisions affecting the administration and enforcement of the Customs and related laws that are not specifically provided for in the preceding section. The language of the statute[57] is broad in scope. It grants the Court of International Trade exclusive jurisdiction of actions commenced against the government or any other of its agencies or officers arising out of any law providing for:

1. Revenue from imports or tonnage;
2. Tariffs, duties, fees, or other taxes on the importation of merchandise for reasons other than the raising of revenue;
3. Embargoes or other quantitative restrictions on the importation of merchandise for reasons other than the protection of public health or safety; or
4. Administration and enforcement with respect to the matters referred to in any of the preceding provisions.[58]

(q) Parties Subject to Suit

The agencies that may be sued under this section include not only the Customs Service but any agency whose administration and enforcement actions may impact upon imports, including such relatively obscure agencies as the United States

[53] 7 CIT 195 (1984).

[54] 718 Fifth Ave. Corp. v. United States, 14 CIT 403, 741 F. Supp. 1577 (1990).

[55] National Juice Products Association v. United States, 10 CIT 48, 628 F. Supp. 978 (1986).

[56] 28 U.S.C. § 1581(i).

[57] *id.*

[58] 19 U.S.C. § 1581.

Foreign Trade Zones Board.[59] While most of the matters reviewable under this section involve imports, even taxes and duties on *exports* have been subject to review under this section. The most notable decision in recent years under this section was the successful challenge to the constitutionality of the Harbor Maintenance Tax on exports in *United States Shoe Corp. v. United States.*[60]

(r) Rejection of Review

Many attempts to obtain judicial review[61] under this section have been frustrated by decisions of the courts, which have confined review under that provision to subjects that are not reviewable.[62] If judicial review can be had under any of the other sections, no matter how circuitous the process, the Courts will be reluctant to promote what would undoubtedly be more expeditious judicial review.[63] Nevertheless, the appellate court in recent decisions[64] has taken a more liberal view of the need to exhaust administrative remedies and has refused to impose restrictions on the use of the residual jurisdictional provision.[65]

In entertaining the suit in that case against the Foreign Trade Zones Board,[66] the Court characterized as "jurisdictional ping-pong" some of the earlier decisions limiting the availability of Section 1581(i).[67] An importer who wishes to challenge a Customs decision or determination that is not reviewable under any of the previously discussed subsections would do well to consider the possibilities of bringing an action under the residual jurisdictional provision.[68] However, before seeking review under this section, careful consideration will have to be given to whether jurisdiction will have to be established under one or more of the more cumbersome provisions for judicial review.[69]

16.6 Appeals

If either the government or the importer is dissatisfied with a decision of the Court of International Trade, it has an automatic right of appeal to the United States Court of Appeals for the Federal Circuit, which is located in Washington. Normally, appeals from decisions of the Court of International Trade are taken only after a

---

[59]Conoco Inc. v. United States Foreign Trade Zones Bd., 18 F. 3d 1581 (Fed. Cir. 1994).

[60]907 F. Supp. 408 (1995).

[61]28 U.S.C. § 1581(i).

[62]28 U.S.C. § 1581 (a)–(h).*See,* for instance, Norcal/Crosetti Foods, Inc. v. United States, 963 F.2d 356 (Fed. Cir. 1992) and United States Cane Sugar Refiners Association v. United States, 12 CIT 907, 698 F.Supp. 266 (1988).

[63]28 U.S.C. § 1581(i).

[64]Conoco Inc. v. United States Foreign Trade Zones Bd., *supra.*

[65]28 U.S.C. § 1581(i).

[66]*id.*

[67]*id.* Conoco Inc. v. United States Foreign Trade Zones Bd., *supra* at 1590.

[68]*id.*

[69]28 U.S.C. § 1581.

final decision of the Court is reached. In limited circumstances, an interlocutory appeal is available, but generally such interlocutory appeals are frowned upon.[70]

(a) Timing

The appeal process is relatively quick in the overall scheme of litigation. The party challenging a Court of International Trade decision, the appellant, must serve and file a brief within 60 days after the appeal is docketed, and the Court does not look kindly upon requests for extensions of time. The appellee must file a brief within 40 days after service of the appellant's brief, and a reply brief may be filed 15 days thereafter. Oral argument will be heard before a three-judge panel of the Court normally within one to two months after the briefs have been filed, and in some cases, in an even shorter period of time. In all but the most unusual cases, decisions are rendered by the Court within six months of oral argument.

(b) Remand

If the Court of Appeals for the Federal Circuit agrees with the decision of the Court of International Trade, the lower Court decision will be affirmed. Otherwise, the decision will be reversed and possibly remanded to the Court of International Trade for further consideration. The decision on remand is itself subject to reappeal to the Court of Appeals for the Federal Circuit. Normally, however, a decision by the Court of Appeals for the Federal Circuit is the final decision in a case challenging a Customs decision. Motions for hearings are not encouraged, and rehearings are virtually never granted.

(c) Supreme Court

The final avenue of appeal for the importer or the government is to the Supreme Court of the United States. Review in the Supreme Court may be had only on a *writ of certiorari.* A dissatisfied party must first file a petition for certiorari in order to obtain permission to file an appeal, and the opposing party has the opportunity to oppose the petition. In all but the rarest of cases, petitions for certiorari involving Customs issues are denied. Only a handful of cases involving Customs issues have been decided by the Supreme Court in the past quarter-century.

16.7 Conclusion

Litigation, especially accompanied by an appeal, can be a costly, complicated, and time-consuming process. Nevertheless, important questions involving the substantial rights of importers do arise that warrant and, in many cases, require litigation in order to achieve a satisfactory resolution. While in many cases a dissatisfied

[70]United States v. Dantzler Lumber & Export Co., 17 CIT 178 (1993).

importer will forgo litigation at the end of the administrative process before Customs or other agencies, it is important to remember that these avenues of judicial review exist and that they provide remedies to importers when all else fails. Fortunately, importers have many steps in both the administrative and judicial processes in which to seek a determination by the government on their imports, as well as the review of such determinations when they are unsatisfactory or adverse. See Exhibits 16.1 and 16.2. Utilization of these procedures will not only provide certainty, but they are likely to ensure that the importer is receiving the most favorable tariff or other administrative treatment possible.

Exhibit 16.1

LEVELS OF REVIEW OF CUSTOMS DECISIONS

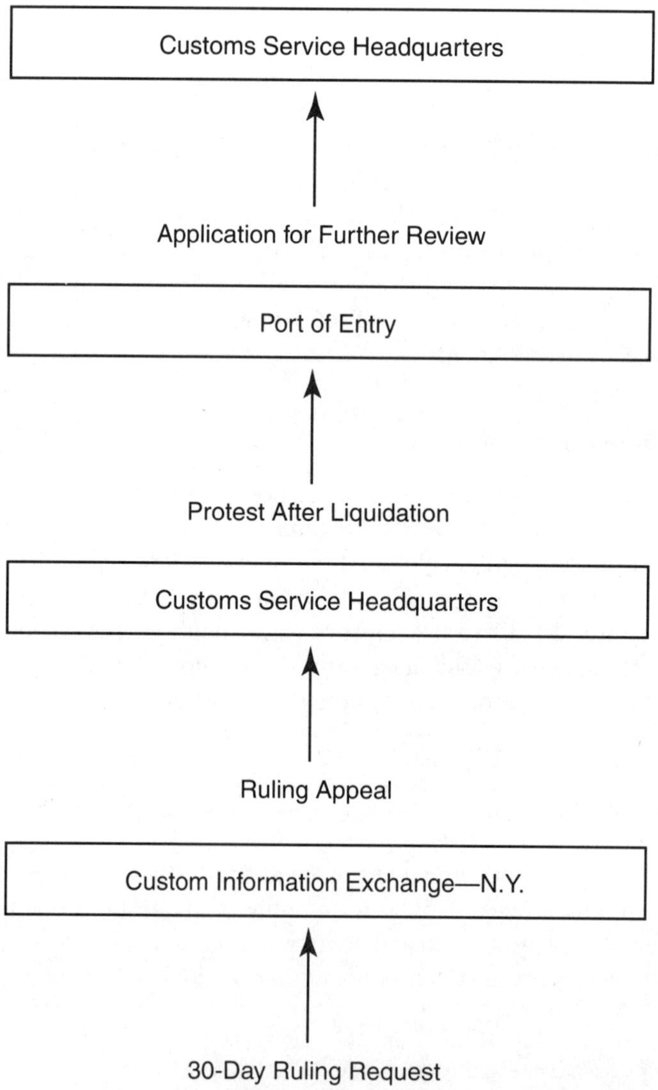

Exhibit 16.2

JUDICIAL REVIEW OF CUSTOMS DECISIONS

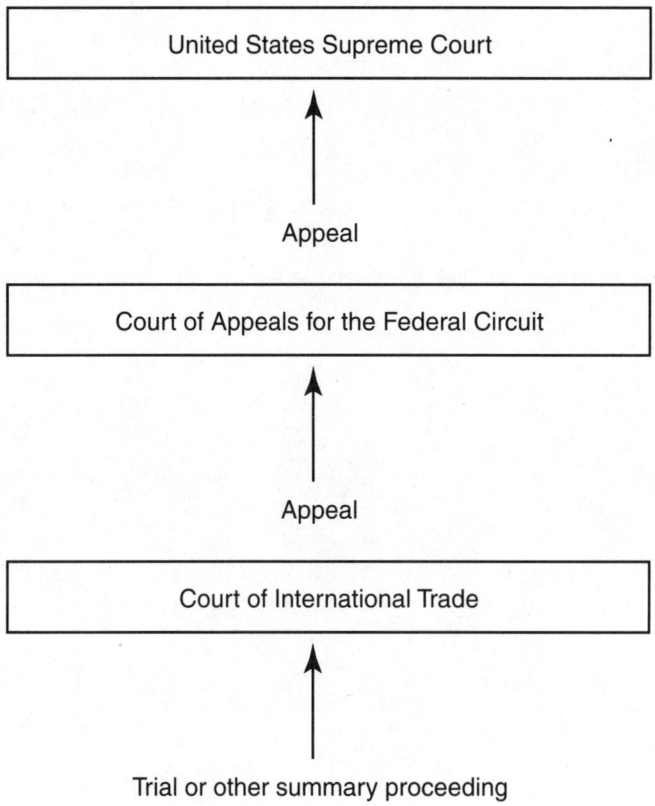

CHAPTER 17

Importing Merchandise—The Tax Issues

Robert Feinschreiber
Steven C. Wrappe

17.1 Introduction
17.2 Differences in the Customs and Tax Approaches
17.3 IRS Transfer Pricing Methodologies
- (a) Comparable Uncontrolled Price
- (b) Resale Price Method
- (c) Cost Plus Method
- (d) Comparable Profits Method
- (e) Profit Split
- (f) Unspecified Methods

17.4 Customs Transfer Pricing Methodologies
- (a) Transaction Value
- (b) Transaction Value of Identical or Similar Merchandise
- (c) Deductive Value
- (d) Computed Value
- (e) Other Approaches

17.5 IRS Enforcement of Section 482
- (a) Statutory Changes
- (b) Regulatory Changes
- (c) Improved Enforcement
- (d) Competent Authority Process

17.6 Procedural Advances
- (a) The APA Process
- (b) Simultaneous Appeals
- (c) Settlement Options
- (d) Acceleration Procedure

(e) Early Referral
(f) Mediation
(g) Arbitration
17.7 Enforcement by Customs
(a) Appraisal
(b) Recordkeeping
(c) Penalties
(d) Recent Guidance
17.8 Problems Created by Lack of Harmonization
(a) Whipsaw by Taxpayers
(b) Customs/IRS Whipsaw
(c) Refund Situations
17.9 Mandatory Coordination
(a) Addressing Taxpayer's Whipsaw
(b) The Statute
(c) Application
(d) First Sale Rule
(e) Private Rulings
17.10 Joint Efforts Between IRS and Customs
(a) Mutual Assistance Agreement
(b) Removal of IRS Disclosure Obstacle
(c) Reconciliation Pilot Program
(d) Joint IRS/Customs APAs
(e) IRS Use of Customs Data
17.11 Conclusion

17.1 Introduction

The Internal Revenue Service (IRS) and the U.S. Customs Service (Customs), as agencies within the Department of the Treasury, have an interest in transfer pricing issues. Until recently, however, little has been done to coordinate tax and customs issues on sales of imported goods. The large volume of cross-border transactions and stepped-up enforcement efforts by U.S. and foreign customs and tax officials make the overlap difficult for importers to ignore.

Both Treasury agencies seek an arm's-length transfer price for transactions between related parties. Despite this goal, the tax and customs rules effectively work at cross-purposes. The IRS asserts pricing adjustments against taxpayers when it believes that the transfer price into the United States is *too high* to prevent the improper shifting of income out of the United States. On the other hand, Customs asserts adjustments against importers when it believes that the transfer price into the United States is *too low* to prevent an understatement of customs duties. This overlap in regulation requires importers to construct a transfer price that satisfies each agency's ideal arm's-length price, yet still produce the lowest possible amount of income tax and customs duties.

17.2 Differences in the Customs and Tax Approaches

Customs and tax rules pursue fundamentally different theoretical goals. This difference of purpose results in practical differences in the customs and tax approach to the item to be taxed, the relevant time for determination, and the level of detailed determination. Differences between customs and tax goals show up in practical application of the relevant transfer pricing rules.

Customs applies duty based on the value of dutiable goods and seeks to *attach the correct dutiable value on specific imported goods.* The relevant time for determination of whether a transfer price is correct for customs purposes is the date of entry of the item into the United States. Customs imposes duty upon classification of goods, including component parts. This approach requires a detailed transaction-by-transaction approach with a determination at the goods classification level.

Tax rules start with gross income and determine taxable income after appropriate deductions. These rules seek to *properly allocate income between related parties* to achieve the clear reflection of income and prevent the shifting of income between tax jurisdictions. The relevant time for determination whether a transfer price is correct for tax purposes is the date on which the tax return is filed.[1] The IRS's goal of clear reflection of income does not require that the valuation be correct for each transaction, but only that the ultimate result of any underpayments and overpayments achieve an appropriate income result in the aggregate. This difference allows for aggregation of transactions and offsetting adjustments for tax purposes.[2]

17.3 IRS Transfer Pricing Methodologies

The transfer pricing regulations under the Internal Revenue Code identify several methodologies for pricing tangible goods.

(a) Comparable Uncontrolled Price

An arm's-length price can be determined from a comparison of sales between the taxpayer and unrelated parties, or sales between two unrelated parties. Comparability exists if substantially similar products are sold under substantially similar circumstances. Differences in the products or circumstances must have no effect on prices, or the effect can be measured and eliminated by adjustment.[3]

(b) Resale Price Method

An arm's-length price can be determined by subtracting the appropriate gross profit from the resale price of the particular product. The appropriate gross profit,

[1]26 U.S.C. §1.482-1(a)(3).

[2]26 U.S.C. §1.482-1(g)(4)(i).

[3]26 U.S.C. §1.482-3(b).

expressed as a percentage of sales, is the gross profit earned by the buyer/reseller on the sale of products bought and resold in uncontrolled transactions similar to the controlled transactions in question. The applicable resale price is the price at which the product bought in the controlled sale would be sold by the buyer in an uncontrolled sale. Adjustments must be made for material differences between controlled and uncontrolled sales and operating expresses if those differences have a definite and reasonably ascertainable impact on price.[4]

(c) Cost Plus Method

The cost plus method determines a transfer price for transactions between a manufacturer and a related buyer based on the markups over costs achieved by a comparable manufacturer in unrelated transactions. Adjustments must be made for material differences between the uncontrolled and controlled transactions if such differences have a definite and reasonably ascertainable effect on the gross margins earned in the unrelated transactions.[5]

(d) Comparable Profits Method

The comparable profits method analyzes the operating profit performance of companies comparable to the taxpayer to determine if the taxpayer's transfer pricing method yields arm's-length results. The sample comparable companies are adjusted individually for differences between the companies and the taxpayer, and a targeted profit range is sought.[6]

(e) Profit Split

Two profit split methods exist: the comparable profit split method and the residual profit split method. The comparable profit split method divides the total operating income of the buyer and the seller in a manner that is consistent with the way comparable unrelated parties divide their operating income in similar transactions. Therefore, data on comparable transactions and resulting profit splits between unrelated parties must be employed. That data must address two independent parties, each having risks, functions, and intangibles substantially comparable to those of the controlled parties.[7]

The residual profit split method operates in a two-step process. Step one assigns an arm's-length return to the routine activities of the buyer and the seller in the controlled transactions based on arm's-length return for functions they perform. Step two allocates the residual profit between the buyer and seller, based on the relative value of their contributions of intangible property to the business activity.[8]

---

[4]26 U.S.C. §1.482-3(c).

[5]26 U.S.C. §1.482-3(d).

[6]26 U.S.C. §1.482-5.

[7]26 U.S.C. §1.482-6(c)(1).

[8]26 U.S.C. §1.482-6(c)(2).

(f) Unspecified Methods

Taxpayers are allowed to use a method other than the specified methods if it provides the most reliable measure of arm's-length result.[9]

17.4 Customs Transfer Pricing Methodologies

Customs law prescribes a hierarchy of methodologies to determine the dutiable value of goods. The primary method is the transaction method. Alternative transaction valuations apply if transaction valuation is unavailable. The process continues with the transaction value of identical merchandise and similar merchandise, deductive value, and computed value.[10]

(a) Transaction Value

The price actually paid or payable for the goods when sold for exportation to the United States is adjusted by adding:

- Packing costs borne by the buyer;
- Selling commission borne by the buyer;
- Value of any "assist," apportioned as necessary;
- Royalty or license fee that the buyer is required to pay with respect to the merchandise; and
- Proceeds of any subsequent resale, disposal, or use of the merchandise that accrue, directly or indirectly, to the seller.[11]

The following items constitute assists:

- Materials, components, parts, and similar items incorporated in the imported merchandise;
- Tools, dies, molds, and similar items used in the production of the imported merchandise;
- Merchandise consumed in the production of the imported merchandise; and
- Engineering, development, artwork, design work, and plans and sketches that are undertaken elsewhere than in the United States and are necessary for the production of the imported merchandise. Incidental services performed overseas do not constitute assists if they are undertaken by U.S. domiciliaries acting in their capacity as employees or agents of the buyer of the merchandise.[12]

---

[9] 26 U.S.C. §1.482-3(e)

[10] 19 U.S.C. §1401a(a).

[11] 19 U.S.C. §1401a(b).

[12] 19 U.S.C. §1401a(h)(1)(A), 19 U.S.C. §1401a(h)(1)(B).

Transaction value may not be used if the buyer and seller are related, except in three situations:

1. The importer relationship did not influence the terms and conditions of sale;
2. The price includes non-cash consideration that cannot be valued; or
3. Compensation is dependent in whole or in part on the price realized upon the occurrence of a future event that cannot be quantified in a reasonable period of time.

(b) Transaction Value of Identical or Similar Merchandise

Identical merchandise is "identical in all respects to, and produced in the same country and (except in the case of related-party transaction) by the same person as, the merchandise being appraised." If there is no merchandise manufactured by the same person, or the buyer and the seller of the goods being appraised are related, merchandise manufactured in the country of exportation by another person are treated as identical.[13]

Similar merchandise is produced in the same country, by the same person as the merchandise under appraisement, and is generally commercially interchangeable with it, taking into account, its quality, reputation, and the existence of a trademark. Similar merchandise manufactured by another manufacturer in the country of exportation may also be used.[14] Generally, sales of identical or similar merchandise must have been made at the same commercial level and quantity to serve as a basis of valuation. If there are no sales in the same quantity at the same level, the transaction value of other sales may be used, but the value is adjusted to reflect the differences in the circumstances of sale, provided such adjustments can be demonstrated with sufficient information.

(c) Deductive Value

Deductive value is determined by reference to the resale price of the merchandise after importation, as reduced by various amounts, including:

1. Any commission or profit associated with the sale in the United States;
2. Transportation and insurance costs;
3. Customs duties and other charges payable upon the importation of the goods; and
4. Any additional processing in the United States.[15]

The deductive value method is broadly similar in approach to the resale price method for tax purposes.

---

[13] 19 C.F.R. §152.102(d); 19 U.S.C. §1401a(h)(2).

[14] 19 U.S.C. §1401a(h)(4).

[15] 19 U.S.C. §1401a(d).

(d) Computed Value

Computed value is derived from the cost of producing the imported merchandise. Computed value is defined as the sum of the following:[16]

- Cost or value of the materials and the fabrication and other processing of any kind employed in the production of the imported merchandise;
- Amount of profit and general expense equal to that usually reflected in sales of merchandise of the same class or kind of the imported merchandise that are made by producers in the country of exportation for export to the United States;
- Assists, if their value is not included under subparagraph (A) or (B); and
- Packing costs.

(e) Other Approaches

Importers can modify methods if the standard methodologies do not apply, "reasonably adjusted" to the extent necessary to arrive at a value. Identical or similar merchandise should be exported at or about the same time as the merchandise being appraised. For deductive value, the 90-day requirement may be administered flexibly.[17]

17.5 IRS Enforcement of Section 482

The IRS experienced difficulty enforcing transfer pricing adjustments during the 1970s and 1980s. A low percentage of proposed adjustments was sustained through administrative appeals. The IRS had little success in transfer pricing litigation. In response to congressional pressure, a number of statutory, regulatory, and enforcement efforts were designed to improve taxpayer compliance with transfer pricing rules.

(a) Statutory Changes

Foreign corporations engaged in a trade or business in the United States and domestic corporations that are foreign-owned are required to maintain and produce specified documentation relevant to related-party transactions on IRS Form 5472.[18] These corporations are also required to produce documentation of foreign affiliates that do not engage in business in the United States. Foreign corporations engaged in a U.S. trade or business are required to designate an agent in the United States to receive summons for the production of records and testimony.

---

[16] 19 U.S.C. §1401a(c).

[17] 19 U.S.C. §1401a(f).

[18] 26 U.S.C. §§6038A and 6038C. *See* R. Feinschreiber, *Tax Reporting for Foreign-Owned U.S. Corporations* (New York: John Wiley & Sons, 1992).

Substantial valuation misstatement and gross valuation misstatement penalties have been extended to Section 482 adjustments. If the U.S. income tax attributable to a substantial valuation misstatement exceeds $10,000, a 20% penalty may be imposed.[19] The penalty is increased to 40% if the substantial valuation misstatement qualifies as a gross valuation misstatement.[20] A substantial valuation misstatement exists if (1) property claimed on a return is clearly valued at more than 200% or less than 50% of the Section 482 value, or (2) the net Section 482 transfer price adjustment is greater than the lesser of $5,000,000 or 10% of gross receipts.[21] A gross valuation misstatement is determined in the same manner, except that 400% is substituted for 200%, 25% for 50%, and $20,000,000 and 20% for $5,000,000 and 10%.[22] Penalties can be avoided if the corporation selects the appropriate transfer pricing method and meets detailed documentation requirements. Penalty exculpation rules for domestic and foreign-owned corporations make use of specific documentation required for foreign-owned corporations.[23]

(b) Regulatory Changes

Following three years of proposed and temporary regulations, the Treasury issued final I.R.C. Section 482 regulations in 1994.[24] These regulations attempt to articulate a standard that could be applied by both taxpayers and the IRS. The new Section 482 regulations contained a number of changes from the earlier regulations, designed to increase flexibility.

The arm's-length result is determined under the transfer pricing method that provides the most reliable result, based on the comparability and quality of data and assumptions. Earlier regulations provided for a strict priority of transfer pricing methods. Contrary to earlier regulations that identified a single point as the appropriate transfer price, the new regulations accept the notion of a range of appropriate arm's-length prices.

The new regulations advanced and refined the "comparable profits method" that determines arm's-length price based on operating margins. Commentors severely criticized an earlier version of this approach because it did not recognize significant factors causing differences in operating profits such as intangible ownership, management efficiency, or varying profitability of product lines. These criticisms were addressed by emphasizing the importance of the comparability analysis in clarifying the focus of the profits analysis on specific transactions.[25]

---

[19]26 U.S.C. §6662(e)(2).

[20]26 U.S.C. §6662(h).

[21]26 U.S.C. §6662(e)(1).

[22]26 U.S.C. §6662(h).

[23]26 U.S.C. §§6664, 1.6662, 26 1.6038A-3(c).

[24]*See* 59 Fed. 26 U.S.C. 34971-35033 (July 8, 1994).

[25]Robert E. Culbertson, *A Rose by Any Other Name: Smelling the Flowers at the OECD's (Last) Resort,* 95 TNT 180-39 (September 11, 1995), p. 5.

(c) Improved Enforcement

The IRS has greatly expanded its technical resources regarding the enforcement of I.R.C. Section 482, nearly doubling the number of international examiners and on-staff economists since 1990. Consequently, the number of transfer pricing examinations has also increased. Armed with the new penalty regulations, examiners are more vigorously requesting documentation to support taxpayers' transfer pricing determinations and setting up proposed adjustments.

(d) Competent Authority Process

Transfer pricing is a zero-sum game between the tax authorities. Whatever income is shifted to the United States comes from the other country, and vice versa. Nearly all U.S. tax treaties contain a "mutual agreement procedure" article (often referred to as the "competent authority process") to prevent economic double taxation in the two countries. The competent authorities of the two countries can agree on allocation of income and deductions between related persons.[26] The competent authority process is available to taxpayers in addition to the administrative appeals rights available in either country.[27]

17.6 Procedural Advances

Statutory, regulatory, and administrative changes, particularly the penalty provisions, greatly increase the likelihood of transfer pricing disputes between the IRS and taxpayers. Fortunately, the IRS has established a number of new procedures that allow taxpayers to avoid transfer pricing disputes or to resolve these disputes in a more effective manner. These new procedures are generally designed either to move a dispute to a more promising forum for resolution or to extend the settlement to cover additional tax years. The following new or revised procedures have been added since 1990.

(a) The APA Process

The APA process allows the taxpayer and the IRS to agree prospectively on three basic issues:

1. The factual nature of the intercompany transactions to which the APA applies;
2. An appropriate transfer pricing methodology; and
3. An expected range of results from applying the methodology to the transactions.[28]

---

[26] *See* Article 25 of the 1981 U.S. Model Treaty.

[27] *See* Rev. Proc. 96-13, 1996-3 I.R.B. 31.

[28] Rev. Proc. 91-22, 1991-1 C.B. 526.

This approach allows taxpayers to reflect a transfer pricing amount that is correct as filed, thus avoiding a transfer pricing dispute.

(b) Simultaneous Appeals

The Simultaneous Appeals Process (SAP) is a major component of the revised competent authority process.[29] The SAP procedure allows active taxpayer involvement in the competent authority process:

1. Appeals works with the taxpayer to prepare an Appeals case memorandum to be considered by the U.S. competent authority in preparing the U.S. position paper.
2. The U.S. competent authority presents the U.S. position paper to the foreign competent authority.

(c) Settlement Options

Delegation Order 236 (Rev. 2)[30] extends limited authority to Examination personnel to settle issues in a manner consistent with an Appeals settlement in prior or subsequent tax years. This change eliminates the need for taxpayers to protest an issue in order to obtain the same result reached with Appeals in prior or subsequent tax years, resulting in considerable resource savings for both taxpayers and the IRS.

(d) Acceleration Procedure

The Accelerated Issue Resolution (AIR) procedure[31] allows taxpayers to advance the resolution of issues arising in tax years under examination to all tax years ending before the date of the AIR agreement. Taxpayers and the IRS could reach agreement regarding the appropriate transfer pricing methodology for all years under Examination jurisdiction, freeing the taxpayer from reconsideration in subsequent examination cycles.

(e) Early Referral

Revenue Procedure 96-9[32] allows taxpayers to request the transfer of developed, unagreed issues from Examination to Appeals while the remaining issues continue to be developed in Examination (Early Referral). Appropriate issues for Early Referral include issues that are not designated for litigation and that, if resolved, are expected to accelerate resolution of the whole case.

---

[29] Rev. Proc. 96-13, 1996-3 I.R.B. 31.

[30] 1996-21 I.R.B. 7.

[31] Rev. Proc. 94-67, 1994-2 C.B. 800.

[32] 1996-2 I.R.B. 15.

(f) Mediation

The IRS announced a one-year test of mediation for nondocketed cases under Appeals jurisdiction in 1995.[33] A recent IRS Chief Counsel memorandum sanctioned the use of mediation for docketed Tax Court cases. Mediation is to result in a more efficient use of judicial and IRS resources in appropriate cases. Mediation should be used when standard settlement procedures, such as Appeals negotiations, have failed and it is cost-effective and otherwise appropriate.[34]

(g) Arbitration

The Tax Court promulgated Tax Court Rule 124 in 1990, allowing voluntary binding arbitration of factual issues under the direction of the Tax Court. Rule 124 both encourages the use of arbitration and standardizes the basic procedure for choosing arbitration. Taxpayers and the IRS invoke Rule 124 by a joint motion to the Tax Court after the case has been docketed.[35] The joint motion contains a statement of issue to be submitted to arbitration, an agreement to be bound by the arbitrator's findings, the names of the arbitrators or a process to select an arbitrator, allocation of the arbitration costs, and a prohibition on ex parte communication.

17.7 Enforcement by Customs

(a) Appraisal

Customs appraises goods at the port of entry.[36] The appropriate Customs officer appraises merchandise by ascertaining or estimating the value "by all reasonable ways and means" notwithstanding any statement of cost or costs of production in any invoice, affidavit, declaration, or other documents. After an appraised value has been determined, the import duty is imposed, based on the rate assigned to the particular item imported, based on the category in which the imported merchandise is classified. The United States adopted a uniform tariff nomenclature known as the Harmonized Tariff Schedule of the United States (HTSUS) in 1989. Under HTSUS, the rates of duty are stated as a percentage of the value of the product, as an amount charged per unit of measure, or as a combination of such methods. Customs has four ways to inspect relevant customs records:

1. Inspect records with the consent of the importer upon reasonable notice;
2. Issue an administrative summons and, if necessary, have the summons enforced by court order;

---

33 IRS Ann. 95-86, 1995-44 I.R.B. 27.

34 This information is taken from a document obtained under the Freedom of Information Act (FOIA), which document is part of the CCDM on mediation, and which was discussed by an IRS official at a public meeting in October 1995.

35 T.C. Rule 124.

36 19 U.S.C.A. § 1500(a).

3. Demand record production through a grand jury subpoena duces tecum; or
4. Seize records pursuant to a judicially issued search warrant.

(b) Recordkeeping

An importer is required to maintain records relating to import transactions for five years under U.S. customs laws.[37] The customs regulations[38] broadly define the term *records* to include statements, declarations, books, papers, correspondence, documents, electronic data, and accounting books. These records are of the type normally kept in the ordinary course of business and that:

- Pertain to any importation of merchandise;
- Establish the right to make entry;
- Establish the correctness of any entry;
- Determine the liability of any person for duties and taxes due or that may be due to the United States.
- Determine the liability of any person for fines, penalties, and forfeitures; or
- Determine whether the person has complied with the laws and regulations administered by Customs.

Customs requires an importer to file forms to disclose the types of merchandise imported into the United States and the importer's relationship to the person selling the goods. For example, Customs Form 7501 asks an importer to disclose whether the relevant transaction is between related parties.

An importer should review its documentation recordkeeping system to ensure compliance with the customs laws. Such a review would also be useful in revealing areas in which the imposition of duty can be minimized. The importer can make a disclosure filing with Customs if such a review reveals prior violations and the importer is not currently under audit. A voluntary disclosure will limit the importer's potential liability, in the absence of fraudulent behavior, to the payment of duties and interest without the imposition of penalties.

(c) Penalties

Civil and criminal penalties enforce customs laws. Civil penalties can be assessed against any person who enters or attempts to enter merchandise into the United States by means of a materially false document or statement.[39] Documents or statements that contain "material misstatements or omissions" are considered materially false. The penalty can be assessed even if the government has not lost any revenue as a result of such material false documents or statements. This pen-

---

[37] 19 U.S.C.A. § 1508.

[38] 19 C.F.R. § 162.1a(a).

[39] 19 U.S.C.A. §1592.

alty can be assessed if the conduct that gives rise to the penalty is fraudulent, negligent, or grossly negligent.

(d) Recent Guidance

Customs provides guidance concerning customs valuations laws and the appraisement of transactions between related parties.[40] The existence of a related party relationship between buyer and seller does not give Customs the right to reject the transaction value. However, such a relationship alerts Customs to inquire as to the circumstances surrounding the sale.

An examination of the circumstances concerning related party relationships is not required in every case, but only in those cases in which Customs has doubts about the acceptability of the price. Customs is not required to communicate its doubts to the importer when seeking information on the circumstances surrounding the sale and may not indicate whether the price has been influenced by the relationship between the buyer and the seller. Customs must communicate its grounds to the importer if it has grounds for maintaining that the transaction value is unacceptable because the relationship has influenced the price. Moreover, the importer must be given a reasonable opportunity to respond and is entitled to be advised in writing of the grounds for Customs' beliefs.

17.8 Problems Created by Lack of Harmonization

(a) Whipsaw by Taxpayers

Early tax cases took little notice of the differences between the tax and customs approaches to transfer pricing. In *Ross Glove Co. v. Commissioner,* the Tax Court found that the "methods adopted by Customs and [IRS] . . . are quite similar."[41] Markups used by Customs to compute the value of gloves purchased from a related party were considered adequate to determine the arm's-length price under I.R.C. Section 482.

According to the Court, the customs markups were the "best available evidence as to the amounts that a seller would receive to cover overhead and product in an arm's length sale."[42] The Court rejected the IRS's arguments that customs valuations are basically unreliable and cannot form the basis for a determination of an arm's-length price for tax purposes. In fact, the Court used the customs valuation to demonstrate the unreasonableness of the IRS position.[43]

In *Brittingham v. Commissioner,*[44] the IRS attempted to use a customs value to establish an arm's-length price for tax purposes. An arm's-length price is the price

---

[40]Customs Directive 4820-02 (Jan. 13, 1993).

[41]60 T.C. 569, 604 (1973), *acq.*, 1974-1 C.B.2.

[42]*Id.* at 605.

[43]*Id.* at 604.

[44]66 T.C. 373 (1976), *aff'd,* 598 F.2d 1375 (5th Cir. 1979).

the unrelated party charges another unrelated party for a product or service. In that case, IRS determined that a U.S. importer paid more than an arm's-length price[45] for ceramic tile imported from a related party in Mexico. The purchase price substantially exceeded the value reported for customs duty purposes.

The Tax Court rejected the IRS argument, holding that the customs value was based on an erroneous assumption that a competitor's product was similar. The Court determined that Customs' determinations were not indicative of an arm's-length price, even though the taxpayer had won a previous dispute with Customs on the same issues.[46]

Congress was concerned that the holding in *Brittingham* encouraged taxpayers to declare a low customs value and a higher tax value. Therefore, in 1986 Congress enacted I.R.C. Section 1059A, specifically to prevent this whipsaw.[47]

(b) Customs/IRS Whipsaw

Despite Congress's demonstrated concerns with taxpayer whipsaw, the opportunity for Customs/IRS whipsaw is genuine, as demonstrated by the following example:

Example

A U.S. distributor, a subsidiary of a Japanese parent company manufacturer, attempts to revise its pricing as a result of the new Section 482 transfer pricing regulations. The U.S. distributor is buying products from the Japanese parent, and the Japanese parent has worldwide trademark rights to the product. The trademark is very valuable in Japan, but even after several years, the trademark is not valuable in the United States.

The distributor is concerned that the IRS may view the U.S. distributor as having "developed" an intangible. The U.S. distributor spends significant advertising and marketing funds and finally develops a significant market in the United States. After having reviewed the proposed and temporary regulations, the U.S. distributor takes the position with the Japanese parent that the price that it pays for the products must decrease because the IRS would likely say that it possesses an intangible, or had developed an intangible in the United States, and that this should be taken into account in the pricing.

The U.S. Customs Service is likely to become aware of the fact that the pricing for the goods has decreased. At the same time, the demand for the goods in the United States has increased. It is unlikely that Customs will understand how the U.S. distributor could be viewed as developing an intangible for which it has no legal rights. As the parties are related, Customs may well scrutinize the price decrease closely and might make a claim for a higher dutiable value.[48]

---

[45]*International Taxation: Problems Persist in Determining Tax Effects of Intercompany Prices* (GAO/GGD-92-89, June 15, 1992).

[46]66 T.C. at 389.

[47]General Explanation of the Tax Reform Act of 1986 (Staff, Joint Committee on Taxation), 100th Cong., 1st Sess. 1061, 1062 (1987).

[48]H. Levine and S. Weisser speech at American Bar Association Tax Section Annual Meeting, Committee on Foreign Investment in the United States, New York (August 6, 1996).

(c) Refund Situations

Customs value generally becomes final 90 days following the date of liquidation of imported goods. By law, customs entries must be liquidated within one year from date of entry unless:

1. The importer requests an extension;
2. Customs has reason to withhold liquidation; or
3. Customs is ordered to do so by the courts.

This timing can create an unfortunate whipsaw situation for importers. Under the IRS's current audit cycle, it is highly likely that, unless an extension is requested, a substantial portion of an importer's import entries will have been liquidated for Customs purposes before completion of an IRS audit.

17.9 Mandatory Coordination

(a) Addressing Taxpayer's Whipsaw

Congress was concerned that the transfer price reported for tax purposes could substantially exceed the transfer price reported for customs purposes, allowing related parties to avoid federal tax or customs duties. In response to this concern, Congress added I.R.C. Section 1059A in 1986.

(b) The Statute

The coordination provisions apply to any property imported into the United States in a transaction, directly or indirectly, between related persons within the meaning of Section 482. Costs taken into account in computing the basis or inventory cost of the property by the purchaser are taken into account in computing the customs value of such property. These amounts, in computing basis or inventory cost, cannot be greater than costs taken into account in computing such customs value.

The strict statutory language prevents an importer from claiming a higher tax basis for imported merchandise than the customs value. Application of this statutory language is complex.

(c) Application

The legislative history to I.R.C. Section 1059A stated that the Secretary of the Treasury would provide rules coordinating customs and tax valuation principles. The Treasury issued I.R.C. Section 1059A regulations in 1989. These regulations apply the customs value basis limitation to all transactions between controlled taxpayers, but imported items that are not subject to customs duties are excluded.[49] If

---

[49]As defined in Treas. Reg. 26 U.S.C. § 1.482-1(a).

an item or a portion of an item is not subject to customs duty, or is subject to a free rate duty, that item or portion of the item is not subject to the provisions of the coordination provision.[50] The coordination provision does not apply to:

1. The portion of an item that is an American good returned and not subject to duty;[51]
2. Imports on which no duty is imposed that are valued by Customs for statistical purposes only;
3. Items subject to a zero rate of duty;[52] and
4. Items subject only to the user fee[53] or the harbor maintenance tax[54] or only to both such levies.

The tax basis may differ from customs value because of legitimate differences between customs and tax valuation rules. Regulations allow certain adjustments to the customs value, and the taxpayers may increase the customs value of imported property by:

1. Freight charges;
2. Insurance charges;
3. The construction, erection, assembly, or technical assistance provided for property after its importation into the United States; and
4. Any other amounts that are not taken into account in determining the customs value, that are not properly included in customs value, and that are appropriately included in the cost basis or inventory cost for income tax purposes.

Section 1059A does not limit the authority of the IRS to increase or decrease the claimed basis or inventory cost under I.R.C. Section 482.[55] The coordination rule applies to merchandise subject to any customs duty or subject to a free rate of duty.[56] Further, the coordination rule does not apply to imported property not subject to customs duty based on value, including property subject only to a per item or duty based on volume.

One of the ways the IRS monitors I.R.C. Section 1059A compliance is through IRS Form 5472 for foreign-owned U.S. corporations and branches. Form 5472 asks whether the corporation imports goods from a foreign related party and whether the basis or inventory costs of the goods is valued at greater than the customs value of the imported goods. The corporation must provide a statement ex-

---

[50]Treas. Reg. 26 U.S.C. § 1.1059A-1(c)(1).

[51]Items 806.20 and 806.30. Tariff Schedules of the United States, 19 U.S.C.A. § 1202.

[52]19 U.S.C.A. § 1202, General Headnote 3.

[53]19 U.S.C.A. § 58(c).

[54]26 U.S.C.A. § 4461.

[55]*Id.* § 1.1059A-1(c)(7).

[56]*Id.* § 1.1059A-1(c)(1).

plaining the reason or reasons for such difference. Documents used to support this treatment of the imported goods must be in existence and available. A statement attached to IRS Form 5472 should explain any disparity between the cost basis of inventory for income tax purposes and the customs value.

(d) First Sale Rule

The appropriate customs valuation is not necessarily the price paid by the importer. If the goods are purchased from a foreign manufacturer by a middleman that imports the goods or resells to the importer, the correct customs value in some circumstances is the price that the middleman paid to the foreign manufacturer, rather than the price paid by the importer to the middleman.

In *United States v. Getz Bros. & Co.,*[57] a U.S. importer purchased plywood from Japanese trading houses that, in turn, purchased the plywood from Japanese manufacturers. The Court determined that the price to the trading houses constituted the "export value"[58] under Customs law. Subsequently, *E. C. McAfee Co. v. United States,*[59] presented a similar issue regarding made-to-measure clothing. Sales representatives for Hong Kong clothing distributors took orders for clothing from U.S. customers. The issue was whether the merchandise, as sold by the tailor to the distributor, was sold "for exportation."[60] The Court held that a sale need not be made to purchasers located in the United States to provide the basis for valuation; the manufacturer's price to the distributor may be used for appraisal purposes, if the sale by the manufacturer falls within the statutory valuation provision.[61]

In a more recent case, *Nissho Iwai American Corp. v. United States*[62] tested the *McAffee* rule. Nissho Iwai Corporation (NIC), sold 205 rapid transit passenger cars to the Metropolitan Transportation Authority of New York City (MTA). The MTA had agreed to purchase the cars from Nissho Iwai American Corporation (NIAC), a wholly-owned U.S. subsidiary of NIC, for use in the New York City transit system.[63] The contract between NIAC and the MTA specified that the cars would be manufactured and produced by Kawasaki Heavy Industries, Ltd., Japan.

The Federal Circuit in *Nissho Iwai* adopted the *McAfee* analysis, selecting the manufacturer's price to the middleman over the resale price, as long as the manufacturer's price falls within the statutory valuation provision.[64] The court held that the manufacturer's price constitutes a viable transaction value when the goods are clearly destined for export to the United States and when the manufacturer and the middleman deal with each other at arm's length.[65]

---

[57]55 C.C.P.A. 11 (1967).

[58]The export value in *Getz* would apparently be equivalent to Customs value in §1059A(b)(1).

[59]842 F.2d 314 (Fed. Cir. 1988).

[60]*Id.* at 318.

[61]*Id.*

[62]982 F.2d 505 (Fed. Cir. 1992).

[63]*Id.* at 506.

[64]982 F.2d at 509.

[65]*id.*

(e) Private Rulings

Private Letter Ruling 9406026 addressed a multitier arrangement with a Cayman Islands middleman. The IRS followed *Nissho Iwai* and recognized that customs law permits an importer to base transaction value for imported goods on the price paid by a foreign reseller rather than the importer. The importer must demonstrate that the sale was at arm's length and that the goods were clearly destined for the United States when sold.[66] The ruling held that if the taxpayer reported the correct customs value, the taxpayer may increase the Section 1059A limitation to its actual purchase price.

Private Letter Ruling 9515011 was directed to the same taxpayer as PLR 9406026 and contained certain modifications. The IRS ruled that no Section 1059A adjustments can be made if the taxpayer reports an equal or higher value to Customs. An importer can base its transaction value for imported goods or the price paid to a foreign middleman if the sale was at arm's length and the goods were clearly destined for the United States when sold.

The taxpayer may increase the I.R.C. Section 1059A limitation to its actual purchase price. The difference between customs value and the purchase price can be attributable to freight, insurance, and American content, which are not includible in dutiable value, and to differences in valuation methods. However, even though the I.R.C. Section 1059A limitation is raised to the actual purchase price, the IRS may assert I.R.C. Section 482 if the purchase price is greater than an arm's-length price.[67]

Private Letter Ruling 953048 presented multitiered purchase structure functionally similar to Private Letter Ruling 9406026 and 9515011. Using slightly different terminology, the ruling expressed a result strikingly similar to Private Letter Ruling 9515011. Both Sections 1059A and 482 are satisfied if the "customs duty is fully paid assuming that Customs does not change duty on the middleman's markup and the purchase price is at arm's length."

17.10 Joint Efforts Between IRS and Customs

Tax authorities from member countries have been able to minimize their differences with regard to transfer pricing and provide consensus guidelines for transfer pricing through the Organization for Economic Cooperation and Development.[68] Although this process does not prevent a certain amount of difference in application, it represents a positive step toward harmonization. The General Agreement on Tariffs and Trade (GATT) and its progeny have achieved a certain level of harmonization of customs treatment among contracting states. Nevertheless, the Department of the Treasury has not reconciled differences between customs and tax treatment of transfer pricing results.

---

[66]Priv. Ltr. Rul. 9406026.

[67]Priv. Ltr. Rul. 9515011.

[68]*Transfer Pricing Guidelines for Multinational Enterprises and Tax Administration*, Report of the OECD Committee on Fiscal Affairs (July 1995).

(a) Mutual Assistance Agreement

Customs and the IRS established a Mutual Assistance Agreement in 1992 as to international compliance and importation issues. The purpose of the agreement was to develop a general framework in providing assistance and exchanging information and data between the respective agencies. The agreement has three objectives:

1. To achieve greater efficiency in the administration and enforcement of federal laws;
2. To promote certainty and objectivity in the administration of issues pertaining to complex international transactions; and
3. To promote an environment conducive to voluntary compliance.

The Mutual Assistance Agreement provides each agency with "the opportunity to seek assistance in the collection and exchange of information, as well as the ability to share knowledge, experiences, and techniques regarding areas of mutual interest." The Mutual Assistance Agreement recites that joint efforts may be beneficial as to functional activities, such as administration, compliance, enforcement, audit, and the regulatory process.

Both agencies are actively seeking methods to collect and track information pertaining to the import of products into the United States. It is expected that the availability of import data will assist both agencies in their enforcement and compliance efforts in the following areas:

1. Verification of quantities and amounts reported as purchases of foreign goods, particularly transactions involving related parties;
2. Identification of entities importing similar foreign-produced goods;
3. Identification of pricing/valuation data on imported foreign products for specific periods; and
4. Determination of international pricing and valuation issues, particularly as to the application of the arm's-length standard to related party transactions.[69]

Each agency agrees that it will make a good faith effort to provide information to the other agency and to be as responsible as possible to requests for information, giving consideration to the strict disclosure guidelines placed on each agency by statute. The Mutual Assistance Agreement provides the opportunity to develop interagency understanding of similarities and differences in transfer pricing approaches. Despite the conflicting goals of the two organizations regarding transfer prices, a sustained effort should be made by these two agencies to minimize the impact of those differences.

---

[69] *Id.*

(b) Removal of IRS Disclosure Obstacle

Uncertainty existed before 1993 as to the scope of restrictions on IRS's ability to disclose taxpayer information to Customs.[70] The North American Free Trade Agreement Implementation Act caused a change in policies.[71] The Treasury has issued regulations delineating the procedure by which Customs may obtain access to tax return information in connection with a Customs audit of the taxpayer or related party. These regulations specifically prohibit the IRS's disclosure of information disclosed in an APA or information that would violate a tax treaty or executive agreement.

(c) Reconciliation Pilot Program

Under a voluntary Customs program announced in 1995, related-party importers who believe that their Customs transfer prices should be adjusted upward to meet the arm's-length standard can make the adjustments without violating I.R.C. Section 1059A.[72] Applicants must be able to provide the electronic entry of merchandise or, on an entry-by-entry basis, an electronic summary of required information. Further, the program does not apply to downward adjustments. Strangely, no importers have taken advantage of this program.

(d) Joint IRS/Customs APAs

Despite support of the Organization for Economic Cooperation and Development (OECD) guidelines, tax authorities from different countries frequently disagree on the transfer pricing results in individual cases. Given the complex factual content, large revenue amounts, and subjective application of transfer pricing rules, government-to-government disputes are common. Advance Pricing Agreements (APAs) enable treaty partners to agree prospectively with taxpayers and each other regarding the appropriate arm's-length pricing. The APA process proceeds much faster than the normal competent authority process.

It has been suggested on a number of occasions that Customs attend IRS APA conferences and attempt to develop a form of joint IRS/Customs APA program whereby both IRS and Customs would agree prospectively with taxpayers regarding transfer pricing determinations. Tax and customs officials have had discussions regarding the potential joint IRS/Customs APAs as early as 1993. One joint IRS/Customs prefiling occurred, but the taxpayer chose not to continue in the APA process. Tax and customs authorities continue to be interested in the prospect of joint APAs, but four concerns exist:

1. Taxpayers have expressed concern that information divulged to Customs officials through the APA would no longer be protected under I.R.C. Section 6103.

---

[70] *See* I.R.C. §6103.

[71] Regs. §1.6103(1)(14)-1T(d). Pub. L. No. 103-182, § 552.

[72] 60 Fed. 26 U.S.C. 46141 (1995).

2. Concerns have been raised as to whether Customs has the authority to enter into private, prospective agreements with taxpayers.
3. Questions arise concerning Customs' reaction to operational transfer pricing methodologies, such as the comparable profits method and the profit split method.
4. Concerns exist as to whether Customs has the requisite resources to pursue APAs with taxpayers.

Until all these concerns have been eliminated, it is unlikely that any joint IRS/Customs APA can be achieved.

(e) IRS Use of Customs Data

The IRS started collecting customs information under a new data-gathering system that allows the IRS to target transactions that appear to fall outside an estimated arm's-length range.[73] The new system, the Outlier Analysis Targeting System (OATS), takes a pool of trade and data and computes a range of prices. The Customs data can be used to provide a preliminary test of related party transactions for audit by the IRS. The OATS system is a result of the joint IRS/Customs policy board established in 1992 to evaluate IRS/Customs issues in transfer pricing compliance.

17.11 Conclusion

Recent events have focused attention on the need to harmonize the tax and customs approaches to transfer pricing issues. This process will take time. Meanwhile, taxpayers should continue to document their transfer pricing decisions and express their results under both tax and customs rules whenever possible.

---

[73]"IRS Using New Customs Data System to Find Transactions That May Fail Arm's Length Test," Transfer Pricing Report 269 (Oct. 2, 1996).

Index

A

Accelerated issue resolution (AIR) procedure, 352
Accounting methods, 139, 166
Administrative protective order (APO), 292–294
Ad valorem, 6, 7, 91, 140, 309
Advanced Pricing Agreements (APAs), 351–352, 362–363
Agreement on Trade in Textiles and Clothing (ATTC), 213, 214
Agricultural Act of 1956, Section 204, 228
America Air Parcel Forwarding Company Ltd. v. United States, 75
American Association of Importers and Exporters, 220
Antidumping, *see* Duties, dumping and antidumping
(a)(1)(A) list, 46, 47, 57, 69
Apparel:
  marking requirements, 42–43, 311–316
  quotas, *see* Quotas, textiles
  temporary importation under bond, 201
Appeals:
  conclusions regarding, 339–340
  introduction to, 338–339
  litigation and, *see* Appeals, litigation and
  remand, 339
  simultaneous, 352
  Supreme Court, 339
  timing, 339
Appeals, litigation and, 70
  actions by other non-importers, 334
  administration and enforcement, 337
  advance determinations, 336–337
  antidumping and countervailing duties, 278, 335–336
  classification of merchandise and, 334
  conclusions regarding, 339–340
  contestable actions, 331
  court procedure, 331
  fact analysis, 332
  interest recovery, 333–334
  introduction to, 330, 353–354
  judicial review, 101–104, 271, 330, 338, 341
  limitation of an unfavorable decision, 332
  multiple protests, 332
  parties subject to suit, 337–338
  protests, 16, 38, 99–101, 193, 329, 330, 332
  rejection of review, 338
  review and decisions, 330–331
  special proceedings, 336
  suspension procedure, 332–333
  timing issues, 333
  trial practice, 333
Appraisement, 72
  bases for, 20–21
  computed value, 7, 21, 29
  conclusions concerning, 30
  deductive value, 7, 21, 28–29
  derivative value, 21, 29–30
  first sale rule, *see* First sale rule
  introduction to, 20
  price determination, 27–28
  transaction value, *see* Transaction value
Arms Export Control Act, 234
Assists, 145
  categories of, 8, 25–26
  drawback on duty payments for, 171, 173, 175–177
  examination of sale requirements, 80
Atomic Energy Act of 1954, 234
Auditors, scope and authority of, 53–54
Audit report, 69–70
Audits:
  assessment of internal controls, 66–67
  benefits of being prepared for, 56–57
  compliance assessment team (CAT), 60, 65–66, 69
  compliance reviews, *see* Audits, compliance reviews
  continuing, 65–67
  controls and procedures, *see* Audits, controls and procedures
  exit conference, 69–70
  introduction to, 52–55
  opening conference, 65
  overview of, 55–58
  periodic reviews, 58–60
  primary objectives of, 53
  protesting, 70
  record-keeping requirements, 57–58
  Regulatory Audit Division, 52–53, 55, 195
  selection process, 54–55

Audits, compliance reviews, 167
agreements affecting importations, 59
cash disbursements journal, 59, 68
chart of accounts, 59
debit and credit notes, 59
entry analysis, 68–69
general journal, 59, 67–69
general ledger, 59, 67, 68
letters of credit schedule, 59
monthly statements, 59
purchase journal, 67–68
supplemental logs and schedules, 60
Audits, controls and procedures:
for compliance assessment team (CAT) reviews, 65–66
consultation with outside consultants, 62
contract and agreement logs, 61–62
coordination within departments, 63
customs compliance and import procedures manual, 62
customs liaison, 63
electronic data, 61
in-house training, 63
marking, 63
periodic internal/independent reviews, 61
post-entry document reviews, 61
preference duties and special tariffs, 64
product classification, 62
transshipment, 63–64
Automated broker interface (ABI), 158, 171, 219
Automated Commercial Service, 161
Automated Commercial System, 219
Automated export system (AES), 44, 171
Average ex-factory price, 281, 282–283

B

Back-to-back sales, 28
Best information available (BIA) rule, 270
Bill of lading, 15, 224
Binding rulings, *see* Rulings, Customs
Blanket permit summary, 189
Bond, posting, 4, 200, 227–228. *See also* Temporary importation under bond
Bonded warehouses, 5
advantages of storing in, 181–183
classes of, 183–184
duty-free store, 184, 198–199
entry requirements, 185–186
establishing, 180–181
foreign trade zones versus, 149
general order, 184–185
manipulation of merchandise, 186, 306–307
materials for use in manufacturing, 196–197
overview of, 10, 11–12, 13
record keeping, 194–196
rewarehouse entry, 193–194
transfers, 186–187
withdrawals from, 187–193, 197–198
Brittingham v. Commissioner, 355
Broker, customs, 3–4, 9
Brosterhous Coleman & Co. v. United States, 76, 77
Bureau of Census, 44, 233
Bureau of Export Administration (BXA), 234, 236

C

Canada, 200, 227, 254, 310
NAFTA and, *see* North American Free Trade Agreement (NAFTA)
Canadian Free Trade Agreement, 160
Caribbean Basin Initiative (CBI), 316
compliance review, 60
documentary requirements, 230–231
import quotas and, 214
overview of, 9, 10, 92
CCC (Customs Cooperation Council), 90, 93
Centralized examination station, 41
Certificate of Delivery (CD), 156, 164
Certificate of Manufacture and Delivery (CMD), 163, 164, 170
Chioccola, Frank, 221
CITA (Committee on the Implementation of Textile Agreements), 212, 214, 219
Civil enforcement issues, *see also* Court of International Trade (CIT); International Trade Administration (ITA), countervailing and antidumping duties; International Trade Commission (ITC):
appeals, *see* Appeals
bond default/cancellation, 201–203
conclusions concerning, 49
copyright protection, 38
detention policy, 39–40
drawback penalties, 48, 159–161, 168
duties, *see* Duties, investigations and enforcement
exports, 44, 48
introduction to, 32–33
liquidated damages, 37–38
litigation, *see* Appeals, litigation and
marking violations, 14, 40–42, 63, 102, 308–310
Mod Act enactment, 44–46. *See also* Customs Modernization and Informed Compliance Act (Mod Act)
NAFTA, 48–49
patents, 39
petitions, 36–37, 38
prior disclosures, 34–36
record keeping, 46–48, 233, 238–240, 354–355
rulings, *see* Rulings, Customs
scenario illustrating penalties, 32, 33–34
seizure of merchandise, 14, 38, 42, 63, 308

textiles, 42–43
trademark infringement, 39
Claims, *see* Drawback, duty; Regulations and forms
Classification, product, *see* Tariff classification
Classification Appeals Division, 326
CMD (Certificate of Manufacture and Delivery), 163, 164, 170
Commerce Department, U.S., 44, 239, 335, 336
Commercial interchangeability, 122–123, 163
Commissioner of Customs, 52, 100, 101, 181, 182, 188, 321
Commissions, agency:
buying, 8, 24–25
selling, 7, 25, 29, 145
Committee on the Implementation of Textile Agreements (CITA), 212, 214, 219
Commodities control list (CCL), 235
Comparable profits method, 346, 350
Comparable uncontrolled price, 345
Comparative profit interval (CPI), 297
Competent authority process, 351
Compliance:
assessment team (CAT), 60, 65–66, 69
drawback, program, 162, 167–168
five core areas of, 60
reviews, *see* Audits
Computed value, 7, 21, 29, 349
Constructed expert price (CEP) sale, 281, 282
Constructed value, 247, 282, 283, 284–286
Consultants, 9, 45, 62
Contract and agreement logs, 61–62
Copyrights, 38
Cost of manufacture (COM), 283, 284
Cost of production (COP), 283–284, 285, 286, 287
Cost plus method, 346
Council for Trade in Goods, 214
Counterfeit goods, 38
Country, definition of, 304
Country Desk Program, 3
Country of origin:
definition of, 307, 310
marking requirements, *see* Marking requirements, country of origin
Court of Customs and Patent Appeals, 74
Court of International Trade (CIT), 16
antidumping regulations and procedures, 278, 335–336
audit resolutions, 70
determining dumping margins, 287
first sale rule, 75, 76, 77, 85
judicial review, 101–104, 271, 321, 329
litigation and appeals, *see* Appeals; Appeals, litigation and
warehouse bonds, 181
Crowley, Charles L., viii
Customs:
appeals, *see* Appeals
appraisement considerations, *see* Appraisement; First sale rule
audits, *see* Audits
bonds, *see* Bond, posting; Bonded warehouses; Temporary importation under bond
documentation, *see* Documentation, export; Documentation, import
duties, *see* Duties
example of levels of review of decisions by, 340
fines and penalties, *see* Civil enforcement issues
forms and regulations, *see* Regulations and forms
liquidation, *see* Liquidation
litigation, *see* Appeals, litigation and
marking requirements, *see* Marking requirements, country of origin
overview of, 2–17
quotas, *see* Quotas
record keeping, *see* Record keeping
rulings, *see* Rulings, Customs
tariffs, *see* Tariffs
tax issues, *see* Tax issues
Customs Bulletin, 98, 99, 161, 325, 327
Customs Commercial Enforcement Branch, 219–220
Customs compliance and import procedures manual, 62
Customs Cooperation Council (CCC), 90, 93
Customs Directive 3550–43, 40
Customs Electronic Bulletin Board, 208, 219, 220
Customs Headquarters Quota Branch, 208, 220
Customs Information Exchange, 320
Customs Modernization and Informed Compliance Act (Mod Act):
compliance review, 60, 62
conclusions concerning, 30
drawbacks
compliance program, 167, 168
electronic data, 158
introduction to, 154, 155
NAFTA and changes to, 169
other technical changes, 163
penalties, 160
revitalization, 156, 157
interpretive rulings, 325
modification and revocation of rulings, 326, 327
overview of, 44–46
record-keeping requirements, 17, 222, 232, 233
Section 632, 157
tariff classification, 88
Customs Web site, 208, 219

D

Deductive value, 7, 21, 28–29, 348
Delegation Order 236, 352
De minimis rule, 112, 117, 123, 260, 278
Denial list, 239
Department of Agriculture, U.S., 211, 212

Department of Commerce (DOC), 3, 5, 228
  antidumping regulations and procedures, 275, 276, 277, 278, 279
  determining dumping margins, 286, 287, 288
  dumping analysis, 280, 283
  injury determination, 279, 280
  market share strategy implementation, 291, 292
  record keeping, 298
  use of confidential data, 292, 293, 294
  use of facts available rule, 295–296
Department of the Treasury, 360
Deputy National Import Specialists (DNIS), 98
Derivative value, 21, 29–30
Detention policy, 39–40
Disclosures, prior, 34–36
Discounts, 27
Disputes, and penalties, 37
Dispute settlement, 271
Disregarded materials, special rules, 123
District Director of Customs, 4, 9, 12
Documentation, export:
  conclusions concerning, 240
  and determination of exporting requirements, 235–236
  export license, 234–235. *See also* Export license (visa)
  introduction, 222, 233
  record keeping, *see* Record keeping, export documentation
  shipper's export declaration, 233–234
Documentation, import:
  bond information, 227–228
  commercial invoice, 15, 224–225
  conclusions concerning, 240
  entry/immediate delivery, 226–227
  entry summary form, 225–226
  evidence of right to make entry, 223–224
  introduction, 222
  list of, 223
  other, *see* Documentation, other
  packing list, 15, 225
  power of attorney, 227
  purchase order, 227
  record keeping, 119, 232–233
Documentation, other:
  Caribbean Basin Initiative, 230–231. *See also* Caribbean Basin Initiative (CBI)
  export license, 228. *See also* Export license (visa)
  GSP declarations, 230. *See also* Generalized system of preferences (GSP)
  multiple country declaration, 229
  NAFTA certificate of origin, 231
  quota charge statement, 5, 229–230
  single country designation, 229
  special footwear invoice, 231–232
  textiles, 228–229. *See also* Textiles
Domestic material, definition of, 120
Donohue, Joseph F., Jr., 127
Drawback, duty, 10, 11
  compliance program, 162, 167–168
  computerization of claims, 170–171
  conclusions concerning, 177
  foreign trade zones versus, 148–149
  introduction to, 152–155
  on lump sum duty payments, 171, 173, 175–177
  manufacturing, 12–13
  Mod Act and, 154, 155, 157, 158, 160, 163, 168, 169
  NAFTA, 154, 155, 160, 168–170
  other changes, *see* Drawback, other technical changes
  penalties, 48, 159–161, 168
  privileges, 13, 161–162, 168
  record-keeping requirements, 47–48, 119–120, 167
  revitalization of, 155–157
  statute and regulation changes, 157–158
  types of, 12–13
  unused merchandise, 13, 165
Drawback, other technical changes:
  accounting methods, 166
  claims filed under wrong provision, 164–165
  completion of drawback claim, 163–164
  fungible versus commercially interchangeable, 122–123, 163
  restructuring claims, 164
  successorship, 165–166
  unused merchandise substitution drawback, 165
Drawback Regulations Team, 152, 173, 177
Drawback Revitalization Study Summary, 155
Dumping, *see* Duties, dumping and antidumping
Dumping, transfer pricing and:
  analysis of sales, 280–284
  confidential data use, 292–295
  constructed value, 283, 284–286
  determining dumping margins, 286–289
  facts available rule, 294, 295–297
  implementing market share strategy, 291–292
  introduction to, 274–275
  pricing methodologies, 299
  record keeping, 297–299
  relational topics, 290
  summary of, 299
Duties, 2, 5–6, 64
  ad valorem, 6, 7, 91, 140, 309
  calculating, 6–9. *See also* Appraisement; Valuation
  classification of goods and services, *see* Tariff classification
  as core area of compliance, 60
  countervailing, *see* Duties, countervailing
  deferral of, *see* Duties, deferral and avoidance mechanisms
  dumping and antidumping, *see* Duties, dumping and antidumping
  investigations and enforcement, *see* Duties, investigations and enforcement
  miscellaneous quota safeguards, 208, 211–212

most favored nation (MFN) rate, 91–92, 107, 206, 217
NAFTA, *see* North American Free Trade Agreement (NAFTA)
types of, 6, 91
valuation, *see* Appraisement; Valuation
Duties, countervailing, 2
administrative review of duty determinations, 267–269
Court of International Trade's review of, 335–336
duty assessment order, 266
Foreign Trade Zones Act, 136
injury to domestic industry, 250–255
introduction to, 5–6, 242–244
investigations and enforcement, *see* Duties, investigations and enforcement
judicial review and dispute settlement, 102, 271
miscellaneous rules, 266–267
practice and procedure rules, 269–270
subsidies and, 244–246
Duties, deferral and avoidance mechanisms, 130
bonded warehouses, *see* Bonded warehouses
drawbacks, *see* Drawback, duty
foreign trade zones, *see* Foreign trade zones
temporary importation under bond, *see* Temporary importation under bond
Duties, dumping and antidumping, 2
administrative review of duty determinations, 267–269
Court of International Trade's review of, 278, 335–336
duty assessment order, 266
Foreign Trade Zones Act, 136
injury determination, 250–255, 279–280
introduction to, 5–6, 242–244
investigations and enforcement, *see* Duties, investigations and enforcement
judicial review and dispute settlement, 102, 271
laws and regulations
adjustments, 247–248, 250
comparisons, 249–250
constructed value, 247
definitions, 248–249, 276
factors of production, 248
fair value, 246
normal value, 246–247, 281–282
overview of, 275–277
miscellaneous rules, 266–267
rules of practice and procedure, 269–270
transfer pricing and, *see* Dumping, transfer pricing and
Duties, investigations and enforcement:
final determinations, 264–266
importance of prior disclosure, 35–36
overview of, 255–256
preliminary determinations, 259–262
procedures for initiating, 256–259, 277–279
termination or suspension of, 262–263
time frame for, 278
Duty-free store, 184, 198–199
Duty-paid delivered price (DDP), 24

E

E. C. McAfee Company v. United States, 73, 75, 76, 77, 78, 80, 81, 359
Electronic Bulletin Board, 208, 219, 220
Electronic data, 4, 61, 158, 171
Electronic Visa Interface System (ELVIS), 218
Evidence of right to make entry, 223–224
Explanatory Notes, 93, 94
Export Administration Act, 234, 236, 239
Export Administration Regulations, 236, 238, 239
Export control classification number (ECCN), 235
Exporter's summary procedure, 162
Exporting, *see* Customs
Export license (visa), 3
civil enforcement and, 37, 42
overview of, 228, 234–235
quota costs and value of, 27
textile, 217–218, 228

F

Factors of production, 248
Facts available rule, 294, 295–297
Fair value, 246, 277
Farrell, Edward L., Jr., 273
Federal Register, 134, 161, 177, 257, 261, 262, 265
Federal Rules of Civil Procedure, 331
Federal Trade Commission, 14
Fees, 60
harbor maintenance, 4, 44, 68, 226
license, 8, 145
merchandise processing, 4, 226
user, 68
Feinschreiber, Robert, vii, 343
FIFO accounting method, 139, 166
Fines, Penalties, and Forfeiture Office, 32, 201–202
enforcement issues, *see* Civil enforcement issues
First sale rule:
background, 73
Customs' acquiescence, 78
Customs' nonacquiescence, 76
early litigation, 74
Hong Kong tailor's litigation, 75–76
1956 amendments, 74
1979 amendments, 74–75
1983 reversal, 75
Nissho Iwai's litigation, 76–77
conclusions concerning, 86

First sale rule, (*Continued*)
evaluation of sale for exportation
admission, 81–82
customer, 82
failure of proof, 84
identification, 81
letter of credit, 83–84
made-to-order factors, 83
notification, 83
physical characteristics, 82–83
shipment in-bond, 84
summary, 84
examination of bona fide sale
assists, 80
establishment of sale, 79
failure of proof, 79–80
manufacturer involvement in resale, 80–81
no-single-factor reasoning, 79
relevant factors, 81
transfer of title and risk of loss, 78
introduction to, 28, 72–73, 359
related parties transactions, 85–86
transaction-at-arm's-length test, 84–86
Food and Drug Administration (FDA), 14, 37
Footwear, 231–232
Foreign-first accounting method, 139
Foreign trade zones, 5
activation, 138
application for zone grant, 132–134
benefits from using, 129–131
comparison of, with other duty-deferral programs, 147–149
conclusions concerning, 150
conditions, prohibitions, and restrictions, 134–136
equipment to be used in, 146–147
establishing, 131–132
introduction to, 10, 11–12, 13, 128–129
manufacturing and processing activities, 136–138
NAFTA and, 147
operations of, *see* Foreign trade zones, operations of
transfer of merchandise, 143–146
Foreign trade zones, operations of:
admission of merchandise, 140
domestic status, 142
handling of merchandise, 143
inventory control and record keeping, 139
nonprivileged foreign status, 141–142
privileged foreign status, 140–141
role of customs, 138
status of zone merchandise, 140
zone restricted status, 142–143
Foreign Trade Zones Act, 134, 135, 136, 147, 148, 154
Foreign Trade Zones Board:
authority of, in establishment of zones, 131
conditions, prohibitions, and restrictions, 134–136, 142
as a party subject to suit, 337–338
two-step review process of, 136–138
zone grants, 132–134, 141
Forms, *see* Regulations and forms
Formula pricing, 27–28
Fraud penalties, 36, 160–161
Freedom of Information Act, 69
Freight:
inland, 8, 23, 24
international, 23
Freight forwarder, 3, 4
Fungible goods, 122–123, 163

G

GAAP (generally accepted accounting principles), contructed value and, 286
General Agreement on Tariffs and Trade (GATT):
antidumping laws and regulations, 275, 276, 277
countervailing and antidumping duties, 243, 275
duty assessment order, 266
initiating investigations, 257, 259
subsidies, 244, 245, 246
harmonization of rules of origin, 311, 360
import quotas, 206, 208, 213
Most Favored Nation (MFN) status, 91–92
General rules of interpretation (GRI), 92–96, 97, 124–125
Generalized system of preferences (GSP), 181
compliance review, 60
documentary requirements, 230
overview of, 9, 10, 92
Geraghty, James A., 19
Gill, Patrick D., 317
Glowzinski, Ronald C., 151
Government Accounting Office (GAO), 156
Gross negligence penalties, 36
GSP, *see* Generalized system of preferences (GSP)
Guaranteed access levels (GALs), 214
Guidelines for Reporting of Imported Products in Various Textile and Apparel Categories, 212

H

Hampco Apparel Inc. v. United States, 333
Harbor maintenance fee (HMF), 4, 44, 68, 226
Harmonized Commodity Description and Coding System, 90
Harmonized System Committee, 90
Harmonized Tariff Code, 89
Harmonized Tariff Schedule of the United States (HTSUS):
appraisement issues, 20, 29
audit compliance reviews, 60, 62
diskette program, 158, 170

general rules of interpretation (GRI), 92–96, 97, 124–125
list of codes, *see* HTSUS classification codes
NAFTA eligibility and, 107–112
overview of, 6–7, 88–92, 353–354
quotas and sources, 206, 208–211
tariff-shift rules of origin, 310, 312, 313, 314
using, to determine rate of duty, 107
HTSUS classification codes:
cotton fiber designations, 218–219
8470.1000, 109
8471.9000, 109
8473.21.00, 110
8473.30.10, 109
8517.10.00, 111
8517.90.12, 111
8540.91.15, 107
8703.23.00, 140
8708.93.34, 140
8741.2000, 109
9405.20.40, 121
9802.00.40, 224
9802.00.60, 224
9802.00.80, 29, 215, 316
9802.00.90, 216
9813.00.20, 200, 201
9813.00.25, 200
9813.00.50, 200, 201
9903.52.13, 219
textile designations, 212, 314–315

I

Importer number, 4–5
Importing, *see* Customs
Incoterms, 23
Industry, injury to domestic, 250–255
Injury:
to domestic industry, 250–255
final determination of, 264
material, 245, 250–251, 252–253, 254–255
review of determinations, 268
Insurance premiums, 23
Intellectual property rights, 38, 39
Interest based problem solving, 177
Interest charges, 8, 24, 334
Interested party, definition of, 258
Internal Revenue Codes (IRCs):
Section 482, 275, 297, 299, 349–351, 355, 357, 358, 360
Section 1059A, 356, 357, 358, 360, 362
Section 5472, 358, 359
Section 6038A record keeping, 297–299
Section 6103, 362
Internal Revenue Service (IRS), *see* Internal Revenue Codes (IRCs); Tax issues; Transfer pricing
Internal Revenue Service (IRS) Form 5472, 349
International Arrangement Regarding Trade in Textiles [Multi-Fiber Arrangement (MFA)], 212–213, 217, 228
International Import Certificate, 228
International Trade Administration (ITA), countervailing and antidumping duties:
administration of, 243
administrative review of duty determinations, 269
duty assessment order, 266
final determinations, 264, 265, 266
initiating investigations, 256, 257, 258, 259
injury to domestic industry, 254, 255
judicial review and dispute settlement, 271
laws and regulations, 276
preliminary determinations, 259, 260, 261, 262
rules of practice and procedure, 269, 270
termination or suspension of investigations, 262
International Trade Commission (ITC):
countervailing and antidumping duties, 335, 336
administration of, 243
administrative review of duty determinations, 268, 269
duty assessment order, 266
final determinations, 264, 265
initiating investigations, 257, 258, 259
injury to domestic industry, 250, 253, 254, 255
judicial review and dispute settlement, 271
miscellaneous rules, 267
preliminary determinations, 259, 260, 262
regulations and procedures, 276, 277, 278, 279
rules of practice and procedure, 269, 270
subsidies, 244
harmonization of rules of origin, 311
injury determination, 279, 280
market share strategy implementation, 291–292
modifications to tariff schedule, 90
patent protection, 39
use of confidential data, 292, 293
International Trade Compliance Division, 201
Inventory methods, 139, 166
Invoice:
commercial, 15, 224–225, 306
footwear, 231–232
Invoice price, 21–22, 27
IRS (Internal Revenue Service), *see* Internal Revenue Codes (IRCs); Tax issues; Transfer pricing
IRS Form 5472, 349
Isacoff, Harry L., 221

J

J-list articles, 14, 305
Judicial review, 101–104, 271, 330, 338. *See also* Appeals, litigation and
exhibit illustrating, of customs decisions, 341

K

Kaplan, Joseph S., 241
Kaplan, Seth T., 273
Klestadt, Peter W., 205, 301
Knit to shape, defining, 313, 315

L

Lapson, Beril J., 273
Levy, M. Barry, 71
License:
  export, *see* Export license (visa)
  fees, 8, 145
  import, 211–212
  individual validated, (IVL), 234
Liquidation, 99
  damages, 37–38, 202
  overview of, 15
  protesting, 16, 38, 193, 329, 332
Litigation and appeals, *see* Appeals, litigation and

M

Major parts, defining, 313, 315
Manhattan Shirt Co. v. United States, 333
Manipulation, of merchandise, 186, 306–307
Margins, determining dumping, 286–289
Marking requirements, country of origin:
  certificate of origin, 231
  conclusions concerning, 316
  delegation of authority, 319
  introduction, 13–14, 301
  proposed simplification, 310–311
  rules governing, 120–125, 311
  statute concerning, *see* Marking statute
  substantial transformation, 306, 307–308
  textiles and apparel, 42–43, 311–316
  violations, 14, 40–42, 63, 102, 308–310
Marking statute:
  English-language names, 13–14, 304
  exceptions to individual marking, 304–305
  location of marking, 302–303
  manner and method of marking, 303–304
  overview of, 302
  repackaging requirements, 306–307
  for ultimate-purchaser's benefit, 13–14, 302, 305–306
Markup, middleman, 8
Materials, definition of, 108
Maxwell, Michael P., 105
Merchandise processing fee, 4, 226
Mexico, 200, 227, 310
  NAFTA and, *see* North American Free Trade Agreement (NAFTA)
  quotas, 215–216
Middleman pricing rule, *see* First sale rule
Mitsui & Co. v. United States, 74, 75
Mod Act, *see* Customs Modernization and Informed Compliance Act (Mod Act)
Most Favored Nation (MFN) rate, 91–92, 107, 206, 217
Multi-Fiber Arrangement (MFA), 212–213, 217, 228
Multiple country declaration, 229
Murphy, David M., 205, 301
Murray, Jill D., 179
Mutual agreement procedure, 351
Mutual Assistance Agreement, 361

N

NAFTA, *see* North American Free Trade Agreement (NAFTA)
National Commodity Specialist Division, 318, 319–320, 321, 323, 324, 325, 326
National Import Specialists (NIS), 98, 318, 323, 324, 326
Negligence penalties, 36
Net cost method, 110, 115–116
Nissho Iwai American Corp. v. United States, 73, 76–77, 78, 80, 81, 82, 85, 86, 359, 360
Non-originating materials, 112, 114–115
Non-qualifying operations, special rules, 124
Normal value, 246–247, 276, 281
North American Free Trade Agreement (NAFTA), 9, 10
  Annexes to,
    308.1, 108
    401 of, 106, 107
    703.2, 108
  audit compliance, 60
  civil enforcement tools provided by, 48–49
  certificate of origin, 231
  conclusions concerning, 125
  delegation of authority, 319
  direct shipment of goods, 117–118
  drawback under, 154, 155, 160, 168–170
  effect of, on foreign trade zones, 147
  introduction to, 106
  Mod Act, *see* Customs Modernization and Informed Compliance Act (Mod Act)
  quota elimination, 205–206, 215–216
  record-keeping requirements, 118–120
  regional-value-content determination, *see* Regional value content (RVC)
  regulations governing marking rules, 120–125, 311. *See also* Marking requirements, country of origin

rules governing eligibility
de minimis rule, 112
overview of basic, 107–108
regional value content (RVC) requirement, 109–110
Rule A (wholly produced goods), 108–109
Rule B (tariff shift), 109
Rule C (goods produced from originating materials), 110–111
Rule D (parts and components), 111–112
Rule E (parts of automatic data processing equipment), 112
Schedule X accounting method, 166
tariff elimination, 106–107
tariff preference levels (TPLs), 216, 217
tariff shift rules of origin, 310–311, 314–315
North American Free Trade Agreement Implementation Act, 362
Notice to Mark as Redeliver, 40, 41
Notice to Redeliver, 37, 309
Notice to Remark, 41

O

Offer in compromise, 36
Office of Enforcement, 52, 55
Office of Export Administration, 239
Office of Export Licensing, 235, 238
Office of Inspector General (OIG), 156, 162
Office of Internal Affairs and Treasury Inspector General, 52
Office of Regulations and Rulings, 70, 98, 201, 318, 319, 326
Organization for Economic Cooperation and Development (OECD), 360, 362
Origin, *see* Country of origin
Outlier Analysis Targeting System (OATS), 363

P

Packing cost, 7, 25, 145
Packing list, 15, 225
Parts, special rules, 123–124
Patent and Trademark Office, U.S., 38
Patents, 39
Penalties, *see* Civil enforcement issues
Period of investigation (POI), 286, 287
Permit summary, blanket, 189
Petitions, 36–37, 38, 257–258
Port of entry, 3, 129
Post-importation costs, 21, 24
Power of attorney, 227
Pre-entry classification program, 98
Pre-Importation Review Program (PIRP), 322–323
Presentation, defining, 207
Pricing, transfer, *see* Transfer pricing, dumping and
Prior disclosures, 34–36
Private Letter Rulings, 360
Privileges, duty drawback and, 13, 161–162, 168
Profit split method, 346
Protests, 16, 38, 99–101, 193, 329, 330, 332
Purchase order, 227

Q

Quota Charge Statement, 5, 229–230
Quotas, 2, 3
absolute, 5, 206, 207, 229
costs, 8, 27
disputes, 37
entitlement to entry, 206–207
HTSUS, and sources, 209–211
introduction to, 205–206
miscellaneous, 208–212
status or fill rates of, 208
textiles, *see* Quotas, textiles
tariff-rate, 5, 206, 207, 218, 229–230
types of, 5, 206
Quotas, textiles, 42, 206
administration of, 217–218
background, 212–214
cotton fiber, 218–219, 228–229
Mexico quotas, 215–216
special access program, 214–215
status and specification information, 219–220
tariff preference levels, 217

R

Reasonable care standard, 45, 60, 167, 259
Record keeping:
(a)(1)(A) list, 46, 47, 57, 69
audit requirements, 57–58, 69
binding rulings procedure, 120
bonded warehouse, 194–196
as core area of compliance, 60
definition of records, 46–47, 354
drawbacks, 47–48, 119–120, 167
electronic data, 61
export, *see* Record keeping, export documentation
foreign trade zones, 139
import documentation, 119, 232–233
Internal Revenue Code (IRC) Section 6038A, 297–299
Mod Act regulations, 17, 46–48
NAFTA requirements, 118–120

Record keeping, (*Continued*)
  notice of violations, 47
  penalties, 49, 233, 354–355
  retention period for records, 233, 236
  summons for records, 47
Record keeping, export documentation:
  criminal sanctions, 239–240
  enforcement, 238
  exempt documents, 237–238
  and NAFTA, 118–119
  prohibitions, 238–239
  record retention period, 236
  records to be maintained, 236–237
Records, *see* Documentation, export; Documentation, import; Record keeping
Regional value content (RVC), 108, 310
  applying the RVC formula, 115
  de minimis rule, 117
  eligibility requirements, 109–110
  net cost method, 115–116
  non-originating materials, 114–115
  overview of, 112–113
  transaction value method, 113–114
Regulations and forms:
  CF 19, 321, 329
  CF 28, 16, 55
  CF 214, 48, 140
  CF 216, 143
  CF 300, 195
  CF 301, 4, 180, 187, 193, 197, 198, 200, 228
  CF 331, 163
  CF 368, 184
  CF 368A, 184
  CF 434, 119
  CF 520(c), 16
  CF 3173, 199
  CF 3461, 15, 60, 184, 200, 223, 226
  CF 3461s, 185
  CF 3495, 200
  CF 3499, 182, 186
  CF 5251, 184
  CF 5291, 4, 227
  CF 6043, 184, 189, 195
  CF 7501, 60, 143, 184, 185, 192, 193, 194, 196, 200, 225, 227
  CF 7505, 186, 187, 188, 192, 197
  CF 7505A, 193
  CF 7506, 187, 188, 189, 190
  CF 7507A, 192
  CF 7512, 189, 190, 197, 198
  CF 7512C, 189, 190
  CF 7525V, 233
  CF 7533, 200, 223
  C.R. 12.130, 312
  C.R. 19.6(d), 189
  C.R. 152.103(a)(3), 80
  C.R. 593A, 160
  Customs Directive 3550–43, 40
  ITA-370P, 214–215
  19 C.F.R. 141.85, 224
  19 C.F.R. 181, 154, 166, 168
  19 C.F.R. 181.45, 169
  19 C.F.R. 181.50(b), 169
  19 C.F.R. 191, 152, 154
  19 C.F.R. 191.12, 157
  19 C.F.R. 191.13, 157
  19 C.F.R. 191.22, 157
  19 C.F.R. 191.32, 157, 165
  19 C.F.R. 191.32(f), 166
  19 C.F.R. 191.33, 165
  19 C.F.R. 191.34, 165
  19 C.F.R. Part 134, 302
  19 C.F.R. Part 353, 243
  19 C.F.R. Part 355, 243, 246
  19 C.F.R. Subparts C, D, Q, 157
  19 C.F.R. Subparts E, G, I, S, 158
  19 U.S.C. 81(c), 154
  19 U.S.C. 1202, 90
  19 U.S.C. 1309, 153
  19 U.S.C. 1313(a), 152
  19 U.S.C. 1313(b), 165, 166
  19 U.S.C. 1313(c), 152, 157
  19 U.S.C. 1313(d), 153
  19 U.S.C. 1313(f), 153
  19 U.S.C. 1313(g), 154
  19 U.S.C. 1313(h), 154
  19 U.S.C. 1313(j), 152, 157, 163, 165
  19 U.S.C. 1313(p), 154, 157
  19 U.S.C. 1313(w)(1), 157
  19 U.S.C. 1401a(g), 77
  19 U.S.C. 1557(a), 154
  19 U.S.C. 1593A, 157
  19 U.S.C. 1671(a), 256
  19 U.S.C. 1671(c), 335
  19 U.S.C. 1671c(h), 336
  19 U.S.C. 1671(d), 335
  19 U.S.C. 1673(a), 256
  19 U.S.C. 1673(c), 335
  19 U.S.C. 1673c(h), 336
  19 U.S.C. 1673(d), 335
  19 U.S.C. 1675, 335
  19 U.S.C. 1675b(a)(1), 336
  19 U.S.C. 3538, 336
  26 U.S.C. 5062(c), 154
  28 U.S.C. 1581(a), 102
  Standard Form 87, 180
  U.S.C. Ruling NY 813637, 95
  U.S.C. Ruling HQ 958995, 94
Regulatory Audit Division, 52–53, 55, 195
Related parties transactions, 22, 23, 85–86
Repackaging requirements, 306–307
Resale price method, 345–346
Resale proceeds, 8, 25
Revenue Canada, 169
Revenue Procedure 96–9, 352
R. J. Saunders & Co. v. United States, 74, 75
Rodriguez v. United States, 74, 75
Ross, Susan Kohn, 31

Ross Glove Co. v. Commissioner, 355
Royalties, 8, 25, 26–27, 145
Rules of Interpretation, 92–97
Rulings, Customs:
  application for further review, 321
  challenges to adverse, 328–330
  delegation of authority, 319
  importance of written binding, 7, 9
  information requirement, 322
  interpretive, 323, 325–326
  introduction to binding, 9, 318
  litigation and appeals, *see* Appeals, litigation and
  modification and revocation, 326–328
  National Commodity Specialized Division, 319–320
  oral rulings, 318–319
  pre-importation review program, 322–323
  procedures for binding, 120
  prospective-transaction requirement, 320–321
  ruling request, 322
  seeking binding, 98–99, 319, 320
  thirty-day, 323–324, 326
  timing issues, 320

S

Schedule X accounting method, 166
Seizure, merchandise, 14, 38, 42, 63, 308
718 Fifth Ave. Corp. v. United States, 337
Shared responsibility approach, 30
Shaw, Matthew G., 1
Shipments, marking violations and in-transit, 42
Shipper's Export Declaration (SED), 233–234
Siciliano, Andrew L., 51
Simultaneous appeals process (SAP), 352
Single country designation, 229
Special access program, 214, 215
Special limit (SL), 214
Special regime goods, 215, 216
Stanhagen, Kenneth C., 273
State Department, U.S., 44
Statutory provisions, *see* Regulations and forms
Subsidies, 244–246
Substantial transformation, concept of, 306, 307–308
Sunset reviews, 268–269, 279
Suppliers, marking violations and multiple, 42
Supreme Court of the United States, 339
Synergy Sport International, Ltd. v. United States, 82

T

Table of Denial Orders, 235, 239
Tariff Act of 1930, 74, 232, 243, 275, 336
  Section 304, 302
  Section 402(b), 72, 73
  Section 402(g), 85, 86
Tariff classification
  additional U.S. Rules of Interpretation, 96–97
  administrative protests, 99–101
  conclusions concerning, 104
  as core area of compliance, 60
  Court of International Trade's review of, 334
  general rules of interpretation (GRI), 92–96, 124–125
  importance of, 62
  judicial review, 101–104
  pre-importation determination, 97–99
  of privileged and nonprivileged foreign merchandise, 144–145
  schedule of, *see* Harmonized Tariff Schedule of the United States (HTSUS)
Tariff preference levels (TPLs), 216, 217
Tariffs:
  classifications, *see* Tariff classification
  duties, *see* Duties
  GATT, *see* General Agreement on Tariffs and Trade (GATT)
  Harmonized Tariff Schedule, *see* Harmonized Tariff Schedule of the United States (HTSUS)
  inverted, 137, 142
  quotas, *see* Quotas
  special preference, *see* Tariffs, special preference programs
Tariffs, special preference programs, 9–10, 64. *See also* Duties, deferral and avoidance mechanisms
  Caribbean Basin Initiative, *see* Caribbean Basin Initiative (CBI)
  generalized system of preferences, *see* Generalized system of preferences (GSP)
  NAFTA, *see* North American Free Trade Agreement (NAFTA)
Tariff-shift rules, 310–311, 314–315
Tax Court Rule 124, 353
Tax issues, 8–9, 29, 36
  benefits of foreign trade zones, 130–131
  conclusions concerning, 363
  differences between goals of Customs and, 345
  enforcement by Customs, 353–355
  introduction to, 344
  IRS enforcement of Section 482, 349–351
  joint efforts by IRS and Customs, 360–363
  mandatory coordination, 357–360
  mutual agreement procedure, 351
  problems created by lack of harmonization, 355–357
  procedural advances, 351–353
  transfer pricing and, 294–295, 297. *See also* Transfer pricing methodologies, Customs; Transfer pricing methodologies, IRS
Temporary importation under bond:
  default or cancellation of bond, 201–203
  entry requirements, 199, 200
  foreign trade zones versus, 149

Temporary importation under bond, (*Continued*)
goods imported under, 201
overview of, 10, 11, 12, 13, 199–200
Textile Fiber Products Identification Act, 303
Textile Monitoring Body (TMB), 213
Textiles:
classification of, 97
de minimis rule for, 117
import documentation, 228–229
marking requirements, 311–316
origin of, 42–43
quotas, *see* Textiles, quotas
Textiles, quotas, 42
administration of, 217–218
background, 212–214
cotton fiber, 218–219, 228–229
Mexico, 215–216
special access program, 214–215
status and specification information, 219–220
tariff preference levels, 217
Textile Surveillance Body (TSB), 213
Theatrical effects, temporary importation under bond, 201
Total zone value, 145
Trade Act of 1974, 6, 336
Trade Agreements Act (TAA) of 1979, 72, 74–75
Trademarks, 38, 39
Trading with the Enemy Act, 234
Training, in-house, 63
Transaction value:
additions to, *see* Transaction value, additions to
determining regional value content (RVC), 110, 113–114
exclusions from, *see* Transaction value, exclusions from
general considerations, 21
invoice prices, 21–22
and price determination, 27–28
as primary basis of appraisement, 20–21
related parties, 22
remedies, 23
valuation methodologies, 7, 9, 347–348
Transaction value, additions to:
assists, 8, 25–26
royalties, 8, 26–27
selling agents' commissions, 7, 25, 29
Transaction value, exclusions from:
buying agents' commissions, 8, 24–25
inland freight, 8, 23, 24
interest charges, 8, 24
limits on exclusions, 24
post-importation costs, 21, 24
Transfer pricing:
dumping and, *see* Transfer pricing, dumping and
IRS and, 294–295, 297. *See also* Transfer pricing methodologies, IRS
methodologies, *see* Transfer pricing methodologies, Customs; Transfer pricing methodologies, IRS
Transfer pricing, dumping and:
analysis of sales, 280–284
confidential data use, 292–295
constructed value, 283, 284–286
determining dumping margins, 286–289
implementing market share strategy, 291–292
introduction to, 274–275
pricing methodologies, 299
record keeping, 297–299
relational topics, 290
summary of, 299
use of facts available rule, 295–297
Transfer pricing methodologies, Customs:
computed value, 349
deductive value, 348
other approaches, 349
transaction value, 347–348
Transfer pricing methodologies, IRS:
comparable profits method, 346, 350
comparable uncontrolled price, 345
cost plus method, 346
profit split, 346
resale price method, 345–346
unspecified methods, 347
Transport international routier (TIR) carnet, 190
Transshipment, 63–64, 108, 117
Trigger price safeguard, 208
Trigger volume safeguard, 208

U

Ultimate purchaser, 13–14, 302, 305–306
Uniroyal Inc. v. United States, 308
United States v. Getz Bros., 74, 75, 359
United States Shoe Corp. v. United States, 338
United States v. S. S. Kresge Co., Inc., 74, 75
Uruguay Round Agreements Act (URAA), 243
antidumping regulations and procedures, 275, 276, 277, 278, 279
constructed value and, 284, 286
determining dumping margins, 287, 288
dumping analysis, 281, 284
harmonization of rules of origin, 311
Section 334, 311–312

V

Valuation, *see also* Regional value content (RVC):
Ad valorem, 6, 7, 91, 140, 309
computed value, 7, 21, 29, 349
constructed value, 247, 282, 283, 284–286
as core area of compliance, 60
Court of International Trade's review of, 334
deductive value, 7, 21, 28–29, 348
derivative value, 21, 29–30

entry analysis of imported merchandise, 68
fair value, 246, 277
introduction to, 20
methodologies, 7–9
normal value, 246–247, 276, 281
privileged and nonprivileged foreign merchandise, 145–146
transfer pricing, *see* Transfer pricing
transaction value, *see* Transaction value
Vehicles, temporary importation under bond, 201
Visa, *see* Export license (visa)

W

Waiver of notice of intent to export or destroy, 162
Waiver of verification, 260
Warehouses, *see* Bonded warehouses
Warranty charges, 27
Web site, Customs, 208, 219
Weiss, Sidney N., 87
Whipsaw, Customs/IRS, 356
Wholly assembled, defining, 314
World Trade Organization (WTO), 316
antidumping laws and regulations, 276, 277
countervailing and antidumping duties, 243, 245, 271
quota safeguards, 208
textile agreements, 213
Wrappe, Steven C., 343
Wulwick, Richard P., 1, 221

Z

Zuvich, Douglas P., 51